IBRAM X. KENDI

Ibram X. Kendi is the Andrew W. Mellon Professor in the Humanities at Boston University, and the founding director of the BU Center for Antiracist Research. He is the author of many books including *Stamped from the Beginning: The Definitive History of Racist Ideas in America*, which won the National Book Award for Non-fiction, and five #1 *New York Times* bestsellers, including *Stamped: Racism, Antiracism, and You*, co-authored with Jason Reynolds; and *Antiracist Baby*, illustrated by Ashley Lukashevsky. His most recent book, *How to Raise an Antiracist*, was also a *New York Times* best-seller. In 2020, *Time* magazine named him one of the 100 most influential people in the world, and in 2021 he was awarded a MacArthur Fellowship, popularly known as the Genius Grant.

ibramxkendi.com
facebook.com/ibramxkendi
Twitter: @dribram
Instagram: @ibramxk

ALSO BY IBRAM X. KENDI

The Black Campus Movement

Stamped from the Beginning:
The Definitive History of Racist Ideas in America

Stamped: Racism, Antiracism, and You
by Ibram X. Kendi and Jason Reynolds

Antiracist Baby
by Ibram X. Kendi, illustrated by Ashley Lukashevsky

Be Antiracist: A Journal for Awareness,
Reflection, and Action

Four Hundred Souls: A Community History
of African America, 1619–2019
edited by Ibram X. Kendi and Keisha N. Blain

Stamped (For Kids): Racism, Antiracism, and You
by Ibram X. Kendi, Jason Reynolds
and Sonja Cherry-Paul

The Antiracist Deck: 100 Meaningful Conversations
on Power, Equity, and Justice

Goodnight Racism
by Ibram X. Kendi, illustrated by Cbabi Bayoc

How to Raise an Antiracist

Magnolia Flower
by Zora Neale Hurston and Ibram X. Kendi,
illustrated by Loveis Wise

The (Young) Antiracist's Workbook: Questions for
Changemakers by Ibram X. Kendi and Nic Stone

How to Be a (Young) Antiracist
by Ibram X. Kendi and Nic Stone

HOW TO
BE AN
ANTIRACIST

IBRAM
X. KENDI

VINTAGE

3 5 7 9 10 8 6 4 2

Vintage is part of the Penguin Random House group of companies
whose addresses can be found at global.penguinrandomhouse.com

Penguin
Random House
UK

Copyright © Ibram X. Kendi 2019, 2023

Ibram X. Kendi has asserted his right to be identified as the author of this
Work in accordance with the Copyright, Designs and Patents Act 1988

First published in Vintage in 2023
First published in hardback by The Bodley Head in 2019
Originally published in hardcover and in different form in the
United States by One World, an imprint of Random House,
a division of Penguin Random House LLC, in 2019

Book design by Jo Anne Metsch

penguin.co.uk/vintage

A CIP catalogue record for this book is available from the British Library

ISBN 9781529111828

Printed and bound in Great Britain by Clays Ltd, Elcograf S.p.A.

The authorised representative in the EEA is Penguin Random House Ireland,
Morrison Chambers, 32 Nassau Street, Dublin D02 YH68

Penguin Random House is committed to a sustainable future
for our business, our readers and our planet. This book is made
from Forest Stewardship Council® certified paper.

MIX
Paper from
responsible sources
FSC
www.fsc.org   FSC® C018179

TO SURVIVAL

TABLE OF CONTENTS

PREFACE TO THE PAPERBACK EDITION

Being antiracist is a journey, not a destination. This book has been on its own journey since it was first published on my birthday: August 13, 2019.

Much has changed about the world and me since then—and thereby some elements needed to change in this paperback edition to reflect all that I've seen, researched, and learned since 2019. Still, I agonized, first over whether I should update the book at all, and then over how transparent I should be about the updates. Since its initial publication, this book has attracted the attention of people whose interest is in delegitimizing antiracism so they can legitimize racism, or their unproven conception of racism, or their flattering conception of themselves. Many of these people are suspicious about the book's success. After all, if a book on being antiracist by a Black scholar becomes a global bestseller, surely it can't be because the book is useful or compelling.

After the experience of the last three years, it does not feel safe for me to be publicly self-reflective and self-critical. It feels dangerous for me to be vulnerable, just as it can be dangerous to be antiracist and challenge the power and policy structure of racism.

But in the end, I decided I didn't fear those dangers as much as I fear other dangers. What happens if we don't strive to be antiracist? What happens if we allow racism to continue to spread like a cancer? What happens if we allow racist power to continue to get a fascist foothold? What happens to you? To me? To all we hold dear? White supremacy is the greatest domestic threat to American lives and the life of democracy in the United States. Racism (and bigotry more broadly) is an existential threat to humans across the world, like nuclear war, climate change, and pandemics. The real danger lies in us *not* challenging racism. It is even more dangerous for us *not* to strive to be antiracist. It is even more dangerous for us—for me—*not* to be vulnerable and self-critical, to find our flaws, and to grow.

I decided to update this new edition, including data whenever possible, refine the notes section, and expand it with more sources. But I also decided to show, in critical moments in the text, how my scholarly ideas have changed or become more precise. Chris Jackson, my editor, and I came up with the idea to show this through annotations. The introduction and chapter one—which frame the book—have the most annotations. The rest of the chapters typically have one or two, until they trail off in the final three chapters.

Amid all the changes, much has remained the same about me, the world, and thereby this book. It still seeks to magnify, define, and clarify the complexities and forms of racism and antiracism. It still weaves this growing clarity with a chronological and vulnerable narrative of my own individual experiences either reinforcing or challenging the structure of racism. It still replaces the fixed binary of "not racist" *or* racist with the peelable descriptors of antiracist *and* racist. It retains the nonbinary of antiracist, assimilationist, and segregationist. It retains the double focus on readers of color and White readers; on individual transformation *for* societal transformation—because powerful forces are still striving to conserve racism.

I am still on this journey, still striving to be antiracist each day. But I am not on this journey for me. We are not on this journey by ourselves. This antiracist work is collective work. This collective work is essential work. This essential work is liberatory and constructive work.

Being antiracist, to liberate humanity from the clutches of racist power.

Being antiracist, to construct an equitable, habitable, and just society.

—IBRAM X. KENDI

HOW TO
BE AN
ANTIRACIST

MY RACIST INTRODUCTION

DESPISED SUITS AND ties. For seventeen years I had been surrounded by suit-wearing, tie-choking, hat-flying church folk. My teenage wardrobe hollered the defiance of a preacher's kid.

It was January 17, 2000. More than three thousand Black people—with a smattering of White folks—arrived that Monday morning in their Sunday best at the Hylton Memorial Chapel in Northern Virginia. My parents arrived in a state of shock. Their floundering son had somehow made it to the final round of the Prince William County Martin Luther King Jr. oratorical contest.

I didn't show up with a white collar under a dark suit and matching dark tie like most of my competitors. I sported a racy golden-brown blazer with a slick black shirt and bright color-streaked tie underneath. The hem of my baggy black slacks crested over my creamy boots. I'd already failed the test of respectability before I opened my mouth, but my parents, Carol and Larry, were all smiles nonetheless. They couldn't remember the last time they saw me wearing a tie and blazer, however loud and unconventional.

But it wasn't just my clothes that didn't fit the scene. My competitors were academic prodigies. I wasn't. I carried a GPA lower than 3.0; my SAT score barely cracked 1000. Colleges were recruiting my competitors. I was riding the high of having received surprise admission letters from the two colleges I'd halfheartedly applied to.

A few weeks before, I was on the basketball court with my high school team, warming up for a home game, cycling through layup lines. My father, all six foot three and two hundred pounds of him, emerged from my high school gym's entrance. He slowly walked onto the basketball court, flailing his long arms to get my attention—and embarrassing me before what we could call the "White judge." Classic Dad. He couldn't care less what judgmental White people thought about him. He rarely if ever put on a happy mask, faked a calmer voice, hid his opinion, or avoided making a scene. I loved and hated my father for living on his own terms in a world that usually denies Black people their own terms. It was the sort of defiance that could have gotten him lynched by a mob in a different time and place—or lynched by men in badges today.

I jogged over to him before he could flail his way right into our layup lines. Weirdly giddy, he handed me a brown manila envelope.

"This came for you today."

He motioned me to open the envelope, right there at half-court as the White students and teachers looked on.

NOTE ON "UNCONVENTIONAL" I changed "crazy" to "unconventional." "Crazy" is too often used in ableist fashion to identify anyone or anything abnormal—as I did here.

My expertise lies in racist language. I am still learning to identify my own ableist language, terms like "crazy" and "stupid" and "dumb," and to catch myself before using these terms and others. I replaced quite a few ableist terms for this paperback edition. I am striving to clean out all forms of bigotry from my vocabulary. It is striking how many terms we routinely use that are dirtied by bigotry.

I pulled out the letter and read it: I had been admitted to Hampton University in southern Virginia. My immediate shock exploded into unspeakable happiness. I embraced Dad and exhaled. Tears mixed with warm-up sweat on my face. The judging White eyes around us faded.

I thought I wasn't smart enough for college. Of course, intelligence is as subjective as beauty. But I kept using so-called "objective" standards, like test scores, to judge myself. No wonder I sent out only two college applications: one to Hampton and the other to the institution I ended up attending, Florida A&M University. Fewer applications meant less rejection—and I fully expected those two historically Black universities to reject me. Why would any university want someone on their campus who can't understand Shakespeare? It never occurred to me that maybe I wasn't really trying to understand Shakespeare and that's why I dropped out of my English II International Baccalaureate class during my senior year. Then again, I did not read much of anything in those years.

Maybe if I'd read history then, I'd have learned about the historical significance of the new town my family had moved to from New York City in 1997. I would have learned about all those Confederate memorials surrounding me in Manassas, Virginia, like Robert E. Lee's dead army. I would have learned why so many tourists trek to Manassas National Battlefield Park to relive the glory of the Confederate victories at the Battles of Bull Run during the Civil War. It was there that General Thomas J. Jackson acquired his nickname, "Stonewall," for his stubborn defense of the Confederacy. Northern Virginians kept the stonewall intact after all these years. Did anyone notice the irony that at this Martin Luther King Jr. oratorical contest, my free Black life represented Stonewall Jackson High School?

THE DELIGHTFUL EVENT organizers from Delta Sigma Theta sorority, the proud dignitaries, and the competitors were all seated on the pulpit. (The group was too large to say we were seated in the pulpit.) The audience sat in rows that curved around the long, arched pulpit, giving room for speakers to pace to the far sides of the chapel while delivering their talks; five stairs also allowed us to descend into the crowd if we wanted.

The middle schoolers had given their surprisingly mature speeches. The exhilarating children's choir had sung behind us. The audience sat back down and went silent in anticipation of the three high school orators.

I went first, finally approaching the climax of an experience that had already changed my life. From winning my high school competition months before to winning "best before the judges" at a countywide competition weeks before—I felt a special rainstorm of academic confidence. If I came out of the experience dripping with confidence for college, then I'd entered from a high school drought. Even now I wonder if it was my poor sense of self that first generated my poor sense of my people. Or was it my poor sense of my people that inflamed a poor sense of myself? Like the famous question about the chicken and the egg, the answer is less important than the cycle it describes. Racist ideas make people of color think less of themselves, which makes them more vulnerable to racist ideas. Racist ideas make White people think more of themselves, which further attracts them to racist ideas.

I thought I was a subpar student and was bombarded by messages—from Black people, White people, the media—that told me that the reason was rooted in my race . . . which made me more discouraged and less motivated as a student . . . which only further reinforced for me the racist idea that Black people just weren't very studious . . . which made me feel even more despair or indifference . . . and on it went. At no point was this cycle interrupted by a deeper analysis of my own specific circumstances and shortcomings or a critical look at the ideas of the society that judged me—instead, the cycle hardened the racist ideas inside me until I was ready to preach them to others.

· · ·

I REMEMBER THE MLK competition so fondly. But when I recall the racist speech I gave, I flush with shame.

"What would be Dr. King's message for the millennium? Let's visualize an angry seventy-one-year-old Dr. King . . ." And I began my remix of King's "I Have a Dream" speech.

It was joyous, I started, our emancipation from enslavement. But "now, one hundred thirty-five years later, the Negro is still not free." I was already thundering, my tone angry. "Our youth's minds are still in captivity!"

I did not say our youth's minds are in captivity of racist ideas, as I would say now.

"They think it's okay to be those who are most feared in our society!" I said, as if it was their fault they were so feared.

"They think it's okay not to think!" I charged, raising the classic racist idea that Black youth don't value education as much as their non-Black counterparts. No one seemed to care that this well-traveled idea had flown on anecdotes but had never been grounded in proof. Still, the crowd encouraged me with their applause. I kept shooting out unproven and disproven racist ideas about all the things wrong with Black youth—ironically, on the day when all the things right about Black youth were on display.

I started pacing wildly back and forth on the runway for the pulpit, gaining momentum.

NOTE ON MARTIN AND MALCOLM For decades, Americans have been misled into viewing Malcolm X as the angry and violent leader, and Martin Luther King Jr. as the loving and nonviolent leader. I have written and spoken against this contrast. But still, I reinforced that false contrast here, which led to my deleting a reference to Malcolm X. Martin was angry at racism and empathized with the violence of urban rebels in the 1960s. He once said, "A riot is the language of the unheard." Malcolm primarily preached self-defense from racist terror and his anger at racism came from a deep well of love for Black people and a belief in human rights for all.

"They think it's okay to climb the high tree of pregnancy!" Applause. "They think it's okay to confine their dreams to sports and music!" Applause.

Had I forgotten that I—not "Black youth"—was the one who had confined his dreams to sports? And I was calling Black youth "they"? Who on earth did I think I was? Apparently, my placement on that illustrious stage had lifted me out of the realm of ordinary—and thus inferior—Black youngsters and into the realm of the rare and extraordinary.

In my applause-stoked flights of oratory, I didn't realize that to say something is wrong about a racial group is to say something is inferior about that racial group. I did not realize that to say something is inferior about a racial group is to say a racist idea. I thought I was serving my people, when in fact I was serving up racist ideas about my people to my people. The Black judge seemed to be eating it up and clapping me on my back for more. I kept giving more.

"Their minds are being held captive, and our adults' minds are right there beside them," I said, motioning to the floor. "Because they somehow think that the cultural revolution that began on the day of my dream's birth is over.

"How can it be over when many times we are unsuccessful because we lack intestinal fortitude?" Applause.

"How can it be over when our kids leave their houses not knowing how to make themselves, only knowing how to not make themselves?" Applause.

"How can it be over if all of this is happening in our community?" I asked, lowering my voice. "So I say to you, my friends, that even though this cultural revolution may never be over, I still have a dream . . ."

I STILL HAVE a nightmare—the memory of this speech whenever I muster the courage to recall it anew. It is hard for me to believe I finished high school in the year 2000 touting so many racist ideas. A racist society had handed me the ammunition to shoot Black people, to shoot myself, and I took and used it. Internalized racist ideas are the real Black on Black crime.

I was a dupe, a chump who saw the ongoing struggles of Black people on MLK Day 2000 and decided that Black people themselves were the problem. This is the consistent function of racist ideas—and of any kind of bigotry more broadly: to manipulate us into seeing people as the problem, instead of the policies that ensnare them.

The language used by the forty-fifth president of the United States offers a clear example of how this sort of racist language and thinking works. Long before he became president in 2017, Donald Trump liked to say, "Laziness is a trait in Blacks." When he decided to run for president, his plan for making America great again: defaming Latinx immigrants as mostly criminals and rapists and demanding billions for a border wall to block them. He promised "a total and complete shutdown of Muslims entering the United States." Once he became president, he routinely called

NOTE ON "RACISM" AND "RACIST" Here, I corrected one of my biggest errors in the hardcover edition: my use, at times, of the terms "racism" and "racist" interchangeably. Many people use "racism" and "racist" interchangeably. But we must stop. I am trying to stop. Because they mean different things.

"Racism" connotes power, policies, *and* ideas. "Racist" connotes a power, a policy, *or* an idea. "Racism" connotes what is structural, systemic, institutional, connected, or plural: a powerful collection of unjust or inequitable policies justified by ideas of racial hierarchy. "Racist" connotes what is individual or singular, such as a single (racist) policy or idea, or a single person who is being racist. I changed "internalized racism" to "internalized racist ideas" because an *individual* cannot have or internalize racism. A group of people can engage in racism, while an individual can be racist.

The common definition of racism can no longer hold. When we define racism as only a belief, philosophy, or ideology that can be internalized by an individual, it undermines two things: (1) the recognition of racism as structural, institutional, and systemic; and (2) the powerful role of policymakers, policies, and practices in the operation of racism. Power and policy are more foundational to racism than ideas (with ideas justifying the policies and practices). When we think *racism,* what comes to mind should be structures. When we think *racist,* what comes to mind should be an individual, an idea, a policy—the elements making up the structure of racism.

his Black critics "stupid." He claimed immigrants from Haiti "all have AIDS," while praising White supremacists as "very fine people" in the summer of 2017.

Through it all, whenever someone pointed out the obvious, Trump responded with variations on a familiar refrain: "No, no. I'm not a racist. I'm the least racist person that you have ever interviewed," that "you've ever met," that "you've ever encountered." Trump's behavior may be exceptional, but his denials are normal. When racist ideas resound, denials that those ideas are racist typically follow. When racist policies resound, denials that those policies are racist also follow.

Denial is the heartbeat of being racist, beating across ideologies, races, and nations. It is beating within us. Many of us who strongly call out Trump's racist ideas will strongly deny our own. How often do we become reflexively defensive when someone calls something we've done or said racist? How many of us would agree with this statement: " 'Racist' isn't a descriptive word. It's a pejorative word. It is the equivalent of saying, 'I don't like you.'" These are actually the words of White supremacist Richard Spencer, who, like Trump, identifies as "not racist." How many of us who despise the Trumps and White supremacists of the world share their self-definition of "not racist"?

What's the problem with being "not racist"? It is a claim that signifies neutrality: "I am not a racist, but neither am I aggressively against racism." But there is no neutrality in the racial struggle. The opposite of "racist" isn't "not racist." It is "antiracist." What's the difference? One endorses either the idea of a racial hierarchy as a racist, or racial equality as an antiracist. One either believes racial inequities are rooted in groups of people, as a racist, or locates the roots of racial inequities in power and policies, as an antiracist. One either allows racial injustice to persevere, as a racist, or confronts racial injustice, as an antiracist. There is no in-between safe space of "not racist." The claim of "not racist" neutrality is a mask for being racist. This may seem harsh, but it's important at the outset that we apply one of the core principles of antiracism, which is to return the word "racist" itself back to its proper usage. "Racist" is not—as Richard Spencer argues—a pejorative. It is not the worst word in the English language; it is not the equivalent of a "slur." It is descriptive, and the only way to undo what is racist is to consistently identify and describe it—and then dismantle it. The attempt to turn this usefully descriptive term into an almost unusable slur is, of course, designed to do the opposite: to freeze us into inaction.

THE COMMON IDEA of claiming "color blindness" is akin to the notion of being "not racist"—as with the "not racist," the color-blind individual, by ostensibly failing to see how people are racialized, fails to see racism and falls into racist passivity. The language of color blindness—like the language of "not racist"—is a mask to hide when someone is being racist. "Our Constitution is color-blind," U.S. Supreme Court Justice John Harlan proclaimed in his dissent to *Plessy v. Ferguson,* the case that legalized Jim Crow segregation in 1896. "The white race deems itself to be the dominant race in this country," Justice Harlan asserted. "I doubt not, it will continue to be for all time, if it remains true to its great heritage." A color-blind Constitution for a White-supremacist America.

THE GOOD NEWS is that racist and antiracist are not fixed identities. We can be a racist one minute and an antiracist the next. What we say about race, what we do about race, in each moment, determines what—not who—we are.

I used to be racist most of the time. I am changing. I am no longer identifying with racists by claiming to be "not racist." I am no longer speaking through the mask of racial neutrality. I am no longer manipulated by racist ideas to see racial groups as problems. I no longer believe a person of color cannot be racist. I am no longer policing my every action around an imagined White or Black judge, trying to convince White people of my equal humanity, trying to convince Black people I am representing the race well. I no longer view race and racism through a Black-White binary that marginalizes Latinx, Asian, Native, and Middle Eastern peoples. I no longer care about how the actions of other Black individuals reflect on me, since none of us are race representatives, nor is any individual responsible for someone else's racist ideas. And I've come to see that the movement from racist to antiracist is always ongoing—it requires understanding and snubbing racist ideas based on biology, ethnicity, body, culture, behavior, color, space, and class. And beyond that, it means standing ready to fight racism at its intersections with other bigotries.

THIS BOOK IS ultimately about the basic struggle we're all in, the struggle to be fully human and to see that others are fully human. I share my own journey of being raised in the dueling racial consciousness of the Reagan-era Black middle class, then right-turning onto the ten-lane highway of anti-Black racism—a highway mysteriously free of speed limits and surveillance—and veering off onto the two-lane highway of anti-White racism, where speed limits and surveillance are everywhere, before finding and turning down the unlit dirt road of antiracism.

After taking this grueling journey to the dirt road of the antiracist, humanity can come upon the clearing of a potential future: an antiracist world in all its imperfect beauty. It can become real

NOTE ON BEING FULLY HUMAN I think we are beginning to understand how being racist prevents us from seeing certain people as fully human. But I don't think we understand how being racist prevents us from *being* fully human. What do I mean by fully human? I'm not talking in a biological or behavioral sense; we are all fully human in a biological and behavioral sense. I'm speaking in a social and political sense. To be fully human, socially, is for us to recognize a fundamental connection between ourself and every human being on earth. Which is to say we see every human being as a member of our extended family; we value the lives of all human groups equally, no matter their skin color. To be fully human, politically, is to think about human rights, about what all humans need to live fulfilling lives, and what powerful forces constrain humans—in this case the force of racism. To be fully human is to use our power to join with other humans to challenge the forces that prevent the full flowering of humanity.

if we focus on power instead of people, if we focus on changing policy instead of groups of people. It's possible if we overcome our cynicism about the permanence of racism.

We know how to be racist. We know how to pretend to be not racist. Now let's know how to be antiracist.

CHAPTER 1

DEFINITIONS

RACIST: One who is expressing an idea of racial hierarchy, or through actions or inaction is supporting a policy that leads to racial inequity or injustice.

ANTIRACIST: One who is expressing an idea of racial equality, or is actively supporting a policy that leads to racial equity or justice.

SOUL LIBERATION SWAYED onstage at the University of Illinois arena, rocking colorful dashikis and Afros that shot up like balled fists—an amazing sight to behold for the eleven thousand college students in the audience. Soul Liberation appeared nothing like the White ensembles in suits who'd been sounding hymns for nearly two days after Jesus's birthday in 1970.

NOTE ON DEFINITIONS In this chapter (and in some of my speeches on the topic), I spend a lot of time explaining and defining the terms "racist policy" and "racist idea" or "antiracist policy" and "antiracist idea." And then I use those definitions to define the terms "racist" and "antiracist" for an individual. I was so adamant about people coming to an understanding of those terms that I inserted them into these seminal definitions of what it means for an individual to be racist and antiracist. But that created circular definitions, where the terms "racist" and "antiracist" are used to define racist and antiracist.

This error happened because I lost sight of something critical: definitions must be able to stand on their own. *Especially* definitions as critical to human beings and as critical to my work as "racist" and "antiracist." I should have simply defined the terms "racist policy," "racist idea," "antiracist policy," and "antiracist idea" within these definitions of "racist" and "antiracist." I have done that now.

Black students had succeeded in pushing the InterVarsity Christian Fellowship, the U.S. evangelical movement's premier college organizer, to devote the second night of the conference to Black theology. More than five hundred Black attendees from across the country were on hand as Soul Liberation began to perform. Two of those Black students were my parents.

They were not sitting together. Days earlier, they had ridden on the same bus for twenty-four hours that felt like forty-two, from Manhattan through Pennsylvania, Ohio, and Indiana, before arriving in central Illinois. About one hundred Black New Yorkers converged on InterVarsity's Urbana '70.

My mother and father had met during the Thanksgiving break weeks earlier when Larry, an accounting student at Manhattan's Baruch College, co-organized a recruiting event for Urbana '70 at his church in Jamaica, Queens. Carol was one of the thirty people who showed up—she had come home to Queens from Nyack College, a small Christian school about thirty miles north of her parents' home in Far Rockaway. The first meeting was uneventful, but Carol noticed Larry, an overly serious student with a towering Afro, his face hidden behind a forest of facial hair, and Larry noticed Carol, a petite nineteen-year-old with dark freckles sprayed over her caramel complexion, even if all they did was exchange small talk. They'd independently decided to go to Urbana '70 when they heard that Tom Skinner would be preaching and Soul Liberation would be performing. At twenty-eight years old, Skinner was growing famous as a young evangelist of Black liberation theology. A former gang member and son of a Baptist preacher, he reached thousands via his weekly radio show and tours, where he delivered sermons at packed iconic venues like the Apollo Theater in his native Harlem. In 1970, Skinner published his third and fourth books, *How Black Is the Gospel?* and *Words of Revolution*.

Carol and Larry devoured both books like a James Brown tune, like a Muhammad Ali fight. Carol had discovered Skinner through his younger brother, Johnnie, who was enrolled with her at Nyack. Larry's connection was more ideological. In the spring of 1970, he had enrolled in "The Black Aesthetic," a class taught by legendary Baruch College literary scholar Addison Gayle Jr. For the first time, Larry read James Baldwin's *The Fire Next Time,* Richard Wright's *Native Son,* Amiri Baraka's wrenching plays, and the banned revolutionary manifesto *The Spook Who Sat by the Door* by Sam Greenlee. It was an awakening. After Gayle's class, Larry started searching for a way to reconcile his faith with his newfound Black consciousness. That search led him to Tom Skinner.

SOUL LIBERATION LAUNCHED into their popular anthem, "Power to the People." The bodies of the Black students who had surged to the front of the arena started moving almost in unison with the sounds of booming drums and heavy bass that, along with the syncopated claps, generated the rhythm and blues of a rural Southern revival.

The wave of rhythm then rushed through the thousands of White bodies in the arena. Before long, they, too, were on their feet, swaying and singing along to the soulful sounds of Black power.

Every chord from Soul Liberation seemed to build up anticipation for the keynote speaker to come. When the music ended, it was time: Tom Skinner, dark-suited with a red tie, stepped behind the podium, his voice serious as he began his history lesson.

"The evangelical church . . . supported the status quo. It supported slavery; it supported segregation; it preached against any attempt of the Black man to stand on his own two feet."

Skinner shared how he came to worship an elite White Jesus Christ, who cleaned people up through "rules and regulations," a savior who prefigured Richard Nixon's vision of law and order. But one day, Skinner realized that he'd gotten Jesus wrong. Jesus wasn't in the Rotary Club and he wasn't a policeman. Jesus was a "radical revolutionary, with hair on his chest and dirt under his fingernails." Skinner's new idea of Jesus was born of and committed to a new reading of the gospel. "Any gospel that does not . . . speak to the issue of enslavement" and "injustice" and "inequality—any gospel that does not want to go where people are hungry and poverty-stricken and set them free in the name of Jesus Christ—is not the gospel."

Back in the days of Jesus, "there was a system working just like today," Skinner declared. But "Jesus was dangerous. He was dangerous because he was changing the system." The Romans locked up this "revolutionary" and "nailed him to a cross" and killed and buried him. But three days later, Jesus Christ "got up out of the grave" to bear witness to us today. "Proclaim liberation to the captives, preach sight to the blind" and "go into the world and tell men who are bound mentally, spiritually, and physically, 'The liberator has come!'"

The last line pulsated through the crowd. "The liberator has come!" Students practically leapt out of their seats in an ovation— taking on the mantle of this fresh gospel. The liberators had come.

My parents were profoundly receptive to Skinner's call for evangelical liberators and attended a series of Black caucuses over the week of the conference that reinforced his call every night. At Urbana '70, Ma and Dad found themselves leaving the civilizing and conserving and racist church they realized they'd been part of. They were saved into Black liberation theology and joined the churchless church of the Black Power movement. Born in the days of Malcolm X, Fannie Lou Hamer, Stokely Carmichael, and other antiracists who confronted segregationists and assimilationists in the 1950s and 1960s, the movement for Black solidarity, Black cultural pride, and Black economic and political self-determination had enraptured the entire Black world. And now, in 1970, Black power had enraptured my parents. They stopped thinking about saving Black people and started thinking about liberating Black people.

In the spring of 1971, Ma returned to Nyack College and helped form a Black student union, an organization that challenged racist theology, the Confederate flags on dorm-room doors, and the paucity of Black students and programming. She started wearing African-print dresses and wrapped her growing

Afro in African-print ties. She dreamed of traveling to the motherland as a missionary.

Dad returned to his church and quit its famed youth choir. He began organizing programs that asked provocative questions: "Is Christianity the White man's religion?" "Is the Black church relevant to the Black community?" He began reading the work of James Cone, the scholarly father of Black liberation theology and author of the influential *Black Theology & Black Power* in 1969.

One day in the spring of 1971, Dad struck up the nerve to go up to Harlem and attend Cone's class at Union Theological Seminary. Cone lectured on his new book, *A Black Theology of Liberation*. After class, Dad approached the professor.

"What is your definition of a Christian?" Dad asked in his deeply earnest way.

Cone looked at Dad with equal seriousness and responded: "A Christian is one who is striving for liberation."

James Cone's working definition of a Christian described a Christianity of the enslaved, not the Christianity of the enslavers. Receiving this definition was a revelatory moment in Dad's life. Ma had her own similar revelation in her Black student union— that Christianity was about struggle and liberation. My parents now had, separately, arrived at a creed with which to shape their lives, to be the type of Christians that Jesus the revolutionary inspired them to be. This new definition of a word that they'd already chosen as their core identity naturally transformed them.

MY OWN, STILL-ONGOING journey toward being an antiracist began at Urbana '70. What changed Ma and Dad led to a chang-

NOTE ON "ENSLAVERS" Words pack meaning. But often words do not contain critical forms of meaning. The terms "slave" and "slaveholder" erase history. These terms convey an almost static station, erasing the constant struggle to force people to labor against their will. The terms "enslave," "enslaver," "enslaved," and "enslavement" better convey the persistent force needed to keep Black people in bondage because the people constantly resisted. I had already started using the term "enslaved," but not "enslaver." I made the change here and throughout this paperback edition.

ing of their two unborn sons—this new definition of the Christian life became the creed that grounded my parents' lives and the lives of their children. I cannot disconnect my parents' religious strivings to be Christian from my secular strivings to be an antiracist. And the key act for both of us was defining our terms so that we could begin to describe the world and our place in it. Definitions anchor us in principles. This is not a light point: If we don't do the basic work of defining the kind of people we want to be in language that is stable and consistent, we can't work toward stable, consistent goals. Some of my most consequential steps toward being an antiracist have been the moments when I arrived at basic definitions. To be an antiracist is to set lucid definitions of racism/antiracism, racist/antiracist policies, racist/antiracist ideas, racist/antiracist people. To be a racist is to constantly redefine racist in a way that exonerates one's changing policies, ideas, and personhood.

So let's set some definitions. What is racism? To understand racism, one must first understand racist policies and racist ideas and how they are married. Okay, so what are racist policies and ideas? We have to define them separately to understand how they are married and why they interact so well together. In fact, let's take one step back and consider the definition of two other important phrases: racial inequity and racial injustice.

Racial inequity (or disparity) is when two or more racial groups are not standing on approximately equal footing. Here's an example of racial inequity: The houselessness rate in 2022 for Black Americans (51.9 per 10,000) and Native Americans (45.2 per 10,000) is more than four times the houselessness rate for White Americans (11.2 per 10,000). Racial equity is when two or more racial groups are standing on a relatively equal footing. An example of racial equity would be if Black, Native, and White people were all experiencing houselessness at a rate close to around 11.2 per 10,000 people.

If racial equity is the start, then racial justice is the end. If racial equity is all racial groups experiencing houselessness at somewhere close to 20 or 10 or 5 per 10,000 people, then racial justice is the abolition of houselessness and housing insecurity for all racial groups. Racial justice is building a society where everyone of every race has an affordable, safe, and comfortable roof over their head. Justice in a structural sense is when people experience nurturing and restorative love from policies and from their makers and defenders, who are being held accountable by the people. Injustice in a structural sense is when people experience destructive harm from policymakers and policies and from people who are usually immune to accountability.

A racist policy is any measure that produces or sustains racial inequity or injustice. An antiracist policy is any measure that produces or sustains racial equity or justice. By policy, I mean written and unwritten laws, rules, procedures, processes, regulations, and guidelines that govern people. There is no such thing as a nonracist or race-neutral policy. Every policy in every institution in every community in every nation is producing or sustaining either racial inequity or equity, racial injustice or justice.

Racist policies have been described by other terms: "institutional racism," "structural racism," and "systemic racism," for instance. But those are vaguer terms than "racist policy." When I use them I find myself having to immediately explain what they mean. "Racist policy" is more tangible and exacting, and more likely to be immediately understood by everyday people, including its victims, who may not have the benefit of extensive fluency in racial terms. "Racist policy" says exactly what the problem is and where the problem is. "Institutional racism" and "structural racism" and "systemic racism" are redundant. Racism itself is institutional, structural, and systemic.

"Racist policy" also cuts to the core of racism better than "racial discrimination," another common phrase. "Racial discrimination" is an immediate and visible manifestation of an underlying racial policy. When someone discriminates against a person in a racial group, they are carrying out a policy or taking advantage of the lack of a protective policy. We all have the power to discriminate. Only an exclusive few have the power to make policy. Focusing on "racial discrimination" puts our eyes on interpersonal actions and everyday people: one person discriminating against another. Focusing on "racial discrimination" takes our eyes off the central agents of racism: racist policy and racist policymakers, or what I call racist power.

Since the 1960s, racist power has commandeered the term "racial discrimination," transforming the act of discriminating on the basis of race into an inherently racist act. But if racial discrimination is defined as treating, considering, or making a distinction in favor of or against an individual based on that person's race, then racial discrimination is not inherently racist. The defining question is whether the discrimination is creating equity or inequity. If discrimination is creating equity, then it is antiracist. If discrimination is creating inequity, then it is racist. Another term for antiracist discrimination that leads to equity is "positive discrimination." Another term for racist discrimination that maintains inequity is "negative discrimination." These terms are perhaps most widely used in Europe and the British Commonwealth of Nations. Positive discrimination has been defined in two ways. I do not think an organization should hire an incapable candidate solely because of that candidate's race, which is how positive discrimination is sometimes defined. But I do think organizations and societies should support practices that seek to remedy inequities, which is another way positive discrimination is defined by organizations like the Australian Human Rights Commission.

An example of positive age discrimination is when a nation with limited supply of a life-saving vaccine provides it *first* to the elderly people dying at the highest rates from a viral disease. An example of positive antiracist discrimination is when a nation with limited supply of a life-saving vaccine provides it *first* to the racial groups dying at the highest rates from the viral disease. Both actions reduce inequities in death rates (whether age or racial), and they result in the most lives being saved, since the people most likely to die from the viral disease receive the protective vaccine first.

An example of negative age discrimination is when a nation with limited supply of a life-saving vaccine provides it *first* to the young people who are dying at the lowest rates from a viral disease. An example of negative racist discrimination is when a nation with limited supply of a life-saving vaccine provides it *first* to the racial groups dying at the lowest rates from the viral disease. Both actions increase inequities in death rates (whether age or racial), and lead to the most people dying, since the people most likely to die from the viral disease do not receive the protective vaccine first.

Another example of negative age discrimination is a nation with limited supply of a vaccine providing it to all age groups at the same time, even as different age groups are dying at different rates. Another example of negative racist discrimination is a nation with limited supply of a vaccine providing it to all racial groups at the same time, even as they are dying at different rates. Both actions lead to less vulnerable individuals receiving the protective vaccine in place of more vulnerable individuals, which maintains inequities in death rates (whether age or racial), and leads to more deaths overall, since the most vulnerable individuals didn't receive the protective vaccine first.

When a limited supply of the COVID-19 vaccine became available in 2021, officials in the United States (and in many countries around the world) engaged in positive age discrimination, getting the vaccine first to vulnerable elders, which research has shown saved lives. But these same officials refused to engage in positive antiracist discrimination, getting the vaccine first to the most vulnerable racial groups, which likely led to more deaths.

The United States routinely engages in positive age discrimination to benefit vulnerable elderly people. *As all nations should.* Could that be because policymakers—particularly politicians—are disproportionately elderly? Could that be because elderly people vote at disproportionately high rates? Or could that be because elderly people are disproportionately White? The most common age of White Americans was fifty-eight in 2018, compared with twenty-nine for Asian Americans, twenty-eight for Native Hawaiian and Pacific Islander Americans, twenty-seven for Black Americans, twenty-six for American Indians and Alaska Natives, and eleven for Latinx Americans.

Engaging in positive age discrimination in cases where elderly people are vulnerable, and refusing to engage in positive antiracist discrimination in cases where certain racial groups are vulnerable, both lead to the persistence of racial inequities. And these actions are justified by legal frameworks that liken what maintains racial inequity (framed as negative discrimination) to what reduces racial inequity (framed as positive discrimination). It is absurd that positive and negative discrimination are rendered no different, when they have different effects. Someone reproducing inequity through permanently assisting an overrepresented racial group into wealth and power is entirely different than someone challenging that inequity by temporarily assisting an underrepresented racial group into relative wealth and power until equity is reached. The height of all absurdities is when one racial group has far fewer resources than another racial group due to the history of racism, and the popular proposal to remedy this historic inequity is providing the same resources to these two unevenly resourced groups. This will never add up to equity or justice.

The only remedy to negative racist discrimination that produces inequity is positive antiracist discrimination that produces equity. The only remedy to past negative racist discrimination that has produced inequity is present positive antiracist discrimination that produces equity. The only remedy to present negative racist discrimination toward inequity is future positive antiracist discrimination toward equity. As President Lyndon B. Johnson said in 1965, "You do not take a person who, for years, has been hobbled by chains and liberate him, bring him up to the starting line of a race and then say, 'You are free to compete with all the

NOTE ON DISCRIMINATION These three sentences—and almost always these three sentences—have been heavily quoted by the conservators of racism to attack me and this book. They strip these sentences of the context and meaning I establish in the paragraphs before and after them. They reject my definition of "discrimination" and the delineation between racist and antiracist discrimination, even as these sentences are predicated on that definition and that delineation. All to substantiate their propaganda that my work is racist, and that antiracism is racist toward White people.

others,' and still justly believe that you have been completely fair." As U.S. Supreme Court Justice Harry Blackmun wrote in 1978, "In order to get beyond racism, we must first take account of race. There is no other way. And in order to treat some persons equally, we must treat them differently."

The racist champions of racist discrimination engineered to maintain racial inequities before the 1960s are now the racist opponents of antiracist discrimination engineered to dismantle those racial inequities. The most threatening racist movement is not the alt right's unlikely drive for a White ethnostate but the regular American's drive for a "race-neutral" one. The construct of race neutrality actually feeds White nationalist victimhood by positing the notion that any policy protecting or advancing non-White Americans toward equity is "reverse discrimination."

That is how racist power can call affirmative action policies that succeed in reducing racial inequities "race conscious" and standardized tests that produce racial inequities "race neutral." That is how they can blame the behavior of entire racial groups for the inequities between different racial groups and still say their ideas are "not racist." But there is no such thing as a not-racist idea, only racist ideas and antiracist ideas.

So what is a racist idea? A racist idea is any notion that suggests one racial group is inferior or superior to another racial group in any way. Racist ideas argue that the inferiorities and superiorities of racial groups explain racial inequities in society. As Thomas Jefferson suspected a decade after declaring White American independence: "The blacks, whether originally a distinct race, or made distinct by time and circumstances, are inferior to the whites in the endowments both of body and mind."

I am talking about "propaganda" and not "criticism" for a reason. Critics explore what a writer actually means and challenge it. Propagandists distort what a writer means and then attack their own distortions. Consumers of the propaganda who haven't read the book will never know that what is being fed to them is misinformation. These edits make it harder to distort the meaning of these sentences. But I am sure the conservators of racism will try. They want us thinking that antiracism, not racism, is the problem. They want us thinking that racism, not antiracism, is the solution.

An antiracist idea is any idea that suggests the racial groups are equals in all their apparent differences—that there is nothing right or wrong with any racial group. Antiracist ideas thereby convey that racist policies and practices are the cause of racial inequities.

Understanding the differences between racist policies and antiracist policies, between racist ideas and antiracist ideas, allows us to return to our fundamental definitions. Racism is a powerful collection of policies that lead to racial inequity and injustice and that are substantiated by ideas of racial hierarchy. Antiracism is a powerful collection of policies that lead to racial equity and justice and that are substantiated by ideas of racial equality.

ONCE WE HAVE a solid definition of racism and antiracism, we can start to make sense of the racialized world around us, before us. My maternal grandparents, Mary Ann and Alvin, moved their family to New York City in the 1950s on the final leg of the Great Migration, happy to get their children away from violent Georgia segregationists and the work of harvesting crops under the increasingly hot Georgia sun.

To think, they were also moving their family away from the effects of climate change. Do-nothing climate policy is racist policy, since the predominantly non-White Global South is being victimized by climate change more than the Whiter Global North, even as the Whiter Global North is contributing more to its acceleration. Land is sinking and temperatures are rising from Florida to Bangladesh. Droughts and food scarcity are ravaging bodies in Southern and Eastern Africa, regions already containing

NOTE ON SCHOLARSHIP What drives me to produce scholarship about being antiracist is learning from the research how and what I can be and do to dismantle the power and policy structure of racism—and knowing I'm not alone in this learning journey. It does not help me—nor, I suspect, you—for scholars to say what we should *not* be doing if scholars do not also use their research expertise to say what we *should* be doing. It is like a nutritionist telling clients to cut back on red meat without suggesting what they should eat instead. We need scholarship that helps us make the world healthy. An equitable and just world is a healthy world.

nearly one-fifth of the world's undernourished population. Human-made environmental catastrophes disproportionately harming bodies of color are not unusual; for instance, nearly four thousand U.S. areas—where mostly impoverished people and people of color live—have higher lead poisoning rates than Flint, Michigan.

I am one generation removed from picking cotton for pocket change under the warming climate in Guyton, outside Savannah, Georgia. That's where we buried my grandmother in 1993. Memories of her comforting calmness, her dark green thumb, and her large trash bags of Christmas gifts lived on as we drove back to New York from her funeral. The next day, my father ventured up to Flushing, Queens, to see his single mother, also named Mary Ann. She had the clearest dark-brown skin, a smile that hugged you, and a wit that smacked you.

When my father opened the door of her apartment, he smelled the fumes coming from the stove she'd left on, and some other fumes. His mother nowhere in sight, he rushed down the hallway and into her back bedroom. That's where he found his mother, as if sleeping, but dead. Her struggle with Alzheimer's, a disease more prevalent among African Americans, was over.

There may be no more consequential White privilege than life itself. White lives matter to the tune of four additional years— and five additional years during the first year of the COVID-19 pandemic in 2020—over Black lives in the United States, which is just the most glaring of a host of health disparities, starting from infancy, where Black infants die at twice the rate of White infants. But at least my grandmothers and I met, we shared, we loved. I never met my paternal grandfather. I never met my maternal grandfather, Alvin, killed by cancer three years before my birth. In the United States, African Americans are 33 percent

NOTE ON "UNDERNOURISHED" I wrongly used the term "malnourished." This was too broad a term to use here, as it is defined as all forms of undernutrition and overnutrition. For example, obesity is a form of malnutrition, but fatphobia prevents us from seeing obesity as a form of malnutrition that necessitates our support and not our derision. I corrected myself with the term "undernourished."

more likely to die of cancer than White people. My father survived prostate cancer, which kills twice as many Black men as it does White men. Breast cancer disproportionately kills Black women.

Three million African Americans and four million Latinx Americans secured health insurance through the Affordable Care Act, dropping uninsured rates for both groups to around 11 percent before President Barack Obama left office. But a staggering 28.5 million Americans remained uninsured, a number that has risen to 31.6 million since Congress repealed the individual mandate in 2017. And it is becoming harder for people of color to vote out of office the politicians crafting these policies designed to shorten their lives. Racist voting policy has evolved from disenfranchising by Jim Crow voting laws to disenfranchising by mass incarceration and voter-ID laws. Sometimes these efforts are so blatant that they are struck down: North Carolina enacted one of these targeted voter-ID laws, but in July 2016 the Court of Appeals for the Fourth Circuit struck it down, ruling that its various provisions "target African Americans with almost surgical precision." But others have remained and been successful. Wisconsin's strict voter-ID law suppressed approximately two hundred thousand votes—again primarily targeting voters of color—in the 2016 election. Donald Trump won that critical swing state by 22,748 votes.

But after Trump lost the presidential election in 2020, voter suppression intensified in 2021. Republicans not only tried to overturn the election results through violently storming the U.S. Capitol on January 6, they led the charge to introduce more than 440 voter suppression bills in 49 states that year. And the U.S. Supreme Court cleared the way for it all. Months after Joe Biden's inauguration in 2021, the court upheld Arizona laws that disproportionately impacted Black and Brown voters, gutting the Voting Rights Act in the process. Justice Samuel Alito, writing for the court's antidemocratic majority, said, "The mere fact that there is some disparity in impact does not necessarily mean that a system is not equally open or that it does not give everyone an equal opportunity to vote." Actually, it does, Justice Alito. If the system was "equally open," then there would not be "some dis-parity in impact."

We are surrounded by racial inequity, as visible as the law, as hidden as our private thoughts. The question for each of us is: What side of history will we stand on? A racist is someone who is expressing an idea of racial hierarchy, or through actions or in-action is supporting a policy that leads to racial inequity or injus-tice. An antiracist is someone who is expressing an idea of racial equality, or is actively supporting a policy that leads to racial eq-uity or justice. "Racist" and "antiracist" are like peelable name tags that are placed and replaced based on what someone is doing or not doing, supporting or expressing in each moment. These are not permanent tattoos. No one becomes a racist or antiracist. We can only strive to be one or the other in each moment. We can unknowingly strive to be a racist. We can knowingly strive to be an antiracist. Like fighting an addiction, being an antiracist requires persistent self-awareness, constant self-criticism, and reg-ular self-examination.

Racist ideas have defined our society since its beginning and can feel so natural and obvious as to be banal, but antiracist ideas remain difficult to comprehend, in part because they go against the flow of history. As Audre Lorde said in 1980, "We have all been programmed to respond to the human differences between us with fear and loathing and to handle that difference in one of three ways: ignore it, and if that is not possible, copy it if we think it is dominant, or destroy it if we think it is subordinate. But we have no patterns for relating across our human differences as equals." To be an antiracist is a radical choice in the face of this history, requiring a radical reorientation of our consciousness.

DUELING CONSCIOUSNESS

ASSIMILATIONIST IDEA: Any notion that suggests that a racial group is culturally or behaviorally inferior, which justifies support for cultural or behavioral enrichment programs to develop that racial group.

SEGREGATIONIST IDEA: Any notion that suggests that a permanently inferior racial group can never be developed, which justifies policies and practices that kill, terrorize, deport, incarcerate, or separate away that racial group.

ANTIRACIST IDEA: Any notion that suggests that racial groups are equals and none needs developing, which justifies policy focused on creating racial equity and justice.

M Y PARENTS HAD not seen each other since Urbana '70. Christmas approached in 1973. Soul Liberation held a concert at the iconic Broadway Presbyterian Church in Harlem that turned into a reunion of sorts for the New York attendees of Ur-

NOTE ON INDIVIDUALS AND IDEAS I defined these terms as persons in the hardcover edition. I should have defined and described them as ideas in this chapter on dueling consciousness. Because it is ideas that are dueling inside a person, that are dueling inside my consciousness.

When the definitions beginning chapters defined racist and antiracist persons in the original hardcover edition—in the chapters "Biology," "Body," "Culture," "Behavior," "White," and "Class"—I also changed these definitions to racist and antiracist ideas. I have leaned into describing ideas and policies, and not identifying who individuals are in a permanent sense. I try to describe what individuals are being in moments of time. Now I usually talk about an individual "being racist" or "being antiracist" based on what a person is doing or not doing, saying or not saying, in any given moment. Are they reinforcing or challenging the structure of racism? Are they building a new structure of antiracism?

bana '70. Dad and Ma showed up. Old friends beckoned, and something new. After the chords of Soul Liberation fell silent, my parents finally spoke again and a spark finally lit.

Days later, Dad called. He asked Ma out. "I've been called to the mission field," Ma responded. "Leaving in March."

Ma and Dad persevered, even after Ma left to teach in a rural Liberian village outside Monrovia for nine months. Eight years later they were married, daring to name me, their second son, "exalted father" when I arrived in a world not in the practice of exalting Black sons. Just before that arrival, as my pregnant mother celebrated her thirty-first birthday on June 24, 1982, President Reagan declared war on her unborn baby. "We can put drug abuse on the run through stronger law enforcement," Reagan said in the Rose Garden.

It wasn't drug abuse that was put on the run, of course, but people like me, born into this regime of "stronger law enforcement." The stiffer sentencing policies for illegal drug activity—not a net increase in harm—caused the American prison population to quadruple between 1980 and 2000. While people convicted of violence typically account for about half of the prison population at any given time, more people were incarcerated for drugs than violence every year from 1993 to 2009. White Americans are more likely than Black and Latinx Americans to sell drugs, and these groups consume drugs at similar rates. Yet Black Americans are far more likely than White Americans to be jailed for drug offenses. Black Americans convicted of nonviolent drug-related activities remain in prisons for about the same length of time (58.7 months) as White Americans convicted of violence (61.7 months). In 2018, Black and Latinx Americans were still grossly overrepresented in the prison population at 56 percent, double their percentage of the U.S. adult population. White Americans were still grossly underrepresented in the prison population at 30 percent, about half their percentage of the U.S. adult population.

Reagan didn't start this so-called war, as historian Elizabeth Hinton recounts. President Lyndon B. Johnson first put us on the run when he named 1965 "the year when this country began a thorough, intelligent, and effective war against crime." My parents were in high school when Johnson's war on crime mocked his undersupported war on poverty, like a heavily armed shooter mocking the underresourced trauma surgeon. President Richard Nixon announced his war on drugs in 1971 to devastate his harshest critics—Black and antiwar activists. "We could arrest their leaders, raid their homes, break up their meetings, and vilify them night after night on the evening news," Nixon's domestic-policy chief, John Ehrlichman, told a *Harper's* reporter years later. "Did we know we were lying about the drugs? Of course we did."

Black Americans joined in the vilification, convinced that homicidal drug dealers, gun toters, and thieving heroin addicts were flushing "down the drain" all "the hard won gains of the civil rights movement," to quote an editorial in *The Washington Afro-American* in 1981. Some, if not most, Black leaders, in an effort to appear as saviors of the people against this menace, turned around and set the Black "criminal" alongside the White racist as the enemies of the people.

Seemingly contradictory calls to lock up and to save Black people dueled in legislatures around the country but also in the minds of Americans. Black leaders joined with Republicans from Nixon to Reagan, and with Democrats from Johnson to Bill Clinton, in calling for and largely receiving more police officers, tougher and mandatory sentencing, and more jails. But they also called for the end of police brutality, more jobs, better schools, and drug-treatment programs. These calls were less enthusiastically received.

By the time I came along in 1982, the shame about "Black on Black crime" was on the verge of overwhelming a generation's pride about "Black is beautiful." Many non-Black Americans looked down on Black Americans struggling with an addiction in revulsion—but too many Black folk looked down on the same people in shame.

Both of my parents emerged from impoverished families, one from Northern urban projects, one from Southern rural fields.

Both framed their rise from poverty into the middle class in the 1980s as a climb up the ladder of education and hard work. As they climbed, they were inundated with racist talking points about Black people refusing to climb, the ones who were irresponsibly strung out on heroin or crack, who enjoyed stealing and being criminally dependent on the hard-earned money of climbing Americans like them.

In 1985, adored civil rights lawyer Eleanor Holmes Norton took to *The New York Times* to claim the "remedy . . . is not as simple as providing necessities and opportunities," as antiracist activists argued. She urged the "overthrow of the complicated, predatory ghetto subculture." She called on people like my parents with "ghetto origins" to save "ghetto males" and women by impressing on them the values of "hard work, education, respect for family" and "achieving a better life for one's children." Norton provided no empirical evidence to substantiate her position that certain "ghetto" Black people were deficient in any of these values.

But my parents, along with many others in the new Black middle class, consumed these ideas. The class that challenged racist policies from the 1950s through the 1970s now began challenging other Black people in the 1980s and 1990s. Antiracism seemed like an indulgence in the face of the self-destructive behavior they were witnessing all around them. My parents followed Norton's directive: They fed me the mantra that education and hard work would uplift me, just as it had uplifted them, and would, in the end, uplift all Black people. My parents—even from within their racial consciousness—were susceptible to the racist idea that it was laziness that kept Black people down, so they paid more attention to chastising Black people than to Reagan's policies, which were chopping the ladder they climbed up and then punishing people for falling.

The Reagan Revolution was just that: a radical revolution for the benefit of the already powerful. It further enriched high-income Americans by cutting their taxes and government regulations, installing a Christmas-tree military budget, and arresting the power of unions. Seventy percent of middle-income Black people said they saw "a great deal of racial discrimination" in 1979, before Reagan revolutionaries rolled back enforcement of civil rights laws and affirmative-action regulations, before they rolled back funding to state and local governments whose contracts and jobs had become safe avenues into the single-family urban home of the Black middle class. In the same month that Reagan announced his war on drugs on Ma's birthday in 1982, he cut the safety net of federal welfare programs and Medicaid, sending more low-income Black people into poverty. His "stronger law enforcement" sent more Black people into the clutches of violent cops, who killed twenty-two Black people for every White person in the early 1980s. Black youth were four times more likely to be unemployed in 1985 than in 1954. But few connected the increase in unemployment to the increase in violence.

Americans have long been trained to see the deficiencies of people rather than policy. It's a pretty easy mistake to make: People are in our faces. Policies are distant. We are particularly poor at seeing the policies lurking behind the struggles of people. And so my parents turned away from the problems of policy to look at the problems of people—and reverted to striving to save and civilize Black people rather than liberate them. Civilizer theology became more attractive to my parents, in the face of the rise of crack and the damage it did to Black people, as it did to so many children of civil rights and Black power. But in many ways, liberation theology remained their philosophical home, the home in which they raised me.

DEEP DOWN, MY parents were still the people who were set on fire by liberation theology back in Urbana. Ma still dreamed of globetrotting the Black world as a liberating missionary, a dream her Liberian friends encouraged in 1974. Dad dreamed of writing liberating poetry, a dream Professor Addison Gayle encouraged in 1971.

I always wonder what would have been if my parents had not

let their reasonable fears stop them from pursuing their dreams. Traveling Ma helping to free the Black world. Dad accompanying her and finding inspiration for his freedom poetry. Instead, Ma settled for a corporate career in healthcare technology. Dad settled for an accounting career. They entered the American middle class—a space then as now defined by its disproportionate White majority—and began to look at themselves and their people not only through their own eyes but also "through the eyes of others." They joined other Black people trying to fit into that White space while still trying to be themselves and save their people. They were not wearing a mask as much as splitting into two minds.

This conceptual duple reflected what W.E.B. Du Bois indelibly voiced in *The Souls of Black Folk* in 1903. "It is a peculiar sensation, this double-consciousness, this sense of always looking at one's self through the eyes of others," Du Bois wrote. He would neither "Africanize America" nor "bleach his Negro soul in a flood of white Americanism." Du Bois wished "to be both a Negro and an American." Du Bois wished to inhabit opposing constructs. To be American is to be White. To be White is to not be a Negro.

What Du Bois termed double consciousness may be more precisely termed *dueling* consciousness. "One ever feels his two-ness," Du Bois explained, "an American, a Negro; two souls, two thoughts, two unreconciled strivings; two warring ideals in one dark body, whose dogged strength alone keeps it from being torn asunder." Du Bois later also explained how this war was being waged within his own dark body, wanting to be a Negro and wanting to "escape into the mass of Americans in the same way that the Irish and Scandinavians" were doing.

These dueling ideas were there in 1903, and the same duel overtook my parents—and it remains today. The duel within Black consciousness seems to usually be between antiracist and assimilationist ideas. Du Bois believed in both the antiracist concept of racial relativity, of every racial group looking at itself with its own eyes, and the assimilationist concept of racial standards, of "looking at one's self through the eyes" of another racial group—in his case, White people. In other words, he wanted to liberate Black people from racism but he also wanted to change them, to save them from their "relic of barbarism." Du Bois argued in 1903 that racism and "the low social level of the mass of the race" were both "responsible" for the "Negro's degradation." Assimilation would be part of the solution to this problem.

Assimilationist ideas are racist ideas. Assimilationist ideas position any racial group as the superior standard that another racial group should be measuring themselves against, the benchmark they should be trying to reach. Assimilationist ideas typically position White people as the superior standard. "Do Americans ever stop to reflect that there are in this land a million men of Negro blood . . . who, judged by any standard, have reached the full measure of the best type of modern European culture? Is it fair, is it decent, is it Christian . . . to belittle such aspiration?" Du Bois asked in 1903.

THE DUELING CONSCIOUSNESS played out in a different way for my parents, who became all about Black self-reliance. In 1985, they were drawn to Floyd H. Flake's Allen African Methodist Episcopal Church in Southside Queens. Flake and his equally magnetic wife, Elaine, grew Allen into a megachurch and one of the area's largest private-sector employers through its liberated kingdom of commercial and social-service enterprises. From its school to its senior-citizen housing complex to its crisis center for victims of domestic abuse, there were no walls to Flake's church. It was exactly the type of ministry that would naturally fascinate those descendants of Urbana '70. My father joined Flake's ministerial staff in 1989.

My favorite church program happened every Thanksgiving. We would arrive as lines of people were hugging the church building, which smelled particularly good that day. Perfumes of gravy and cranberry sauce warmed the November air. The aromas multiplied in deliciousness as we entered the basement fellowship hall, where the ovens were. I usually found my spot in the endless assembly line of servers. I could barely see over the food. But I strained up on my toes to help feed every bit of five thousand people. I tried to be as kind to these hungry people as my mother's peach cobbler. This program of Black people feeding Black people embodied the gospel of Black self-reliance that the adults in my life were feeding me.

Black self-reliance was a double-edged sword. One side was an abhorrence of White supremacy and White paternalism, White rulers and White saviors. On the other, a love of Black rulers and Black saviors, of Black paternalism. On one side was the antiracist belief that Black people were entirely capable of ruling themselves, of relying on themselves. On the other, the assimilationist idea that Black people should focus on pulling themselves up by their baggy jeans and tight halter tops, getting off crack, street corners, and government "handouts," as if those were the things holding their incomes down. This dueling consciousness nourished Black pride by insisting that there was nothing wrong with Black people, but it also cultivated shame with its implication that there was something behaviorally wrong with Black people . . . well, at least those other Black people. If the problem was in our own behavior, then Reagan revolutionaries were not keeping Black people down—we were keeping ourselves down.

WHITE PEOPLE HAVE their own dueling consciousness, between the ideas of the segregationist and the assimilationist: the human trader and the missionary, the proslavery exploiter and the antislavery civilizer, the eugenicist and the melting pot-ter, the mass incarcerator and the mass developer, the Blue Lives Matter and the All Lives Matter, the not-racist nationalist and the not-racist liberal.

Assimilationist ideas and segregationist ideas are the two types of racist ideas, the duel within racist thought. White assimilationist ideas challenge segregationist ideas that claim people of color are incapable of development, incapable of reaching the superior standard, incapable of becoming White and therefore fully human. Assimilationist ideas convey that people of color can, in fact, be developed, become fully human, just like White people. Assimilationist ideas reduce people of color to the level of children needing instruction on how to act. Segregationist ideas cast people of color as "animals," to use Trump's descriptor for Latinx immigrants—unteachable after a point. The history of the racialized world is a three-way ideological fight between assimilationist, segregationist, and antiracist ideas. Antiracist ideas are based on the notion of racial equality, assimilationist ideas are rooted in the notion that certain racial groups are culturally or behaviorally inferior, and segregationist ideas spring from a belief in genetic racial distinction and fixed hierarchy. "I am apt to suspect the negroes and in general all the other species of men (for there are four or five different kinds) to be naturally inferior to the whites," Enlightenment philosopher David Hume wrote in 1753. "There never was a civilized nation of any other complexion than white. . . . Such a uniform and constant difference could not happen, in so many countries and ages, if nature had not made an original distinction between these breeds of men."

David Hume declared that all races are created unequal, but Thomas Jefferson seemed to disagree in 1776 when he declared "all men are created equal." But Thomas Jefferson never made the antiracist declaration: All racial groups are equals. While segregationist ideas suggest a racial group is permanently inferior, assimilationist ideas suggest a racial group is temporarily inferior. "It would be hazardous to affirm that, equally cultivated for a few generations," the Negro "would not become" equal, Jefferson once wrote, in assimilationist fashion.

The dueling White consciousness fashioned two types of racist policies, reflecting the duel of racist ideas. With assimilationist ideas positing cultural and behavioral hierarchy, assimilationist policies and programs are geared toward developing, civilizing, and integrating a racial group (to distinguish from programs that uplift individuals). With segregationist ideas positing the incapability of a racial group to be civilized and developed, segregationist policies are geared toward segregating, enslaving, incarcerating, deporting, and killing. With antiracist ideas positing that the racial groups are already civilized, antiracist policies are geared toward reducing racial inequities and creating equal opportunity.

White people have generally advocated for both assimilationist and segregationist policies. People of color have generally advocated for both antiracist and assimilationist policies. The "history of the American Negro is the history of this strife," to quote Du Bois—the strife between assimilationist and antiracist ideas, between mass civilizing and mass equalizing. In Du Bois's Black mind, in my parents' Black minds, in my young Black mind, this double desire, this dueling consciousness, yielded an inner strife between Black pride and a yearning to be White. My own assimilationist ideas stopped me from noticing the racist policies really getting high during Reagan's drug war.

THE DUELING WHITE consciousness has, from its position of relative power, shaped the struggle within Black consciousness. Despite the cold truth that America was founded "by white men for white men," as segregationist Jefferson Davis said on the floor of the U.S. Senate in 1860, Black people have often expressed a desire to be American and have been encouraged in this by America's undeniable history of antiracist progress, away from chattel slavery and Jim Crow. Despite the cold instructions from the likes of Nobel laureate Gunnar Myrdal to "become assimilated into American culture," Black people have also, as Du Bois said, desired to remain Negro, discouraged by America's undeniable history of racist progress, from advancing police violence and voter suppression, to widening racial inequities in areas ranging from health to wealth.

History duels: the undeniable history of antiracist progress, the undeniable history of racist progress. Before and after the Civil War, before and after civil rights, before and after the first

Black presidency, the White consciousness duels. The White body defines the American body. The White body segregates the Black body from the American body. The White body instructs the Black body to assimilate into the American body. The White body rejects the Black body assimilating into the American body—and history and consciousness duel anew.

The Black body in turn experiences the same duel. The Black body is instructed to become an American body. The American body is the White body. The Black body strives to assimilate into the American body. The American body rejects the Black body. The Black body separates from the American body. The Black body is instructed to assimilate into the American body—and history and consciousness duel anew.

But there is a way to get free. To be antiracist is to emancipate oneself from the dueling consciousness. To be antiracist is to conquer the assimilationist consciousness and the segregationist consciousness. The White body no longer presents itself as the American body; the Black body no longer strives to be the American body, knowing there is no such thing as the American body, only American bodies, racialized by power.

POWER

RACE: A power construct of blended difference that lives socially.

W E PULLED INTO the parking lot, looking for signs of life. But the daily life of the school had ended hours ago. It was pushing four o'clock on that warm April day in 1990, on Long Island, New York.

The car was parked and I could see the unease in my parents' faces as they freed themselves from their seatbelts. Maybe they were just trying to wrap their heads around making this thirty-minute drive out to Long Island twice a day, every weekday, year after year—on top of their hour-long job commutes to Manhattan. I sensed their discomfort and felt my own. Nerves about changing schools. Wishing P.S. 251 went past second grade. Feeling sick being so far from home in this foreign neighborhood. My seven-year-old feelings were roiling.

Several public elementary schools resided within walking distance of my house in Queens Village. But middle-income Black New Yorkers with the wherewithal to do it were separating their children from low-income Black children in low-income Black neighborhoods, just like White New Yorkers were separating their children from Black children. The dueling consciousness of

White parents did not mind spending more money on housing in order to send their kids to White public schools—and keep them away from the purportedly bad schools and bad children. The dueling consciousness of Black parents did not mind paying for private Black schools to keep their children away from those same public schools and children.

A Black woman greeted us at the front door of Grace Lutheran School. She had been waiting. She was the school's third-grade teacher, and after a quick greeting, she took us down a corridor. Classrooms stood on both sides, but I fixated on the class photos outside the rooms: all those adult White faces and young Black faces looking back at us. We occasionally peeked inside nicely decorated classrooms. No sounds. No students. No teachers. Just footsteps.

She took us to her third-grade classroom, a long throw from the entrance. We could see the materials laid out for a science project, the details of which she explained to us. I couldn't care less about raising chicks. Then she took us over to a round table and asked if we had any questions. Sitting down, my mother asked a question about the curriculum. I did not care much about that, either. I started looking more intently around the classroom. A pause in the discussion caught my attention—Dad had just asked about the racial makeup of the student body. Majority Black. I took note. My mind drifted away again, this time wandering around the classroom and around the school, trying to imagine the students and teachers, remembering those pictures in the hallway. A pause caught my attention again. A question popped out of me.

"Are you the only Black teacher?"

"Yes, but—"

I cut her off. "Why are you the only Black teacher?"

Puzzled, she looked away at my parents. My parents exchanged curious looks. I kept staring at the teacher, wondering why she was looking at my parents. Ma ended the awkward silence. "He has been reading biographies of Black leaders."

Ma was talking about the critically acclaimed Junior Black Americans of Achievement series, promoted by Coretta Scott King. Dad had bought a stack of these biographies, towering over one hundred now. Martin Luther King Jr. Frederick Douglass. Mary McLeod Bethune. Richard Allen. Ida B. Wells. Dad kept urging me to pull from the tower for every writing project.

These gripping biographies were as exciting to me as new video games on my Sega Genesis. Once I started reading, I could not stop. Discovering through these books the long history of harm done to Black Americans left me seething and brought to life a kind of racial consciousness I could articulate for the first time.

"He is very much aware of being Black," Ma made sure to add, looking at Dad. She did not look for confirmation. Dad nodded in agreement anyway, as I stared at the teacher, awaiting my answer.

In that classroom, on that April day in 1990, my parents discovered that I had entered racial puberty. At seven years old, I began to feel the encroaching fog of racism overtaking my dark body. It felt big, bigger than me, bigger than my parents or anything in my world, and threatening. What a powerful construction race is—powerful enough to consume us. And it comes for us early.

NOTE ON KIDS AND RACE After writing this book, I started researching precisely how early it comes for us. I realized it likely came for me much earlier than seven years old. Scholars have found that kids can have an "adult-like" concept of race by three years old, as I share in my book *How to Raise an Antiracist*. Studies show that kids can conceive of something years before they have the language to articulate that conception. If they are conceiving of race by three years old, then studies show that by seven years old they have the language to talk about race, to ask questions about race. But when kids start asking questions—as I did in this moment—their questions often go unanswered or are shut down. The first lesson kids receive about race is not to talk about it. When it comes for our kids, who is going to be there to protect them? It must be us, and that's why I followed up this book with *How to Raise an Antiracist*.

But for all of that life-shaping power, race is a mirage, which doesn't lessen its force. We are what we see ourselves as, whether what we see exists or not. We are what people see us as, whether what they see exists or not. What people see in themselves and others has meaning and manifests itself in ideas and actions and policies, even if what they are seeing is an illusion. Race is a mirage but one that we do well to see, while never forgetting it is a mirage, never forgetting that it's the powerful light of racist power that makes the mirage.

So I do not pity my seven-year-old self for identifying racially as Black. I still identify as Black. Not because I believe Blackness, or race, is a meaningful scientific category but because our societies, our policies, our ideas and our histories and our cultures have rendered race and made it matter. I am among those who have been degraded by racist ideas, suffered under racist policies, and who have nevertheless endured and built movements and cultures to resist or at least persist through this madness. I see myself culturally and historically and politically in Blackness, in being an African American, an African, a member of the forced and unforced African diaspora. I see myself historically and politically as a person of color, as a member of the Global South, as a close ally of Latinx, Asian, Middle Eastern, and Native peoples and all the world's degraded peoples, from the Roma and Jews of Europe to the Aboriginals of Australia, to the stateless Palestinians and Kurds in the Middle East, to the White people battered for their religion, class, gender, transgender identity, ethnicity, sexuality, body size, age, and disability. The gift of seeing myself as Black instead of being color-blind is that it allows me to clearly see myself historically and politically as being an antiracist, as a member of the interracial body striving to accept and equate and empower racial difference of all kinds.

Some White people do not identify as White for the same reason they identify as not-racist: to avoid reckoning with the ways that Whiteness—even as a construction and mirage—has informed their notions of America and identity and offered them privilege, the primary one being the privilege of being inherently

normal, standard, and legal. It is a racial crime to be yourself if
you are not White in America. It is a racial crime to look like
yourself or empower yourself if you are not White. I guess I became a criminal at seven years old.

It is one of the ironies of antiracism that we must identify racially in order to identify the racial privileges and dangers of being
in our bodies. Latinx and Asian and African and European and
Indigenous and Middle Eastern: These six races—at least in the
U.S. context—are fundamentally power identities, because race is
fundamentally a power construct of blended difference that lives
socially. Race creates new forms of power: the power to categorize and judge, elevate and downgrade, include and exclude.
Race makers use that power to process distinct individuals, ethnicities, and nationalities into monolithic races.

THE FIRST GLOBAL power to construct race happened to be the
first racist power and the first exclusive human trader of the constructed race of African people. The individual who orchestrated
this trading of an invented people was nicknamed the "Navigator," though he did not leave Portugal in the fifteenth century.
The only thing he navigated was Europe's political-economic
seas, in order to create the first transatlantic human-trading policies. Hailed for something he was not (and ignored for what he
was)—it is fitting that Prince Henry the Navigator, the brother
and then uncle of Portuguese kings, is the first character in the
history of racist power.

Prince Henry lived in me. The name Henry had traveled
down through the centuries and over the Atlantic Ocean and
eventually into my father's family. After my mother gave my older
brother a middle name from her family, Dad chose a middle name
for me from his family. He chose the name of his enslaved great-
great-grandfather, Henry. Dad did not know that this ancestor
shared the name of the Navigator, but when I learned the history,
I knew it had to go. My middle name is now Xolani, meaning
peace, the very thing Henry's human traders snatched from Africa

(and the Americas and Europe), the thing they snatched from my ancestor Henry.

Until his death in 1460, Prince Henry sponsored Atlantic voyages to West Africa by the Portuguese, to circumvent Islamic human traders, and in doing so created a different sort of slavery than had existed before. Premodern Islamic human traders, like their Christian counterparts in premodern Italy, were not pursuing racist policies—they were enslaving what we now consider to be Africans, Arabs, and Europeans alike. At the dawn of the modern world, the Portuguese began to exclusively trade people from Africa. Prince Henry's sailors made history when they navigated past the feared "black" hole of Cape Bojador, off Western Sahara, and brought enslaved Africans back to Portugal.

Prince Henry's first biographer—and apologist—became the first race maker and crafter of racist ideas. King Afonso V commissioned Gomes Eanes de Zurara, a royal chronicler and a loyal commander in Prince Henry's Military Order of Christ, to compose a glowing biography of the African adventures of his "beloved uncle." Zurara finished *The Chronicle of the Discovery and Conquest of Guinea* in 1453, the first European book on Africa.

One of Zurara's stories chronicled Prince Henry's first major human auction in Lagos, Portugal, in 1444. Some people from Africa were "white enough, fair to look upon, and well proportioned," while others were "like mulattoes" or "as black as Ethiops, and so ugly." Despite their different skin colors and languages and ethnic groups, Zurara blended them into one single group of people, worthy of enslavement.

Unlike babies in some cultures, phenomena are typically born long before humans give them names. Zurara did not call Black people a race. French poet Jacques de Brézé first used the term "race" in a 1481 hunting poem. In 1606, the same diplomat who brought the addictive tobacco plant to France formally defined race for the first time in a major European dictionary. "Race . . . means descent," Jean Nicot wrote in the *Trésor de la langue française*. "Therefore, it is said that a man, a horse, a dog, or another animal is from [a] good or bad race." From the beginning, to make races was to make racial hierarchy.

Gomes Eanes de Zurara grouped all those peoples from Africa into a single race for that very reason: to create hierarchy, the first racist idea. Racist ideas have been an essential ingredient in the making of races. Zurara constructed the Black race with negative traits to justify Prince Henry's evangelical mission to the world. This Black race of people was lost, living "like beasts, without any custom of reasonable beings," Zurara wrote. "They had no understanding of good, but only knew how to live in a bestial sloth."

After Spanish and Portuguese colonizers arrived in the Americas in the fifteenth century, they took to race making all the different Indigenous peoples, calling them one people, "Indians," or *negros da terra* (Blacks from the land) in sixteenth-century Brazil. Spanish lawyer Alonso de Zuazo in 1510 contrasted the beastly African race as "strong for work, the opposite of the natives, so weak who can work only in undemanding tasks." Both racist constructions normalized and rationalized the increased importing of the supposedly "strong" enslaved Africans and the ongoing genocide of the supposedly "weak" Indigenous people in the Americas.

The other races, save Latinx and Middle Eastern people, had been completely made and distinguished by the Age of Enlightenment in the eighteenth century. Beginning in 1758, Swedish botanist and physician Carl Linnaeus locked in the racial hierarchy of humankind in the tenth edition of *Systema Naturae*. He color-coded the races as White, Yellow, Red, and Black. He attached each race to one of the four regions of the world and described their characteristics. The Linnaean taxonomy became the blueprint that nearly every enlightened race maker followed and that race makers still follow today. And, of course, these were not simply neutral categories, because races were not meant to be neutral categories. Racist power constructed them for a purpose.

Linnaeus positioned *Homo sapiens europaeus* at the top of the racial hierarchy, making up the most superior character traits.

"Vigorous, muscular. Flowing blond hair. Blue eyes. Very smart, inventive. Covered by tight clothing. Ruled by law." He made up the middling racial character of *Homo sapiens asiaticus*: "Melancholy, stern. Black hair; dark eyes. Strict, haughty, greedy. Covered by loose garments. Ruled by opinion." He granted the racial character of *Homo sapiens americanus* a mixed set of attributes: "Ill-tempered, impassive. Thick straight black hair; wide nostrils; harsh face; beardless. Stubborn, contented, free. Paints himself with red lines. Ruled by custom." At the bottom of the racial hierarchy, Linnaeus positioned *Homo sapiens afer*: "Sluggish, lazy. Black kinky hair. Silky skin. Flat nose. Thick lips. Females with genital flap and elongated breasts. Crafty, slow, careless. Covered by grease. Ruled by caprice."

FROM 1434 TO 1448, Gomes Eanes de Zurara estimated, 927 enslaved Africans landed in Portugal, "the greater part of whom were turned into the true path of salvation." It was, according to Zurara, Prince Henry's paramount achievement, an achievement blessed by successive popes. No mention of Prince Henry's royal fifth (*quinto*), the 185 or so of those captives he was given, a fortune in bodies.

The obedient Gomes Eanes de Zurara created racial difference to convince the world that Prince Henry (and thus Portugal) did not enslave and trade humans for money, only to save souls. The liberators had come to Africa? Zurara personally sent a copy of *The Chronicle of the Discovery and Conquest of Guinea* to King Afonso V with an introductory letter in 1453. He hoped the book would "keep" Prince Henry's name "before" the "eyes" of the world, "to the great praise of his memory." Gomes Eanes de Zurara secured Prince Henry's memory as surely as Prince Henry secured the wealth of the royal court. King Afonso was accumulating more capital from selling enslaved Africans to foreigners "than from all the taxes levied on the entire kingdom," observed a traveler in 1466. Racism had served its purpose.

Prince Henry's racist policy of human trading came first—a

cunning invention for the practical purpose of bypassing Muslim traders. After nearly two decades of slave trading, King Afonso asked Gomes Eanes de Zurara to defend the lucrative commerce in human lives, which he did through the construction of a Black race, an invented group, invented through racist ideas. This cause and effect—a racist power creates racist policies out of raw self-interest; the racist policies necessitate racist ideas to justify them— lingers over the life of racism.

FROM THE JUNIOR Black Americans of Achievement series on- ward, I had been taught that racist ideas cause racist policies. That ignorance and hate cause racist ideas. That the root problem of racism is ignorance and hate.

But that gets the chain of events exactly wrong. The root problem—from Henry to Trump—has always been the self- interest of racist power. Powerful economic, political, and cultural self-interest—the primitive accumulation of capital in the case of royal Portugal and subsequent human traders—has been behind racist policies. Powerful and brilliant intellectuals in the tradition of Gomes Eanes de Zurara then produced racist ideas and races to justify the racist policies of their era, to redirect the blame for their era's racial inequities and injustices away from those policies and onto people.

THE TEACHER SOON overcame her surprise at a seven-year-old questioning her about the paucity of Black teachers. After search- ing my parents' faces, she looked back at me. "Why are you ask- ing that question?" she asked nicely.

"If you have so many Black kids, you should have more Black teachers," I said.

"The school hasn't hired more Black teachers."

"Why?"

"I don't know."

"Why don't you know?"

My parents could see my agitation growing. Dad changed the subject. I didn't mind. My train of thought had taken me away, anyway. I was thinking about what Ma had just said. I am Black. I am Black.

I ended up attending a private Lutheran school closer to home, White third-grade teacher and all. I did not mind until I noticed.

CHAPTER 4

BIOLOGY

BIOLOGICAL RACIST IDEA: Any notion that suggests that the races are meaningfully different in their biology and that these differences create a hierarchy of value.

BIOLOGICAL ANTIRACIST IDEA: Any notion that suggests that the races are meaningfully the same in their biology and there are no genetic racial differences.

CANNOT RECALL HER name. So very odd. I can recite the names of my Black fourth-, fifth-, and sixth-grade teachers. But the name of my White third-grade teacher is lost in my memory like the names of so many racist White people over the years who interrupted my peace with their sirens. Forgetting her may have been a coping mechanism. People of color sometimes cope with abuse from White individuals by hiding those individuals behind the generalized banner of Whiteness. "She acted that way," we say, "because she is White."

But generalizing the behavior of racist White individuals to all White people is as perilous as generalizing the individual faults of people of color to entire races. "He acted that way because he is Black." "She acted that way because she is Asian." We often see and remember the race and not the individual. This is racist categorizing, this stuffing of our experiences with individuals into color-marked racial closets. An antiracist treats and remembers individuals as individuals. "She acted that way," we should say, "because she was being racist."

I know that now, but that knowledge won't bring back the specific memory of that teacher. My parents do not remember her name, either. All we remember is what she did.

My third-grade class was mostly made up of Black kids, with a handful of Asian and Latinx kids. Three White kids—two girls and a boy—kept to themselves and sat toward the front of the class. I sat toward the back near the door, where I could see everything. I could see when the White teacher overlooked raised Asian, Latinx, and Black hands and called on White hands. I could see her punish Asian, Latinx, and Black students for something she didn't punish White students for doing.

This was not a problem specific to my school or my childhood—it's a problem that cuts from private to public schools and through time. During the 2017–18 school year, Black students were twice as likely as White students to be suspended from public schools. The suspension rate of Black students was more than double their share of student enrollment.

Back in my third-grade class, the unfair punishments and overlooking did not seem to bother the other Black students, so I did not let them bother me. But one day, before Christmas break in 1990, it became unavoidable.

A tiny and quiet girl—tinier and quieter than me—sat on the other side of the back of the room. The teacher asked a question and I saw her slowly raise her dark-skinned hand, which was a rare occurrence. Her shyness, or something else, generally kept her mouth closed and arm down. But something roused her today. I smiled as I saw her small hand rising for the teacher's attention.

The teacher looked at her, looked away, and instead called on a White hand as soon as it was raised. As the Black girl's arm came down, I could see her head going down. As I saw her head going down, I could see her spirits going down. I turned and looked up at the teacher, who, of course, was not looking at me. She was too busy engaging a favored White child to notice what was happening in the back row—neither my fury nor the sadness of the girl registered for her.

Scholars call what I saw a "microaggression," a term coined by eminent Harvard psychiatrist Chester Pierce in 1970. Pierce employed the term to describe the constant verbal and nonverbal abuse racist White individuals unleash on Black individuals wherever we go, day after day. A White woman grabs her purse when a Black person sits next to her. The seat next to a Black person stays empty on a crowded bus. A White woman calls the cops at the sight of Black people barbecuing in the park. White individuals telling us that our firmness is anger or that our practiced talents are natural. Mistaking us for the only other Black person around. Calling the cops on our children for selling lemonade on the street. Butchering Ebonics for sport. Assuming we are the help. Assuming the help isn't brilliant. Asking us questions about the entire Black race. Not giving us the benefit of the doubt. Calling the cops on us for jogging down the street.

As an African American, Pierce suffered from and witnessed this sort of everyday abuse. He identified these individual abuses as microaggressions to distinguish from the macroaggressions of racist violence and policies.

Since 1970, the concept of microaggressions has expanded to apply to interpersonal abuses against all marginalized groups, not just Black people. In the last decade, the term has become popular in social-justice spaces through the defining work of psychologist Derald Wing Sue. He defines microaggressions as "brief, everyday exchanges that send denigrating messages to certain individuals because of their group membership."

I don't think it's coincidental that the term "microaggression" emerged in popularity during the so-called post-racial era that some people assumed we'd entered with the election of the first Black president. The word "racism" went out of fashion in the bipartisan haze of racial progress—Obama's political brand—and many Republicans and Democrats started to treat "racist" as the equivalent to the N-word, a vicious pejorative rather than a descriptive term. With the word itself becoming radioactive to some, passé to others, some well-meaning people started consciously and perhaps unconsciously looking for other terms to identify racism. "Microaggression" became part of a whole vocabulary of old and new words—like "cultural wars" and "stereotype" and "implicit bias" and "economic anxiety" and "tribalism"—that made it easier to talk about or around the R-word.

I do not use "microaggression" anymore. I detest the post-racial platform that supported its sudden popularity. I detest its component parts—"micro" and "aggression." A persistent daily low hum of racist abuse is not minor. I use the term "abuse" because aggression is not as exacting a term. Abuse accurately describes the action and its effects on people: distress, anger, worry, depression, anxiety, pain, fatigue, and suicide.

What other people call racial microaggressions I call racist abuse. And I call the zero-tolerance policies holding these abusers accountable what they are: antiracist. To be racist is to shy away from the R-word, steeped in denial.

BACK IN THE classroom, I needed some time to think about the racist abuse I saw. I watched my dejected classmate with her head down when we all began the walk through the long hall that led to the adjoining chapel, where we were to have our weekly service. Her sadness did not seem to let up. My fury did not, either.

The chapel had a postmodern design but was simple inside: a small pulpit and dozens of rows of brown pews, with a cross looming over it all from the back wall. When the morning service ended, the teacher began motioning my classmates out. I didn't move. I sat at the edge of the pew and stared at the teacher as she approached.

"Ibram, time to go," she said pleasantly.

"I'm not going anywhere!" I faintly replied, and looked straight ahead at the cross.

"What?"

I looked up at her, eyes wide and burning: "I'm not going anywhere!"

"No! You need to leave, right now."

Looking back, I wonder, if I had been one of her White kids would she have asked me: "What's wrong?" Would she have wondered if I was hurting? I wonder. I wonder if her racist ideas chalked up my resistance to my Blackness and therefore categorized it as misbehavior, not distress. With racist teachers, misbehaving Black kids do not receive inquiry and empathy and legitimacy. We receive orders and punishments and "no excuses," as if we are adults. The Black child is ill-treated like an adult, and the Black adult is ill-treated like a child.

My classmates were nearly out of the chapel. An observant handful stopped near the door, gazing and speculating. Irate and perplexed at this disruption, the teacher tried again to command me. She failed again. She grabbed my shoulder.

"Don't touch me!" I yelled.

"I'm calling the principal," she said, turning toward the exit.

"I don't care! Call her! Call her right now," I shouted, looking straight ahead as she walked away behind me. I felt a single tear falling from each eye.

It was chapel-quiet now. I wiped my eyes. I started rehearsing what I was going to tell the principal. When she came, she offered more commands that she thought could move me. She learned her lesson like her predecessor. I was not going to move until I recited my first dissertation on racism, until I had a chance to defend our Blackness.

OUR BLACKNESS. I am Black. I looked at the girl's dark skin and saw my skin color. Saw her kinky hair, split down the middle in cornrows held by barrettes, and saw my kinky hair, my small Afro. Saw her broad nose and saw my nose. Saw her thicker lips and saw my lips. Heard her talk and heard the way I talk. I did not see a mirage. We were the same. Those three favored White kids—they were different to my eight-year-old racial understanding. Their whiter skin color, straighter hair, skinnier noses and lips, their different way of speaking, even the way they wore their uniforms—all marked a different species to me. The difference was not skin deep.

No one taught me that these differences were meaningless to our underlying humanity—the essence of biological antiracist ideas. Adults had in so many ways taught me that these superficial differences signified different forms of humanity—the essence of biological racist ideas.

To essentialize race is to express a biological racist idea. To express a biological racist idea is to be segregationist. Biological racist ideas rest on two notions: that the races are meaningfully different in their biology and that these differences create a hierarchy of value. I grew up believing the first idea of biological racial difference. I grew up disbelieving the second idea of biological racial hierarchy, which conflicted with the biblical creation story I'd learned through biblical study, in which all humans descend from Adam and Eve. It also conflicted with the secular creed I'd been taught, the U.S. creation story that "all men are created equal."

My acceptance of biological racial distinction and rejection of biological racial hierarchy was like accepting water and rejecting its wetness. But that is precisely what I learned to do, what so many of us have learned to do in our dueling racial consciousness.

Biological racial difference is one of those widely held racist beliefs that few people realize they hold—nor do they realize that those beliefs are rooted in racist ideas. I grew up hearing about how Black people had "more natural physical ability," as half of respondents replied in a 1991 survey. How "Black blood" differed from "White blood." How "one drop of Negro blood makes a Negro" and "puts out the light of intellect," as wrote Thomas Dixon in *The Leopard's Spots* (1902). How Black people have natural gifts of improvisation. How "if blacks have certain inherited abilities, such as improvisational decision making, that could explain why they predominate in certain fields such as jazz, rap, and basketball, and not in other fields, such as classical music, chess, and astronomy," as suggested by Dinesh D'Souza in his 1995 book with the laughably dishonest title *The End of Racism*. How Black women had naturally large buttocks and Black men had naturally large penises. How the "increase of rape of white women" stems from the "large size of the negro's penis" and their "birthright" of "sexual madness and excess," as a doctor wrote in a 1903 issue of *Medicine*.

How Black people are biologically distinct because of slavery. At the 1988 American Heart Association conference, a Black hypertension researcher said African Americans had higher hypertension rates because only those able to retain high levels of salt survived consuming the salt water of the Atlantic Ocean during the Middle Passage. "I've bounced this off a number of colleagues and . . . it seems certainly plausible," Clarence Grim told swooning reporters. Plausibility became proof, and the slavery/hypertension thesis received the red-carpet treatment in the cardiovascular community in the early 1990s. Grim did not arrive at the thesis in his research lab. It came to him as he read *Roots* by Alex Haley. Who needs scientific proof when a biological racial distinction can be imagined by reading fiction? By reading the Bible?

THE SAME BIBLE that taught me that all humans descended from the first pair was also used to argue for immutable human difference, the result of a divine curse. "The people who were scattered over the earth came from Noah's three sons," according to the biblical story of the Great Flood in the ninth chapter of Genesis. Noah planted a vineyard, drank some of its wine, and fell asleep, naked and drunk, in his tent. Ham saw his father's nakedness and alerted his brothers. Shem and Japheth refused to look at Noah's nakedness, walked backward into his tent, and covered him. When Noah awoke, he learned that Ham, the father of Canaan, had viewed him in all his nakedness. "May a curse be put on Canaan," Noah raged. "May Canaan be the slave of Shem."

Who are the cursed descendants of Canaan? In 1578, English travel writer George Best provided an answer that, not coincidentally, justified expanding European enslavement of African people. God willed that Ham's son and "all his posteritie after him should be so blacke and loathsome," Best writes, "that it might remain a spectacle of disobedience to all the worlde."

Racist power at once made biological racial distinction and biological racial hierarchy the components of biological racist ideas. This curse theory lived prominently on the justifying lips of enslavers until Black chattel slavery died in Christian countries in the nineteenth century. Proof did not matter when biological racial difference could be created by misreading the Bible.

But science can also be misread to essentialize race. After Christopher Columbus came upon a people unmentioned in the Bible, speculations arose about Native Americans and soon about Africans descending from "a different Adam." But Christian Europe regarded polygenesis—the theory that the races are separate species with distinct creations—as heresy. When Isaac La Peyrère released *Men Before Adam* in 1655, authorities threw him in prison and ordered his books burned in Paris. But powerful enslavers in places like Barbados "preferred" the proslavery belief that there existed a "race of Men, not derivable from Adam" over "the Curse of Ham."

Polygenesis became a source of intellectual debate throughout the Age of Enlightenment. The debate climaxed in the 1770s, during the first transatlantic antislavery movement. Writing the Declaration of Independence in 1776, Thomas Jefferson seemingly came down on the side of monogenesis. Still, he expressed openness to the idea that Black people may have been created differently than White and Native peoples. And over the next few decades, polygenesis came to rule racial thought in the United States through scholars like Samuel Morton and Louis Agassiz, prompting biologist Charles Darwin to write in the opening

NOTE ON "CAME UPON" I changed "discovered" in the hardcover edition to "came upon." I fell for this conceptual trap. It is quite striking to recognize the level of anti-Native racist ideas within me, how the narrative of White colonists has infected my language, particularly this language of discovery. I am striving to unlearn these ideas and this language. I am striving to learn more about settler colonialism and the history of Native nations.

pages of *On the Origin of Species* in 1859, "The view which most naturalists entertain, and which I formerly entertained—namely, that each species has been independently created—is erroneous." He offered a theory of natural selection that was soon used as another method to biologically distinguish and rank the races.

The naturally selected White race was winning the struggle, was evolving, was headed toward perfection, according to social Darwinists. The only three outcomes available for the "weaker" races were extinction, slavery, or assimilation, explained the social Darwinist who founded American sociology. "Many fear the first possibility for the Indians," Albion Small co-wrote in 1894; "the second fate is often predicted for the negroes; while the third is anticipated for the Chinese and other Eastern peoples."

The transatlantic eugenics movement, powered by Darwin's half cousin Francis Galton, aimed to speed up natural selection with policies encouraging reproduction among those considered to have superior genes and discouraging reproduction among those considered to have inferior genes. Global outrage after the genocidal eugenics-driven policies of Nazi Germany in the mid-twentieth century led to the marginalization of biological racist ideas within academic thought for the first time in four hundred years. Biological racist ideas—curse theory, polygenesis, and eugenics—had held strong for that long. And yet marginalization in academic thought did not mean marginalization in common thought, including the kind of common thinking that surrounded me as a child.

SCIENTISTS AND APPLAUSE accompanied the president of the United States as he walked into the East Room of the White House on June 26, 2000. Bill Clinton took his position behind a podium in the middle of two screens featuring this headline: DE-CODING THE BOOK OF LIFE / A MILESTONE FOR HUMANITY. Geneticists had started decoding the book of life in 1990, the same year I identified myself in that book as Black.

After thanking politicians and scientists from around the

world, Clinton harkened back two hundred years, to the day Thomas Jefferson "spread out a magnificent map" of the continental United States "in this room, on this floor."

"Today, the world is joining us here in the East Room to behold a map of even greater significance," Clinton announced. "We are here to celebrate the completion of the first survey of the entire human genome. Without a doubt, this is the most important, most wondrous map ever produced by humankind." When scientists finished drawing the map of "our miraculous genetic code," when they stepped back and looked at the map, one of the "great truths" they saw was "that in genetic terms, all human beings, regardless of race, are more than 99.9 percent the same," Clinton declared. "What that means is that modern science has confirmed what we first learned from ancient faiths. The most important fact of life on this Earth is our common humanity."

No one told me the defining investigation in modern human history was unfolding behind the racist wars of the 1990s. It was arguably one of the most important scientific announcements ever made by a sitting head of state—perhaps as important to humans as landing on the moon—but the news of our fundamental equality was overtaken by more-familiar arguments.

"Scientists planning the next phase of the human genome project are being forced to confront a treacherous issue: the genetic differences between human races," science writer Nicholas Wade reported in *The New York Times* a year after Clinton's announcement. In his 2014 bestseller, *A Troublesome Inheritance,* Wade made the case that "there is a genetic component to human social behavior." This connecting of biology to behavior is the cradle of biological racist ideas—it leads to biological ranking of the races and the supposition that the biology of certain races yields superior behavioral traits, like intelligence.

But there is no such thing as racial ancestry. Ethnic ancestry does exist. Camara Jones, a prominent medical researcher of health disparities, explained it this way to bioethics scholar Dorothy Roberts: "People are born with ancestry that comes from their parents but are assigned a race." People from the same ethnic groups that are native to certain geographic regions typically share the same genetic profile. Geneticists call them "populations." When geneticists compare these ethnic populations, they find there is more genetic diversity between populations within Africa than between Africa and the rest of the world. Ethnic groups in Western Africa are more genetically similar to ethnic groups in Western Europe than to ethnic groups in Eastern Africa. Race is a genetic mirage.

Segregationist ideas, like those espoused by Nicholas Wade, figure if humans are 99.9 percent genetically alike, then they must be 0.1 percent distinct. And this distinction must be racial. And that 0.1 percent of racial distinction has multiplied exponentially over the millennia. And it is their job to search heaven and earth for proof of these exponentially distinct races.

To be assimilationist is to accept a different job, which has been in the works for decades. "What should we be teaching inside our churches and beyond their four walls?" Christian fundamentalist Ken Ham, the co-author of *One Race One Blood,* asked in an op-ed in 2017. "For one, point out the common ground of both evolutionists and creationists: the mapping of the human genome concluded that there is only one race, the human race."

Singular-race makers push for the end of categorizing and identifying by race. They wag their fingers at people like me identifying as Black—but the unfortunate truth is that their post-racial strategy makes no sense in our racist world. Race is a mirage but one that humanity has organized itself around in very real ways. Imagining away the existence of races in a racist world is as conserving and harmful as imagining away classes in a capitalistic world—it allows the inequality to exist and persist undetected.

To be assimilationist is to believe in the post-racial myth that talking about race constitutes racism, or that if we stop identifying by race, then racism will miraculously go away. They fail to realize that if we stop using racial categories, then we will not be able to identify racial inequity. If we cannot identify racial inequity, then we will not be able to identify racist policies. If we cannot identify racist policies, then we cannot challenge racist policies. If we cannot challenge racist policies, then racist power's final solution will be achieved: an unjust world of inequity none of us can see, let alone resist. Terminating racial categories is potentially the last, not the first, step in the antiracist struggle.

To be segregationist is to see several biologically distinct races. The assimilationist sees one biological human race. But there is another way of looking: through the lens of biological antiracist ideas. To be antiracist is to challenge those ideas essentializing race and racial identity. To be antiracist is to recognize one human race and the reality of biological equality, that skin color is as meaningless to our underlying humanity as the clothes we wear over that skin. To be antiracist is to recognize there is no such thing as White blood or Black diseases or natural Latinx athleticism. To be antiracist is to also recognize the living, breathing reality of the mirage of race, which makes our skin colors more meaningful than our individuality. To be antiracist is to focus on ending the racism that shapes the mirages, not ignoring the mirages that shape people's lives.

THE PRINCIPAL FINALLY sat down next to me. Maybe she suddenly saw me not as the misbehaving Black boy but as a boy, a student under her care, with a problem. Maybe not. In any case, I was allowed to speak. I defended my dissertation. I did not use terms like "racist abuse" and "racist ideas." I used terms like "fair" and "unfair," "sad" and "happy." She listened and surprised me with questions. My one-boy sit-in ended after she heard me out and agreed to talk to that teacher.

I expected to be punished when the principal summoned Ma that afternoon. After describing what happened, the principal told her my behavior was prohibited at the school. Ma did not say it would never happen again, as the principal expected. Ma told her she would have to speak to me.

"If you are going to protest, then you're going to have to deal with the consequences," Ma said that night, as she would on future nights after my activism.

"Okay," I replied. But no consequences came this time. And the teacher eased up on the Black, Asian, and Latinx students.

Third grade ended it. My parents took me out of that school. One year was enough. They looked for a Christian private school that could better nurture a Black student. They found the Black teaching staff at St. Joseph's Parish Day School, an Episcopalian school closer to our home in Queens Village, where I attended fourth, fifth, and sixth grades.

For seventh grade and the yearlong comedy show that kept my eighth-grade classroom filled with laughs and hurt feelings, I transferred to a private Lutheran school around the corner from St. Joseph's. Almost all my Black eighth-grade classmates were jokesters. Almost everyone got joked on for something. But one joke stung more than others.

CHAPTER 5

ETHNICITY

ETHNIC RACIST IDEA: Any notion that suggests that a racialized ethnic group is superior or inferior to another racialized ethnic group in any way, or justifies policies that lead to injustice or inequity between racialized ethnic groups.

ETHNIC ANTIRACIST IDEA: Any notion that suggests that the racialized ethnic groups are equals or substantiates policies that lead to justice and equity between racialized ethnic groups.

NOTE ON RACIST IDEAS AND STRUCTURES I decided to change these definitions from "racism"/"antiracism" to "racist ideas"/"antiracist ideas." I made similar changes to the definitions opening the chapters "Color," "Space," "Gender," and "Sexuality." I kept the definitions of these forms of racism/antiracism in the notes section for reference, but I made these changes to the main body of the text to double down on the thesis of this book: how individuals can all strive to *be* antiracist by challenging the structure of racism and constructing anew. I strive to explain that individuals are facing the power and policy structures of racism; that individuals are seeing if not feeling the ravages of this structure in racial inequities and injustices; and that racist ideas function to rationalize and normalize those racial inequities and injustices. This all leads to individuals thinking, for example, that Indigenous people or Black people, rather than racist power and policy, are the racial problem, thus resulting in individuals supporting the structure of racism through their actions or inaction. It is difficult for individuals to see the structure if their worldview is clouded by racist ideas. But antiracist ideas can bring clarity, as they have for me. As the structure becomes clearer for us through the lens of antiracist ideas, we gain the ability to challenge that structure, to be antiracist. That is why these chapters focus on the ideas, and it is important for the definitions opening the chapters to emphasize that focus. The structure of racism is not going to construct and deconstruct itself. Individuals organized together created the structure. Individuals organized together will ultimately abolish this structure and construct an equitable and just structure of antiracism.

E DISSED SPEEDO because he was so uptight. We rode camel jokes on another boy for the divot on the top of his head. We pointed mercilessly at one girl's skyscrapers for legs. "You expecting?" we kept asking the obese boy. "We know you expecting," we kept saying to the obese girl. They renamed me Bonk, after the video-game character whose only weapon was his large head, which made a rhythmic "Bonk. Bonk. Bonk" as he attacked his enemies.

I dished out as many jokes as anyone—the eight-year-old third-grade dissident had turned into a popular teenager with a penchant for cruel jokes. Maybe my empathetic sensibilities would have been rekindled if I'd gotten on the bus and Million Man–marched in Washington, D.C., that fall of 1995. But my father, caring for his ailing sibling, did not take us.

None of us attended that fall's other big event, either: the O. J. Simpson trial in Los Angeles. Two weeks before the Million Man March, I sat in my eighth-grade classroom, waiting patiently with my Black classmates, listening to the radio. When "not guilty" sliced the silence like a cleaver, we leapt from behind our desks, shouting, hugging each other, wanting to call our friends and parents to celebrate. (Too bad we didn't have cellphones.)

Over in Manhattan, my father assembled with his accounting co-workers in a stuffed, stiff, and silent conference room to watch the verdict on television. After the not-guilty verdict was read, my father and his Black co-workers migrated out of the room with grins under their frowns, leaving their baffled White co-workers behind.

Back in my classroom, amid the hugging happiness, I glanced over at my White eighth-grade teacher. Her red face shook as she held back tears, maybe feeling that same overwhelming sensation of hopelessness and discouragement that Black people feel all too many times. I smiled at her—I didn't really care. I wanted O.J. to run free. I had been listening to what the Black adults around me had been lecturing about for months in 1995. They did not think O.J. was innocent of murder any more than they thought he was innocent of selling out his people. But they knew the criminal punishment system was guilty, too. Guilty for freeing the White cops who beat Rodney King in 1991 and the Korean storekeeper who killed fifteen-year-old Latasha Harlins that same year after falsely accusing her of stealing orange juice. But the O.J. verdict didn't stop justice from miscarrying when it came to Black bodies—all kinds of Black bodies. New Yorkers saw it two years later, when NYPD officers inside a Brooklyn police station rammed a wooden stick up the rectum of a thirty-year-old Haitian immigrant named Abner Louima, after viciously beating him on the ride to the station. And two years after that, the punishment system freed another group of NYPD officers who'd blasted forty-one bullets at the body of Amadou Diallo, an unarmed twenty-three-year-old immigrant from Guinea. It did not matter if Black people breathed first in the United States or abroad. In the end, racist violence did not differentiate.

But back in my eighth-grade class, my fellow African Americans did differentiate. Kwame probably bore the nastiest beating of jokes. He was popular, funny, good-looking, athletic, and cool—yet his Ghanaian ethnicity trumped all. We relentlessly joked on Kwame like he was Akeem, from the kingdom of Zamunda, and we were Darryl, Lisa's obnoxious boyfriend, in the 1988 romantic comedy *Coming to America*. After all, we lived in Queens, where Akeem came in search of a wife and fell for Lisa in the movie.

In *Coming to America*, Darryl, Lisa, Akeem, and Patrice (Lisa's sister) are sitting in the stands, watching a basketball game. "Wearing clothes must be a new experience for you," Darryl quips with a glance at Akeem. An annoyed Lisa, sitting between the two men, changes the subject. Darryl brings it back. "What kind of games do y'all play in Africa? Chase the monkey?" Darryl grins. African Americans in the audience were expected to grin with Darryl and laugh at Akeem. Back in our classrooms, we paraphrased Darryl's jokes about barbaric and animalistic Africans to the Kwames in our midst.

These were racist jokes whose point of origin—the human trade—was no laughing matter. When African Americans make jokes that dehumanize other branches of the African diaspora, we allow that horror story to live again in our laughs. Ethnic racist ideas are the resurrected script of the human trader.

The origins of ethnic racism can be found in the human trade's supply-and-demand market for human products. Different enslavers preferred different ethnic groups in Africa, believing they made "better slaves." And they considered the "better slaves" to be the better Africans. Some French enslavers thought of the Congolese as "magnificent blacks" since they were "born to serve." Other French enslavers joined with Spanish enslavers and considered captives from Senegambia "the best slaves." But most enslavers in the Americas considered the ethnic groups from the Gold Coast—modern-day Ghana—to be "the best and most faithful of our slaves," as relayed by one of Antigua's wealthiest enslavers and governors, Christopher Codrington.

Enslavers and human traders least valued Angolans, considering them the worst slaves, the lowest step on the ladder of ethnic racist ideas, just above animals. In the 1740s, captives from the Gold Coast were sold for nearly twice as much as captives from Angola. Maybe Angolans' low value was based on their oversupply: Angolans were traded more than any other African ethnic group. The twenty or so captives hauled into Jamestown, Virginia, in August 1619, symbolically beginning African American history, were from Angola.

Enslavers had no problem devising explanations for their ethnic racist ideas. "The Negroes from the Gold Coast, Popa, and Whydah," wrote one Frenchman, "are born in a part of Africa which is very barren." As a result, "they are obliged to go and cultivate the land for their subsistence" and "have become used to hard labour from their infancy," he wrote. "On the other hand . . . Angola Negroes are brought from those parts of Africa . . . where everything grows almost spontaneously." And so "the men never work but live an indolent life and are in general of a lazy disposition and tender constitution."

My friends and I may have been following an old script when it came to ethnic racist ideas, but our motivations weren't the same as those old enslavers'. Under our laughs at Kwame and Akeem was probably some anger at continental Africans. "African chiefs were the ones waging war on each other and capturing their own people and selling them," President Yoweri Museveni of Uganda said during President Bill Clinton's trip to Africa, taking a page out of African American memory of the human trade. I still remember an argument I had with some friends in college years later—they told me to leave them alone with my "Africa shit." Those "African motherfuckers sold us down the river," they said. They sold their "own people."

The idea that "African chiefs" sold their "own people" is an anachronistic memory, overlaying our present ideas about race onto an ethnic past. When European intellectuals created the races between the fifteenth and eighteenth centuries, lumping diverse ethnic groups into monolithic races, it didn't necessarily change the way the people saw themselves. Africa's residents in the seventeenth and eighteenth centuries didn't look at the various ethnic groups around them and suddenly see them all as one people, as the same race, as "African" or "Black." People in West Africa involved in the human trade did not believe they were selling their own people—they were usually selling people as different to them as the Europeans waiting on the coast. Ordinary people in West Africa—like ordinary people in Western Europe—identified themselves in ethnic terms during the life of the human trade. It took a long time, perhaps until the twentieth century, for race making to cast its pall over the entire globe.

THROUGHOUT THE 1990S, the number of immigrants of color in the United States grew, due to the combined effects of the Immigration and Nationality Act of 1965, the Refugee Act of 1980, and the Immigration Act of 1990. Taken together, these bills encouraged family reunification, immigration from conflict areas, and a diversity visa program that spiked immigration from countries outside Europe. Between 1980 and 2000, the Latinx immigrant population ballooned from 4.2 million to 14.1 million. As of 2022, Black immigrants account for 10 percent of the nation's Black population, more than triple their share (3 percent) in 1980. As an early-eighties baby, I witnessed this upsurge of immigrants of color firsthand.

While some African Americans were wary of this immigrant influx from the Black world, my parents were not. A Haitian couple with three boys lived across the street from us, and I befriended the youngest boy, Gil, and his cousin Cliff. I spent many days over there eating rice and peas, fried plantains, and chicken dishes with names I couldn't pronounce. I learned a little Haitian Creole. Gil's father pastored a Haitian church in Flatbush, Brooklyn, the heart of New York's West Indian community. I often joined them for church, taking in large helpings of Haitian American culture along with the day's sermon.

Gil and Cliff held me close, but Gil's parents not as much. They were nice and accommodating, but there was always a distance between us. I never felt part of the extended family, despite how many times I ate at their dinner table. Maybe they kept me at arm's length because I was African American, at a time when Haitian immigrants were feeling the sting of African American bigotry. Maybe not. Maybe I am making something out of nothing. But that same feeling recurred in other encounters. West Indian immigrants in the 1990s tended to categorize African Americans as "lazy, unambitious, uneducated, unfriendly, welfare-dependent, and lacking in family values," Mary C. Waters found in her interview-rich study of West Indian attitudes. African Americans tended to categorize West Indians as "selfish, lacking in race awareness, being lackeys of whites, and [having] a sense of inflated superiority."

I grew up with different ethnic groups of Black people all around me—I never knew anything else. But being surrounded by Black immigrants was new for my parents' and grandparents' generations.

The loosening immigration laws of the 1960s through 1990s were designed to undo a previous generation of immigration laws that limited non-White immigration to the United States. The

1882 Chinese Exclusion Act was extended to an even broader act, encompassing a larger "Asiatic Barred Zone," in 1917. The 1921 Emergency Quota Act and the Immigration Act of 1924 severely restricted the immigration of people from Africa and Eastern and Southern Europe and practically banned the immigration of Asians until 1965. "America must be kept American," President Calvin Coolidge said when he signed the 1924 law. Of course, by then "American" included millions of Negro, Asian, Native, Middle Eastern, and Latinx peoples (who would, at least in the case of Mexican Americans, be forcibly repatriated to Mexico by the hundreds of thousands). But Coolidge and congressional supporters determined that only immigrants from northwestern Europe—Scandinavia, the British Isles, Germany—could keep America American, meaning White. The United States was "a mighty land settled by northern Europeans from the United Kingdom, the Norsemen, and the Saxon," proclaimed Maine representative Ira Hersey, to applause, during debate over the Immigration Act of 1924.

Nearly a century later, U.S. senator Jeff Sessions lamented the growth of the non-native-born population. "When the numbers reached about this high in 1924, the president and Congress changed the policy. And it slowed down immigration significantly," he told Breitbart's Steve Bannon in 2015. "We then assimilated through to 1965 and created really the solid middle class of America with assimilated immigrants. And it was good for America." A year later, as attorney general, Sessions began carrying out the Trump administration's anti-Latinx, anti-Arab, and anti-Black immigrant policies geared toward making America White again. "We should have more people from places like Norway," Trump told lawmakers in 2018. There were already enough people of color like me, apparently.

THE TRUMP ADMINISTRATION'S throwback to early-twentieth-century immigration policies—built on racist ideas of what constitutes an American—were meant to roll back the years of immigration that saw America dramatically diversify, including a new diversity within its Black population, which now included Africans and West Indians in addition to the descendants of enslaved people in the United States. But regardless of where they came from, they were all racialized as Black.

The fact is, all ethnic groups, once they fall under the gaze and power of race makers, become racialized. I am a descendant of enslaved Africans in the United States. My ethnic group is African American. My race, as an African American, is Black. Kenyans are racialized as a Black ethnic group, while Italians are White, Japanese are Asian, Syrians are Middle Eastern, Puerto Ricans are Latinx, and Choctaws are Native American. The racializing serves the core mandate of race: to create hierarchies of value.

Across history, racist power has produced racist ideas about the racialized ethnic groups in its colonial sphere and ranked them—across the globe and within their own nations. The history of the United States offers a parade of intraracial ethnic power relationships: Anglo-Saxons terrorizing Irish Catholics and Jews; Cuban immigrants being privileged over Mexican immigrants; the model-minority construction that includes East Asians and excludes Muslims from South Asia. It's a history that began with early European colonizers referring to the Cherokee, Chickasaw, Choctaw, Creek, and Seminole as the "Five Civilized Tribes" of Native Americans, as compared to other "wild" tribes. This ranking of racialized ethnic groups within the ranking of the races creates a racial-ethnic hierarchy, a ladder of ethnic racist ideas within the larger schema of racist ideas.

We express ethnic racist ideas when we express a racist idea about an ethnic group or support a racist policy toward an ethnic group. Ethnic racist ideas point to group behavior, instead of policies, as the cause of disparities between ethnic groups. When Ghanaian immigrants to the United States join with White Americans and say African Americans are lazy, they are recycling the ethnic racist ideas of White Americans about African Americans.

The face of ethnic racist ideas bares itself in the form of a persistent question:

"Where are you from?"

I am often asked this question by people who see me through an ethnic racist lens. They presume I—a scholar—cannot be a so-called lowly, lazy, lackluster African American.

"I am from Queens, New York," I respond.

"No, no, where are you really from?"

"I am really from New York."

Frustrated, the person slightly alters the line of inquiry. "Where are your parents from?" When I say, "My dad's family is from New York, and my ma's family is from Georgia," the questioner freezes up in confusion. When I add, "I am a descendant of enslaved Africans in the United States," the questions cease. They must resign themselves to the fact that I am an African American. Perhaps the next move is for the person to look at me as extraordinary—not like those ordinary inferior African Americans—so they can leave quietly, their ethnic-racist lens intact.

But sometimes they do not leave quietly. Sometimes they take the opportunity to lecture down at my ethnic group, like a bold Ghanaian student early in my professorial career in upstate New York. He delivered a monologue to a classroom full of African Americans that touched on everything from our supposed laziness to our imagined dependence on welfare. I offered data that disproved his ethnic racist ideas—e.g., the facts that Black (31.3 percent), White (30.3 percent), and Latinx (29.8 percent) people receive welfare at similar rates, and states with larger Black populations tend to offer the lowest welfare benefits. But he held tightly to his ethnic racist ideas and spoke on as the snickering of the African American students slowly turned to anger (while many of the children of Black immigrants remained quiet). To calm my African American students, I recited the ethnic racist ideas African Americans express about West Africans, to show them that this absurdity is universal. It backfired. The African American students started nodding their heads to the litany of stereotypes about African immigrants.

To be antiracist is to view national and transnational ethnic groups as equals in all their differences. To be antiracist is to challenge the racist policies that plague racialized ethnic groups across the world. To be antiracist is to view the inequities between all racialized ethnic groups as a problem of power and policy.

The Ghanaian student confronted me after class as I packed up (and as some of his African American classmates glared sharply at him while leaving the room). When he finished his second monologue to me, I asked if he minded answering some questions. He agreed to. I really just wanted to keep him talking to me for a while longer, in case there were any angry students still waiting for him outside the classroom. Fights—or worse—were occasionally erupting between Black ethnic groups in New York, just as they had a century prior between White ethnic groups.

"What are some of the racist ideas the British say about Ghanaians?" I asked.

He offered a blank stare before blurting out, "I don't know."

"Yes, you do. Tell me some. It's okay."

He was silent for a moment and then started speaking again, now much more slowly and nervously than in his earlier rants, seemingly wondering where this was going. When he finished listing racist ideas, I spoke again.

"Now, are those ideas true?" I asked. "Are the British superior to Ghanaians?"

NOTE ON "EQUALS" I have started using the term "equals" instead of "equal." "Equals" better connotes racial groups, in this case racialized ethnic groups, being on the same level.

I have found that for some people "equal" connotes what is the same or identical, and does not account for color and cultural and ethnic differences. The races *are* equal—pretty much identical from a biological or genetic standpoint. But from a cultural standpoint, the racial groups are not identical. They are equals, on the same level. When we don't account for cultural differences—I did not originally do so in this passage—we are laying the foundation for assimilationist ideas. These assimilationist ideas imagine that people should be color-blind and all racial groups are identical, or have the capability to be the same—that is, White.

"No!" he said proudly. I was proud, too, that he had not internalized these racist ideas about his own racialized ethnic group.

"When African Americans repeat British racist ideas about Ghanaians, do you defend your people?"

"Yes. Because they are not true!"

"So these ideas about African Americans: Who did you get these ideas from?"

He thought. "My family, my friends, and my observations," he said.

"Who do you think your fellow Ghanaian Americans got these ideas about African Americans from?"

He thought much longer this time. From the side of his eye he saw another student waiting to speak to me, which seemed to rush his thoughts—he was a polite kid in spite of his urge to lecture. But I did not rush him. The other student was Jamaican and listening intently, maybe thinking about who Jamaicans got their ideas about Haitians from.

"Probably American Whites," he said, looking me straight in the eye for the first time.

His mind seemed open, so I jumped on in. "So if African Americans went to Ghana, consumed British racist ideas about Ghanaians, and started expressing those ideas to Ghanaians, what would Ghanaians think about that? What would you think about that?"

He smiled, surprising me. "I got it," he said, turning to walk out of the classroom.

"Are you sure?" I said, raising my voice over the Jamaican student's head.

He turned back to me. "Yes, sir. Thanks, Prof."

I respected him for his willingness to reflect on his own hypocrisy. And I didn't want to overreact when he trashed African Americans, because I knew where he was coming from: I had been there myself. When I learned the history of ethnic racist ideas, of African Americans commonly degrading Africans as "barbaric" or routinely calling West Indians in 1920s Harlem "monkey chasers"—or when I remembered my own taunts of Kwame back in eighth grade—I tried not to run away from the hypocrisy, either. How can I get upset at immigrants from Africa and South America for looking down on African Americans when African Americans have historically looked down on immigrants from Africa and South America? How can I critique their ethnic racist ideas and ignore my own? That is the central double standard in ethnic racist ideas: loving one's position on the ladder above other ethnic groups and hating one's position below that of other ethnic groups. It is angrily trashing the racist ideas about one's own group but happily consuming the racist ideas about other ethnic groups. It is failing to recognize that the racist ideas we consume about others came from the same restaurant and the same cook who used the same ingredients to make different degrading dishes for us all.

WHEN STUDIES STARTED to show that the median family income of African Americans is far lower than that of foreign-born Black people and that African Americans have higher rates of poverty and unemployment, numerous commentators wondered why Black immigrants do so much better than African Americans. They also answered their own questions: Black immigrants are more motivated, more hardworking, and "more entrepreneurial than native-born blacks," wrote one commentator in *The Economist* in 1996. Their success shows "that racism does not account for all, or even most, of the difficulties encountered by native-born blacks."

Ethnic racist ideas, like all racist ideas, cover up the racist policies wielded against African Americans and Black immigrants. Whenever Black immigrants in the United States compare their economic standing to that of African Americans, whenever they agree that their success stories show that antiracist Americans are overstating racist policies against African Americans, they are tightening the handcuffs of racist policy around their own wrists. Black immigrants' comparisons with African Americans conceal the racial inequities between Black immigrants and non-Black immigrants.

Despite studies showing Black immigrants, on average, earn college degrees at rates comparable to the overall immigrant population in the United States, they earn lower wages than similarly trained non-Black immigrants and have the highest unemployment rate of any immigrant group. An ethnic racist asks, Why are Black immigrants doing better than African Americans? An ethnic antiracist asks, Why are Black immigrants not doing as well as other immigrant groups?

The reason Black immigrants generally have higher educational levels and economic pictures than African Americans is not that their transnational ethnicities are superior. The reason resides in the circumstances of human migration. Not all individuals migrate, but those who do, in what's called "immigrant self-selection," are typically individuals with an exceptional internal drive for material success and/or they possess exceptional external resources. Generally speaking, individual Black and Latinx and Asian and Middle Eastern and European immigrants are uniquely resilient and resourceful—not because they are Nigerian or Cuban or Japanese or Saudi Arabian or German but because they are immigrants. In fact, immigrants and migrants of all races tend to be more resilient and resourceful when compared with the natives of their own countries and the natives of their new countries. Sociologists call this the "migrant advantage." As sociologist Suzanne Model explained in her book on West Indian immigrants, "West Indians are not a black success story but an *immigrant* success story." As such, policies from those of Calvin Coolidge to Donald Trump's limiting immigration to the United States from China or Italy or Palestine or Senegal or Haiti or Mexico have been self-destructive to the country. With ethnic racism, no one wins, except the racist power at the top. As with all racism, that is the entire point.

∙ ∙ ∙

THERE WERE NO winners in eighth grade, either. In class, I'd randomly shout, *"Ref!"* A friend would scream, *"Uuuuuu!"* Another friend would scream, *"Geeeeee!"* And the whole class of African Americans would burst out laughing as the three of us pointed at Kwame and chanted, *"Ref-u-gee! Ref-u-gee! Ref-u-gee!"* The smirking White teacher would tell us to be quiet. Kwame would break the quietness with defensive jokes. The cycle would repeat, day after day.

Kwame never seemed to let the jokes bother him. In that way, he resembled Akeem in *Coming to America,* a prince so powerful, so sophisticated, so self-assured, that he was able to ignore demeaning jokes like an elite athlete ignoring a hostile crowd. Kwame had a smugness about him that maybe, subconsciously, we were trying to shatter by pulling him down to earth. As scholar Rosemary Traoré found in a study of an urban high school, "African students wondered why their fellow African American brothers and sisters treated them as second-class citizens, while the African Americans wondered why the African students [seemed] to feel or act so superior to them." The tensions created by ethnic racist ideas didn't produce any winners, just confusion and hurt on both sides.

Don't get me wrong, Kwame joked back. Kwame and others never let me forget that I had a big-ass head. I never knew why. My head wasn't that big—maybe a little out of proportion.

But a high school growth spurt was coming.

CHAPTER 6

BODY

BODILY RACIST IDEA: Any notion that a group of racialized bodies is more animal-like and violent than others.

BODILY ANTIRACIST IDEA: Any notion that is humanizing, deracializing, and individualizing nonviolent and violent behavior.

DONE. FINISHED WEARING uniforms. Through with attending chapel service. The older I became, the more I despised the conformity of private schooling and churching. After eighth grade, I was finally free of them. I enrolled in John Bowne High School, a public school that my Haitian neighbor Gil attended. It was in Flushing, in central Queens, just across the street from Queens College. We bathed in the ambient noise of the nearby Long Island Expressway.

In the mid-1950s, public-housing authorities allowed my grandmother to move into the predominantly White Pomonok Houses, due south of John Bowne. Dad went through all of his local elementary schooling in the late 1950s without noticing another Black student, only the kids of working-class White families, who were even then fixing to flee to suburban Long Island. By 1996 they were nearly all gone.

After school, John Bowne students jammed into public buses like clothes jammed into a drawer. As my bus made its way toward Southside Queens, it slowly emptied. On this day, I stood near the back door, facing a teenage boy we called Smurf, a nickname he earned from his short, skinny frame, blue-black skin, thick ears, and big round eyes that nearly met in the center of his face.

As I stood near him, Smurf reached into his pants and pulled out a black pistol. He stared at it and I stared at it, too. Everyone did. Smurf looked up and pointed the gun—loaded or unloaded?—directly at me. "You scared, yo?" he asked with almost brotherly warmth, a smirk resting on his face.

"BLACKS MUST UNDERSTAND and acknowledge the roots of White fear in America," President Bill Clinton said in a speech on October 16, 1995, the same day as the Million Man March. He'd escaped the march and the Black men assembling practically on the White House lawn for the Austin campus of the University of Texas. "There is a legitimate fear of the violence that is too prevalent in our urban areas," he added. "By experience or at least what people see on the news at night, violence for those White people too often has a Black face."

History tells the same story: Violence for White people really has too often had a Black face—and the consequences have landed on the Black body across the span of American history. In 1631, Captain John Smith warned the first English colonizers of New England that the Black body was as devilish as any people in the world. Boston pastor Cotton Mather preached compliance to slavery in 1696: Do not "make yourself infinitely Blacker than you are already." Virginia lieutenant-governor Hugh Drysdale spoke of "the Cruel dispositions of those Creatures" who planned a freedom revolt in 1723. Seceding Texas legislators in 1861 complained of not receiving more federal "appropriations for protecting . . . against ruthless savages." U.S. senator Benjamin Tillman told his colleagues in 1903, "The poor African has become a fiend, a wild beast, seeking whom he may devour." Two leading criminologists posited in 1967 that the "large . . . criminal display of the violence among minority groups such as Negroes" stems from their "subculture-of-violence." Manhattan Institute fellow Heather Mac Donald wrote "The core criminal-justice population is the black underclass" in *The War on Cops* in 2016.

This is the living legacy of racist power, constructing the Black race biologically and ethnically and presenting the Black body to the world first and foremost as a "beast," to use Gomes Eanes de Zurara's term, as violently dangerous, as the dark embodiment of evil. Americans today see the Black body as larger, more threatening, more potentially harmful, and more likely to require force to control than a similarly sized White body, according to researchers. No wonder the Black body had to be lynched by the thousands, deported by the tens of thousands, incarcerated by the millions, segregated by the tens of millions.

WHEN I FIRST picked up a basketball, at around eight years old, I also picked up on my parents' fears for my Black body. My parents hated when I played ball at nearby parks, worried I'd get shot, and tried to discourage me by warning me of the dangers waiting for me out there. In their constant fearmongering about Black drug dealers, robbers, killers, they nurtured in me a fear of my own Black neighbors. When I proposed laying concrete in our grassy backyard and putting up a basketball hoop there, my father built a court faster than a house flipper, a nicer one than the courts at nearby parks. But the new basketball court could not keep me away from my own dangerous Black body. Or from Smurf on the bus.

"NAW, YO," I coolly responded to Smurf's question about my fear. My eyes locked on the gun.

"Whatever, man," he snickered. "You scared, yo." Then he jammed the gun in my ribs and offered a hard smile.

I looked him straight in the eye, scared as hell. "Naw, yo," I said, giggling a little, "but that's a nice piece, though."

"It is, ain't it?"

Satisfied, Smurf turned, gun in hand, and looked for somebody else to scare. I exhaled relief but knew I could have been harmed that day, as I could have other days. Especially, I thought, inside John Bowne High School, surrounded by other Black and Latinx and Asian teens.

Moving through John Bowne's hallways, eyes sharper than my pencils, I avoided stepping on new sneakers like they were land mines (though when I did accidentally step on one, nothing exploded). I avoided bumping into people, worried a bump could become a hole in my head (though when I did inevitably bump into someone, my head stayed intact). I avoided making eye contact, as if my classmates were wolves (though when I did, my body did not get attacked). I avoided crews, fearing they would flock at me at any moment (though when I did have to pass through a crew, I didn't get jumped). What could happen based on my deepest fears mattered more than what did happen to me. I believed violence was stalking me—but in truth I was being stalked inside my own head by racist ideas.

Crews ran my high school—like crews run the United States—and I considered joining the Zulu Nation, awed by its history and reach. Witnessing an initiation changed my mind. The perverse mix of punches and stomps, handshakes and hugs, turned me off. But I did have an informal crew, bound by an ironclad loyalty that required us to fight for each other, should the occasion arise.

One day we met another crew on a block near the Long Island Expressway—maybe five of us and fifteen of them, all staring menacingly at each other as we approached. This was new to me, the showdown, the curses flying and landing, the escalating displays of anger. Threats slamming like fists. I was in the mix with the rest of them—but passing drivers glancing over could not see that I was fighting my nervousness more than anything.

One threat led to another. No one rushed me, as small and unassuming as I was. I saw big Gil fighting off punches. I wanted to help him, but then I saw a tall, skinny, solitary teen looking around nervously. He reminded me of myself. I crept up behind him and jump-threw a vicious right hook. He went down hard on the pavement and I skittered off. Soon we heard sirens and scattered like ants, fearful of getting smashed by the NYPD.

WE WERE UNARMED, but we knew that Blackness armed us even though we had no guns. Whiteness disarmed the cops—turned them into fearful potential victims—even when they were approaching a group of clearly outstrapped and anxious high school kids. Black people comprise 13 percent of the U.S. population. And yet, in 2015, when *The Washington Post* began logging every known fatal police shooting, Black bodies accounted for 26 percent of those killed by police, declining slightly to 23 percent in 2018, before increasing to 24 percent in 2020, when the police murder of George Floyd sparked the largest series of demonstrations in U.S. history. Unarmed Black bodies—which apparently look armed to fearful officers—are more than three times as likely to be killed as unarmed White bodies.

Gil and I ran over the Long Island Expressway overpass and hopped onto a departing bus, feeling lucky, catching our breath. I could have gone to jail, or worse, that day.

More than the times I risked jail, I am still haunted by the times I did not help the victims of violence. My refusal to help them jailed me in fear. I was as scared of the Black body as the White body was scared of me. I could not muster the strength to do right. Like that time on another packed bus after school. A small Indian teen—tinier than me!—sat near me at the back of the bus that day. My seat faced the back door, and the Indian teen sat in the single seat right next to the back door. I kept staring at him, trying to catch his eye so I could give him a nod that would direct him to the front of the bus. I saw other Black and Indian kids on the bus trying to do the same with their eyes. We wanted so badly for him to move. But he was fixated on whatever was playing on his fresh new Walkman. His eyes were closed and his head bobbed.

Smurf and his boys were on the bus that day, too. For the moment, they were blocked from the Indian teen by the bodies of other kids—they couldn't see him sitting there. But when the bus cleared enough for them to have a clear lane to him, Smurf, as expected, focused in on the thing we didn't want him to see.

He did not have his pistol that day. Or maybe he did.

Smurf motioned to his boys and stood up. He walked a few feet and stood over the Indian teen, his back to me, his head turned to face his boys.

"What the fuck!"

He pointed his finger, gun-like, at the seated teen's head. "Look at this motherfucker!"

IN 1993, A bipartisan group of White legislators introduced the Violent Crime Control and Law Enforcement Act. They were thinking about Smurf—and me. The Congressional Black Caucus was also thinking about Smurf and me. They asked for $2 billion more in the act for drug treatment and $3 billion more for violence-prevention programs. When Republicans called those items "welfare for criminals" and demanded they be scaled back for their votes, Democratic leaders caved. Twenty-six of the thirty-eight voting members of the Congressional Black Caucus caved, too. After all, the bill reflected their fear for my Black body—and of it. The policy decision reflected their dueling consciousness—and their practical desire to not lose the prevention funding entirely in a rewrite of the bill. On top of its new prisons, capital offenses, minimum sentences, federal three-strike laws, police officers, and police weaponry, the law made me eligible, when I turned thirteen in 1995, to be tried as an adult. "Never again should Washington put politics and party above law and order," President Bill Clinton said upon signing the bipartisan, biracial bill on September 13, 1994.

"YO, NIGGA, RUN that Walkman," Smurf said rather gently. The kid did not look up, still captivated by the beat coming from his headphones. Smurf punch-tapped him on the shoulder. "Yo, nigga, run that Walkman," he shouted.

I wanted to stand up and yell, "Leave that nigga alone. Why you always fucking with people, Smurf? What the fuck is wrong with you?" But my fear caged me. I remained seated and quiet.

The kid finally looked up, startled. "What!" The shock of Smurf looming over him and the loudness of the music made him raise his voice. I shook my head but without shaking my head. I remained still.

CLINTON DEMOCRATS THOUGHT they had won the political turf war to own crime as an issue—to war on the Black body for votes. But it took little time for racist Americans to complain that even the most expensive crime bill in U.S. history was not enough to stop the beast, the devil, the gun, Smurf, me. Around Thanksgiving in 1995, Princeton political scientist John J. DiIulio Jr. warned of the "coming of the super-predators," especially young bodies like mine in "Black inner-city neighborhoods." DiIulio later said he regretted using the term. But DiIulio never had to internalize this racist idea and look at his own body in fear. He never had to deal with being hunted. My friends at John Bowne did. I did. In 1996, I turned fourteen. A super-predator was growing in me, in Smurf, they said. I believed what I heard.

"Most inner-city children grow up surrounded by teenagers and adults who are themselves deviant, delinquent or criminal," DiIulio and two co-authors wrote in 1996. Watch out. "A new generation of street criminals is upon us—the youngest, biggest and baddest generation any society has ever known," he warned. My band of "juvenile 'super-predators'" were "radically impulsive, brutally remorseless youngsters, including ever more preteenage boys, who murder, assault, rape, rob, burglarize, deal deadly drugs, join gun-toting gangs and create serious communal disorders." We, the young Black super-predators, were apparently being raised with an unprecedented inclination toward

violence—in a nation that presumably did not raise White enslavers, lynchers, mass incarcerators, police officers, corporate
officials, venture capitalists, financiers, drunk drivers, and war
hawks to be violent.

This swarm of super-predators never materialized in the late
1990s. Violence had already begun its dramatic decline by the
time I stared at Smurf demanding that Walkman in 1996. Homicides had dropped to their lowest levels since the Reagan era,
when intense crack-market competition and unregulated gun
trafficking spiked the rate.

But crime bills have never correlated to harm any more than
fear has correlated to actual violence. We are not meant to fear
suits with policies that kill. We are not meant to fear good White
males with AR-15s. No, we are to fear the weary, unarmed
Latinx body from Latin America. The body kneeling to Allah is
to be feared. The Black body from hell is to be feared. Adept
politicians and police and prison entrepreneurs manufacture the
fear and stand before voters to deliver them—messiahs who will
liberate them from fear of these other bodies.

NOTE ON "VIOLENCE" AND "CRIME" In this paperback edition, I replaced the term "violent crime" with the term "violence" and the term "crime" with
"harm." I've learned from abolitionist writers like Mariame Kaba and Derecka Purnell
that "violence" and "harm" are more precise terms than "crime," because what is
considered a crime does not always overlap with what is harmful and violent. Which
is to say we tend to focus on individual violence, and neglect the more severe violence that policy choices inflict on whole communities. Policymakers choose to criminalize certain harmful actions and not criminalize other harmful actions (especially
their own). For example, lawmakers in the United States have long criminalized marijuana use and not alcohol use, even though alcohol use is more harmful to the body
and to society. Robbing a woman's purse is criminalized while what is not criminalized
is an elected official robbing millions of impoverished mothers of public assistance or
an executive robbing workers of wages, even as the latter two induce more societal
harm. Shooting someone is considered a violent crime, but an elected official supporting the easy availability of guns—which has been proven to spur gun violence—is
not considered a violent crime. We must recognize and strive to eliminate all forms
of harm and violence, whether structural or individual, whether criminalized or not.

. . .

"NIGGA, YOU DIDN'T hear me!" Smurf fumed. "I said run that fucking Walkman!"

In my mind I tried to devise a strategy for the poor kid, imagining myself in his place. I had a bit of a gift for staying calm and defusing potentially volatile situations, which served me well whether I was dealing with the violently finicky Smurfs of the world or capriciously violent police officers. I learned to disarm or avoid the individual Smurfs around town—those bent on mayhem. But I also saw that strangers were doing the same calculations when they saw me coming—I'd see the fear in their eyes. They'd see me and decide they were looking at Smurf. We scared them just the same—all they saw were our dangerous Black bodies. One as all. Cops seemed especially fearful. Just as I learned to avoid the Smurfs of the world, I had to learn to keep racist police officers from getting nervous. Black people are apparently responsible for calming the fears of violent cops in the way women are supposedly responsible for calming the sexual desires of male rapists. If we don't, then we are blamed for our own assaults, our own deaths.

But at that point, the kid across from me was out of options—there was probably no way to defuse the situation. "Run that fucking Walkman!" Smurf yelled, now turning heads at the front of the bus and most likely prompting the bus driver to call the ruckus in. The shocked teen started to stand up, saying nothing, just shaking his head. He probably intended to relocate to the front, near the relative safety of the bus driver. But as soon as he straightened his body, Smurf landed a side haymaker to the kid's temple—his head bounced into the window and then onto the bus's floor. Smurf snatched the tumbling Walkman, and then his boys got up to join in. The kid covered his face when the stomps from Timberland boots came pummeling down. It all happened right in front of me. I did nothing. I did nothing.

The bus stopped. The back door opened. Smurf and his boys

leapt off and ran away, lighthearted, grinning. But I noticed that four-eyes from Smurf's crew remained on the bus, lurking and looking, seemingly waiting for somebody to help this kid laid out in agony. I did nothing.

THE RESPONSIBILITY OF keeping myself safe followed me like the stray dogs in my neighborhood, barking fear into my consciousness. I never wanted to arrive home to my parents with empty pockets and no shoes, with a leaking, beaten body like the Indian kid. Or worse, no arrival at all, only a letter from the police reporting my murder, or a phone call from the hospital. I convinced my parents (or so I thought) I was safe. But I did not convince myself. The acts of violence I saw from Smurf and others combined with the racist ideas all around me to convince me that more violence lurked than there actually was. I believed that violence didn't define just Smurf but all the Black people around me, my school, my neighborhood. I believed it defined me—that I should fear all darkness, up to and including my own Black body.

Those of us Black writers who grew up in "inner city" Black neighborhoods too often recall the violence we experienced more than the nonviolence. We don't write about all those days we were not faced with guns in our ribs. We don't retell all those days we did not fight, the days we didn't watch someone get beaten in front of us. We become exactly like the nightly local-news shows—if it bleeds, it leads—and our stories center on violent Black bodies instead of the overwhelming majority of nonviolent Black bodies. In 1993, near the height of urban violence, for every thousand urban residents, seventy-four, or 7.4 percent, reported being victims of violence, a percentage that declined further thereafter. In 2020, for every thousand urban residents, nineteen, or 1.9 percent, reported being victims of violence. These numbers are not precise. Researchers estimate that more than half of violent incidents in 2020 went unreported to law enforcement. And even being around violence can create adverse effects. But the idea that directly experienced violence is endemic and everywhere, affecting everyone, or even most people—that Black neighborhoods, as a whole, are more dangerous than "war zones," to use President Trump's term—is not reality. This justification for all the prisons and police in the criminal punishment system is not based in reality.

It all makes sense that this is the story we so often tell—the fist-swinging and gunshots and early deaths cling to us like a second skin, while the hugs and dances and good times fall away. But the writer's work reflects, and the reader consumes, those vivid, searing memories, not the everyday lived reality of the Black body.

As many moments as I had of anxiety and fear from other Black bodies, I probably lived many more moments in serenity and peace. As much as I feared that violence stalked me, my daily life was not organized around that fear. I played baseball for years with White kids on Long Island and always wondered why they never wanted to visit my neighborhood, my home. When I would ask, the looks of horror on their faces, and even more on their parents' faces, startled and confused me. I knew there were dangers on my block; I also thought it was safe.

I did not connect the whole or even most of Southside Queens with violence, just as I did not connect all or even most of my Black neighbors with violence. Certain people like Smurf, cer-

NOTE ON THE CRIMINAL PUNISHMENT SYSTEM As abolitionists have pointed out in recent years, this system is hardly a justice system. It is not oriented toward justice, meaning it is not oriented toward accountability, toward healing or eliminating the root causes of harm, whether structural or individual. One reason for this: the widespread racist ideas that Black people are inherently criminals, and Black neighborhoods are inherently dangerous. The "crime" is there because the Black people are there. So there's no way to stop the "crime." There's only the surveillance, policing, and punishment of these "Black criminals" to deter more "crime." This is an orientation toward punishment.

It is no longer accurate to call it the criminal justice system. It is more precise to call it the criminal "punishment" system. And this system must be abolished to bring into being antiracism, safety, and justice for the people.

tain blocks, and certain neighborhoods I knew to avoid. But not because they were Black—we were almost all Black. I knew in a vague way that Black neighborhoods with high-rise public housing like 40P (the South Jamaica Houses) or Baisley Park Houses were known to have more violence than neighborhoods like mine, Queens Village, with more single-family homes, but I never really thought about why. I knew it wasn't Blackness—Blackness was a constant.

A study that used National Longitudinal Survey of Youth data from 1976 to 1989 found that young Black males engaged in more violent acts than young White males. But when the researchers compared only employed young males of both races, the differences in violent behavior vanished. Or, as the Urban Institute stated in a more recent report on long-term unemployment, "Communities with a higher share of long-term unemployed workers also tend to have higher rates of crime and violence."

Another study found that the 2.5 percentage-point decrease in unemployment between 1992 and 1997 resulted in a decrease of 4.3 percentage points for robbery, 2.5 percentage points for auto theft, 5 percentage points for burglary, and 3.7 percentage points for larceny. Sociologist Karen F. Parker strongly linked the growth of Black-owned businesses to a reduction in Black youth violence between 1990 and 2000. In recent years, the University of Chicago Crime Lab worked with the One Summer Chicago Plus jobs program and found a 43 percent reduction in violence-related arrests for Black youths who worked eight-week-long part-time summer jobs, compared with a control group of teens who did not.

In other words, researchers have found a much stronger and clearer correlation between violence levels and unemployment levels than between violence and race. Black neighborhoods do not all have similar levels of violence. If the cause of the violence is the Black body, if Black people are violent demons, then the violence levels would be relatively the same no matter where Black people live. But Black upper-income and middle-income neighborhoods tend to have less violence than Black low-income neighborhoods—as is the case in non-Black communities. But that does not mean low-income Black people are more violent than high-income Black people. That means low-income neighborhoods struggle with unemployment and poverty—and their typical byproduct, violence.

For decades, there have been three main strategies in reducing violence in Black neighborhoods. Segregationist ideas consider Black neighborhoods to be war zones, substantiating calls for tougher and more policing and the mass incarceration of "super-predators." Assimilationist ideas substantiate calls to civilize these "super-predators" back to nonviolence through tough laws and tough love from mentors and fathers. Antiracist ideas substantiate the recognition that Black people, like all people, don't need surveillance, policing, and prisons; they need more higher-paying jobs within their reach, especially Black youngsters, who have consistently had the highest rates of unemployment of any demographic group, topping 50 percent in the early to mid-1980s.

There is no such thing as a dangerous racial group. But there are, of course, individuals who do violent things, like Smurf. There is the violence of racism—manifest in poverty and policing and prisons—that fears the Black body. And there is the nonviolence of antiracism that does not fear the Black body, that fears, if anything, the violence of the racism that has been set on the Black body through poverty and prisons and police; that strives to abolish poverty and police and prisons and all the structural sources of harm in Black communities, in all communities. All to create public safety. All to address what's truly dangerous.

Perceptions of danger and actual threats met me each day at John Bowne, in various forms. There was the dangerous disinterest of some teachers. Or the school's dangerous overcrowding: three thousand students packed into a school built for far fewer. The classes were so large—twice as large as in my private schools—that detached students like me were able to hold our own back-of-the-room classes before detached teachers. I do not remember a single teacher or class or lesson or assignment from ninth grade.

I was dangerously checked out—following the lead of most of the teachers, administrators, and politicians who were ostensibly in charge of my education. I attended John Bowne like someone who clocked in to his job with no intention of working. I only worked hard on my first love.

CHAPTER 7

CULTURE

CULTURAL RACIST IDEA: Any notion that creates a cultural standard and imposes a cultural hierarchy among racialized ethnic groups.

CULTURAL ANTIRACIST IDEA: Any notion that rejects cultural standards and equalizes cultural differences among racialized ethnic groups.

M Y DAD DRAGGED me to see the 1994 documentary *Hoop Dreams*, a film about the perils of two young boys pursuing the exceedingly unlikely possibility of an NBA career. His intervention failed, like the dreams of the kids in the film. For me, basketball was life.

It was a cool early-winter day in 1996 and I sat warm in the locker room after practice, getting dressed and exchanging jokes with my new teammates on John Bowne's junior-varsity basketball team. Suddenly, our White coach burst into the locker room like something was wrong. We muted the jokes as he looked hopelessly at our dark faces. He leaned against a locker as if a lecture was building up inside him.

"You all need to post two Cs and three Ds to remain on the team. Okay? Okay?" Everyone nodded or stared back, perhaps expecting more. But that was all he had to say. Our jokes resumed again.

I had neither loved nor hated middle school. But a few months in high school had changed me. I cannot pinpoint what triggered my hatred of school. My difficulty separating the harassing cop from the harassing teacher? A heightened sensitivity to the glares from teachers who saw my Black body not as a plant to be culti- vated but as a weed to be plucked out of their school and thrown into their prison? Freshman year I posted what grades I needed to stay on the basketball team: two Cs and three Ds. Only basketball and parental shame stopped me from dropping out like some other teens.

When I climbed onto the crowded public buses after school, I felt like a runaway. Most days, Smurf was nowhere to be found. Stopping and going, the bus headed south, until the last stop—my cultural home away from home.

We called the central artery of Southside Queens the Ave, the place where Jamaica Avenue crosses 164th Street. On weekends, I'd walk out of my house, strut a block up 209th Street to Jamaica Avenue, and hail a dollar cab down those three dozen blocks to the Ave. One dollar, one ride, one random driver. Little did I know, similar privately run cheap cars or vans, stuffed with sweat- ing and content and tired and recharged and traumatized Black bodies, were hurrying through neighborhoods all over the Black world. I have since traveled on these fast-moving cultural prod- ucts in other parts of the world, from Ghana to Jamaica (the island nation, not the Ave). The ride always takes me back to Queens.

Nothing compared to arriving at the Ave. A couple dozen city blocks lined with stores, this enormous shopping district was crowded with wide-eyed teens. We never knew what we were going to see—what kicks (sneakers) were going to be on sale; what beef (conflict) was going to be cooking; what guads (boys) and shorties (girls) were going to be rocking (wearing). This is my Ebonics—a term coined by psychologist Robert Williams in 1973 to replace racist terms like "Nonstandard Negro English." I must use the language of the culture to express the culture.

Some Americans despised my Ebonics in 1996. In that year the Oakland school board recognized Black people like me as bilingual, and in a cultural antiracist act recognized "the legiti- macy and richness" of Ebonics as a language. They resolved to use Ebonics with students "to facilitate their acquisition and mastery of English language skills." The reaction was fierce. Jesse Jackson at first called it "an unacceptable surrender, bordering on disgrace. It's teaching down to our children."

Was it? It helps to dig back into the origins of Ebonics. Enslaved Africans formulated new languages in nearly every European colony in the Americas, including African American Ebonics, Jamaican Patois, Haitian Creole, Brazilian Calunga, and Cubano. In every one of these countries, racist power—those in control of government, academia, education, and media—has demeaned these African languages as dialects, as "broken" or "improper" or "nonstandard" French, Spanish, Dutch, Portuguese, or English. Assimilationists have always urged Africans in the Americas to forget the "broken" languages of our ancestors and master the apparently "fixed" languages of Europeans—to speak "properly." But what was the difference between Ebonics and so-called "standard" English? Ebonics had grown from the roots of African languages and modern English just as modern English had grown from Latin, Greek, and Germanic roots. Why is Ebonics broken English but English is not broken German? Why is Ebonics a dialect of English if English is not a dialect of Latin? The idea that Black languages outside Africa are broken is as culturally racist as the idea that languages inside Europe are fixed.

WHEN THE REACTION to the Nazi Holocaust marginalized biological racist ideas, cultural racist ideas stepped into their place. "In practically all its divergences," African American culture "is a distorted development, or a pathological condition, of the general American culture," Gunnar Myrdal wrote in *An American Dilemma,* his 1944 landmark treatise on race and racism in the United States, which has been called the "bible" of the civil rights movement. Myrdal's scripture standardized the general (White) American culture, then judged African American culture as distorted or pathological from that standard. Whoever makes the cultural standard makes the cultural hierarchy. The act of making a cultural standard and hierarchy is what creates cultural racist ideas.

To be antiracist is to reject cultural standards and level cultural difference. Segregationist ideas say racial groups cannot reach their superior cultural standard. Assimilationist ideas say racial groups can, with effort and intention, reach superior cultural standards. "It is to the advantage of American Negroes as individuals and as a group to become assimilated into American culture" and "to acquire the traits held in esteem by the dominant white Americans," Myrdal suggested. Or, as President Theodore Roosevelt said in 1905, the goal should be to assimilate "the backward race . . . so it may enter into the possession of true freedom, while the forward race is enabled to preserve unharmed the high civilization wrought out by its forefathers."

Even Alexander Crummell, the stately Episcopalian priest who founded the first formal Black intellectual society in 1897, urged his fellow Black Americans to assimilate. He agreed with those racist Americans who classed Africans as fundamentally imitative. "This quality of imitation has been the grand preservative of the Negro in all the lands of his thraldom," Crummell preached in 1877.

WE CERTAINLY WEREN'T imitating anything on the Ave—to the contrary. The wider culture was avidly imitating and appropriating from us; our music and fashion and language were transforming the so-called mainstream. We did not care if older or richer or Whiter Americans despised our nonstandard dress like our nonstandard Ebonics. We were fresh like they just took the plastic off us, as Jadakiss rapped. Fresh baggy jeans sagging down. Fresh button-down shirts or designer sweatshirts in the winter under our bubble coats. Fresh T's or sports jerseys in the summer above our baggy jean shorts. Dangling chains shining like our smiles. Piercings and tattoos and bold colors told the mainstream world just how little we wanted to imitate them.

Freshness was about not just getting the hottest gear but devising fresh ways to wear it, in the best tradition of fashion: experimentation, elaboration, and impeccable precision. Timberland boots and Nike Air Force 1s were our cars of choice in New York City. It seems as if everyone—girl or boy—had wheat-colored Tims in their closets if they could afford or snatch them. Our black Air Force 1s had to be blacker than the prison populations. Our white Air Force 1s had to be whiter than the NYPD. Had to be as smooth as baby skin. No blemishes. No creases. We kept them black or white through regular touch-ups from paint sticks. We stuffed our shoes at night with paper or socks to ward off creasing in the front. Time to put on the shoes in the morning. Many of us knew the trick to keep the creases away all day. Put on a second sock halfway and fold the other half twice on top of my toes to fill the front of the sneaker. It hurt like those tight Guess jeans around the waists of shorties. But who cared about pain when fresh brought so much joy.

Jason Riley, a *Wall Street Journal* columnist, did not see us or our disciples in the twenty-first century as fresh cultural innovators. "Black culture today not only condones delinquency and thuggery but celebrates it to the point where black youths have adopted jail fashion in the form of baggy, low-slung pants and oversize T-shirts." But there was a solution. "If blacks can close the civilization gap, the race problem in this country is likely to become insignificant," Dinesh D'Souza once reasoned. "Civilization" is often a polite euphemism for cultural racist ideas.

I HATED WHAT they called civilization, represented most immediately by school. I loved what they considered dysfunctional—African American culture, which defined my life outside school. My first taste of culture was the Black church. Hearing strangers identify as sister and brother. Listening to sermonic conversations, all those calls from preachers, responses from congregants. Bodies swaying in choirs like branches on a tree, following the winds and twists of a soloist. The Holy Ghost mounting women for wild shouts and basketball sprints up and down aisles. Flying hats covering the new wigs of old ladies who were keeping it fresh for Jee-susss-sa. Funerals livelier than weddings. Watching Ma dust off her African garb and Dad his dashikis for Kwanzaa celebrations livelier than funerals.

I loved being in the midst of a culture created by my ancestors, who found ways to re-create the ideas and practices of their African ancestors with what was available to them in the United States, through what psychologist Linda James Myers calls the "outward physical manifestations of culture." These outward physical manifestations our ancestors encountered included Christianity, the English language, and popular European food, instruments, fashion, and customs. Cultural racist ideas presuppose that since African Americans exhibit outward physical manifestations of European culture, "North American negroes . . . in culture and language" are "essentially European," to quote anthropologist Franz Boas in 1911. "It is very difficult to find in the South today anything that can be traced directly back to Africa," attested sociologist Robert Park in 1919. "Stripped of his cultural heritage," the Negro's reemergence "as a human being was facilitated by his assimilation" of "white civilization," wrote sociologist E. Franklin Frazier in 1939. As such, "the Negro is only an American, and nothing else," argued sociologist Nathan Glazer in 1963. "He has no values and culture to guard and protect." In the final analysis, "we are not Africans," Bill Cosby told the NAACP in 2004.

It is difficult to find the survival and revival of African cultural forms using our surface-sighted cultural eyes. Those surface-sighted eyes assess a cultural body by its skin. They do not look behind, inside, below. Those surface-sighted eyes have historically looked for traditional African religions, languages, foods, fashion, and customs to appear in the Americas just as they appear in Africa. When they did not find them, they assumed African cultures had been overwhelmed by the "stronger" European cultures. Surface-sighted people have no sense of what psychologist

Wade Nobles calls "the deep structure of culture," the philoso-phies and values that change outward physical forms. It is this "deep structure" that transforms European Christianity into a new African religion, with mounting spirits, calls and responses, and Holy Ghost worship; it changes English into Ebonics, Euro-pean ingredients into soul food. The cultural African survived in the Americas, created a strong and complex culture with Western "outward" forms "while retaining inner [African] values," anthro-pologist Melville Herskovits avowed in 1941. The same cultural African breathed life into the African American culture that raised me.

THE AVE. I just loved being surrounded by all those Black people—or was it all that culture?—moving fast and slow, or just standing still. The Ave had an organic choir, that interplay of blasting tunes from the store to the car trunk, to the teen walking by, practicing her rhymes, to the cipher of rappers on the corners. Gil would freestyle; I would listen and bob my head. The sound of hip-hop was all around us.

"Son, they shook / Cause ain't no such things as halfway crooks / Scared to death, scared to look, they shook." "Shook Ones" was the Queens anthem in the mid-nineties from the self-proclaimed "official Queensbridge murderers"—Mobb Deep. They promised to get their listeners "stuck off the realness," and indeed I was. I despised the teen actors hiding their fear under a tough veneer. They seemed so real to racist cops and outsiders, who could not make distinctions among Black bodies, anyway. But we could tell. "He ain't a crook son / he's just a shook one."

I heard the booming rhymes of Queens's finest: Nas, Salt-N-Pepa, Lost Boyz, A Tribe Called Quest, Onyx, and LL Cool J's "Hey lover, hey lover / This is more than a crush"; and a couple of Brooklyn cats like Biggie Smalls and the whole Junior M.A.F.I.A. and the newbie Jay-Z; and that ill Staten Island crew, the Wu-Tang Clan, learning "life is hell / living in the world no different from a cell"; and that Harlem genius, Big L; and those guads from outside the city, from Queen Latifah setting it off, to Bone Thugs-N-Harmony fast-rapping—"Wake up, wake up, wake up it's the first of tha month"—to Tupac Shakur writing a letter to his mama. I related when Tupac confessed, "I hung around with the thugs, and even though they sold drugs / They showed a young brother love."

Hip-hop has had the most sophisticated vocabulary of any American musical genre. I read endlessly its poetic text. But parents and grandparents did not see us listening to and memorizing gripping works of oral poetry and urban reporting and short stories and autobiographies and sexual boasting and adventure fantasies. They saw—and still see—words that would lead my mind into deviance. "By reinforcing the stereotypes that long hindered blacks, and by teaching young blacks that a thuggish adversarial stance is the properly 'authentic' response to a presumptively racist society, rap retards black success," linguist John McWhorter once claimed. C. Delores Tucker campaigned against rap in the mid-1990s. "You can't listen to all that language and filth without it affecting you," Tucker liked to say—just like our parents and grandparents liked to say. The sixty-six-year-old chair of the National Political Congress of Black Women, the venerable veteran of the civil rights movement, kept coming at us like a Biggie Smalls battle rap.

THE NEXT YEAR we left Queens, left the Ave behind, to start our new life in the South. At the end of a school day sometime in the fall of 1997, I nervously made my way to the gymnasium to see who'd made the cut for Stonewall Jackson High School's junior-varsity basketball team.

I walked over to the gym alone. I hated being alone all the time. I did not have any friends at my new high school in Manassas, Virginia. I'd arrived weeks before at our new house in a predominantly White suburban neighborhood. Manassas wasn't the Deep South, but it was unquestionably south of Jamaica, Queens. Our first night there, I stayed up all night, occasionally looking out the window, worried the Ku Klux Klan would arrive any minute. Why did Aunt Rena have to move here and entice my parents?

The word had spread quickly in school that the quiet, skinny kid wearing baggy clothes, Air Force 1s, and Tims, with a weird accent and a slow strut, was from New York. Girls and boys alike were fascinated—but not necessarily reaching out to be my friend. Basketball was my only companion.

I opened a door to the gym, walked slowly across the dark court to the other side, and came upon the JV list. I confidently looked for my name. I did not see it. Startled, I looked again, pointing my index finger as I slowly read each name. I did not see my name.

Tears welled up. I turned around and fast-walked away, holding back my tears. I made my way to the school bus and plopped down like I've never plopped down on a seat before.

My sadness about being cut was overwhelmed by a deeper agony: Not making the team had fully cut off my one route to finding friends in my new school. I was suffering but held it together on my short walk home from the bus stop.

When I opened the front door, I saw Dad coming down the stairs of our split-level home—I stepped inside and fell into his surprised arms. We sat down together on the stairs, the front door still flung open. I cried uncontrollably, alarming my father. After a few minutes, I gathered myself and said, "I didn't make the team," only to start crying again and blurt out, "Now I'm never going to have any friends!"

Basketball had been life. It all changed when those tears finally passed.

AT FIFTEEN, I was an intuitive believer in multiculturalism, unlike assimilationist sociologists such as Nathan Glazer, who lamented in his 1997 book, *We Are All Multiculturalists Now*. I opposed racist ideas that belittled the cultures of urban Black people, of hip-hop—of me. I sensed that to ridicule the Black cultures I knew would be to ridicule myself.

At the same time, though, as an urban Black Northerner, I looked down on the cultures of non-urban Black Southerners, the very people I was now surrounded by. I measured their beloved go-go music—then popular in D.C. and Virginia—against what I considered to be the gold standard of Black music, Queens hip-hop, and despised it like C. Delores Tucker despised hip-hop. The guys in Virginia could not dress. I hated their Ebonics. I thought the basketball players were scrubs who I had to patronize, a belief that cost me the spot on the JV squad. I walked around during those early months at Stonewall Jackson with an unspoken arrogance. I suspect potential friends heard my nonverbal cues of snobbery and rightly stayed away.

When we refer to a group as Black or White or another racial identity—Black Southerners as opposed to Southerners—we are racializing that group. When we racialize any group and then render that group's culture inferior, we are articulating cultural racist ideas. When I defended Black culture in my mind, I was treating culture in a general sense, not a specific sense, just as I understood race in a general sense, not a specific (or intersectional) sense. I knew it was wrong to say Black people were culturally inferior. But I was quick to judge specific Black cultures practiced by specific Black racial groups. Judging the culture I saw in Manassas from the cultural standards of Black New York was no different than White New York judging Black New York from White New York's cultural standards. That is no different than White America judging Latinx America from White America's cultural standards. That is no different than Europe judging the rest of the world from European cultural standards, which is where the problem started, back during the so-called Age of Enlightenment.

"That every practice and sentiment is barbarous, which is not according to the usages of modern Europe, seems to be a fundamental maxim with many of our critics and philosophers," wrote critical Scottish Enlightenment philosopher James Beattie in 1770. "Their remarks often put us in mind of the fable of the man and the lion." In the fable, a man and lion travel together, arguing over who is superior. They pass a statue that shows a lion strangled by a man. The man says, "See there! How strong we are, and how we prevail over even the king of beasts." The lion replies, "This statue was made by one of you men. If we lions knew how to erect statues, you would see the man placed under the paw of the lion." Whoever creates the cultural standard usually puts themselves at the top of the hierarchy.

"All cultures must be judged in relation to their own history, and all individuals and groups in relation to their cultural history, and definitely not by the arbitrary standard of any single culture," wrote anthropologist Ashley Montagu in 1942, a clear expression of cultural relativity, the essence of cultural antiracist ideas. To be antiracist is to see all cultures in all their differences as on the same level, as equals. When we see cultural difference, we are seeing cultural difference—nothing more, nothing less.

It took me a while. Months of loneliness—really almost two years, if we are talking about making true friends. But I slowly but surely started to respect African American culture in Northern Virginia. I slowly but surely came down from the clouds of my culturally racist conceit. But I could not rise above my behaviorally racist insecurity.

CHAPTER 8

BEHAVIOR

BEHAVIORAL RACIST IDEA: Any notion that makes individuals responsible for the perceived behavior of racial groups and makes racial
groups responsible for the behavior of individuals.

BEHAVIORAL ANTIRACIST IDEA: Any notion that makes racial group behavior fictional and individual behavior real.

DID EVENTUALLY MAKE friends, an interracial group who arrived just as my old gear from the Ave became too small for my
growing body. I lost the purity of my New York accent and
jump shot, but I found living, breathing, laughing friends, like
Chris, Maya, Jovan, and Brandon.

My schoolwork did not recover. I never bothered much
with class back in Queens—I skipped classes at John Bowne
to play spades in the lunchroom and tuned out teachers like
they were bad commercials, doing just enough classwork to
stay married to basketball. I was definitely not living up to
my academic potential—and as a Black teenager in the nineties, my shortcomings didn't go unnoticed or unjudged. The
first to notice were the adults around me of my parents' and
grandparents' generations. As legal scholar James Forman Jr.
documents, the civil rights generation usually evoked Martin Luther King Jr. to shame us. "Did Martin Luther King
successfully fight the likes of Bull Connor so that we could
ultimately lose the struggle for civil rights to misguided or

malicious members of our own race?" asked Washington, D.C., prosecutor Eric Holder at an MLK birthday celebration in 1995. "You are costing everybody's freedom," Jesse Jackson told a group of people incarcerated in Alabama that year. "You can rise above this if you change your mind," he added. "I appeal to you. Your mother appealed to you. Dr. King died for you."

The so-called "first Black president" followed suit. "It isn't racist for Whites to say they don't understand why people put up with gangs on the corner or in the projects or with drugs being sold in the schools or in the open," said President Clinton in 1995. "It's not racist for Whites to assert that the culture of welfare dependency, out of wedlock pregnancy, and absent fatherhood cannot be broken by social programs, unless there is first more personal responsibility."

Black people needed to stop playing "race cards," the phrase Peter Collier and David Horowitz used to brand "talk of race and racism" in 1997. The issue was personal irresponsibility.

Indeed, I was irresponsible in high school. It makes antiracist sense to talk about the personal irresponsibility of individuals like me of all races. I screwed up. I could have studied harder. But some of my White friends could have studied harder, too, and their failures and irresponsibility didn't somehow tarnish their race.

My problems with personal irresponsibility were exacerbated—or perhaps even caused—by the additional struggles that racism added to my school life, from a history of disinterested, racist teachers, to overcrowded schools, to the daily racist attacks that fell on young Black boys and girls. There's no question that I could have hurdled that racism and kept on running. But asking every nonathletic Black person to become an Olympic hurdler, and blaming them when they can't keep up, is racist. One of racism's harms is the way it falls on the unexceptional Black person who is asked to be extraordinary just to survive—and, even worse, when a Black person screws up, she faces the abyss after one error, while a White person who screws up in the same way is handed second chances and empathy. This shouldn't be surprising: One of the fundamental values of racism to White people is that it makes success attainable for even unexceptional Whites, while success, even moderate success, is usually reserved for extraordinary Black individuals or unexceptional Black individuals willing to rise on the debasement of Black people.

How do we think about my young self, the C or D student, in antiracist terms? The truth is that I should be critiqued as a student—I was undermotivated and distracted and undisciplined. In other words, a bad student. But I shouldn't be critiqued as a bad *Black* student. I did not represent my race any more than my irresponsible White classmates represented their race. It makes racist sense to talk about personal irresponsibility as it applies to an entire racial group. Racial-group behavior is a figment of the racist's imagination. Individual behaviors can shape the success of individuals. But policies determine the success of groups. And it is racist power that creates the policies that cause racial inequities and injustices.

Making individuals responsible for the perceived behavior of racial groups and making whole racial groups responsible for the behavior of individuals are the two ways that behavioral racist ideas infect our perception of the world. In other words, when we believe that a racial group's seeming positive or negative attributes redound to each of its individual members, we've accepted a racist idea. Likewise, when we believe that an individual's positive or negative attributes redound to an entire group, we've accepted a racist idea. These two racist ideas were common currency in the 1990s. Progressive Americans—the ones who self-identified as "not racist"—had abandoned biological racist ideas by the mid-1990s. They had gone further: Mostly they'd abandoned ethnic racist, bodily racist, and cultural racist ideas. But they were still sold on behavioral racist ideas. And they carried that torch unwaveringly, right up to the present.

The same behavioral racist ideas drove many of the Trump voters whom these same "not racist" progressives vociferously opposed in the 2016 election. They, too, ascribed qualities to entire groups—these were voters whose political choice correlated with their belief that Black people are ruder, lazier, less intelligent, and crueler than White people. "America's Black community . . . has turned America's major cities into slums because of laziness, drug use, and sexual promiscuity," fancied Reverend Jamie Johnson, director of a faith-based center in Trump's Department of Homeland Security, after the election. "Although black civil rights leaders like to point to a supposedly racist criminal justice system to explain why our prisons house so many black men, it's been obvious for decades that the real culprit is black behavior," argued Jason Riley in 2016.

Every time someone racializes behavior—describes something as "Black behavior"—they are expressing a racist idea. To be an antiracist is to recognize there is no such thing as racial behavior. To be an antiracist is to recognize there is no such thing as Black behavior, let alone irresponsible Black behavior. Black behavior is

NOTE ON BEHAVIORAL RACIST IDEAS There is a critical message that I failed to state explicitly in the hardcover edition. For much of history, racist theorists spoke about specific racial *groups* having superior and inferior behaviors. But by the twenty-first century, with growing awareness of such ideas as racist, racist theorists evolved their rhetoric for renewed circulation and consumption. They now speak about *individual* behaviors to explain racial disparities between *groups*. They use the terms "culture" and "behavior" interchangeably. For example, when newly released datasets revealed in April 2020 that Black Americans *as a group* were dying at the highest rates from COVID-19, some commentators dismissed racist policies as the cause and pointed to irresponsible personal behaviors. They didn't realize—or, as propagandists, perhaps they did—that to explain a racial disparity by speaking about the deficient behaviors of individuals of a particular race is to say that particular race is behaviorally deficient. And to suggest that a race is behaviorally deficient is a racist idea. In other words, the new focus on individual behaviors to explain group disparity is intended to ensure the deniability of racist ideas, when in fact it is proof of racist ideas.

as fictitious as Black genes. There is no "Black gene." No one has ever scientifically established a single "Black behavioral trait." No evidence has ever been produced, for instance, to prove that Black people are louder, angrier, nicer, funnier, lazier, less punctual, more immoral, religious, or dependent; that Asian people are more subservient; that White people are greedier. All we have are stories of individual behavior. But individual stories are only proof of the behavior of individuals. Just as race doesn't exist biologically, race doesn't exist behaviorally.

But what about the argument that clusters of Black people in the South, or Asian Americans in New York's Chinatown, or White people in the Texas suburbs seem to act in ways that follow coherent, definable practices? To be antiracist is to separate the idea of a culture from the idea of behavior. Culture defines a group tradition that a particular racial group might share but that is not shared among all individuals in that racial group or among all racial groups. Behavior defines the inherent human traits and potential that everyone shares. Humans are intelligent and lazy, even as that intelligence and laziness might appear differently across cultural groups.

BEHAVIORAL RACIST IDEAS are different from antiracist ideas, and even from each other. In the decades before the Civil War, behavioral racist ideas clashed over whether freedom or slavery caused supposed mediocre Black behavior. To proslavery theorists, Black behavioral deficiencies stemmed from freedom, either in Africa or among formerly enslaved people in the United States. In the states that "retained the ancient relation" between White mastery and Black slavery, enslaved Black people "had improved greatly in every respect—in numbers, comfort, intelligence, and morals," Secretary of State John C. Calhoun argued to a British critic in 1844. This proslavery position held after slavery. Freed Black people "cut off" "from the spirit of White society"—their civilizing masters—had degenerated into the "original African type," with behavioral traits ranging from hypersexuality, immorality, criminality, and laziness to poor parenting, Philip Alexander Bruce maintained in his popular 1889 book, *The Plantation Negro as a Freeman*.

In contrast, abolitionists, including Benjamin Rush in 1773, argued, "All the vices which are charged upon the Negroes in the southern colonies and the West-Indies, such as Idleness, Treachery, Theft, and the like, are the genuine offspring of slavery." A year later, Rush founded the budding nation's first White antislavery society. Prefacing Frederick Douglass's slave narrative in 1845, abolitionist William Lloyd Garrison stated that slavery "degraded" Black people "in the scale of humanity. . . . Nothing has been left undone to cripple their intellects, darken their minds, debase their moral nature, obliterate all traces of their relationship to mankind."

These abolitionists—or, rather, progressive assimilationists—conjured what I call the oppression-inferiority thesis. In their well-meaning efforts to persuade people about the horrors of oppression, assimilationist ideas now as then maintain that oppression has degraded the behaviors of oppressed people.

This belief extended into the period after slavery. In his address to the founding meeting of Alexander Crummell's American Negro Academy in 1897, W.E.B. Du Bois pictured "the first and greatest step toward the settlement of the present friction between the races . . . lies in the correction of the immorality, crime, and laziness among the Negroes themselves, which still remains as a heritage of slavery." This framing of slavery as a demoralizing force was the mirror image of the Jim Crow historian's framing of slavery as a civilizing force. Both positions led Americans toward behavioral racist ideas: Black behavior demoralized by freedom—or freed Black behavior demoralized by slavery.

The latest expression of the oppression-inferiority thesis is known as post-traumatic slave syndrome, or PTSS. Black "infighting," materialism, poor parenting, colorism, defeatism, rage—these "dysfunctional" and "negative" behaviors "as well as many others are in large part related to trans-generational behavioral adaptations associated with the past traumas of slavery and on-going oppression," maintains psychologist Joy DeGruy in her 2005 book, *Post Traumatic Slave Syndrome*. (Some people believe, based on misleading studies, that these trans-generational adaptations are genetic.)

DeGruy claimed "many, many" African Americans suffer from PTSS. She built this theory on anecdotal evidence and modeled it on post-traumatic stress disorder (PTSD). But studies show that many, many people who endure traumatic environments don't contract post-traumatic stress disorder. Researchers found that among soldiers returning from Iraq and Afghanistan, PTSD rates ranged from 13.5 to 30 percent.

Black individuals have, of course, suffered trauma from slavery and ongoing oppression. Some individuals throughout history have exhibited negative behaviors related to this trauma. DeGruy is a hero for ushering the constructs of trauma, damage, and healing into our understanding of Black life. But there is a thin line between an antiracist idea that says individual Black people have suffered trauma and a racist idea that says Black people are a traumatized people. There is similarly a thin line between an antiracist idea saying slavery was debilitating and a racist idea saying Black people are a debilitated people. The latter constructions erase whole swaths of history: for instance, the story of even the first generation of emancipated Black people, who moved straight from plantations into the Union army, politics, labor organizing, Union leagues, artistry, entrepreneurship, club building, church building, school building, community building—buildings more commonly razed by the fiery hand of racist terrorism than by any self-destructive hand of behavioral deficiencies derived from the trauma of slavery.

Increasingly in the twentieth century, social scientists replaced slavery with segregation and poverty as the oppressive hand ravaging Black behavior. Psychoanalysts Abram Kardiner and Lionel Ovesey expressed this alarm in their 1951 tome, *The Mark of Oppression: A Psychosocial Study of the American Negro*. "There is not one personality trait of the Negro the source of which cannot be traced to his difficult living conditions," they wrote. "The final result is a wretched internal life," a diminished "self-esteem," a vicious "self-hatred," "the conviction of unlovability, the diminution of affectivity, and the uncontrolled hostility." Widely taken as scientific fact, these sweeping generalizations were based on the authors' interviews with all of twenty-five subjects.

AS A STRUGGLING Black teenager in the nineties, I felt suffocated by a sense of being judged, primarily by the people I was closest to: other Black people, particularly older Black people who worried over my entire generation. The Black judge in my mind did not leave any room for the mistakes of Black individuals—I didn't just have to deal with the consequences of my personal failings, I had the added burden of letting down the entire race. Our mistakes were generalized as the mistakes of the race. It seemed that White people were free to misbehave, make mistakes. But if we failed—or failed to be twice as good—then the Black judge handed down a hard sentence. No probation or parole. There was no middle ground—we were either King's disciples or thugs killing King's dream.

But, of course, while that may have felt true in a larger social sense, individual Black parents responded as individuals. My own parents privately etched out probationary middle grounds for their own children. I did not make Ma and Dad proud. But they didn't treat me as a thug and lock me away—they kept trying. When I was in eleventh grade at Stonewall Jackson, my parents nudged me into International Baccalaureate (IB) classes, and even though I didn't have particularly high expectations for myself, I went along with it. I entered the sanctimonious world of IB, surrounded by a sea of White and Asian students. This environment only made my hatred of school more intense, if now for a different reason. I felt stranded, save for an occasional class with my friend Maya, a Black teen preparing for Spelman College. None of my White and Asian classmates came to save me. Rarely opening my lips or raising my hand, I shaped myself according to what I thought they believed about me. I felt like a person in a leaky boat as they sailed by me every day on their way to standardized-test prep sessions, Ivy League dreams, and competitions for teachers' praises. I saw myself through their eyes: an impostor, deserving of invisibility. My drowning in the supposed sea of advanced intelligence was imminent.

I internalized my academic struggles as indicative of something wrong not just with my behavior but with Black behavior as a whole, since I represented the race, both in their eyes—or what I thought I saw in their eyes—and in my own.

The so-called Nation's Report Card told Americans the same story. It first reported the math scores of eighth- and fourth-graders in 1990, the year I entered third grade. Asian fourth-graders scored thirty-seven points, White fourth-graders thirty-two points, and Latinx fourth-graders twelve points higher than Black fourth-graders on the standardized math test. By 2019, the scoring gaps in fourth-grade mathematics had slightly narrowed. The racial "achievement gap" in reading between White and Black fourth-graders also narrowed between 1992 and 2019 but widened between White and Black twelfth-graders. Among students who graduated high school in 2019, Blacks received average total SAT scores 290 points lower than Asians and 181 points lower than Whites; they had the second-lowest average SAT scores of any racial group, scoring higher than only their Native American peers.

As a high school student, I believed standardized tests effectively measured smarts and therefore my White and Asian classmates were smarter than me. I thought I was a fool. Clearly, I needed another shaming lesson about how King died for me.

NOT UNTIL MY senior year in college did I realize I was a fool for thinking I was a fool. I was preparing for my last major standardized test, the Graduate Record Exam, or GRE. I had already forked over $1,000 for a preparatory course, feeding the U.S. test-prep and private tutoring industry that was evaluated at $26 billion in 2022 (the global industry is projected to reach

$201.8 billion by 2026). The courses and private tutors are concentrated in Asian and White communities, who, not surprisingly, score the highest on standardized tests. My GRE prep course, for instance, was not taught on my historically Black campus. I had to trek over to the campus of a historically White college in Tallahassee.

I sat surrounded by White students before a White teacher at Florida State University, a flashback to my lonely boat at Stonewall Jackson. I wondered why I was the only Black student in the room and about my own economic privilege and the presumed economic privilege of my fellow students. I wondered about another stratum of students, who weren't even in the room, the ones who could pay for private tutoring with this teacher.

The teacher boasted the course would boost our GRE scores by two hundred points, which I didn't pay much attention to at first—it seemed an unlikely advertising pitch. But with each class, the technique behind the teacher's confidence became clearer. She wasn't making us smarter so we'd ace the test—she was teaching us *how* to take the test.

On the way home from the class, I typically stopped by the gym to lift weights. When I first started weight lifting, I naturally assumed the people lifting the heaviest weights were the strongest people. I assumed wrong. To lift the most required a combination of strength and the best form; one was based on ability, the other on access to the best information and training. Well-trained lifters with exquisite form lifted heavier weights than similarly or even better-endowed lifters with poorer form.

This regular commute from the GRE prep course to the weight room eventually jarred me into clarity: The teacher was not making us stronger. She was giving us form and technique so we'd know precisely how to carry the weight of the test.

It revealed the bait and switch at the heart of standardized tests—the exact thing that made them unfair: She was teaching test-taking form for standardized exams that purportedly measured intellectual strength. My classmates and I would get higher scores—two hundred points, as promised—than poorer students, who might be equivalent in intellectual strength but did not have the resources or, in some cases, even the awareness to acquire better form through high-priced prep courses. Because of the way the human mind works—the so-called "attribution effect," which drives us to take personal credit for any success—those of us who prepped for the test would score higher and then walk into better opportunities thinking it was all about us: that we were better and smarter than the rest and we even had inarguable, quantifiable proof. Look at our scores! Admissions counselors and professors would assume we were better qualified and admit us to their graduate schools (while also boosting their institutional rankings). And because we're talking about featureless, objective numbers, no one would ever think that racism could have played a role.

The use of standardized tests to measure aptitude and intelligence is one of the most effective racist policies ever devised to degrade Black minds and legally exclude Black bodies. We degrade Black minds every time we speak of an "academic-achievement gap" based on these numbers. The acceptance of an academic-achievement gap is just the latest method of reinforcing the oldest racist idea: Black intellectual inferiority. The idea of an achievement gap means there is a disparity in academic performance between groups of students; implicit in this idea is that academic "achievement" can only be measured by statistical instruments like test scores and dropout rates. There is an even more sinister implication in achievement-gap talk—that disparities in standardized test scores accurately reflect disparities in intelligence among racial groups. Intellect is the linchpin of behavior, and the racist idea of the achievement gap is the linchpin of behavioral racist ideas.

Remember, to believe in a racial hierarchy is to believe in a racist idea. The idea of an achievement gap between the races—with Whites and Asians at the top and Blacks and Latinx people and Natives at the bottom—creates a racial hierarchy, with its implication that the racial gap in test scores means something is wrong with the Black and Latinx and Native test takers and not the tests. From the beginning, the tests, not groups of people, have been the racial problem. I know this is a hard idea to accept—so many well-meaning people have tried to "solve" this problem of the racial achievement gap—but once we understand the history and policies behind it, it becomes clear.

The history of racist ideas and standardized testing begins in 1869, when English statistician Francis Galton—a half cousin of Charles Darwin—hypothesized in *Hereditary Genius* that the "average intellectual standard of the negro race is some two grades below our own." Galton pioneered eugenics decades later but failed to develop a testing mechanism that verified his racist hypothesis. Where Galton failed, France's Alfred Binet and Theodore Simon succeeded, when they developed an IQ test in 1905 that Stanford psychologist Lewis Terman revised and delivered to Americans in 1916. These "experimental" tests would show "enormously significant racial differences in general intelligence, differences which cannot be wiped out by any scheme of mental culture," the eugenicist said in his 1916 book, *The Measurement of Intelligence.*

Terman's IQ test was first administered on a major scale to 1.7 million U.S. soldiers during World War I. Princeton psychologist Carl C. Brigham presented the soldiers' racial scoring gap as evidence of genetic racial hierarchy in *A Study of American Intelligence,* published three years before he created the Scholastic Aptitude Test, or SAT, in 1926. Aptitude means natural ability. Brigham, like other eugenicists, believed the SAT would reveal the natural intellectual ability of White people.

Physicist William Shockley and psychologist Arthur Jensen carried these eugenic ideas into the 1960s. By then, genetic explanations—if not the tests and the achievement gap itself—had largely been discredited. Segregationist ideas pointing to inferior genes had been overwhelmed in the racist debate over the cause of the achievement gap by assimilationist ideas pointing to inferior environments.

The rising assimilationist position shifted the discourse to "closing the achievement gap," powering the testing movement into the nineties, when *The Bell Curve* controversy erupted in 1994 over whether the gap could be closed. "It seems highly likely to us that both genes and the environment have something to do with racial differences" in test scores, wrote Harvard psychologist Richard Herrnstein and political scientist Charles Murray in *The Bell Curve*. The racist idea of an achievement gap lived on into the new millennium through George W. Bush's No Child Left Behind Act and Obama's Race to the Top and Common Core—initiatives that further enlarged the role of standardized testing in determining the success and failure of students and the schools they attended. Through these initiatives and many, many others, education reformers banged the drum of the "achievement gap" to get attention and funding for their equalizing efforts.

But what if, all along, these well-meaning efforts at closing the achievement gap have been opening the door to racist ideas? What if different environments lead to different kinds of achievement rather than different levels of achievement? What if the intellect of a low-testing Black child in an impoverished Black school is different from—and not inferior to—the intellect of a high-testing White child in a rich White school? What if we measured intelligence by how knowledgeable individuals are about their own environments? What if we measured intellect by an individual's desire to know? What if we realized the best way to ensure an effective educational system is not by standardizing our curricula and tests but by standardizing the opportunities available to all students?

A recent nationwide study found that at any given poverty level, districts with a higher proportion of White students receive significantly more funding than districts with more students of color. Low-income White school districts annually receive $150 less per student than the national average, but approximately $1,500 more than low-income school districts where students of color make up at least three-quarters of the student body. Schools lack basic supplies, basic textbooks, healthy food and water. The lack of resources leads directly to diminished opportunities for learning. In other words, the racial problem is the opportunity gap, as antiracist reformers call it, not the achievement gap.

· · ·

BACK IN HIGH school, those final days in 1999 were taking forever. I sat bored during free time in my government class. As my mind wandered, my eyes wandered and latched on to Angela, sitting behind me. Brown-skinned with high cheekbones and a sweet disposition, Angela appeared to be writing intently.

"What are you doing?" I asked.

"I'm writing my speech," she said with her usual smile, not looking up from her writing.

"Speech for what?"

"For the MLK contest. You haven't heard?"

I shook my head, and so she told me all about the Prince William County Martin Luther King Jr. oratorical contest. Stonewall Jackson participants would give their speeches in two days. Stonewall's winner would go on to the county competition. The top three finalists would speak at the Hylton Chapel on MLK Day in 2000.

She urged me to participate. At first, I declined. But by the time she finished with me, I was in. The prompt for the contest was "What would be Dr. King's message for the millennium?" and what came to my pen were all the racist ideas about Black youth behavior circulating in the 1990s that, without realizing, I had deeply internalized. I started writing an anti-Black message that would have filled King with indignity—less like King himself and more like the shaming speeches about King that I heard so often from adults of my parents' generation. If only I'd spent more time listening to King instead of all the adults who claimed to speak for him. "We must no longer be ashamed of being Black," King would have told me, as he told a gathering of Black people in 1967. "As long as the mind is enslaved, the body can never be free."

As long as the mind thinks there is something behaviorally wrong with a racial group, the mind can never be antiracist. As long as the mind oppresses the oppressed by thinking their oppressive environment has led to inferior behaviors, the mind can never be antiracist. As long as the mind is racist, the mind can never be free.

To be antiracist is to think nothing is behaviorally wrong or right—inferior or superior—with any of the racial groups. Whenever the antiracist sees individuals behaving positively or negatively, the antiracist sees exactly that: individuals behaving positively or negatively, not representatives of whole races. To be antiracist is to deracialize behavior, to remove the tattooed stereotype from every racialized body. Behavior is something humans do, not races do.

I FINISHED A draft of the speech that night. "Let me hear it!" Angela excitedly asked the next day, before our government class.

"Hear what?" I said shyly, turning around, knowing exactly what.

"Your speech!" She beamed. "I know you got it there. Let me hear it!"

Feeling obligated, I slowly recited my speech. The more I read, the more confidence I felt. The racist ideas sounded so good, so right, as racist ideas normally do. When I finished, Angela was ecstatic.

"You're going to win! You're going to win!" she chanted softly as class started. I kept turning around and telling her to stop. Angela saw my smiles and did not.

I did not sleep much that night. Between fine-tuning my speech and quieting my nerves and fears, I had too much going in my mind. I fell eventually into a deep sleep, so deep I did not hear my alarm. When I awoke, I realized I had missed the competition. Upset but also relieved, I made my way to school.

Angela was waiting for me at the competition all morning. After the last participant had spoken to the Stonewall judges, Angela demanded they reconvene when I arrived at school and she did not take no from them—the same as she didn't take no from me.

And sure enough, when I got to school, the judges reconvened for me. Hearing all that Angela did, a storm surge of gratitude washed away my fears and nerves. I was determined to give the speech of my life. And I did. I won, racist ideas and all.

WINNING STARTED TO melt away the shame I felt for myself and my race regarding my academic struggles. The Black judge was proud of me. I was more than proud of myself. But my racist insecurity started transforming into racist conceit. The transformation had actually already started when I decided to attend Florida A&M University. "It felt right," I told people. I did not disclose to anyone or myself why this historically Black university felt right.

On my visit during the summer of 1999, everyone gushed about Florida A&M as the biggest and baddest HBCU—historically Black college and university—in the land. *Time* magazine and *The Princeton Review* had named it College of the Year in 1997. For the second time in three years, Florida A&M had outpaced Harvard in its recruitment of National Achievement Scholars (the best of the best of Black high school students). President Frederick S. Humphries, a six-foot-five-inch bundle of charisma, had personally recruited many of those students, while growing his university into the nation's largest HBCU.

Whenever we say something just feels right or wrong we're evading the deeper, perhaps hidden, ideas that inform our feelings. But in those hidden places, we find what we really think if we have the courage to face our own naked truths. I did not look within myself to see why Florida A&M just felt right—a reason beyond my desire to be around Black excellence. The truth is, I wanted to flee misbehaving Black folk.

Florida A&M became for me the best of Blackness, all right. I never could have imagined the enrapturing sound of Blackness at its peak. Two weeks after landing on campus, I heard it in all its glory.

COLOR

COLORIST IDEA: Any notion that suggests that Dark people or Light people are superior or inferior in any way, or justifies racist policies that lead to injustice or inequity between Light people and Dark people.

COLOR ANTIRACIST IDEA: Any notion that suggests that Dark people and Light people are equals, or defends policies that lead to justice and equity between Light people and Dark people.

M Y VOICE CREAKED like an old staircase. My arms flailed sluggishly as I stood on the highest of the seven hills in Tallahassee, Florida. I wasn't tired from climbing on that September day in 2000. I'd been on campus for a few weeks and the school spirit had already mounted me and worn me out, just as it had the thousands of people around me—my fellow Rattlers of Florida A&M University. We called our school FAMU, pronounced as in "family," FAM-YOU.

I looked again at Bragg Stadium's football scoreboard. FAMU 39. MORGAN STATE 7. But I had no time to rest my tiring arms and screams. Halftime approached.

I should have saved my energy, but as a freshman I did not know any better. I had never seen a performance by the Marching 100, the high-stepping pride of FAMU, arguably the most accomplished marching band in history and certainly the most imitated marching band in the land. I'm biased, but see my receipts. William P. Foster had just retired after fifty-two years of raising what *Sports Illustrated* dubbed "the best college marching band in the country." FAMU band members hit the Grammy

Awards stage in 2006. But nothing compared to that Super Bowl in 2007, when I bragged incessantly and danced horribly as my friends and I watched the Marching 100 play for The Artist Formerly Known as Prince.

Back in 2000, though, the Marching 100 confused me on first sight in the first quarter. Winter-clothed in thick pants and long-sleeved orange, green, and white uniforms, adorned with capes and towering hats, they made me hot just watching them roast in the Florida sun. They played off the heat like jam sessions between plays. But nothing prepared me for what I was about to see at halftime.

My roommate, Clarence, stood next to me. Clarence and I arrived at FAMU from different places, had come running from different trails that converged in friendship. Him: an academic titan from Birmingham, Alabama. Me: an academic minion from up north. My daring, untethered ideas complemented his methodical analyses. My fuzzy sense of self and direction embraced his clarity. Clarence considered FAMU a pit stop on a mapped-out trail to a top law school and corporate law and wealth. I considered FAMU an inclusive Black commune to explore and find myself. My explorations amused Clarence. But nothing entertained him more than my eyes.

Clarence's hazelnut skin matched his hazel eyes, an eye color that is rare for anyone around the world but most commonly found among people in North Africa, the Middle East, Brazil, and those with Spanish heritage. Not African Americans. When I first saw his lighter eyes, I assumed they were fake. It turned out, his genes provided him what I had to buy.

Before arriving at FAMU, I'd started wearing "honey" contact lenses, or "orange eyes," as my friends joked on them. My colored contacts were hard to miss on me. Hazel contacts were perhaps the most popular colored contact lens among Black folk, but I picked one shade even lighter. It seemed okay to me to play with my eye color. I knew some Black people who wore blue or green contacts, which I thought was shameful. I saw them—but not me—as straining to not look Black.

Above my orange eyes, Clarence did not see a low haircut, sometimes with fading up the back and sides, all times a brush flattening the kinks that struggled to stand and band in freedom before the next killa haircut. I started cornrowing my hair in college, twisting them up in small locs, or letting the kinks stretch out, hardly caring that racist ideas judged these hairstyles as the unprofessional uniform of thugs. My cornrows signified an antiracist idea. My honey eyes a capitulation to assimilation. Together, they braided the assimilationist and antiracist ideas of my dueling consciousness.

Did I think my honey eyes meant I was striving to be White? No way. I was simply refining a cuter version of myself, which studies show is the explanation of most buyers of artificial contact lenses, complexion, hair, facial features, or bodily changes. I never asked myself the antiracist question. Why? Why did I think lighter eyes were more attractive on me? What did I truly want?

I wanted to be Black but did not want to look Black. I looked up to the new post-racial beauty ideal, an outgrowth of the old White beauty ideal. Lightening eye color. Killing kinks. Lightening skin color. Thinning or thickening facial features. All to reach an ideal we did not label White. This post-racial beauty ideal is Lightness: the race of lighter skin and eyes, straighter hair, thinner noses, and semi-thick lips and buttocks, perceived as biracial or racially ambiguous.

The dueling consciousness of antiracist pride in one's own race and assimilationist desire to be another race stirs this paradoxical post-racial beauty ideal. "It is simultaneously inclusive, multicultural, and new, while remaining exclusive, Eurocentric, and . . . old-fashioned," sociologist Margaret Hunter explains. It is "white beauty repackaged with dark hair."

I had no idea my light eyes embodied the latest form of "colorism," a term coined by novelist Alice Walker in 1983. The post-racial beauty ideal hides colorism, veils it in euphemism. Colorism is a form of racism. To recognize colorism, we must first recognize that Light people and Dark people are two distinct racialized groups shaped by their own histories. Dark people—the unidentified racial group of darker skins, kinky hair, broader noses and lips—span many races, ethnicities, and nationalities. Light people sometimes pass for White and may yet be accepted into Whiteness so that White people can maintain majorities in countries like the United States, where demographic trends threaten to relegate them to minority status. Some reformers project Light people as the biracial key to racial harmony, an embodiment of a post-racial future.

Colorism is a collection of racist policies that cause injustices and inequities between Light people and Dark people, and these injustices and inequities are substantiated by racist ideas about Light and Dark people. Colorism, like all forms of racism, rationalizes injustices and inequities with racist ideas, claiming the inequities are not due to racist policy but are based in what is wrong or right with each group of people. Colorist ideas are also assimilationist ideas, encouraging assimilation into—or transformation into something close to—the White body.

To be an antiracist is to focus on color lines as much as racial lines, knowing that color lines are especially harmful for Dark people. When the gains of a multicolored race disproportionately flow to Light people and the losses disproportionately flow to Dark people, inequities between the races mirror inequities within the races. But because inequities between the races overshadow inequities within the races, Dark people often fail to see colorism as they regularly experience it. Therefore, Dark people rarely protest policies that benefit Light people, a "skin color paradox," as termed by political scientists Jennifer L. Hochschild and Vesla Weaver.

Anti-Dark colorist ideas follow the logic of behavioral racist ideas, linking behavior to color, studies show. White children attribute positivity to lighter skin and negativity to Dark skin, a colorist worldview that continues as they get older. White people usually favor lighter-skinned politicians over darker-skinned ones. Dark African Americans are disproportionately at risk of hypertension. Dark students generally receive significantly lower GPAs than Light students. Maybe because racist Americans have higher expectations for Light students, people tend to remember educated Black men as Light-skinned even when their skin is Dark. Is that why employers prefer Light Black men over Dark Black men regardless of qualifications? Even Dark Filipino men have lower incomes than their lighter peers in the United States. Dark immigrants to the United States, no matter their place of origin, tend to have less wealth and income than Light immigrants. When they arrive, Light Latinas receive higher wages, and Dark Latinx people are more likely to be employed at ethnically homogeneous jobsites.

Dark sons and Light daughters receive higher-quality parenting than Light sons and Dark daughters. Skin color influences perceptions of attractiveness most often for Black women. As skin tone lightens, levels of self-esteem among Black women rise, especially among low- and middle-income Black women.

Dark Black women receive the harshest prison sentences and more time behind bars. White men with African facial features who are convicted of felonies receive harsher sentences than their European-presenting peers. Dark female students are nearly twice as likely to be suspended as White female students, while researchers found no disparity between Light and White female students. Inequities between Light and Dark African Americans can be almost as wide as inequities between Black and White Americans.

THE SECOND QUARTER ticked away. I stared as the world's longest multicolored Rattler uncurled itself. The Marching 100 should have been named the Marching 400. Hundreds of band members slowly stepped onto the field, one after another, into lines of instruments, into a rhythmic strut. Lines low-stepped behind FAMU's team on our side of the field, to the other side of the field behind Morgan State's team, and into the end zones. The line colors draped over the green field like strokes of paint on a canvas. Skin color didn't matter in this procession. It never should have mattered.

I watched the spreading lines of cymbals, trumpets, trombones, saxophones, clarinets, French horns, flutes, and those big tubas. Instruments rhythmically swayed in unison with bodies. The half ended. Football players ran through band lines and departed the field. Instead of a rush out to the concession stands, people rushed to their seats to stand and wait.

Some male students didn't care about watching the Marching 100's first performance of the season and instead prowled inside the shaded concourse or outside the stadium, searching for a new friend, hoping they had more game than football. If they were anything like my heterosexual friends, then Light women were their favorite, and it showed up in the words they spit. "Ugly-Black," they called darker women. "Nappy-headed." But straight and long hair was "good hair."

"She's cute . . . for a Dark girl," was the best some of them could muster for darker-skinned women. Even Dark gay men heard it: "I don't normally date Dark-skin men, but . . ."

The first woman I dated at FAMU was lighter than me, with almost caramel-colored skin. Straight hair fell down her petite body. I liked her (or did I like that she liked me?). But I did not like how my friends fawned over her and overlooked her darker roommate and best friend. The more my friends ignored or denigrated the Dark woman, the more I resented myself for liking the Light woman. After a few months, I had enough. I abruptly cut off the Light woman. My friends thought I had lost my mind. To this day, they deem the Light woman the prettiest woman I dated at FAMU. After her, they say, I rolled downhill into the Dark abyss.

They are right about the Darkness—if not the abyss. That first Light college girlfriend ended up being the last at FAMU. I pledged to date only Dark women. Only my Light friend Terrell did not think I had lost my mind. He preferred Dark women, too. I looked down on the rest—anyone who did not prefer Dark women, as well. I hardly realized my own racist hypocrisy: I was turning the color hierarchy upside down, but the color hierarchy remained. Dark people degraded and alienated Light people with names: light bright, high yellow, redbone. "You're never Black enough," a Light woman once told Oprah about her feelings of rejection. Light people constantly report their struggle to integrate with Dark people, to prove their Blackness to Dark people, as if Dark people are the judge and standard of Blackness. The irony is that many Dark people—read me, circa 2000—do think of themselves as the judge and standard of Blackness, while at the same time meekly aspiring to the standard of Lightness or Whiteness.

White people and Dark people reject and envy Light people. White people have historically employed the one-drop rule—that even one drop of Black blood makes you Black—to bar Light people from pure Whiteness. Dark people employ the two-drop rule, as I call it—two drops of White blood make you less Black—to bar Light people from pure Blackness. Light people employ the three-drop rule, as I call it—three drops of Black blood mean you're too Dark—to bar Dark people from pure Lightness. The "drop" rules of racial purity were mirages, just like the races themselves and the idea of racial blood. No racial group was pure.

When people look at my chocolate-brown skin, broad nose, thick lips, and the long hair I locked during my junior year at FAMU, around the time I retired my orange eyes for good, they do not see a biracial man. They do not see my White great-great-grandfather.

Nothing has been passed down about this White man except that he impregnated my great-great-grandmother, who bore him a Light child named Eliza in 1875. In the 1890s, Eliza married the Dark-skinned Lewis, who had recently arrived in Guyton, Georgia, from Sylvania, West Virginia. In 1920, they bore my grandfather Alvin. Eliza, Alvin, and Ma, all lighter-skinned, all married Dark people.

An ancestral pull toward Dark people? Wishful thinking to exonerate my anti-Light colorism. I had antiracist intentions, unmindful that the car of racism can drive just as far with the right intentions. To be an antiracist is not to reverse the beauty standard. To be an antiracist is to eliminate any beauty standard based on skin and eye color, hair texture, facial and bodily features shared by groups. To be an antiracist is to diversify our standards of beauty like our standards of culture or intelligence, to see beauty equally in all skin colors, broad and thin noses, kinky and straight hair, light and dark eyes. To be an antiracist is to build and live in a beauty culture that accentuates instead of erases our natural beauty.

"FOR IT IS well known," attested Anglican missionary Morgan Godwyn in an antislavery pamphlet in 1680, "that the Negro's . . . do entertain as high thoughts of themselves and of their Complexion, as our Europeans do." Johann Joachim Winckelmann, the so-called "father" of Western art history, endeavored, like his fellow Enlightenment intellectuals, to bring down my ancestors' high thoughts. African people must accept the "correct conception" of beauty, Winckelmann demanded in *History of the Art of Antiquity* in 1764. "A beautiful body will be all the more beautiful the whiter it is."

The enslaver's philosophy extended this further: A body will be all the more superior the Whiter it is. An enslaved body will be closer to the enslaver the Whiter it is. Enslavers more often worked Light people in the house and Dark people in the fields, reasoning that Light people were suited for skilled tasks and Dark people for more physically demanding tasks. A body will be all the more animalistic the darker it is. Enslavers crafted a hierarchy that descended from the intellectually strong White down to the Light, then to the Dark, and, finally, to the physically strong Animal. "Ferocity and stupidity are the characteristics of those tribes in which the peculiar Negro features are found most developed," intoned one writer.

The U.S. father of colorist ideas is Samuel Stanhope Smith, a longtime theologian who taught at and then presided over Princeton University in early America. In early 1787, the young Princeton professor gave the annual oration to the new nation's most distinguished scholarly group, the American Philosophical Society. He spoke before the White men who wrote the U.S. Constitution that year, pledging to use "the genuine light of truth." Smith's racist light: "domestic servants . . . who remain near the [White] persons" have "advanced far before ['field slaves'] in acquiring the regular and agreeable features." Since "field slaves" live "remote from . . . their superiors," their bodies "are frequently ill shaped," and their kinky hair is "the farthest removed from the ordinary laws of nature." In an 1851 book, lawyer and naturalist Peter Browne leaned on his unrivaled human-hair collection to classify the "hair" of White people and "wool" of Black people, to swear, "The hair of the white man is *more perfect* than that of the Negro."

Some enslavers considered Dark people more perfect than the so-called human mule, or mulatto. The biracial "hybrid" is "a degenerate, unnatural offspring, doomed by nature to work out its own destruction," wrote Alabama physician Josiah Nott in the *Boston Medical and Surgical Journal* in 1843.

Enslavers' public racist ideas sometimes clashed with their private racist ideas, which typically described Light women as smarter, kinder, gentler, and more beautiful than Dark women. Enslavers paid much more for enslaved Light females than for their Dark counterparts. From long before the United States even existed until long after American slavery ended, men cast these "yaller gals" and "Jezebels" as seductresses to cover up their centuries of attempted and actual rapes.

Some abolitionists framed biracial Light people as "tragic mulattoes," imprisoned by their "one drop" of "Black blood." In Harriet Beecher Stowe's 1852 bestseller, *Uncle Tom's Cabin,* the only runaways are the biracial captives. Stowe contrasts the biracial runaway George, "of fine European features and a high, indomitable spirit," with a docile enslaved Black man named Tom. "Sons of white fathers . . . will not always be bought and sold and traded," Tom's enslaver says.

Freed sons of White fathers will always be "more likely to enlist themselves under the banners of the whites," *Charleston Times* editor Edwin Clifford Holland contended in 1822. Maybe

Holland had the Brown Fellowship Society in mind, a biracial mutual-aid organization dedicated to "Social Purity" in Charleston. Or maybe he foresaw the White and Light only barbershops owned by Light people in Washington, D.C., before the Civil War.

When emancipation in 1865 thrust all Black people into the land of freedom, White communities built higher walls of segregation to keep Black people out. Light communities, too, built higher walls of segregation to keep Dark people out. To maintain Light privilege, the segregated Light people further segregated Dark people, preserving prewar racial disparities between Light and Dark people. After slavery, Light people were wealthier than Dark people and more likely to have good-paying jobs and schooling.

By the end of the nineteenth century, dozens of cities had "Blue Vein" societies, which barred Dark people "not white enough to show blue veins," as Charles Chesnutt put it in an 1898 short story. Light people reproduced the paper-bag test, pencil test, door test, and comb test to bar Dark people from their churches, businesses, parties, organizations, schools, and HBCUs.

But these segregators were still segregated from Whiteness. In 1896, shoemaker Homer Plessy—of the *Plessy v. Ferguson* case, which deemed constitutional "equal but separate accommodations"—hailed from a proud Light community in New Orleans. But Mississippi professor Charles Carroll considered the interracial intercourse of the White human and the Black "beast" the most diabolical of all sins. Naturally rebellious Light men were raping White women, leading to lynchings, Carroll warned in his 1900 book, *The Negro a Beast*. In 1901, North Carolina State University president George T. Winston disagreed, framing Dark people as committing "more horrible crimes." Sociologist Edward Byron Reuter added to Winston's position, declaring that biracial people were responsible for all Black achievements, in his 1918 book, *The Mulatto in the United States*. Reuter made Light people a sort of racial middle class, below White people and above Dark people.

Reuter defended Light people from the wrath of eugenicists

demanding "racial purity" and from Dark people challenging their colorist ideas. By the final days of 1920, the famous grandson of a biracial man had enough of Dark activists, especially Marcus Garvey and his fast-growing Universal Negro Improvement Association. "American Negroes recognize no color line in or out of the race, and they will in the end punish the man who attempts to establish it," W.E.B. Du Bois declared in *The Crisis*. This from a man who probably heard the Black children's rhyme: "If you're white, you're right / If you're yellow, you're mellow / If you're brown, stick around / If you're black, get back." This from a man who in his own "Talented Tenth" essay in 1903 listed twenty-one Black leaders, all but one of whom was biracial. This from a man who heard Light people say over and over again that the Dark masses needed "proper grooming," as imparted by North Carolina educator Charlotte Hawkins Brown, who took pride in her English ancestry.

Du Bois's avowal of a post-color Black America in 1921 was as out of touch as John McWhorter's avowal of a post-racial America after Barack Obama's presidential election in 2008. Either racist policies or Black inferiority explains why White people are wealthier, healthier, and more powerful than Black people today. Either racist policies or Dark inferiority explained why Light people were wealthier, healthier, and more powerful than

NOTE ON COLORISM When people of color claim they can't be racist, I do not think they realize that they are denying and erasing colorism today, as Du Bois did a century ago. Then again, the mass erasure makes sense. If there's one form of racism that White people and people of color most commonly ignore and deny, it is colorism. Colorism is so old and widespread that it probably seems normal to most people. I had no idea I held colorist ideas. I had no idea about this history of colorism inside the Black community. I suspect many Light people cannot see their privileges, just as many White people cannot see their privileges. They are like fish in water. Surrounded by water their whole lives, how can fish possibly see it? It isn't until they are removed from water that they realize what they were in. It isn't until people develop antiracist empathy and strive to put themselves in waters inhabited by a person of another complexion that they can see the privileges or even deprivations of living in their own Dark or Light skin.

Dark people in 1921. Du Bois snubbed the existence of colorism, claiming it had been "absolutely repudiated by every thinking Negro."

Du Bois had changed his thinking by the 1930s, moving closer to the deported Garvey. He replaced Garvey as the chief antiracist critic of the NAACP, which initially shied away from defending the Dark and impoverished Scottsboro Boys, who were falsely accused of raping two Alabama White women in 1931. Du Bois could not stand the NAACP's new executive secretary, Walter White. The blue-eyed, blond-haired son of biracial parents had advocated assimilation and reportedly believed that "unmixed" Negroes were "inferior, infinitely inferior now." In *The Crisis* in 1934, months before leaving the NAACP, Du Bois bristled: "Walter White is white."

Entrepreneurs were hard at work figuring out a way for Black people, through changing their color and hair, to pass as Light or White, as Walter White had in his earlier investigations of lynchings. The post–World War I craze of the conk—short for the gel called congolene—made it as fashionable for Black men to straighten their hair as for Black women. "I had joined that multitude of Negro men and women in America" trying "to look 'pretty' by white standards," Malcolm X recalled after receiving his first conk as a teenager. Skin-lightening products received a boost after the discovery in 1938 that monobenzyl ether of hydroquinone (HQ) lightened Dark skin.

By the early 1970s, Black power activists inspired by Malcolm X and Angela Davis—including my parents—were liberating their kinks. No more killa cuts for the Black men. No more straight hair for Black women. The higher the better was in. Not many men had a higher Afro than my father. Dark people like my father were saying it loud: "I'm Dark and I'm proud."

SOME DARK PEOPLE took too much pride in Darkness, inverting the color hierarchy as I did at FAMU, deploying the two-drop rule to disavow the Blackness of Light people even as they adored

the Light Malcolm X, Angela Davis, Huey P. Newton, and Kath-
leen Cleaver. And, eventually, the Light ideal came back with a
vengeance, if it had ever left. In his 1988 film *School Daze,* Spike
Lee satirized his experiences in the late 1970s at historically Black
Morehouse College as a battle between the Dark-skinned "jiga-
boos" and the Light-skinned "wannabes." My father slowly cut
his Afro over the years, and my mother straightened her kinks by
the time I arrived.

In the 1980s, Light children were adopted first, had higher
incomes, and were less likely to be trapped in public housing
and prisons. "The lighter the skin, the lighter the sentence" became a popular antiracist saying as the era of mass incarceration
surged in the 1990s. In 2007, MSNBC's Don Imus compared
Rutgers's Dark basketball players—"that's some nappy-headed
hos there"—to Tennessee's Light players—"they all look cute"—
after they played in the NCAA women's championship. In a 2014
casting call for the movie *Straight Outta Compton,* Sande Alessi
Casting ranked extras: "A GIRLS: . . . Must have real hair . . . B
GIRLS: . . . You should be light-skinned . . . C GIRLS: These
are African American girls, medium to light skinned with a
weave . . . D GIRLS: These are African American girls . . . Medium to dark skin tone. Character types."

By then, singer Michael Jackson had paved the skin-bleaching
boulevard traveled by rapper Lil' Kim, baseball player Sammy
Sosa, and so many more. Skin-bleaching products were raking in
millions for U.S. companies. In India, the manufacturer of the
bestselling "fairness" cream saw revenues top $300 million in
2020. Today, skin lighteners are used by 70 percent of women in
Nigeria; 35 percent in South Africa; 59 percent in Togo; and
nearly 40 percent in China, Malaysia, the Philippines, and South
Korea.

Some White people have their own skin-care "addiction" to
reach a post-racial ideal: tanning. In 2016, the United States
elected the "orange man," as NeNe Leakes calls Trump, who reportedly uses a tanning bed every morning. Paradoxically, some
tanning White people look down on bleaching Black people, as

if there's a difference. Research shows that people consider tanned skin—the replica color of Light people—more attractive than naturally pale skin and Dark skin.

HALFTIME ARRIVED. LINES of musicians linked together and outlined the entire football field. The largest human-made rectangle I had ever seen. Colored orange and green. Not Dark and Light. My eyes widened in awe at the length of the FAMU Rattler. On the far side, seven tall and slender drum majors, five yards apart, slowly low-stepped to the center of the field as announcer Joe Bullard yelled their names over our screams. They stopped when they reached the center of the field, facing us. Slowly, they twirled. The drum line sounded. The drum majors sat and then stood, leading the band in a twerk, twerk, twerk, twerk, twerk. We went mad.

"Please welcome what has become known as America's band," Bullard said as the band played and high-stepped around the field, knees folding into their chests with the ease of folding chairs.

"The innnnn-credible, the maaaaagnificent, the number-one band innnnnnnn the woooorld. The faaaantastic Florida A&M University Marching Band!"

Band members stopped in straight lines and faced us. They kissed their instruments.

"First the souuund!"

Daaaa . . . da, da, daaaaaaaa—the trumpets blew Twentieth Century Fox's thunderous movie introduction, blasting our ears off.

Then the show. High-stepping band members changed in and out of intricate formations and played choruses by Destiny's Child, Carl Thomas, and Sisqó, as the tens of thousands of people sang backup as the world's biggest choir. The R&B ballads warmed us up for the climax—the rap songs. Bucking and twerking and twisting and jumping and swaying all in unison, the band and the backup dancers were one as the crowd rapped. I kept rubbing my eyes, thinking they were deceiving me. I could not play an instrument anymore and could barely dance. How could all these heavy-coated students play tough songs and dance sophisticated routines in harmony? Ludacris, Trick Daddy, Three 6 Mafia, Outkast—the band paraded these Southern rappers before high-stepping off the field to the theme song of *Good Times*, to our booming applause. Utterly exhilarated, I don't know if I ever clapped and stomped harder and louder.

Halftime over, the exodus out of the student section startled me. The people had come to see what the people had come to see.

I HAD COME to see Clarence. I walked into our off-campus apartment, all giddy, like after watching the Marching 100 that first time. Quietness shrouded the afternoon. Dirty dishes sat in the open kitchen. Clarence had to be in his room, finishing homework.

The door was open; I knocked on it anyway, disturbing him at his desk. He looked up in wonder. We had roomed together for nearly two years. Clarence had gotten used to my midday interruptions. He braced himself for my latest epiphany.

WHITE

ANTI-WHITE RACIST IDEA: Any notion that classifies White people as inferior or that focuses hatred toward everyday White people, which distracts from and reinforces an inequitable and unjust power and policy structure that harms people of color and everyday White people.

ANTIRACIST IDEA (ABOUT WHITE PEOPLE): Any notion that acknowledges racial equality, or that everyday White people are harmed by inequitable and unjust policies targeted at people of color (though not as severely as people of color) or that fosters interracial organizing toward an equitable and just society.

STOOD IN THE doorframe, sometime in March 2002. Clarence probably sensed another argument coming. We were tailor-made to argue against each other. Intensely cynical, Clarence seemed to believe nothing. Intensely gullible, I was liable to believe anything, a believer more than a thinker. Racist ideas love believers, not thinkers.

"So what you want to tell me?" Clarence asked.

"I think I figured White people out," I said.

"What is it now?"

I'D ARRIVED AT FAMU trying to figure Black people out. "I had never seen so many Black people together with positive motives," I wrote in an English 101 essay in October 2000. The sentence seemed out of place, sandwiched nastily between "I had never heard the world famous 'Marching 100' perform" and "This was my first ever college football game." The idea—even more out of place. How did I overlook all those Black people who came together with positive motives in all those places and spaces of my upbringing? How did I become the Black judge? Racist ideas suspend reality and retrofit history, including our individual histories.

Anti-Black racist ideas covered my freshman eyes like my orange contacts when I first moved into Gibbs Hall at FAMU. When you entered the lobby, to the right you'd see a busy, tired-looking office. If you took a slight left, you'd find yourself walking down the hallway to my dorm room; a sharper left would take you to the television room, where our dorm's cluster of basketball fans regularly lost bitter arguments to the army of football fans over television rights.

There were no arguments on, or games on, in the television room on the evening of November 7, 2000. We still had our game faces on, though. Rookie voters, we were watching the election results unfold, hoping that our votes would help keep the brother of Florida's governor out of the White House. Black Floridians had not forgotten Jeb Bush's termination of affirmative-action programs earlier in the year. We had voted to save the rest of America from the racist Bushes.

The election was coming down to the winner of Florida. The polls closed, and before long we saw Al Gore's winning face flash on the screen. Game over. We rejoiced. I joined a joyful exodus out of the television room. We marched to our dorm rooms like fans streaming from the stadium when the Marching 100's half-time show ended. The people had come to see what the people had come to see.

The next morning, I awoke to learn that George W. Bush somehow held a narrow lead in Florida of 1,784 votes. Too close to call, and Jeb Bush's appointees were overseeing the recount.

The unfairness of it all crashed on me that November. My anti-Black racist ideas were no consolation. I walked out of my dorm room that morning into a world of anguish. In the weeks that followed, I heard and overheard, read and reread, angry, tearful, first- and secondhand stories of FAMU students and their families back home not being able to vote. Complaints from Black Floridians who'd registered but never received their registration cards. Or their voting location had been changed. Or they were unlawfully denied a ballot without a registration card or ordered to leave the long line when polls closed. Or they were told that as people convicted of felonies, they could not vote. Earlier in the year, Florida purged fifty-eight thousand people alleged to have felony convictions from the voting rolls. Black people were only 11 percent of registered voters but comprised 44 percent of the purge list. And about twelve thousand of those people purged did *not* have felonies on their record.

Reporters and campaign officials seemed more focused on Floridians whose votes were not counted or counted the wrong way. Palm Beach County used confusing ballots that caused about nineteen thousand spoiled ballots and perhaps three thousand Gore voters to mistakenly vote for Pat Buchanan. Gadsden County, next to Tallahassee, had Florida's highest percentage of Black voters and the highest spoilage rate. Black people in the state were ten times more likely than their White peers to have their ballots rejected. The racial inequity could not be explained by income or educational levels or bad ballot design, according to a *New York Times* statistical analysis. That left one explanation, one that at first I could not readily admit: racism. A total of 179,855 ballots were invalidated by Florida election officials in a race ultimately won by 537 votes.

A twenty-nine-year-old Ted Cruz served on Bush's legal team that resisted efforts at manual recounts in Democratic counties that could have netted Gore tens of thousands of votes while pushing for manual recounts in Republican counties that netted Bush 185 additional votes.

Watching this horror flick unfold, I recoiled in fear for days after the election. But not some of my peers at FAMU. They amassed the courage I did not have, that one must have to be antiracist. "Courage is not the absence of fear, but the strength to do what is right in the face of it," as the anonymous philosopher tells us. Some of us are restrained by fear of what could happen to us if we resist. In our naïveté, we are less fearful of what could happen to us—or is already happening to us—if we don't resist.

On November 9, 2000, FAMU's courageous student-government leaders directed a silent march of two thousand FAMU and Florida State University students from campus to Florida's nearby capitol, where they conducted a sit-in. The sit-in lasted for about twenty-four hours, but the witch hunt we launched back at campus lasted for weeks, if not months. We hunted out those thousands of FAMU students who did not vote. We shamed those nonvoters with stories of people who marched so we could vote. I participated in this foolish hunt—one seems to recur every time an election is lost. The shaming ignores the real source of our loss and heartbreak. The fact was that Black people delivered enough voters to win, but those voters were sent home or their votes spoiled. Racist ideas often lead to this silly psychological inversion, where we blame the victimized race for their own victimization.

When on December 12, 2000, the U.S. Supreme Court stopped Florida's recount, I no longer saw the United States as a democracy. When Gore conceded the next day, when White Democrats stood aside and let Bush steal the presidency on the strength of destroyed Black votes, I was shot back into the binary thinking of Sunday school, where I was taught about good and evil, God and the Devil. As Bush's team transitioned that winter, I transitioned into hating White people.

White people became devils to me, but I had to figure out how they came to be devils. I read "The Making of Devil," a chapter in Elijah Muhammad's *Message to the Blackman in America,* written in 1965. Muhammad led the unorthodox Nation of Islam (NOI) from 1934 until his death in 1975. According to the theology he espoused, more than six thousand years ago, in an all-Black world, a wicked Black scientist named Yakub was exiled alongside his 59,999 followers to an island in the Aegean Sea. Yakub plotted his revenge against his enemies: "to create upon the earth a devil race."

Yakub established a brutal island regime of selective breeding—eugenics meeting colorism. He killed all Dark babies and forced Light people to breed. When Yakub died, his followers carried on, creating the Brown race from the Black race, the Red race from the Brown race, the Yellow race from the Red race, and the White race from the Yellow race. After six hundred years, "on the island of Patmos was nothing but these blond, pale-skinned, cold-blue-eyed devils—savages."

White people invaded the mainland and turned "what had been a peaceful heaven on earth into a hell torn by quarreling and fighting." Black authorities chained the White people and marched them to the prison caves of Europe. When the Bible says, "Moses lifted up the serpent in the wilderness," NOI theologians say the "serpent is symbolic of the devil white race Moses lifted up out of the caves of Europe, teaching them civilization" to rule for the next six thousand years.

Aside from the White rule for six thousand years, this history of White people sounded eerily similar to the history of Black people I'd learned piecemeal in White schools of racist thought. White racist ideas cast Black people as living in the bushes of Africa, instead of in caves, until Moses, in the form of White enslavers and colonizers, arrived as a civilizer. Slavery and colonization ended before Black people—and Africa—became civilized in the ways of White people. Black people descended into criminality and ended up lynched, segregated, and mass-incarcerated by noble officers of the law in "developed" White nations. "Developing" Black nations became riddled with corruption, ethnic strife, and incompetence, keeping them impoverished and unstable, despite all sorts of "aid" from the former mother countries in Europe. The NOI's history of White people was the racist history of Black people in Whiteface.

According to NOI mythology, God appeared on earth in the form of Wallace Fard Muhammad. In 1931, Fard sent Elijah Muhammad on the divine mission to save the "Lost-Found Nation of Islam" in the United States—to redeem Black people with knowledge of this true history.

My first time reading this story, I sat there in my dorm room, sweating, mesmerized, scared. It felt like I had climbed up and consumed forbidden fruit. Every White person who'd mistreated me, since my third-grade teacher, suddenly rushed back into my memory like a locomotive blaring its horn in the middle of the forest. But my attention remained focused on all those White people who'd railroaded the election of 2000 in Florida. All those White policemen intimidating voters, White poll officials turning away voters, White state officials purging voters, White lawyers and judges defending the voter suppression. All those White politicians echoing Gore's call to, "for the sake of our unity as a people and the strength of our democracy," concede the election to Bush. White people showed me they did not actually care about national unity or democracy, only unity among and democracy for White people!

I lay in my dorm room, staring up at the ceiling, silently raging at the White people walking away into the wilderness to plan Bush's presidency.

ELIJAH MUHAMMAD'S WHITE creation story made so much sense to me as a college freshman. Half a century earlier, it also made sense to a calculating and cursing young imprisoned man nicknamed "Satan." One day, in 1948, Satan's brother, Reginald, whispered to him during a visit, "The white man is the devil." When he returned to his Massachusetts cell, a line of White people appeared before his eyes. He saw White people lynching his activist father, committing his activist mother to an asylum, splitting up his siblings, telling him being a lawyer was "no realistic goal for a nigger," degrading him on eastern railroads, trapping him for the police, sentencing him to ten years for robbery because his girlfriend was White. His brothers and sisters, clutching their sore necks from a similar rope of White racism, had already converted to the Nation of Islam. In no time, they turned Satan back into Malcolm Little, and Malcolm Little into Malcolm X.

Malcolm X left prison in 1952 and quickly began to grow

Elijah Muhammad's Nation of Islam, through his powerful speaking and organizing. The suddenly resurgent NOI caught the attention of the media, and in 1959 Louis Lomax and Mike Wallace produced a television documentary on the NOI, *The Hate That Hate Produced,* which ran on CBS. It made Malcolm X a household name.

In 1964, after leaving the Nation of Islam, Malcolm X made the hajj to Mecca and changed his name again, to el-Hajj Malik el-Shabazz, and converted to orthodox Islam. "Never have I witnessed such" an "overwhelming spirit of true brotherhood as is practiced by people of all colors and races here in this Ancient Holy Land," he wrote home on April 20. He acknowledged that his family and friends "may be shocked by these words coming from me," but what he had "seen, and experienced" had caused him to "*toss aside* some of my previous conclusions [about White people]. . . . I have always been a man who tries to face facts, and to accept the reality of life as new experience and new knowledge unfolds it." On September 22, 1964, Malcolm made no mistake about his conversion. "I totally reject Elijah Muhammad's racist philosophy, which he has labeled 'Islam' only to fool and misuse gullible people, as he fooled and misused me," he wrote. "But I blame only myself, and no one else for the fool that I was, and the harm that my evangelic foolishness in his behalf has done to others."

Months before being assassinated, Malcolm X faced a fact many admirers of Malcolm X still refuse to face: Black individuals can be racist toward White people. But since White people remain on the higher end of nearly every racial disparity, we can conclude that Black people (and non-Black people) hardly wield racist policy when being racist toward White people. And the instances of Black people engaging in anti-White discrimination are as negligible as Black people engaging in voter fraud, even as propagandists keep fearmongering about both. Equitable actions—actions that do not reinforce White supremacy, and which White supremacists have historically framed as anti-White—are, in fact, antiracist. When I say Black individuals can be racist toward White people, I am specifically calling attention to anti-White racist ideas.

The NOI's White-devil idea is a classic example. Whenever someone classifies people of European descent as biologically, culturally, or behaviorally inferior, someone is articulating a *racist* idea. Some people consider "assumptions and stereotypes about White people" to be "racial prejudice, not racism." They define "racial prejudice" in a similar way to how I define racist ideas: "a set of . . . derogatory attitudes based on assumptions derived from perceptions about race." They define racism as "prejudice plus power." There isn't a corresponding definition of racist. There is a conflation of racism and the racist, which I can relate to. But saying a Black individual is being racist toward White people when he calls them "devilish" is very different from saying Black people are engaging in racism toward White people. I am saying the former. I am *not* saying the latter. If anything, it seems to me that Black people—through their general support of antiracist policies—have been engaging in antiracism toward White people. Everyday White Americans—and other non-Black people—have benefitted from the equitable and just policies and practices for which Black people have struggled over the course of U.S. history.

This definition of "prejudice plus power" does not explain how people become prejudiced, and it falsely positions power as secondary. It maintains this notion that people of all races have prejudice, but only White people have the addition—power—which is why their "prejudice results in acts of discrimination and oppression against groups or individuals." This suggests: Racism is the result of prejudice *and then* power. This formulation reinforces the myth of racial prejudice (or racist ideas) as the foundation of racism. In fact, powerful self-interest is the foundation of racism, a self-interest that leads to racist policies, and those policies lead to racial inequity and injustice, which are then justified and normalized by racist ideas (or racial prejudice). The consumption of racist ideas leads to ignorance and hate—all this ignorance about racist power and policy: the actual source of pain.

And this ignorance opens the door for people to blame other racial groups for their pain, thus reinforcing hate for other racial groups. Whenever there is common ignorance and mutual hate, it prevents individuals and groups from organizing together to challenge racist policies especially harming people of color and harming most White people, too, at lesser levels.

I don't think people realize that "racial prejudice" or racist ideas *about any racial group* do not cause racism, they conserve racism. They cause people to use their power to fight other people rather than power and policy. Whatever breeds common ignorance and mutual hate conserves racism. Whatever breeds notions of racial hierarchy conserves racism. That is the function of racist ideas: to conserve racist power and policy. Any idea that conserves racist power and policy is racist. An individual conserving racist power and policy is being racist. It is dangerously conserving of racist *policy* for a White person to think there is something wrong with people of color. It is dangerously conserving of racist *power* for a person of color to think there is something wrong with everyday White people.

The only thing wrong with people, including White people, is when they embrace racist ideas and policies and then deny their ideas and policies are racist. This is not to ignore that White people have massacred and enslaved millions of Indigenous and African peoples, colonized and impoverished millions of people

NOTE ON "PREJUDICE PLUS POWER" I have thought many times about exiting my vocation as a scholar who studies racism. Because I am not only contending with White people saying, "I'm not racist," and people of color saying, "I can't be racist." I am not only contending with popular definitional myths about racial groups. I am contending with popular definitional myths about racism. People believe their definitions of racism as firmly as they believe their ideas about racial groups.

One of the more popular definitions of racism is "prejudice plus power." I did not engage with this definition in the hardcover edition. I did not show precisely how this definition does not explain racism—and if anything, conserves it. And that was a mistake. I added a few paragraphs to engage with this definition. Just as this book makes the case for being antiracist, it makes the case for a new way of defining and understanding the terms "racism" and "racist."

of color around the globe as their nations grew rich, all the while producing racist ideas that blame the victims. This is to say their history of pillaging is not the result of the evil genes or cultures of White people. There's no such thing as White genes. We must separate the warlike, greedy, bigoted, and individualist cultures of modern imperialism and racial capitalism (more on that later) from the cultures of White people. They are not one and the same, as the resistance within White nations shows, resistance admittedly often tempered by racist ideas.

To be antiracist is to never mistake the global march of White racism for the global march of White people. To be antiracist is to never mistake the antiracist hate of White racism for the racist hate of White people. To be antiracist is to never conflate racist individuals with White people, knowing there are antiracist White individuals and racist individuals of color. To be antiracist is to see everyday White people as the frequent victimizers of people of color and the frequent victims of racist power. Donald Trump's economic policies are geared toward enriching elite White male power—but at the expense of most of his White male followers, along with the rest of us.

We must discern the difference between racist power (racist

NOTE ON ANTIRACIST WORK AND CRT In the summer of 2020, after the police murders of Breonna Taylor and George Floyd, approximately three in four White Americans recognized racism as a big problem. The growing recognition of racism among White Americans, their growing efforts to be antiracist, no doubt scared Trump operatives who relied on the racist ideas of White Americans to garner their support.

To reinflame the racist ideas of White people, Trump operatives named all antiracist work "critical race theory," and named *me* one of the fathers of CRT, even though CRT was born in 1981 and I was born in 1982. And then these operatives went about falsely defining CRT. Senator Ted Cruz said, "Critical race theory says every white person is a racist." It doesn't matter to this senator that the founders of CRT never made such a claim, or that I wrote: "To be antiracist is to never conflate racist people with White people, knowing there are antiracist Whites and racist non-Whites."

Alabama state legislator Chris Pringle misleadingly said that critical race theory "basically teaches that certain children are inherently bad people because of the color of their skin." But to be antiracist is to condemn this idea. No racial group is inherently bad or good, racist or antiracist.

policymakers) and White people. For decades, racist power contributed to stagnating wages, destroying unions, deregulating banks and corporations, and steering funding for schools into prison and military budgets, policies that have deepened injustices and inequities and often drawn a backlash from some White people. White economic inequality, for instance, soared to the point that the "99 percenters" occupied Wall Street in 2011, and Vermont senator Bernie Sanders ran a popular presidential campaign against the "billionaire class" in 2016.

Of course, working-class White people benefit from racist policies, though not nearly as much as wealthy White people and not nearly as much as they could from a just society. In a just society, everyday White people (along with the rest of us), instead of superrich White men, would be deciding elections and shaping policies. Their kids' first-class schools would resemble the private-jet prep schools of today's superrich. High-quality universal healthcare could save millions of White lives. A national basic income program would pull millions of White people out of poverty. Building out of the ashes of our criminal punishment system a humane justice system that roots out the structural causes of harm and violence, and facilitates mediation, healing, and restoration when harm and violence occur, would save countless White people from harm, violence, surveillance, and incarceration. White people would no longer face the cronies of racism that attack them: sexism, ethnocentrism, homophobia, xenophobia, ableism, transphobia, and capitalism.

Racist power, hoarding wealth and resources, has the most to lose in the building of a just society. As we've learned, racist power produces racist policies out of self-interest and then produces racist ideas to justify those policies. But racist ideas also suppress the resistance to policies that are detrimental to White people, by convincing everyday White people that injustice and inequity are rooted in "personal failure" and are unrelated to policies. Racist power manipulates everyday White people into resisting equitable and just policies by drilling them on what they are losing with equitable and just policies and how those policies are anti-White. In 2017, most White people identified anti-White discrimination as a serious problem. "If you apply for a job, they seem to give the Blacks the first crack at it," said sixty-eight-year-old Tim Hershman of Ohio to an NPR reporter. African Americans are getting unfair handouts, "and it's been getting worse for Whites," Hershman said. Hershman was complaining of losing a promotion to a Black finalist, even though it was actually another White person who got the job.

Claims of anti-White racism in response to antiracism are as old as civil rights. When Congress passed the (first) Civil Rights Act of 1866, it made Black people citizens of the United States, stipulated their civil rights, and stated that state law could not deprive a person of these rights "by reason of [their] color or race." President Andrew Johnson reframed this Civil Rights Act as a "bill made to operate in favor of the colored against the white race." Racist Americans a century later framed supporters of affirmative action as "hard-core racists of reverse discrimination," to quote former U.S. solicitor general Robert Bork in The Wall Street Journal in 1978. When Alicia Garza typed "Black Lives Matter" on Facebook in 2013 and when that love letter crested into a movement in 2015, former New York City mayor Rudy Giuliani called the movement "inherently racist."

Racist White people do not want to define racial hierarchy or policies that yield racial injustices as racist. To do so would be to define their ideas and policies as racist. Instead, they define policies leading to justice as racist. Ideas not centering White lives are racist. Beleaguered racist White people who can't imagine their lives not being the focus of any movement respond to "Black Lives Matter" with "All Lives Matter." Embattled police officers who can't imagine losing their right to profile and brutalize respond with "Blue Lives Matter."

Ordinary racist White people function as soldiers of racist power. With these ground troops shelling out racist abuse each day, it is hard for people of color not to hate ordinary White people. Anti-White racist ideas are usually a reflexive reaction to virulent White racism. Anti-White racism is indeed the hate that hate produced, attractive to the victims of White racism.

And yet racist power thrives on anti-White racist ideas—more hatred only makes their power greater. When Black people recoil from White racism and concentrate their hatred on everyday White people, as I did freshman year in college, they are not fighting racist power. In losing focus on racist power, they fail to challenge anti-Black racist policies, which means those policies are more likely to flourish. Going after White people instead of racist power prolongs the policies harming Black life. In the end, anti-White racist ideas, in taking some or all of the focus off racist power, become anti-Black. In the end, hating White people becomes hating Black people.

IN THE END, hating Black people becomes hating White people.

On October 15, 2013, workers unveiled a twelve-by-twenty-four-foot sign near a major roadway in Harrison, Arkansas, known in those parts as Klan territory. The same sign showed up on billboards overlooking major roadways from Alabama to Oregon. Passing drivers saw bold black letters against a yellow background: ANTI-RACIST IS A CODE WORD FOR ANTI-WHITE.

Robert Whitaker, who ran for vice president of the United States in 2016 on the American Freedom Party's ticket, popularized this declaration in a 2006 piece called "The Mantra." This mantra has become scripture to the self-identified "swarm" of White supremacists who hate people of color and Jews and fear the "ongoing program of genocide against my race, the white race," as Whitaker claimed.

History tells a different story. Contrary to "the mantra," White supremacists are the ones supporting unjust policies that benefit racist power against the interests of the majority of White people. White supremacists claim to be pro-White but refuse to acknowledge that climate change is having a disastrous impact on the earth White people inhabit. They oppose affirmative-action programs, despite White women being their primary beneficiaries. White supremacists rage against Obamacare even as 43 percent of the people who gained lifesaving health insurance from 2010 to 2015 were White. They heil Adolf Hitler's Nazis, even though it was the Nazis who launched a world war that destroyed the lives of more than forty million White people and ruined Europe. They wave Confederate flags and defend Confederate monuments, even though the Confederacy started a civil war that ended with more than five hundred thousand White American lives lost—more than every other American war combined until the Vietnam War. White supremacists "welcomed" the spread of COVID-19, even though it has killed approximately half a million White Americans to date. White supremacists love what America used to be, even though America used to be—and still is—teeming with 15.9 million White people living below the poverty line. White supremacists blame non-White people for the struggles of White people when any objective analysis of their plight primarily implicates the rich White Trumps they support.

White supremacist is code for anti-White, and White supremacy is nothing short of an ongoing program of genocide against the White race. In fact, it's more than that: White supremacist is code for anti-human, a nuclear ideology that poses an existential threat to human existence.

I CARRIED THE White hate into my sophomore year, as anti-Muslim and anti–Middle Eastern hate filled the American atmosphere like a storm cloud after 9/11. Many Americans did not see any problem with their growing hate of Muslims in the spring of 2002. And I did not see any problem with my growing hate of White people. Same justifications. "They are violent evildoers." "They hate our freedoms."

I kept reading, trying to find the source of White evil. I found more answers in Senegalese scholar Cheikh Anta Diop's two-cradle theory, long before I learned about his antiracist work on the African ancestry of the ancient Egyptians. Diop's two-cradle theory suggested the harsh climate and lack of resources in the northern cradle nurtured in Europeans barbaric, individualistic, materialist, and warlike behaviors, which brought destruction to the world. The amenable climate and abundance of resources in the southern cradle nurtured the African behaviors of community, spirituality, equanimity, and peace, which brought civilization to the world.

I blended Diop's environmental determinism with Michael Bradley's version of the same, his theory in *The Iceman Inheritance* that the White race's ruthlessness is the product of its upbringing in the Ice Age. But I still thirsted for biological theories. How we frame the problem—and who we frame as the problem—shapes the answers we find. I was looking for a biological theory of why White people are evil. I found it in *The Isis Papers* by psychiatrist Frances Cress Welsing.

The global White minority's "profound sense of numerical inadequacy and color inferiority" causes their "uncontrollable sense of hostility and aggression," Welsing wrote. White people are defending against their own genetic annihilation. Melanin-packing "color always 'annihilates' . . . the non-color, white." Ironically, Welsing's theory reflects fears of genetic annihilation that White supremacists around the Western world have been expressing these days in the "great replacement" conspiracy theory, in their fears of "white genocide"—an idea with a deep history, as in the work of eugenicists like Lothrop Stoddard and his 1920 bestseller, *The Rising Tide of Color Against White World-Supremacy*.

I devoured Welsing, but later, when I learned melanin did not give me any Black superpower, I felt deflated. It turns out, it's the racist one-drop rule that made Black identity dominant in biracial people, not any genetic distinction or melanin superpower. My search continued.

I DID NOT knock on Clarence's door that day to discuss Welsing's "color confrontation theory." Or Diop's two-cradle theory.

He had snickered at those theories many times before. I came to share another theory, the one that finally figured White people out.

"They are aliens," I told Clarence, confidently resting on the doorframe, arms crossed. "I just saw this documentary that laid out the evidence. That's why they are so intent on White supremacy. That's why they seem to not have a conscience. They are aliens."

Clarence listened, face expressionless.

"You can't be serious."

"I'm dead serious. This explains slavery and colonization. This explains why the Bush family is so evil. This explains why Whites don't give a damn. This explains why they hate us so damn much. They are aliens!" I'd lifted off the doorframe and was in full argumentative mode.

"You really are serious about this," Clarence said with a chuckle. "If you're serious, then that has got to be the dumbest thing I ever heard in my life! I mean, seriously, I can't believe you are that gullible." The chuckle turned to a grimace.

"Why do you spend so much time trying to figure out White people?" he asked after a long pause. Clarence had asked this question before. I always answered the same way.

"Because figuring them out is the key! Black people need to figure out what we are dealing with!"

"If you say so. But answer me this: If Whites are aliens, why is it that Whites and Blacks can reproduce? Humans can't reproduce with animals on this planet, but Black people can reproduce with aliens from another planet? Come on, man, let's get real."

"I am being real," I replied. But I really had no comeback. I stood and turned around awkwardly, walked to my room, plopped down on my bed, and returned to staring at the ceiling. Maybe White people were not aliens. Maybe they became this way on earth. Maybe I needed to read more Frances Cress Welsing. I looked over at *The Isis Papers* on my nightstand.

· · ·

BY THE FALL of 2003, Clarence had graduated and I decided to share my ideas with the world. I began my public writing career on race with a column in FAMU's student newspaper, *The Famuan*. On September 9, 2003, I wrote a piece counseling Black people to stop hating White people for being themselves. Really, I was counseling myself. "I certainly understand blacks who have been wrapped up in a tornado of hate because they could not escape the encircling winds of truth about the destructive hand of the white man." Wrapped in this tornado, I could not escape the fallacious idea that "Europeans are simply a different breed of human," as I wrote, drawing on ideas in *The Isis Papers*. White people "make up only 10 percent of the world's population" and they "have recessive genes. Therefore they're facing extinction." That's why they are trying to "destroy my people," I concluded. "Europeans are trying to survive and I can't hate them for that."

The piece circulated widely in Tallahassee, alarming White readers. Their threats hit close to home. My new roommates, Devan, Brandon, and Jean, half-jokingly urged me to watch my back from the Klan. FAMU's new president, Fred Gainous, called me into his office to scold me. I scolded him back, calling him Jeb's boy.

The editor of the *Tallahassee Democrat* summoned me to his office, too. I needed to complete this required internship to graduate with my journalism degree. I walked into his office in fear. It felt like walking into a termination, the termination of my future. And, indeed, something would be terminated that day.

BLACK

POWERLESS DEFENSE: The illusory, concealing, disempowering, and racist idea that Black individuals can't be racist because they don't have any power or agency.

WALKED INTO HIS office. Every time I looked at Mizell Stewart, the *Tallahassee Democrat* editor, in the autumn of 2003, I saw the tall, slim, light-skinned actor Christopher Duncan. His tense energy reminded me of Braxton, Duncan's character on *The Jamie Foxx Show*.

I sat down. He swiveled back in his chair. "Let's talk about this piece," he said.

He darted from critique to critique, surprised at my defenses. I could debate without getting upset. So could he. Black people were problematic to me, but he realized White evil ached in the forefront of my mind.

He became quiet, clearly mulling something over. I was not going to confront him, just defend myself as respectfully as I could. He held my graduation in his hands.

"You know, I have a nice car," he said slowly, "and I hate it when I get pulled over and I'm treated like I am one of them niggers."

I took a deep inaudible breath, turned my lips inside, licked them, and mentally ordered my silence. "Them niggers" hung in the air between our probing eye contact. He waited for my response. I stayed silent.

I wanted to stand up and point and yell, "Who the fuck do you think you are?" I would have cut off his answer: "Clearly you don't think you are a nigger! What makes them niggers and you not a nigger? Am I one of 'them niggers'?" My air quotes struck the air over his head.

He separated himself from "them niggers," racialized them, looked down on them. He directed his disdain not toward the police officers who profiled him, who mistreated him, but to "them niggers."

NO ONE POPULARIZED this racial construct of "them niggers" quite like comedian Chris Rock in his 1996 HBO special, *Bring the Pain*. Rock began the show on an antiracist note, mocking reactions among White people to the O. J. Simpson verdict. He then turned to talk about Black people and "our own personal civil war." He picked a side: "I love Black people, but I hate niggers." It was a familiar refrain for me—my own dueling consciousness had often settled on the same formula, adding after the 2000 election: "I love Black people, but I hate niggers and White people."

While hip-hop artists recast "nigga" as an endearing term, "nigger" remained a derisive term. Rock helped Black people remake the racial group "niggers" and assigned qualities to this group, as all race makers have done. "Niggers" always stop Black people from having a good time, Rock said. Niggers are too loud. Niggers are always talking, demanding credit for taking care of their kids and staying out of prison. "The worst thing about niggers is that they love to not know," Rock teased. "Books are like Kryptonite to a nigger." He rejected the antiracist claim that "the media has distorted our image to make us look bad." Forget that! It was niggers' fault. When he'd go to get money, he wasn't "looking over my shoulders for the media. I'm looking for niggers."

We were laughing as Chris Rock shared the great truth that the nigger is not equal to the Black man (a remix of "the great truth that the negro is not equal to the white man," expressed by Confederate vice president Alexander Stephens in 1861). Racist White people had schooled us well in generalizing the individual characteristics we see in a particular Black person. We were not seeing and treating Black people as individuals, some of whom do bad things: We created a group identity, niggers, that in turn created a hierarchy, as all race making does. We added the hypocritical audacity of raging when White people called all of us niggers (Chris Rock stopped performing this routine when he realized racist White people were using it as license to say the N-word).

We did not place loud people who happened to be Black into an interracial group of loud people—as antiracists. We racialized the negative behavior and attached loudness to niggers, like White racists, as Black racists. We did not place negligent Black parents into an interracial group of negligent parents—as antiracists. We racialized the negative behavior and attached negligent parenting to niggers, like White racists, as Black racists. We did not place Black people who harm people into an interracial group of people who harm people—as antiracists. We racialized the negative behavior and attached harmful behavior to niggers, like White racists, as Black racists. We did not place Black people who were being lazy into an interracial group of people who were being lazy—as antiracists. We racialized the negative behavior and attached laziness to niggers, like White racists, as Black racists.

And after all that, we self-identified as "not-racist," like White racists, as Black racists.

Chris Rock met Black Americans where all too many of us were at the turn of the millennium, stationed within the dueling consciousness of assimilationist and antiracist ideas, distinguishing ourselves from them niggers as White racists were distinguishing themselves from us niggers. We felt a tremendous antiracist pride in Black excellence and a tremendously racist shame in being connected to them niggers. We recognized the racist policy we were facing and were ignorant of the racist policy them niggers were facing. We looked at them niggers as felons of the race when our anti-Black racist ideas were the real Black on Black crime.

In 2003, as I sat in the Black editor's office, 53 percent of Black people were surveyed as saying that something other than racism mostly explained why Black people had worse jobs, income, and housing than White people, up from 48 percent a decade earlier. Only 40 percent of Black respondents described racism as the source of these inequities in 2003. By 2013, in the middle of Obama's presidency, only 37 percent of Black people were pointing to "mostly racism" as the cause of racial inequities. A whopping 60 percent of Black people had joined with the 83 percent of White people that year who found explanations other than racist policy and practices to explain persisting racial inequities. The internalizing of racist ideas was likely the reason.

Black minds were awakened to the ongoing reality of racism by the series of televised police killings and flimsy exonerations that followed the Obama election, the movement for Black Lives, the racist ascendancy of Donald Trump, and the national uprising that followed the police murders of Breonna Taylor and George Floyd. By 2017, 59 percent of Black people expressed the antiracist position that racism is the main reason Black people can't get ahead (compared to 35 percent of White people and 45 percent of Latinx people). But even then, about a third of Black people still expressed the racist position that Black people are mostly responsible for their own condition, compared to 54 percent of White people, 48 percent of Latinx people, and 75 percent of Republicans. In early 2021, less than a year after George Floyd's murder, 95 percent of Black Americans, 83 percent of Latinx Americans, 82 percent of Asian Americans, and 76 percent of White Americans recognized that Black people face racism. However, Black Americans were most likely (80 percent) to state that Black people face "a lot" of discrimination, while White Americans were least likely (38 percent) to share this view.

Clearly, some Black people hold anti-Black racist ideas. But I still wanted to believe Stewart's "them niggers" comment was abnormal. The truth is, though, Stewart had put up a mirror. I had to face it. I hated what I saw. He was saying what I had been thinking for years. He had the courage to say it. I hated him for that.

How was his criticism of Black people different than my criticism of Black people when I blamed them for their own votes being stolen or accused them of lethargy and self-sabotage? How was our criticism of Black people any different from the anti-Black criticism of racist White people? I learned in that office that day that every time I say something is wrong with Black people, I am simultaneously separating myself from them, essentially saying "them niggers." When I do this, I am being racist.

I THOUGHT ONLY White people could be racist and that Black people could not be racist, because Black people as a group did not have power. I thought Latinx, Asian, Middle Eastern, and Native people could not be racist, because their racial groups did not have power. I conflated the (structural) term "racism" with the (individual) term "racist." I conflated Black people as a group with a Black individual. Black people, as a group, have not had enough power (or desire) to institutionalize policies that put Black people on the higher end of inequities, while justifying their higher status by spreading ideas that Black people *should* be on the higher end because they are superior. In actuality, I'd argue that Black people as a group have been a force for antiracism: for promoting policies that create equity and justice for all based on ideas of the racial equality of all. But the question is not whether Black people as a group can engage in racism. The oft-asked question is: Can Black people be racist? This question is based on a false premise. An individual can be racist. A group can engage in racism. Instead of, Can Black people be racist?, the question should be: Can a Black individual be racist? And this question is usually asking whether Black individuals can be racist toward White people. But instead of asking, Can a Black individual be racist toward White people?, the question should also be: Can a Black individual be racist toward Black people? What about a

Latinx, Asian, Native, or Middle Eastern individual? Can a Latino American be racist toward Black people? Can a Native American be racist toward Middle Eastern Americans? Can an Asian American be racist to Latina Americans? Does any Latinx, Asian, Native, or Middle Eastern person have any power to harm Black people, or any other racial group? According to recent works on Asian Americans, Native Americans, and Latinx Americans, these individuals of color can be racist toward Black people. But Black individuals can't be racist toward non–Black people? Black individuals can't be racist toward Black people?

Does a Black individual—do I—have the power to reinforce the structure of anti–Black racism through my actions or inaction? Does a Black individual—do I—have the power to express racist ideas about Black people or any other racial group (which reinforces the structure)? Does a Black individual—do I—have the power to make, manage, support, or protest racist policies that harm Black people or any other racial group (which reinforces the structure)? Or are all Black individuals powerless (*and therefore we all need White saviors*)? Do Black individuals have no power or agency to reinforce or challenge the structure? Am I powerless? I thought I was. I had no sense of the reactionary history of this construction, of its racist bearing.

This powerless defense, as I call it, emerged in the wake of racist power dismissing antiracist policies and ideas as racist in the late 1960s. In subsequent decades, Black voices critical of White racism defended themselves from these charges by saying, "Black people can't be racist, because Black people don't have power."

Quietly, though, this defense shields Black individuals and other individuals of color in positions of power from having to make antiracist policy, since even they are apparently powerless, since apparently White people have all the power. This means

NOTE ON DENIAL The heartbeat of being racist is denial. If the sound of that denial is "I'm not racist" for White individuals, then the sound of that denial for individuals of color is "I can't be racist." I have heard both sounds time and again from people reacting to this book.

that individuals of color are powerless to roll back racist policies and eliminate racial injustice even in their own spheres of influence, the places where they actually do have some power to effect change. The powerless defense shields individuals of color from charges of racism even when these individuals are reproducing racist policies and justifying them with the same racist ideas as the White individuals they call racist. The powerless defense shields its believers from the history of racist White people empowering individuals of color to oppress people of color and of individuals of color using their limited power to oppress people of color for their own personal gain.

Like every other racist idea, the powerless defense underestimates Black people and overestimates White people. It erases the small amount of power that Black individuals have and expands the already expansive reach of power that White individuals have.

The powerless defense does not consider individuals at all levels of power, from policymakers like politicians and executives who have the power to institute and eliminate racist and antiracist policies, to policy managers like officers and middle managers empowered to execute or not execute racist and antiracist policies. Every single person actually has the power to protest racist and antiracist policies, to advance them, or, in some small way, to stall them. Nation-states, sectors, communities, institutions are run by policymakers and policies and policy managers. "Institutional power" or "systemic power" or "structural power" is the policymaking and managing power of people, in groups or individually. When someone says Black individuals can't be racist because Black people don't have "institutional power," they are flouting reality.

The powerless defense strips Black policymakers and managers of all their power. The powerless defense says the 175 Black Americans who have served in Congress from 1870 to 2022 had no legislative power. It says none of the thousands of state and local Black politicians have any lawmaking power. It says U.S. Supreme Court justice Clarence Thomas never had the power to put his vote to antiracist purposes. The powerless defense says the more than two hundred Black judges on federal courts have had no power during the trials and sentencing processes that built our system of mass incarceration. It says the more than fifty thousand Black police officers do not have the power to brutalize and kill the Black body. It says the hundreds of Black police chiefs, assistant chiefs, and commanders have no power to shield the racist officers under their command. The powerless defense says the more than forty-five thousand full-time Black faculty at U.S. colleges and universities in 2018 did not have the power to pass and fail Black students, hire and tenure Black faculty, or shape the minds of Black people. It says the world's fifteen Black billionaires and the 340,000 Black millionaire families in the United States have no economic power, to use in racist or antiracist ways. It says the eighteen Black CEOs who've run Fortune 500 companies since 1999 had no power to diversify their workforces. When a Black man stepped into the most powerful office in the world in 2009, his policies were often excused by apologists who said he didn't have executive power. As if none of his executive orders were carried out, neither of his Black attorneys general had any power to roll back mass incarceration, or his Black national security adviser had no power. The truth is: Black individuals can be racist because Black individuals do have power, even if limited.

Note that I say *limited* Black power rather than no power. White individuals control the United States. But not absolutely. Absolute power necessitates complete control over all levels of power. All policies. All policy managers. All minds. Ironically, the only way that White individuals can gain full control is by convincing us that White people already have all the power. If Black people accept the idea that we have no power, we are falling under the sort of mind control that will, in fact, rob us of any power to resist. As Black History Month father Carter G. Woodson once wrote: "When you control a man's thinking you do not have to worry about his actions. You do not have to tell him not to stand here or go yonder. He will find his 'proper place' and will stay in it."

Racist ideas are constantly produced to cage the power of individuals to come together to resist. Racist ideas make Black individuals believe White people have all the power, elevating them to gods. And so segregationist Black people lash out at these all-powerful gods as fallen devils, as I did in college, while assimilationist Black people worship their all-powerful White angels, strive to become them, to curry their favor, reproducing their racist ideas and defending their racist policies.

Aside from Justice Clarence Thomas's murderous gang of anti-Black judgments over the years, another series of egregiously racist actions by a Black individual decided the 2004 presidential election. George W. Bush narrowly won reelection by taking Ohio with the crucial help of Ohio's ambitious Black secretary of state, Ken Blackwell, who operated simultaneously as Bush's Ohio campaign co-chair.

Blackwell directed county boards to limit voters' access to the provisional ballots that ensured that anyone improperly purged from voting rolls could cast their ballot. He ordered voter-registration forms accepted only on expensive eighty-pound stock paper, a sly technique to exclude newly registered voters (who he almost certainly knew were more likely to be Black). Under Blackwell's supervision, county boards were falsely telling formerly incarcerated people they could not vote. County boards allocated fewer voting machines to heavily Democratic cities. Black Ohio voters on average waited fifty-two minutes to vote, thirty-four minutes longer than White voters, according to one post-election study. Long lines caused about 3 percent of Ohio voters to leave before voting or discouraged them from even going to the polls, meaning approximately 129,000 potential votes walked away, larger than Bush's 118,000 margin of victory. "Blackwell made Katherine Harris look like a cupcake," Representative John Conyers said after investigating Ohio's voter suppression, referring to the Florida secretary of state who certified Bush as winner of the election in 2000. But according to the theory that Black individuals can't be racist because they lack power, Blackwell didn't have the power to suppress Black votes. Remember, we are all either being racist or antiracist. How can Florida's Katherine Harris be racist in 2000 and Blackwell be antiracist in 2004?

After unsuccessfully running for Ohio governor in 2006 and chairman of the Republican National Committee in 2009, Blackwell joined Trump's Presidential Advisory Commission on Election Integrity in May 2017. The commission had clearly been set up, although Trump would never admit it, to find new ways to suppress the voting power of Trump's opponents, especially the Democratic Party's most loyal voters: Black people. Clearly, even thirteen years later, Trump officials had not forgotten Blackwell's state-of-the-art racist work suppressing Black votes for Bush's re-election.

With the popularity of the powerless defense, racist Black policymakers like Blackwell get away with their racist policies and ideas. Black people call them Uncle Toms, sellouts, Oreos, puppets—everything but the right thing: racist.

The saying "Black people can't be racist" reproduces the false duality of racist and not-racist promoted by racist White people in denial. By this theory, Black people can hate them niggers, value Light people over Dark people, support anti-Latinx immigration policies, defend the anti-Native team mascots, back bans against Middle Eastern Muslims, and deny they are being racist. By this theory, Latinx, Asian, and Native people can fear unknown Black bodies, support mass-incarcerating policies, and deny they are being racist. By this theory, I could have looked upon White people as devils and aliens and denied that I was being racist.

When we stop denying the duality of racist and antiracist, we can take an accurate accounting of the racial ideas and policies we support. For the better part of my life I held both racist and anti-racist ideas, supported both racist and antiracist policies; I've been antiracist one moment, racist in many more moments. To say individuals of color can't be racist is to say people of color are being antiracist at all times. To say Black individuals can't be racist is to say all Black individuals are being antiracist at all times. My own story tells me that is not true. History agrees.

THE RECORDED HISTORY of Black individuals being racist begins in 1526 in *Della descrittione dell'Africa (Description of Africa),* authored by a Berber Andalusi diplomat who was kidnapped after he visited sub-Saharan Africa. His enslavers presented him to Pope Leo X, who converted him to Christianity, freed him, and renamed him Leo Africanus. *Description of Africa* was translated into multiple European languages and emerged as the most influential book of anti-Black racist ideas in the sixteenth century, when the British, French, and Dutch were diving into human trading. "Negroes . . . leade a beastly kind of life, being utterly destitute of the use of reason, of dexterities of wit, and of all arts," Africanus wrote. "They so behave themselves, as if they had continually lived in a forrest among wild beasts." Africanus may have made up his travels to sub-Saharan Africa to secure favor from the pope.

Englishman Richard Ligon may have made up the stories in *A True and Exact History of the Island of Barbadoes,* published in 1657. Led by Sambo, a group of enslaved people disclosed a plot for an uprising. They refused their enslaver's rewards. A confused enslaver asked why. It was "but an act of Justice," replied Sambo, according to Ligon. Their duty. They were "sufficiently rewarded in the Act."

Slavery was justified in Sambo's narrative, because some Black individuals believed they were supposed to be enslaved. The same was true of Ukawsaw Gronniosaw, who authored the first known slave narrative, in 1772. Born to Nigerian royalty, Gronniosaw was enslaved at fifteen by an ivory merchant, who sold him to a Dutch captain. "My master grew very fond of me, and I loved him exceedingly" and "endeavoured to convince him, by every action, that my only pleasure was to serve him well." The ship reached Barbados. A New Yorker purchased Gronniosaw and brought him home, where he came to believe there was "a black man called the Devil that lives in hell." Gronniosaw was sold again to a minister, who transformed him from "a poor heathen" into an enslaved Christian. He was apparently happy to escape the Black Devil.

Enslavers welcomed ministers preaching the gospel of eternal Black enslavement, derived from the fraught reading of the Bible where all Black people were the cursed descendants of Ham. A fifty-one-year-old free Black carpenter had to first teach away these racist ideas in 1818 as he began recruiting thousands of enslaved Black people around Charleston, South Carolina, to join his freedom revolt. Denmark Vesey set the date of the revolt for July 14, 1822, the anniversary of the storming of the Bastille during the French Revolution. The aim of the revolt was to take down slavery, as in the successful 1804 Haitian revolution that inspired Vesey.

But the revolt had to remain a secret, even from some enslaved people. Don't mention it "to those waiting men who receive presents of old coats from their masters," Vesey's chief lieutenants told recruiters. "They'll betray us." One recruiter did not listen and told house slave Peter Prioleau, who promptly told his master in May. By late June 1822, South Carolina enslavers had destroyed Vesey's army, which one estimate placed as high as nine thousand strong. Vesey, hung on July 2, 1822, remained defiant to the very end.

The South Carolina legislature emancipated Peter Prioleau on Christmas Day 1822, and bestowed on him a lifetime annual pension. By 1840, he'd acquired seven enslaved people of his own and lived comfortably in Charleston's free Light community. Even when he was a slave, this Black man had no desire to get rid of his enslaver. He used his power to spoil one of the most well-organized freedom revolts in American history. He used his power to fully take on the qualities of his enslaver, to become him: enslaving, racist ideas, and all.

PETER PRIOLEAU RESEMBLED William Hannibal Thomas, who wanted to be accepted by White people as one of their own. But as Jim Crow spread in the 1890s, Thomas was shoved more deeply into Blackness. He finally deployed the tactic self-interested racist Black individuals have been using from the beginning to secure White patronage: He attacked Black people as inferior. When Thomas's *The American Negro* appeared weeks before Booker T. Washington's *Up from Slavery* in 1901, *The New York Times* placed Thomas "next to Mr. Booker T. Washington, the best American authority on the negro question."

Black people are an "intrinsically inferior type of humanity," Thomas wrote. Black history is a "record of lawless existence." Blacks are mentally undeveloped, immoral savages, "unable practically to discern between right and wrong," Thomas wrote. Ninety percent of Black women are "in bondage to physical pleasure." The "social degradation of our freedwomen is without parallel in modern civilization." In the end, Thomas's "list of negative qualities of Negroes seemed limitless," as his biographer concluded.

Thomas believed himself to be among a minority of Light people who had overcome their inferior biological heritage. But this "saving remnant" was set "apart from their white fellowmen." We show, Thomas pleaded to White people, that "the redemption of the negro is . . . possible and assured through a thorough assimilation of the thought and ideals of American civilization." To speed up this "national assimilation," Thomas advised restricting the voting rights of and intensely policing Black adults whom he considered to be natural criminals, and placing all Black children with White guardians.

Black people stamped William Hannibal Thomas as the "Black Judas." Black critics ruined his credibility and soon racist White people could no longer use him. So they tossed him away like a paper plate, as they have done to so many disposable racist Black individuals over the years. Thomas found work as a janitor, before dying in obscurity in 1935.

Black people would be harmed by racist Black individuals again and again in the twentieth century. In the 1960s, the diversifying of America's police forces was presented as a solution to the scourge of police brutality against Black victims. The fruit of decades of activism, a new crop of Black officers were expected to treat Black citizens better than their White counterparts did. But reports immediately surfaced in the 1960s that Black officers were as abusive as White officers. One report noted "in some places, low-income Negroes prefer white policemen because of the severe conduct of Negro officers." A 1966 study found Black officers were not as likely to be racist as White officers, but a significant minority expressed anti-Black racist ideas like, "I'm telling you these people are savages. And they're real dirty." Or the Black officer who said, "There have always been jobs for Negroes, but the f—— people are too stupid to go out and get an education. They all want the easy way out."

To color racist police violence as White on the pretext that only White people can be racist is to ignore the Black officer's history of profiling and killing "them niggers." It is to ignore that the police killer in 2012 of Brooklyn's Shantel Davis was Black, that three of the six officers involved in the 2015 death of Freddie Gray were Black, that the police killer in 2016 of Charlotte's Keith Lamont Scott was Black, that one of the police killers in 2018 of Sacramento's Stephon Clark was Black, and that one of the two police officers who assisted George Floyd's murderer in 2020 was Black (another was Asian). How can the White officers involved in the deaths of Terence Crutcher, Sandra Bland, Walter L. Scott, Michael Brown, Laquan McDonald, Decynthia Clements, and Breonna Taylor be racist but their Black counterparts be antiracist?

To be fair, one survey of nearly eight thousand sworn officers in 2017 makes strikingly clear that White officers are far and away more likely to be racist than Black officers these days. Nearly all (92 percent) of White officers surveyed agreed with the post-racial idea that "our country has made the changes needed to give Blacks equal rights with Whites." Only 6 percent of White officers co-signed the antiracist idea that "our country needs to continue making changes to give Blacks equal rights with Whites," compared to 69 percent of Black officers. But the disparity shrinks concerning deadly police encounters. Black officers (57 percent) are only twice as likely as White officers (27 percent) to say "the deaths of Blacks during encounters with police in recent years are signs of a broader problem."

The new crop of Black politicians, judges, police chiefs, and officers in the 1960s and subsequent decades helped to create a new problem. Rising levels of violence engulfed impoverished neighborhoods. Black residents in some of these impoverished neighborhoods bombarded their politicians and police departments with their racist fears of their *Black* neighbors—as opposed to their neighborhood's poverty. Neither the residents nor the politicians nor the police departments wholly saw the heroin and crack problem as a public-health crisis or the violence in impoverished neighborhoods where Black people lived as a poverty problem. Black people (like most Americans) seemed to be more worried about other people killing them in drug wars or homicides or robberies by the thousands each year than about the cancers, heart diseases, and respiratory diseases killing them by the hundreds of thousands each year. Those illnesses were not mentioned, but "Black on Black crime has reached a critical level that threatens our existence as a people," wrote *Ebony* publisher John H. Johnson, in a 1979 special issue on the topic. If anything, the Black on Black crime of internalized racist ideas had indeed reached a critical level—this renewed focus on the crisis of "Black crime" helped feed the growth of the movement toward mass incarceration that would devastate generations.

The rise of mass incarceration was partially fueled by Black people who, even as they adopted racist ideas, did so ostensibly out of trying to save the Black community in the 1970s. But the

NOTE ON "CRIMINAL" I have moved away from using the term "criminal." This term implies that there are inherently bad people who commit crimes. This implication substantiates our criminal punishment system: that bad people must be locked away. But what about people who occasionally do bad things? And what if they do bad things largely as a result of bad conditions? Like poverty. Like the easy availability of guns. Like toxic masculinity. Should we be locking people away? Or should we be locking away the bad conditions?

1980s brought a more premeditated form of racism, as channeled through the Black administrators Ronald Reagan appointed to his cabinet. Under Clarence Thomas's directorship from 1980 to 1986, the Equal Employment Opportunity Commission doubled the number of racist discrimination cases it dismissed as "no cause." Samuel Pierce, Reagan's secretary of the Department of Housing and Urban Development (HUD), redirected billions of dollars in federal funds allotted for low-income housing to corporate interests and Republican donors. Under Pierce's watch in the first half of the 1980s, the number of public-housing units in non-White neighborhoods dropped severely. Impoverished Black people faced a housing crisis in the 1980s that Pierce made worse, even though he had the power to alleviate it, setting the stage for future secretaries of HUD like Trump's appointee, Ben Carson. These were Black men who used the power they'd been given—no matter how limited and conditional—in inarguably racist ways that harmed Black people.

AS THE EDITOR and I stared each other down, I had a heated conversation—and conversion—in my mind. Eventually, the silence broke and the editor excused me from his office. I received an ultimatum before the end of the workday: Terminate my race column for *The Famuan* or be terminated from my internship at the *Tallahassee Democrat*. I terminated my column in absolute bitterness, feeling as if I terminated a part of myself.

And I did begin to terminate a part of myself—for the better. I began to silence one half of the war within me, the duel between antiracist and assimilationist ideas that W.E.B. Du Bois gave voice to, and started embracing the struggle toward a singular antiracist consciousness. I picked up a second major, African American studies.

I took my first Black history course that fall of 2003, the first of four African and African American history courses I would take over three semesters with FAMU professor David Jackson. His precise, detailed, engaging, but somehow funny lectures systematically walked me back through history for the first time. I had imagined history as a battle: on one side Black folks, on the other a team of "them niggers" and White folks. I started to see for the first time that it was a battle between racist and antiracist power.

Ending one confusion started another: what to do with my life. As a senior in the fall of 2004, I found that sports journalism no longer moved me. At least not like this thrilling new history I was discovering. I ended up abandoning the press box for what Americans were saying was the most "dangerous" box.

CHAPTER 12

CLASS

CLASS RACIST IDEA: Any notion that suggests that a race-class is superior or inferior to another race-class in any way, to justify the relative disparities in poverty and wealth between the race-classes brought on by racial capitalism.

CLASS ANTIRACIST IDEA: Any notion that suggests that the race-classes are equals and the economic disparities between them are the result of the policies of racial capitalism.

EXCITED TO BEGIN graduate school in African American studies at Temple University, I moved to North Philadelphia in the early days of August 2005. Hunting Park to be exact, steps away from Allegheny Avenue and the neighborhood of Allegheny West. My second-floor one-bedroom apartment overlooked North Broad Street: White people driving by, Black people walking by, Latinx people turning right on Allegheny. None of the people outside my building, a drab chocolate tenement adjoining an Exxon station, could tell that a few windows up over its vacant ground-floor storefront was home to a real human life. Its covered windows looked like shut eyes in a casket.

Death resided there, too, apparently. My new Black neighbors had been told for years that Hunting Park and Allegheny West were two of the most dangerous neighborhoods in Philadelphia—the most impoverished, with some of the highest reported rates of violence.

I unpacked myself in the "ghetto," as people flippantly called my new neighborhood. The so-called ghetto had expanded in the twentieth century as it swallowed millions of Black people migrating from the South to Western and Northern cities like Philadelphia. White flight followed. The combination of government welfare—in the form of subsidies, highway construction, and loan guarantees—along with often racist developers opened new wealth-building urban and suburban homes to the fleeing White people, while largely confining Black natives and new Black migrants to the so-called ghettos, now overcrowded and designed to extract wealth from their residents. But the word "ghetto," as it migrated to the Main Street of American vocabulary, did not conjure a series of racist policies that enabled White flight and Black abandonment—instead, "ghetto" began to describe unrespectable Black behavior on the North Broad Streets of the country.

"The dark ghetto is institutionalized pathology; it is chronic, self-perpetuating pathology; and it is the futile attempt by those with power to confine that pathology so as to prevent the spread of its contagion to the 'larger community,'" wrote psychologist Kenneth Clark in his 1965 book, *Dark Ghetto*. "Pathology," meaning a deviation from the norm. Impoverished Black people in the "ghetto" are pathological, abnormal? Abnormal from whom? What group is the norm? White elites? Black elites? Impoverished White people? Impoverished Latinx people? Asian elites? Impoverished Native people?

All of these groups—like the group "Black poor"—are distinct race-classes, racial groups at the intersection of race and class. Impoverished people are a class, Black people a race. Black impoverished people are a race-class. When we say impoverished people are lazy, we are expressing a classist idea. When we say Black people are lazy, we are expressing a racist idea. When we say impoverished Black people are lazier than impoverished White people, White elites, and Black elites, we are speaking at the intersection of classist and racist ideas—an ideological intersection that forms class racist ideas. When Dinesh D'Souza writes, "the behavior of the African American underclass . . . flagrantly violates and scandalizes basic codes of responsibility, decency, and civility," he is expressing class racist ideas.

When a policy exploits impoverished people, it is a classist policy. When a policy exploits Black people, it is a racist policy. When a policy exploits Black impoverished people, the policy exploits at the intersection of classist and racist policies—a policy intersection of class racist policies. When we racialize classes, support racist policies against those race-classes, and justify them by racist ideas, we are engaging in class racism. To be antiracist is to equalize the race-classes. To be antiracist is to root the economic disparities between the equal race-classes in policies, not people.

Class racist ideas are as ripe among White elites—who castigate impoverished White people as "White trash"—as they are among Black elites, who degrade impoverished Black people as "them niggers" who live in the "ghetto." Constructs of "ghetto Blacks" (and "White trash") are perhaps the most popular class racist ideas. Pathological people made the pathological ghetto, segregationist ideas say. The pathological ghetto made pathological people, assimilationist ideas say. To be antiracist is to say the political and economic conditions, not the people, in impoverished Black neighborhoods are pathological. Pathological conditions are making the residents sicker and poorer while they strive to survive and thrive, while they invent and reinvent cultures and behaviors that may be different but never inferior to those of residents in richer neighborhoods. But if the elite race-classes are judging the impoverished race-classes by their own cultural and behavioral norms, then the impoverished race-classes appear inferior. Whoever creates the norm creates the hierarchy and positions their own race-class at the top of the hierarchy.

DARK GHETTO WAS a groundbreaking study of the Black poor during President Johnson's war on poverty in the 1960s, when scholarship on poverty was ascendant, like the work of anthropologist Oscar Lewis. Lewis argued that the children of impoverished people, namely impoverished people of color, were raised on behaviors that prevented their escape from poverty, perpetuating generations of poverty. He introduced the term "culture of poverty" in a 1959 ethnography of Mexican families. Unlike some economists, who explored the role of policy in the "cycle of poverty"—predatory exploitation moving in lockstep with meager income and opportunities, which kept even the hardest-working people in poverty and made poverty expensive—Lewis reproduced the classist idea that poor behaviors keep poor people poor. "People with a culture of poverty," Lewis later wrote, "are a marginal people who know only their own troubles, their own local conditions, their own neighborhood, their own way of life."

Racist White elected officials still drag out the culture of poverty thesis. "We have got this tailspin of culture in our inner cities in particular of men not working, and just generations of men not even thinking about working, and not learning the value and the culture of work," Wisconsin representative Paul Ryan said in 2014. "So there's a real culture problem here that has to be dealt with."

Unlike Lewis and Ryan, Kenneth Clark presented the hidden hand of racism activating the culture of poverty, or what he called "pathology." In Clark's work, the dueling consciousness of the oppression-inferiority thesis resurfaced. First slavery, then segregation, and now poverty and life in the "ghetto" made Black people inferior, according to this latest update of the thesis. Yet again, it wasn't just the oppressive conditions—in this case, poverty—that were the problem: Impoverished Black people were the problem. Poverty became perhaps the most enduring injustice to fit into the oppression-inferiority thesis.

Something was making poor people poor, according to theorists. And it was welfare. Welfare "transforms the individual from a dignified, industrious, self-reliant *spiritual* being into a dependent animal creature without his knowing it," U.S. senator Barry Goldwater wrote in *The Conscience of the Conservative* in 1960. Goldwater and his ideological descendants said little to nothing about rich White people who depended on the welfare of inheritances, tax cuts, government contracts, hookups, and bailouts. They said little to nothing about the White middle class depending on the welfare of the New Deal, the GI Bill, subsidized suburbs, and exclusive White networks. Welfare for middle- and upper-income people remained out of the discourse on "handouts," as welfare for the Black poor became the true oppressor in this conservative version of the oppression-inferiority thesis. "The evidence of this failure is all around us," wrote Heritage Foundation president Kay Coles James in 2018. "Being black and the daughter of a former welfare recipient, I know firsthand the unintended harm welfare has caused."

Kenneth Clark was an unrelenting chronicler of the racist policies that made "the dark ghetto," but at the same time he reinforced the racial-class hierarchy. He positioned the Black poor as inferior to Black elites like himself, who had also long lived "within the walls of the ghetto," desperately attempting "to escape its creeping blight." Clark considered the Black poor less stable than the White poor. "The white poor and slum dweller have the advantage of . . . the belief that they can rise economically and escape from the slums," he wrote. "The Negro believes himself to be closely confined to the pervasive low status of the ghetto." Obama made a similar case during his campaign speech on race in 2008. "For all those who scratched and clawed their way to get a piece of the American Dream, there were many who didn't make it—those who were ultimately defeated, in one way or another, by discrimination. That legacy of defeat was passed on to future generations—those young men and increasingly young women who we see standing on street corners or languishing in our prisons, without hope or prospects for the future." This stereotype of hopeless, defeated, unmotivated impoverished Black people is without evidence. Research shows, in fact, that impoverished Black people are more optimistic about their prospects than impoverished White people are.

For ages, racist impoverished White people have enriched their sense of self on the stepladder of racist ideas, what W.E.B. Du Bois famously called the "wage" of Whiteness. I may not be rich, but at least I am not a nigger. Racist Black elites, meanwhile, heightened their sense of self on the stepladder of racist ideas, on what we can call the wage of Black elitism. I may not be White, but at least I am not them niggers.

Racist Black elites thought about low-income Black people the way racist non-Black people thought about Black people. We thought we had more than higher incomes. We thought we were higher people. We saw ourselves as the "Talented Tenth," as Du Bois named Black elites from the penthouse of his class racist ideas in 1903. "The Negro race, like all races, is going to be saved by its exceptional men," Du Bois projected. "Was there ever a nation on God's fair earth civilized from the bottom upward? Never; it is, ever was, and ever will be from the top downward that culture filters."

I had come a long way by 2005. So had the Talented Tenth and the term "ghetto" in America's racial vocabulary. In the forty years since Clark's *Dark Ghetto,* dark had married ghetto in the chapel of inferiority and took her name as his own—the ghetto was now so definitively dark, to call it a dark ghetto would be redundant. Ghetto also became as much an adjective—ghetto culture, ghetto people—as a noun, loaded with racist ideas, unleashing and justifying all sorts of racism onto impoverished Black communities.

IN MY NEW Philly home, I did not care what people thought about the impoverished Black people in my neighborhood. Call them ghetto if you want. Run away if you want. I wanted to be there. To live the effects of racism firsthand!

I saw impoverished Black people as the product of racism and not capitalism, largely because I thought I knew racism but knew I did not know capitalism. But it is impossible to know racism without understanding its intersection with capitalism. As Martin Luther King Jr. said in his critique of capitalism in 1967, "It means ultimately coming to see that the problem of racism, the problem of economic exploitation, and the problem of war are all tied together. These are the triple evils that are interrelated."

Capitalism emerged during what world-systems theorists term the "long sixteenth century," a cradling period that begins around 1450 with Portugal sailing into the unknown Atlantic. Prince Henry's Portugal birthed conjoined twins—capitalism and racism—when it initiated the transatlantic human trade of African people. These newborns looked up with tender eyes to their ancient siblings of sexism, imperialism, ethnocentrism, and homophobia. The conjoined twins developed different personalities through the new class and racial formations of the modern world. As the principal customers of Portuguese human traders, first in their home country and then in their American colonies, Spain adopted and raised the toddlers among the genocides of Indigenous people that laid the foundational seminaries and cemeteries on which Western Europe's Atlantic empire grew in the sixteenth century. England, France, and the Netherlands competed for dominance in the transatlantic human trade, raising the conjoined twins into their vigorous adolescence in the seventeenth and eighteenth centuries. The conjoined twins entered adulthood through Indigenous and Black and Asian and White enslavement and forced labor in the Americas, which powered industrial revolutions from Boston to London that financed still-greater empires in the eighteenth and nineteenth centuries. The hot and cold wars in the twentieth century over resources and markets, rights and powers, weakened the conjoined twins—but eventually they would grow stronger under the guidance of the United States, the European Union, Russia, China, and the satellite nations beholden to them, colonies in everything but name. The conjoined twins are again struggling to stay alive and thrive as their own offspring—inequality, war, pandemics, and climate change—threaten to kill them, and all of us, off.

In the twenty-first century, persisting racial injustices and inequities in poverty, unemployment, and wealth show the lifework of the conjoined twins. The Black poverty rate in 2020 stood at 19.8 percent, more than double the White poverty rate. Both rates signified economic injustice. The Black unemployment rate has consistently been about twice as high as the White unemployment rate for the last fifty years. The wage gap between Black and White people is about as large as it was in 1950. The median net worth of White families is about eight times that of Black families. The disparity stands to only get worse if racist housing policies, tax policies benefiting the rich, and mass incarceration continue unabated, according to forecasters. By 2053, the median wealth of Black households is expected to fall to $0, and Latinx households will zero out two decades later.

The injustices and inequities wrought by anti-Black racism and capitalism are not restricted to the United States. Africa's unprecedented capitalist growth over the past two decades has enriched foreign investors and a handful of Africans, while the number of people living in extreme poverty is growing in Sub-Saharan Africa. With extreme poverty falling rapidly elsewhere, forecasters project that nearly nine in ten extremely impoverished people will live in Sub-Saharan Africa by 2030. In Latin America, people of African descent remain disproportionately impoverished. The global gap between the richest (and Whitest) regions of the world and the poorest (and Blackest) regions of the world has tripled in size since the 1960s—at the same time as the global non-White middle class has grown.

It is a persisting injustice that upward mobility is a struggle for all racial groups. Upward mobility is still greater for White people, and downward mobility is greater for Black people. And equity is nonexistent on the race-class ladder in the United States. In the highest-income quintile, White median wealth is about $444,500, around $300,000 more than for upper-income Black and Latinx people. Black middle-income households have less wealth than White middle-income households, whose homes are valued higher. Indeed, the wealth distribution of Black middle-class families is comparable to the wealth distribution of White low-income families. White poverty is not as distressing as Black poverty. Impoverished Black people are much more likely to live in neighborhoods where other families are impoverished, creating a poverty of resources and opportunities. Sociologists refer to this as the "double burden." Impoverished Black people in metropolitan Chicago are ten times more likely than impoverished White people to live in high-poverty areas. With Black poverty dense and White poverty scattered, Black poverty is visible and surrounds its victims; White poverty blends in.

Attributing these injustices and inequities solely to capitalism is as faulty as attributing them solely to racism. Believing these injustices and inequities will be eliminated through eliminating capitalism is as faulty as believing they will be eliminated through eliminating racism. Rolling back racism in a capitalist nation can eliminate the inequities between the Black and White poor, middle-income Latinx and Asian people, rich White and Native people. Antiracist policies in the 1960s and 1970s narrowed these inequities on some measures. But the injustice of widespread poverty remains. And antiracist policies alone cannot eliminate the inequities between rich and impoverished Asian people or between rich White people and "White trash"—the intraracial inequities between race-classes. As racial disparities within the classes narrowed in recent decades, the economic inequities within the races have broadened, as have the class racist ideas justifying those inequities.

Antiracist policies cannot eliminate class racism without anticapitalist policies. Anticapitalism cannot eliminate class racism without antiracism. Case in point is the persistent racism Afro-Cubans faced in socialist Cuba after revolutionaries eliminated capitalism there in 1959, as chronicled by historian Devyn Spence Benson. Revolutionaries demanded Afro-Cubans assimilate into an imagined post-racial Cuba—"Not Blacks, but Citizens"—built on White Cuban social norms after a three-year campaign against racism abruptly ended in 1961.

Socialist and communist spaces are not automatically antiracist. Some socialists and communists have pushed a segregationist or assimilationist program in order not to alienate racist White workers. For example, delegates at the founding meeting of the Socialist Party of America (SPA) in 1901 refused to adopt an anti-lynching petition. Assimilationist leaders of some socialist and communist organizations have asked people of color to leave their racial identities and antiracist battle plans at the door, decrying "identity politics." Some of these socialists and communists may not be familiar with their ideological guide's writings on race. "The discovery of gold and silver in America," Karl Marx once wrote, "the extirpation, enslavement and entombment in mines of the aboriginal population, the beginning of the conquest and looting of the East Indies, the turning of Africa into a warren for the commercial hunting of black-skins, signalised the rosy dawn of the era of capitalist production." Marx recognized the birth of the conjoined twins.

In the 1920s, W.E.B. Du Bois started binge-reading Karl Marx. By the time the Great Depression depressed the Black poor worse than the White poor, and he saw in the New Deal the same old deal of government racism for Black workers, Du Bois conceived of an antiracist anticapitalism. Howard University economist Abram Harris, steeped in a post-racial Marxism that ignores the color line as stubbornly as any color-blind racist, pleaded with Du Bois to reconsider his intersecting of anticapitalism and antiracism. But the reality of what scholars now call racial capitalism—the singular name of the conjoined twins—made up Du Bois's mind.

"The lowest and most fatal degree" of Black workers' "suffering comes not from capitalists but from fellow white workers," Du Bois stated. "White labor . . . deprives the Negro of his right to vote, denies him education, denies him affiliation with trade unions, expels him from decent houses, and neighborhoods, and heaps upon him the public insults of open color discrimination." Du Bois described the development of a "petty bourgeoisie" within the working class in the United States as a "post-Marxian phenomenon." As such, Marxism could not fully explain U.S. political economy. He started to think beyond Marx and Russian communists at the time, as antiracist and anticapitalist Black scholars have ever since. "Instead of a horizontal division of classes, there was a vertical fissure, a complete separation of classes by race, cutting square across the economic layers," Du Bois wrote. The vertical cutting knife? Racism, sharpened through the centuries. "This flat and incontrovertible fact, imported Russian Communism ignored, would not discuss."

But Du Bois discussed it. An antiracist anticapitalism could seal the horizontal class fissures and vertical race fissures—and, importantly, their intersections—with equalizing racial and economic policies for working people. In 1948, Du Bois officially abandoned the idea of a vanguard Talented Tenth of Black elites and called for a "Guiding One Hundredth." Du Bois helped breed a new crop of antiracist anticapitalists before they were driven underground or into prison by the red scares of the 1950s, before resurfacing in the 1960s. They are resurfacing again in the twenty-first century in the wake of the Great Recession, the Occupy movement, the movement for Black Lives, and the campaigns of democratic socialists, recognizing "there is an inextricable link between racism and capitalism," to quote Northwestern scholar Keeanga-Yamahtta Taylor. They are winning elections, rushing into anticapitalist organizations, and struggles against racial capitalism.

I keep using the term "anticapitalist" as opposed to socialist or communist or Marxist to include the people who publicly or privately question or loathe capitalism but do not identify as socialist or communist or Marxist. I use "anticapitalist" because the conservative defenders of capitalism, particularly Republicans, regularly say their opponents fighting for economic justice for all people are against capitalism. They say efforts to provide a safety net for all people are "anticapitalist." They say attempts to prevent monopolies are "anticapitalist." They say efforts that strengthen

NOTE ON MARXISM One of the ways the conservators of racism have tried to fearmonger people away from this book was by identifying me as a Marxist. It was part of their decades-long propaganda campaign that the people who are challenging racism are part of a "Marxist" conspiracy to take over society. It didn't matter to them that there are Marxists who refuse to challenge racism, or that many people who challenge racism refuse to challenge capitalism—both of which I challenge in this chapter. It does not matter to them that my critique of capitalism did not come from reading Marx. It came from my reading of Black scholars like Angela Davis, Robin D. G. Kelley, and W.E.B. Du Bois. But for propagandists, accuracy does not matter. Just fearmongering. It reminds me of when segregationists called Martin Luther King Jr. a "communist" to "red scare" people away from supporting the civil rights movement. And now, the very people who claim to revere King are doing the same thing to those of us who, like King, are challenging racial capitalism.

weak unions and weaken exploitative owners are "anticapitalist."
They say plans to normalize worker ownership and regulations
protecting consumers, workers, and environments from big business are "anticapitalist." They say laws taxing the richest more
than the middle class, redistributing pilfered wealth, and guaran-
teeing basic incomes are "anticapitalist." They say wars to end
poverty are "anticapitalist." They say campaigns to remove the
profit motive from essential life sectors like education, healthcare,
utilities, mass media, and public safety are "anticapitalist."

In doing so, these "conservative" defenders are defining capitalism. They define capitalism as the freedom to exploit people
into economic ruin; the freedom to assassinate unions; the freedom to prey on unprotected consumers, workers, and environments; the freedom to value quarterly profits over responding to
the climate crisis; the freedom to undermine small businesses
and cushion corporations; the freedom from competition; the
freedom not to pay taxes; the freedom to heave the tax burden
onto the middle and lower classes; the freedom to commodify
everything and everyone; the freedom to keep impoverished
people impoverished and middle-income people struggling to
stay middle income, and make rich people richer. The history of
capitalism—of world warring, classing, human trading, enslaving, colonizing, depressing wages, and dispossessing land and
labor and resources and rights—bears out the conservative definition of capitalism.

"Liberals" who are "capitalist to the bone," as U.S. senator
Elizabeth Warren identifies herself, present a different definition
of capitalism. "I believe in markets and the benefits they can
produce when they work," Warren said when asked what that
identity meant to her. "I love the competition that comes with
a market that has decent rules. . . . The problem is when the
rules are not enforced, when the markets are not level playing
fields, all that wealth is scraped in one direction," leading to de-
ception and theft. "Theft is not capitalism," Warren said. She
has proposed a series of regulations and rules that her conservative opponents class as "anticapitalist." Conservatives say other

countries that have these rules are not capitalist. Warren should be applauded for her efforts to establish and enforce rules that end the theft and level the playing field for, hopefully, all race-classes, not just the White middle class. But if Warren succeeds, then the new economic system will operate in a fundamentally different way than it has ever operated before in American history. Either the new economic system will not be capitalist or the old system it replaces was not capitalist. They cannot both be capitalist.

When Senator Warren and others define capitalism in this way—as markets and market rules and competition and benefits from winning—they are disentangling capitalism from theft and racism and sexism and imperialism. If that's their capitalism, I can see how they can remain capitalist to the bone. However, history does not affirm this definition of capitalism. Markets and market rules and competition and benefits from winning existed long before the origins of capitalism in the fifteenth century. What capitalism introduced to the world was global theft in the guise of capital accumulation, racially uneven playing fields, unidirectional wealth that rushes upward in unprecedented amounts, wealth that allows capital to free people from work or force people to work. Since the dawn of racial capitalism, when were markets level playing fields? When could working people compete equally with capitalists? When could Black people compete equally with White people? When could African nations compete equally with European nations? When did the rules not generally benefit the wealthy and White nations? Humanity needs honest definitions of capitalism and racism based in the actual living history of the conjoined twins.

The top 1 percent now own around half of the world's wealth, up from 42.5 percent at the height of the Great Recession in 2008. The world's 2.9 billion poorest adults, comprising 55 percent of the world's working-age population, own 1.3 percent of global wealth. Most of these impoverished adults live in non-White countries that were subjected to centuries of human trading and colonizing and resource dispossessing, which created the modern wealth of the West and increasingly of the East. The wealth extraction continues today via foreign companies that own or control key natural resources in the Global South, taken through force with the threat of "economic sanctions" or granted by "elected" politicians. Racial capitalism makes countries like the Democratic Republic of the Congo one of the richest countries in the world belowground and one of the poorest countries in the world aboveground.

To love capitalism, which inescapably includes all the racial injustices and inequities it has spawned, is to end up loving racism. To love racism, which inescapably includes all the economic injustices and inequities it has spawned, is to end up loving capitalism. The conjoined twins are two sides of the same destructive body. The idea that capitalism is merely free markets, competition, free trade, supplying and demanding, and private ownership of the means of production operating for a profit is as whimsical and ahistorical and conserving as the idea that racism is "prejudice plus power." Popular definitions of capitalism, like popular definitions of racism, do not live in historical or material reality. Capitalism, in producing racial injustices and inequities between race-classes, is essentially racist; racism, in also producing economic injustices and inequities between race-classes, is essentially capitalist. They were birthed together from the same unnatural causes, and they shall one day die together from unnatural causes. Or racial capitalism will live into another epoch of theft and rapacious injustice, especially if activists naïvely fight the conjoined twins independently, as if they are not connected.

. . .

NOTE ON CAPITALISM To attack this book, the conservators of racism have often plucked sentences in this paragraph and the next paragraph to delegitimize me. They usually inject these sentences with meaning that diverges from the evidentiary and historical context I provide throughout. I added language to make my meaning unmistakable.

MY PARENTS WERE worried. I felt alive when I moved into this Black neighborhood. I felt I needed to live around Black people in order to study and uplift Black people. Not just any Black people: impoverished Black people. I considered the Black poor to be the truest and most authentic representatives of Black people. I made urban poverty an entryway into the supposedly crime-riddled and impoverished house of authentic Blackness.

For Lerone Bennett Jr., the longtime executive editor of *Ebony* magazine, my identifying of poverty, hustling, criminality, sex, and gambling in the urban world as the most authentic Black world probably would have reminded him of the Blaxploitation films of the late 1960s and early 1970s. The Black Power movement of the era, in shattering the White standard of assimilationist ideas, sent creative Black people on a mission to erect Black standards, a new Black aesthetic. Blaxploitation films arrived right on time, with Black casts, urban settings, and Black heroes and heroines: pimps, gangsters, prostitutes, and rapists.

Both of my parents saw *Shaft* (1971) and *Super Fly* (1972) upon their release. But their Christian theology, even in its liberational form, halted them from seeing *Sweet Sweetback's Baadasssss Song* in 1971. It was a movie about a male brothel worker who is brutalized by LAPD officers but then beats them up in retaliation, eludes a police manhunt in impoverished communities, uses his sexual prowess to secure aid from women, and reaches freedom in Mexico. "I made this film for the Black aesthetic," Melvin Van Peebles said. "White critics aren't used to that. The movie is Black life, unpandered."

I wanted to experience Black life, unpandered. I had moved to North Philadelphia in 2005 carrying dueling bags of Blackness: "Black is Beautiful," and "Black is Misery," to use the phrase Lerone Bennett Jr. tendered in his *Ebony* review of *Sweet Sweetback's Baadasssss Song*. Bennett blasted Van Peebles for his cinematic ode to the Black "cult of poverty," for imagining poverty "as the incubator of wisdom and soul," for "foolishly" identifying "the black aesthetic with empty bellies and big-bottomed prostitutes. . . . To romanticize the tears and the agony of the people," Bennett wrote, "is to play them cheap as human beings."

I thought I was so real, so Black, in choosing this apartment in this neighborhood. In truth, I was being racist, playing impoverished Black people cheap as human beings. While others had fled from impoverished Black people in racist fear of their dangerous inferiority, I was fleeing to impoverished Black people in racist assurance of the superiority conferred by their danger, their superior authenticity. I was the Black gentrifier, a distinct creature from the White gentrifier. If the White gentrifier moves to the impoverished Black neighborhood to be a developer, the Black gentrifier is moving back to the impoverished Black neighborhood to be developed.

To be antiracist is to recognize neither impoverished Black people nor elite Black people as the truest representative of Black people. But at the time I believed culture filtered upward, that Black elites, in all our materialism, individualism, and assimilationism, needed to go to the "bottom" to be civilized. I understood impoverished Black people as simultaneously the bottom and the foundation of Blackness. I wanted their authenticity to rub off on me, a spoiled—in both senses—middle-income Black man. Rap music made by people from "the bottom" was no longer enough to keep me stuck on the realness.

I was in full agreement with E. Franklin Frazier's *Black Bourgeoisie,* published in 1957. Situating White elites as the norm, Frazier dubbed Black elites as inferior: as quicker sellouts, as bigger conspicuous consumers, as more politically corrupt, as more exploitative, as more irrational for looking up to the very people oppressing them. This inverted class racist idea about inferior Black elites quickly became a widespread belief, joining the widespread belief about the Black masses being more pathological. In the bestselling *Beyond the Melting Pot,* written with Daniel Patrick Moynihan in 1963, sociologist Nathan Glazer argued that, unlike the other middle classes, "the Negro middle class contributes very little . . . to the solution of Negro social programs." Without any supporting data, Glazer positioned the Black bourgeoisie as inferior, in the scale of social responsibility, to other bourgeoisies. These racist ideas were wrong, of course—a decade earlier, Martin Luther King Jr. and a generation of elite Black youngsters from the Black bourgeoisie began the epic struggle for civil rights, economic justice, and desegregation. My generation of elite and non-elite Black youngsters rushed into our own struggle—into Black studies, a Black space.

CHAPTER 13

SPACE

SPACE RACIST IDEA: Any notion that suggests that a racialized space is superior or inferior to another racialized space in any way, or justifies policies that lead to injustice or resource inequity between racialized spaces or the elimination of certain racialized spaces.

SPACE ANTIRACIST IDEA: Any notion that suggests that racialized spaces are equals or substantiates policies that lead to racial justice and equity between integrated and protected racialized spaces.

W E CALLED OUR African American studies space a Black space—it was, after all, governed primarily by Black bodies, Black thoughts, Black cultures, and Black histories. Of course, the spaces at Temple University governed primarily by White bodies, White thoughts, White cultures, and White histories were not labeled White. They hid the Whiteness of their spaces behind the veil of color blindness.

The most prominent person in our Black space at Temple had been piercing this unspoken veil since 1971, when he first printed the *Journal of Black Studies*. Molefi Kete Asante, who in 1980 would publish the seminal work *Afrocentricity*, railed against assimilationist ideas and called for Afrocentric Black people. There were multiple ways of seeing the world, he argued. But too many Black people were "looking out" at the world from a European "center," which was taken as the only point from which to see the world—through European cultures masquerading as world cultures, European religions masquerading as world religions, European history masquerading as world history. Theories gleaned from European subjects masquerading as universal theories. "The rejection of European particularism as universal is the first stage of our coming intellectual struggle," Professor Asante wrote. In 1987, he established the nation's first African American studies doctoral program at Temple to wage the struggle, the program I entered twenty years later.

Asante's right-hand woman in our department was Professor Ama Mazama. A product of Guadeloupe and recipient of a doctorate in linguistics from La Sorbonne in Paris, Professor Mazama may have been more well-known outside the United States. Not minding, she enjoyed bolting the States to speak on her research on the Afrocentric paradigm, African religion, Caribbean culture and languages, and African American homeschooling. She loved African traditions deep in her soul. That same soul hated to see African people worshipping European traditions. "Negroes," she called them in disgust.

Professor Mazama spoke as softly as the African garb that draped her body. I remember her publicly debating an animated Maulana Karenga, the founder of Kwanzaa, with the same tranquility with which she spoke to her homeschooled children afterward. She taught me that the power of the spoken word is in the power of the word spoken.

Professor Mazama gave criticism the way she received it: unflappably. She almost welcomed ideological divergence from the people she held dear. We didn't agree on everything, but we shared a deep love of African people and scholarly combat. Professor Mazama was as intellectually confident, fearless, and clear as anyone I had ever met. I asked her to be my dissertation adviser and she obliged. I hoped at least a few of these intellectual qualities would rub off on me.

In my first course with Mazama, she lectured on Asante's contention that objectivity was really "collective subjectivity." She concluded, "It is impossible to be objective."

It was an idea that shifted my view of the world immediately. It made so much sense to me as I recalled the subjective choices I'd made as an aspiring journalist and then scholar. If objectivity was dead, though, I needed a replacement. I flung up my hand like an eighth-grader.

"Yes?"

"If we can't be objective, then what should we strive to do?" She stared at me as she gathered her words. Not a woman of many words, it did not take long.

"Just tell the truth. That's what we should strive to do. Tell the truth."

AFRICAN AMERICAN STUDIES took up part of the eighth floor of Gladfelter Hall at Temple University, which stoically faced its equally imposing twin, Anderson Hall. The two skyscrapers filled with middle-income White faculty and students loomed over North Philadelphia blocks teeming with low-income Black people. Temple's poorly paid security guards required anyone entering Gladfelter Hall or other campus buildings to show their university IDs to prevent those two worlds from meeting. Racist White people saw danger in the "ghetto" walking on campus. They worried about safeguarding their White space inside North Philadelphia's Black space. But they could not understand why we worried about safeguarding our Black space inside Temple's White space. They branded Black studies a "ghetto," like my neighborhood in North Philadelphia, but insisted it was a ghetto of our making.

The defining character of Harlem's "dark ghetto," where Kenneth Clark lived and studied during the early 1960s, and of the North Philadelphia where I lived and studied four decades later was "creeping blight," according to Clark, "juvenile delinquency" and "widespread violence"—characteristics that exist in different forms in all racialized spaces. The idea of the dangerous Black neighborhood is the most dangerous racist idea. And it is powerfully misleading. For instance, people steer away from and stigmatize Black neighborhoods as crime-ridden streets where you might have your wallet stolen. But they aspire to move into upscale White neighborhoods, home to white-collar exploiters and "banksters," as radio personality Thom Hartmann calls them, who might steal your life savings. Americans lost trillions during the Great Recession, which was largely triggered by financial harms of staggering enormity. White-collar harms increased during the COVID-19 pandemic, at the same time that American billionaires saw their collective wealth become "roughly double" the wealth of the 165 million poorest Americans. Estimated losses from white-collar harms are believed to be between $300 and $800 billion per year, according to experts. By comparison, near the height of violence in 1995, the FBI reported the combined costs of burglary and robbery to be $4 billion.

Racist Americans stigmatize entire Black neighborhoods as places of homicide and mortal violence but don't similarly connect White neighborhoods to the disproportionate number of White males who engage in mass shootings. And they don't even see the daily violence that unfolds on the highways that deliver mostly White suburbanites to their homes. In 1986, during the violent crack crisis 3,380 more Americans died from alcohol-related traffic deaths than from homicides. None of this is to say that White spaces or Black spaces are more or less violent—this isn't about creating a hierarchy. The point is that when we unchain ourselves from the space racist ideas that deracialize and normalize and elevate elite White spaces, while doing the opposite to Black spaces, we will find good and bad, violence and nonviolence, in all spaces, no matter how impoverished or rich, Black or non-Black. No matter the effect of the conjoined twins.

Just as racist power racializes people, racist power racializes space. The ghetto. The inner city. The developing world. A space is racialized when a racial group is known to either govern the space or make up the clear majority in the space. A Black space, for instance, is either a space publicly run by Black people or a space where Black people stand in the majority. Policies of space racism overresource White spaces and underresource non-White spaces. Space racist ideas justify resource inequity through creating a racial hierarchy of space, lifting up White spaces as heaven, downgrading non-White spaces as hell. "We have a situation where we have our inner cities, African Americans, Hispanics, are living in hell, because it's so dangerous," candidate Donald Trump said during a presidential debate in 2016. In an Oval Office meeting in 2018 about Black and Latinx immigrants, President Trump asked: "Why are we having all these people from shithole countries come here?"

AFTER EXITING THE elevator onto Gladfelter's eighth floor, no one could miss the glassed-in classroom known as the fishbowl. Inside the glass walls often sat, in a circle, a motley bunch of mostly Black fish—many of whom had swum into Philadelphia from historically Black colleges and universities (HBCUs) and were still soaked in school pride. One day before class, a Jackson State alum had the audacity to announce the Sonic Boom as the best marching band in the land. He looked at me. I fell out laughing, a deep and long and booming laugh that said everything I needed to say. Almost all of us were boosting our school bands and academic feats and homecomings and histories and alumni. Even Ali from Fisk University. "There are more PhDs," Ali declared one day, "walking around who went to Fisk for undergrad than any other HBCU." We all knew Fisk used to be illustrious, but these days small private HBCUs like Fisk were hemorrhaging students and revenue and donations and respect. "This is 2006, not 1906!" someone blurted. "All of Fisk's doctorates could easily fit in this fishbowl," someone shouted. "What y'all got, two hundred students right now?"

Jokes aside, I respected Ali's pride in Fisk and all my classmates' HBCU pride, no matter how outlandish they sometimes sounded. I had no respect for those who hated their HBCUs. And no one hated their HBCU more than the only other FAMU alum in our graduate program.

Every time I lifted up FAMU's examples of Black excellence, Nashay shot them down. She complained about the incompetence lurking on FAMU's campus the way Temple students complained about the dangers lurking off campus. One day, as we awaited class in the fishbowl, I'd had enough. "Why you always dogging out FAMU?"

"Don't worry about it."

I pressed. She resisted. Finally, she opened.

"FAMU messed up my transcript!"

"What?" I asked, confused.

"I had them send my transcript and they messed it up. How can you have incompetent people working in the transcript office?"

She closed up. Class started, but I could not let it go. How could she use one horrible error from one person in one office to condemn the entire university—my university—as horrible? But I had said it all, heard it all before. I heard and heaped blame on HBCU administrators for the scarcity of resources. I heard Black students and faculty at historically White colleges and universities (HWCUs) say they could never go to HBCUs, those poorly run ghettos. I heard HBCU faculty and staff talk about escaping the dark ghettos and moving to HWCUs.

I heard my uncle say, like Dartmouth alum Aisha Tyler, that HBCUs do not represent "the real world." The argument: Black students are better served learning how to operate in a majority-White nation by attending a majority-White university. The reality: A large percentage of—perhaps most—Black Americans live in majority-Black neighborhoods, work in majority-Black sites of employment, organize in majority-Black associations, socialize in majority-Black spaces, attend majority-Black churches, and send their children to majority-Black schools. When people contend that Black spaces do not represent reality, they are speaking from the White worldview of Black people in the minority. They are conceptualizing the real American world as White. To be antiracist is to recognize there is no such thing as the "real world," only real worlds, multiple worldviews.

I heard people say, "Even the best black colleges and universities do not approach the standards of quality of respectable institutions," as economist Thomas Sowell wrote in 1974. Sowell's "description remains accurate," Jason Riley wrote in *The Wall*

Street Journal on September 28, 2010. Selective HBCUs lag behind "decent state schools like the University of Texas at Austin,
never mind a Stanford or Yale."

Riley had pulled out the familiar weapon safeguarding space
racism and menacing Black spaces: unfairly comparing Black
spaces to substantially richer White spaces. The endowment of
the richest HBCU, Howard, was forty-five times less than the
University of Texas at Austin's endowment in 2020, never mind
being forty-one and forty-four times less than the endowment of
Stanford and Yale, respectively. The racial wealth gap produces a
giving gap. For public HBCUs, the giving gap extends to state-
funding gaps, as racist policies steer more funds to HWCUs, like
the current "performance based" state models.

Resources define a space, resources the conjoined twins divvy
up. People make spaces from resources. Comparing spaces across
race-classes is like matching fighters of different weight classes,
which fighting sports consider unfair. Impoverished Black neighborhoods should be compared to equally impoverished White
neighborhoods, not to considerably richer White neighborhoods.
Small Black businesses should be compared to equally small White
businesses, not to wealthy White corporations. Indeed, when researchers compare HBCUs to HWCUs, HBCUs have equal rates
of Black graduation. This parity is remarkable given that Black
HBCU students are less likely than their Black peers at HWCUs
to have had high school GPAs above 2.5 and to have taken advanced placement courses. Not to mention, Black HBCU graduates are, on average, more likely than their Black peers from
HWCUs to be thriving financially, socially, and physically.

NASHAY FORCED ME to reckon with my own space racist ideas,
but I would learn there was more to her story.

A financial-aid officer had stolen thousands from her as an
undergraduate student at a White university, but she still held that
university in high regard. A botched transcript and she con-
demned her Black university. What hypocrisy. At the time, I

could not be angry at her without being angrier at myself. How many times did I individualize the error in White spaces, blaming the individual and not the White space? How many times did I generalize the error in the Black space—in the Black church or at a Black gathering—and blame the Black space instead of the individual? How many times did I have a bad experience at a Black business and then walk away complaining about not the individuals involved but Black businesses as a whole?

Banks remain twice as likely to offer loans to White entrepreneurs as to Black entrepreneurs. Customers avoid businesses in Black neighborhoods like they are "ghetto," like the "White man's ice is colder," as antiracist Black people have joked for years. I knew this then. But my dueling consciousness still led me to think like one young Black writer wrote in Blavity in 2017: "On an intellectual level, I know that Black people have been denied equal access to capital, training, and physical space. But does that inequitable treatment excuse bad service?" Does not good service, like every other commodity, typically cost more money? How can we acknowledge the clouds of racism over Black spaces and be shocked when it rains on our heads?

I felt Black was beautiful, but Black spaces were not? Nearly everything I am I owe to Black spaces. Black neighborhood. Black church. Black college. Black studies. I was like a plant devaluing the soil that made me.

THE HISTORY OF anti-Black space racism is long. It is a United States history that begins with Thomas Jefferson's solution to the "Negro problem." Civilize and emancipate the Negro. Send the Negro to Africa to "carry back to the country of their origin, the seeds of civilization," as Jefferson proposed in a letter in 1811. But the Negro commonly wanted no part in returning and redeeming Africa "from ignorance and barbarism." We do not want to go to the "savage wilds of Africa," free Black Philadelphians resolved in 1817. Enslavers were, meanwhile, decrying the savage wilds of free Black communities. A writer for the

South's *De Bow's Review* searched around the world, through a series of articles in 1859 and 1860, for "a moral, happy, and voluntarily industrious community of free negroes," but concluded, "no such community exists upon the face of the earth."

On January 12, 1865, in the midst of the Civil War, General William T. Sherman and U.S. secretary of war Edwin M. Stanton met with twenty Black leaders in Savannah, Georgia. After their spokesman, Garrison Frazier, said they needed land to be free so "we could reap the fruit of our labor, take care of ourselves," Stanton asked if they would "rather live . . . scattered among the whites or in colonies by yourselves?"

"Live by ourselves," Frazier responded, "for there is a prejudice against us in the South that will take years to get over."

Four days later, General Sherman issued Special Field Order No. 15 to punish Confederate landowners and rid his army camps of runaways. Black people received an army mule and "not more than forty acres" on coastal plains of South Carolina and Georgia. "The sole and exclusive management of affairs will be left to the freed people themselves," Sherman ordered.

Horace Greeley, the most eminent newspaper editor of the day, thought Sherman's order deprived the Negroes "of the advantage of white teachers and neighbors, who would lead them to an understanding and enjoyment of that higher civilization of which hitherto they have been deprived as slaves." Freed Southern Black people "like their fellows at the North" will be "aided by contact with white civilization," Greeley wrote in his *New-York Tribune* on January 30, 1865.

Black people were rejecting Greeley's assimilationist assumptions about integration. And the new Johnson administration did

NOTE ON "ASSIMILATIONIST" I think the terminology in this chapter could have been much clearer. I changed "integrationist" to "assimilationist" as part of an overall effort to provide more clarity. I wanted to clarify that two ideological assumptions underlie integration: the assimilationist and the antiracist assumptions. Integration can be harmful if advanced from an assimilationist standpoint; I want people to advance integration from an antiracist standpoint.

the same after Lincoln's assassination. By June 1865, roughly forty thousand Black people had settled on four hundred thousand acres of land before Confederate landowners started taking back "their" land.

Assumptions underlying integration—the placing of people of all racial backgrounds in the same spaces—can be antiracist, or assimilationist, like Greeley's. The antiracist assumption underlying integration is that in a multiracial nation, all racial groups can live together in harmony and equity where biological and behavioral sameness is acknowledged, ethnic and cultural differences are respected, and the diversity of it all benefits all. Greeley's assimilationist assumption underlying integration is that White people can cultivate away the barbarism of people of color while upstanding people of color can cultivate away the racist ideas of White people. In a historically racist society, integration, whether assimilationist or antiracist, expects Black bodies harmed by racism to heal in proximity to racist White people who haven't yet stopped harming them. After enduring slavery's violence, Frazier and his brethren had enough. They desired to separate, not from White people but from White racism. Separation is not always segregation. The antiracist desire to separate from racist neighbors is different from the segregationist desire to separate from "inferior" Black people.

Whenever Black people voluntarily gather among themselves, assimilationists do not see spaces of Black solidarity created to separate Black people from racism. They see spaces of White hate. They do not see spaces of cultural solidarity, of solidarity against racism. They see spaces of segregation against White people. Assimilationists do not see these spaces as the movement of Black people toward Black people. Assimilationists think about them as a movement away from White people. They then equate that supposed movement away from White people with the White segregationist movement away from Black people. Assimilationist ideas equate spaces for the survival of Black bodies with spaces for the survival of White supremacy.

When assimilationists use segregation and separation interchangeably, they are using the vocabulary of Jim Crow. Segregationist ideas, too, blur the lines between segregation and separation by justifying segregationist policies as standing "on the platform of equal accommodations for each race but separate," to quote Atlanta newspaper editor Henry W. Grady in 1885. The U.S. Supreme Court sanctioned this spoken veil in the 1896 *Plessy v. Ferguson* decision. Separate but equal covered up the segregationist policies that diverted resources toward exclusively White spaces. In 1930, segregationist Alabama spent $37 for each White student, compared to $7 for each Black student; Georgia, $32 to $7; and South Carolina, $53 to $5. High school was unavailable for my maternal grandparents around this time in Georgia.

"Equal," thought to be the soft target of the "separate but equal" ruling, ended up being a formidable foe for civil rights activists—it was nearly impossible to get equal resources for Black institutions. The NAACP Legal Defense Fund switched tactics to taking down "separate." Lawyers revived the old assimilationist assumption about integration: that "the enforced separation of the two races stamps the colored race with a badge of inferiority," which Associate Justice Henry Billings Brown called a "fallacy" in his *Plessy v. Ferguson* decision.

In the landmark *Brown v. Board of Education* case in 1954, NAACP lawyer Thurgood Marshall attempted to prove the assumption using the new integrationist social science. Marshall asked psychologists Kenneth and Mamie Clark to repeat their famous doll tests for the case. Presented with dolls with different skin colors, the majority of Black children preferred White dolls, which the Clarks saw as proof of the negative psychological harm of segregation. White social scientists argued the harm could be permanent. The U.S. Supreme Court unanimously agreed. "To separate [colored children] from others of similar age and qualifications solely because of their race generates a feeling of inferiority as to their status in the community that may affect their hearts and minds in a way unlikely ever to be undone," Chief Justice Earl Warren wrote.

Justice Warren did not judge White schools to be having a detrimental effect upon White children. He wrote the "segregation of white and colored children in public schools has a detrimental effect upon the colored children." It delays their "education and mental development," Warren explained. "We conclude that, in the field of public education, the doctrine of 'separate but equal' has no place. Separate educational facilities are inherently unequal."

What really made the schools unequal were the dramatically unequal resources provided to them, not the mere fact of racial separation. The Supreme Court justices deciding both *Plessy* and *Brown* avowed the segregationist lie that the "Negro and white schools involved have been equalized, or are being equalized," to quote Justice Warren. By 1973, when the resource inequities between the public schools had become too obvious to deny, the Supreme Court ruled, in *San Antonio Independent School District v. Rodriguez,* that property-tax allocations yielding inequities in public schools do not violate the equal-protection clause of the U.S. Constitution.

THE 1973 SUPREME Court ruling reified the only solution emanating from the *Brown* decision in 1954: busing Black bodies from detrimental Black spaces to worthwhile White spaces. Since "there are adequate Negro schools and prepared instructors and instructions, then there is nothing different except the presence of white people," wrote an insulted Zora Neale Hurston in the *Orlando Sentinel* in 1955. Martin Luther King Jr. also privately disagreed. "I favor integration on buses and in all areas of public accommodation and travel. . . . I think integration in our public schools is different," King told two Black teachers in Montgomery, Alabama, in 1959. "White people view black people as inferior. . . . People with such a low view of the black race cannot be given free rein and put in charge of the intellectual care and development of our boys and girls."

King had a nightmare that came to pass. Students of color fill most of the seats in today's public school classrooms but are taught by a 79 percent–White teaching force, which often has, however unconsciously, lower expectations for students of color. When Black and White teachers look at the same Black student, White teachers are about 40 percent less likely to believe the student will finish high school. Low-income Black students who have at least one Black teacher in elementary school are 29 percent less likely to drop out of school, 39 percent less likely among very low-income Black boys.

King's nightmare is a product of the dueling *Brown* decision. The court rightly undermined the legitimacy of segregated White spaces that hoard public resources, exclude all people of color, and are wholly dominated by White power and cultures. But the court also reinforced the legitimacy of integrated White spaces that hoard public resources, include some people of color, and are generally, though not wholly, dominated by White power and cultures. White majorities, White power, and White culture dominate both the segregated and the integrated spaces, making both White. But the unspoken veil claims there is no such thing as integrated White spaces, or for that matter integrated Black spaces that are underresourced, include some non-Black people, and are generally, though not wholly, dominated by Black peoples and cultures. The court ruled Black spaces, segregated or integrated, to be inherently unequal and inferior.

After *Brown,* the integrated White space came to define the ideal integrated space where inferior people of color could be developed. The integrated Black space became a de facto segregated space where inferior Black bodies were left behind by White flight. Integration had turned into "a one-way street," a young Chicago lawyer observed in 1995. "The minority assimilated into the dominant culture, not the other way around," Barack Obama wrote. "Only white culture could be neutral and objective. Only white culture could be nonracial." Integration (into Whiteness) became racial progress.

. . .

PERSISTENT SEGREGATION IS not limited to the South or any single racial or ethnic group, though White students experience the highest rates of segregation. During the 2018–2019 school year, one Pew Research Center study found that "79 percent of White elementary and secondary public school students went to schools where at least half of their peers were also White. In that year, more than half of Hispanic students (56 percent) and 42 percent of Black students also attended schools where half the students or more shared their race or ethnicity." But over the decades, the focus has been on the segregation and integration of Black and Latinx students.

"The experience of an integrated education made all the difference in the lives of black children," wrote Cal Berkeley professor David L. Kirp in *The New York Times* in 2012, speaking from the new low of integration's roller-coaster history. The "academic-achievement gap" followed a similar roller coaster, closing with the integration of White schools, before opening back up, proving that "African-American students who attended integrated schools fared better academically than those left behind in segregated schools," Kirp argued. Standardized tests "proved" White students and White spaces were smarter. And yet, what if the scoring gap closed because, as Black students integrated White schools, more students received the same education and test prep?

Assimilationist White Americans have resented the rise in what they call segregated schools. "Like many whites who grew up in the 1960s and 1970s, I had always thought the ultimate goal of better race relations was integration," wrote Manhattan Institute fellow Tamar Jacoby in 1998. "The very word had a kind of magic to it," but now "few of us talk about it anymore." We are not pursuing Martin Luther King Jr.'s "color-blind dream" of "a more or less race-neutral America."

The assimilationist transformation of King as color-blind and race-neutral erases the actual King. He did not live to integrate Black spaces and people into White oblivion. If he did, then why did he plan to build low-income Atlanta apartments "using Negro workmen, Negro architects, Negro attorneys, and Negro financial institutions throughout," as he proudly reported in 1967? Why did he urge Black people to stop being "ashamed of being Black," to invest in their own spaces? The child of a Black neighborhood, church, college, and organization lived to ensure equal access to public accommodations and equal resources for all racialized spaces, an antiracist strategy as culture-saving as his nonviolence was body-saving.

Through lynching Black bodies, the segregationist approach is, in the end, more harmful to Black *bodies* than the assimilationist approach. Through lynching Black cultures, the assimilationist approach is, in the end, more harmful to *Black* bodies than the segregationist approach. And the assimilationist approach reasons, the more integration the better for people of color. But think about the logical conclusion of integrationist strategy: every race being represented in every U.S. space according to their percentage in the national population. A Black (13.4 percent) person would not see another until after seeing seven or so non-Black people. A Latinx (18.5 percent) person would not see another until after seeing five or so non-Latinx people. An Asian (5.9 percent) person would not see another until after seeing seventeen non-Asian people. A Native (1.3 percent) person would not see another until after seeing seventy-seven non-Native people. A White (60.1 percent) person would always see more White people around than non-White people. The effects would be everything from the expansion of integrated White spaces to White people gentrifying all the non-White institutions, associations, and neighborhoods. No more spatial wombs for the cultures of peoples of color. Only White spatial wombs of assimilation. We would all become "only white men" with different "skins," to quote historian Kenneth Stampp in 1956.

Americans have seen the logical conclusion of segregationist strategy, from slavery to Jim Crow to mass incarceration and border walls. The logical conclusion of antiracist strategy is open and equal access to all public accommodations, open access to all integrated White spaces, integrated Middle Eastern spaces, integrated Black spaces, integrated Latinx spaces, integrated Native spaces, and integrated Asian spaces that are as equally resourced as they are culturally different. All these spaces adjoin civic spaces of interracial political and economic and cultural power, from a House of Representatives to a school board to a newspaper editorial board where no race predominates, where shared antiracist power predominates. This is diversity, something assimilationists value only in name.

Antiracist strategy fuses desegregation with an antiracist form of integration and racial solidarity. Desegregation: eliminating all barriers to all racialized spaces. To be antiracist is to support the voluntary integration of bodies attracted by cultural solidarity, a shared humanity. Integration: resources rather than bodies. To be an antiracist is to champion resource equity by challenging the racist policies that produce resource inequity. Racial solidarity: openly identifying, supporting, and protecting integrated racial spaces. To be antiracist is to equate ethnic and cultural and color differences among racial groups.

But antiracist strategy is beyond the assimilationist conception that claims Black spaces could never be equal to White spaces, that believes Black spaces have a "detrimental effect upon" Black people, to quote Chief Justice Warren in *Brown*. My Black studies space was supposed to have a detrimental effect on me. Quite the opposite. My professors made sure of that, as did two Black students, answering questions I never thought to ask.

GENDER

GENDER RACIST IDEA: Any notion that suggests that one race-gender is superior or inferior to another race-gender in any way, or justifies policies that lead to injustice or inequity between race-genders.

GENDER ANTIRACIST IDEA: Any notion that suggests that race-genders are equals, or substantiates policies that lead to justice and equity between race-genders.

N O ONE OVERLOOKED the sheer size of her intellect, which was even more immediately apparent than her tall, full build and striking makeup. No one overlooked Kaila at all. She did not tuck away a single aspect of herself by the time I met her at Temple. No self-censoring. No closeting of her lesbian feminism in a Black space that could be antagonizing to lesbianism and feminism. No ambiguity for misinterpretation. All badass Joan Morgan "chickenhead" giving no fucks. All warrior poet giving all fucks, like her idol, Audre Lorde. Kaila was entirely herself, and her Laila Ali intellect wished for the world to voice a problem with what they saw.

Kaila had no problem telling you about yourself. Her legendary impersonations of African American studies students and faculty were as funny as they were accurate. I always wanted her to do an impersonation of me, but I was too scared and insecure to see what she saw.

Kaila held court with Yaba, whose roaring, full-bodied laughter often filled the room. Their back-and-forth jokes were as bad for victims as Venus and Serena Williams's matches were bad for tennis balls. When I sat down for a long talk—or, rather, to listen and learn—my mouth seemed to always be open, in laughter at their jokes or jaw-dropping wonder over their insights. They sat as the royal court of African American studies graduate students. Everyone feared or respected or battled them. I feared and respected them, too scared and awed to battle.

Yaba's irrepressible Blackness governed our Blacker-than-thou space. Blacker than thou not because of her Ghanaian features, her down-home New Orleans air, or her mixes of African garb and African American fashion. Not because she danced as comfortably to the beat of West Indian cultures as she did to her own. She seemed to have an encyclopedic knowledge of Black people: the most ethnically antiracist person in my new world. As up to date on Black American popular culture as African politics, as equipped to debate the intricacies of the rise of Beyoncé as she could the third rise of Black feminism, as comfortable explaining the origins of Haitian Creole as the conflicts between the Yoruba and Igbo of Nigeria. I always felt so ignorant around her.

I ARRIVED AT Temple as a racist, sexist homophobe. Not exactly friend material for these two women. But they saw the potential in me I did not see in myself. They created the space for me that we must create for people willing to acknowledge their attachment to racist, sexist, and homophobic ideas and policies. A forgiving space where we can bring people closer and develop mutual trust. A learning space where we can help friends and relatives unlearn their bigotry and learn feminist and antiracist ideas. A nurturing space for growth and change.

My ideas of gender and sexual orientation reflected those of my parents. They did not actively and explicitly promote distrust of queer people (just as many parents do not actively and explicitly promote distrust of people of color). They rarely talked about queer people (just as many parents rarely talk explicitly about people of color). Ideas often dance a cappella. Their silence erased queer existence as thoroughly as assimilationist ideas erased the different cultures of peoples of color.

On gender, Dad's perception of masculine strength did not derive from the perceived weakness of women. Maybe because Ma made no bones about her strength. She'd weight-lifted ever since I could remember. She carried heavy bags into the house, letting the three six-footers she lived with know that even at five foot three and 120 pounds, she was no physical slouch. Dad had always been more emotional and affectionate than Ma. Dad comforted my brother and me when we got hurt. Ma told us to suck it up, like the time I came in crying about breaking my wrist. She ordered me back outside to finish the basketball game.

Dad often joked at church about Ma being the CFO of the family. While other patriarchal men laughed, Dad was serious. She was. At other times, Dad's sexist ideas demanded he lead and Ma's sexist ideas submitted. She would call him the head of the household. He would accept the calling.

My parents did not strictly raise me to be a Black patriarch. I became a Black patriarch because my parents and the world around me did not strictly raise me to be a Black feminist. Neither my parents nor I came up in an age conducive to teaching Black feminism to a Black boy, if there ever was such an age. There seemed to be a low-level war being waged between the genders, maybe most clearly articulated in our popular culture. I was born the year of Alice Walker's *The Color Purple,* a seminal work of Black feminist art, but one that many Black male critics saw as a hit job on Black masculinity. I entered adolescence the year Black women were hitting theaters for a cathartic tour of Black male maltreatment, *Waiting to Exhale.* But the latest conflict had deeper roots, perhaps germinating in the summer of 1965, when the media got ahold of *The Negro Family: The Case for National Action,* a government report written by President Johnson's assistant secretary of labor, Daniel Patrick Moynihan.

Nearly one-fourth of Black families were headed by women, twice the rate for White families, Moynihan warned, as the media swooned about the "broken" Black family. "The Negro community has been forced into a matriarchal structure which . . . imposes a crushing burden on the Negro male," producing a "tangle of pathology," Moynihan asserted. Moynihan called for national action to employ and empower Black men, who had been emasculated by racism and matriarchal Black women. "Keeping the Negro 'in his place' can be translated as keeping the Negro male in his place: The female was not a threat to anyone," Moynihan wrote.

"The reverberations" from the Moynihan report "were disastrous," historian Deborah Gray White once wrote. Racist patriarchs, from White social scientists to Black husbands, demanded the submission of Black women to uplift the race. A command in *Ebony* magazine became popular: The "immediate goal of the Negro woman today should be the establishment of a strong family unit in which the father is the dominant person." A decade later, Black patriarchs and White social scientists were still touting the idea that Black men had it worse than Black women. Racism had "clearly" and "largely focused" on the Black male, sociologist Charles Herbert Stember argued in his 1976 book, *Sexual Racism: The Emotional Barrier to an Integrated Society*. An America of integrated (White) spaces had not been achieved because at racism's core was the "sexual rejection of the racial minority, the conscious attempt on the part of the majority to prevent interracial cohabitation," he wrote. The White man's sexual jealousy of the Black man was the key.

For too many Black men, the Black Power movement that emerged after the Moynihan report became a struggle against White men for Black power over Black women. Dad witnessed this power struggle, after being raised by a single Black mother who never called him or his brother the head of the household, like other patriarchal single moms did. One day in 1969, Dad had been singing inside a storefront church. He stepped outside for air and confronted a Black Panther assaulting his girlfriend. On another day, in the summer of 1971, Dad and a girlfriend before Ma ventured up to the Harlem Temple of the Nation of Islam. The Nation had piqued Dad's interest. They were eating with one of the ministers. Dad's girlfriend said something. The minister smacked her and smacked from his mouth, "Women are not to speak in the presence of men." Dad sprang out of his chair and had to be restrained and strong-armed out of the temple.

In spite of everything, Dad and Ma could not help but join the interracial force policing the sexuality of young Black mothers. They were two of the millions of Democrats and Republicans aghast at the growing percentage of Black children being born into single-parent households in the 1970s and 1980s—aghast even though my dad turned out just fine. The panic around the reported numbers of single-parent households was based on a host of faulty or untested premises: that two bad parents would be better than one good one, that the presence of an abusive Black father is better for the child than his absence, that having a second income for a child trumps all other factors, that all of the single parents were Black women, that none of these absent mothers or fathers were in prison or the grave, that Black mothers never hid the presence of Black fathers in their household to keep their welfare assistance for the child.

In time for the midterm elections in 1994, political scientist Charles Murray made sure Americans knew the percentage of Black children born into single-parent households "has now reached 68 percent." Murray blamed the "welfare system." My parents and other liberals blamed sexual irresponsibility, a shameful disregard for the opportunities born of 1960s activism, pathologizing poverty, and a disconnect from the premarital abstinence of Christian theology. They were all wrong on so many levels. The increasing percentage of Black babies born into single-parent households was not due to single Black mothers having more children but to married Black women having fewer children over the course of the twentieth century. Ma could see that decline in her family. Ma's married paternal grandmother had sixteen children in the 1910s and 1920s. Ma's married mother had six children in the 1940s and 1950s. My mother had two children in the early 1980s—as did two of her three married sisters.

Ma and Dad and countless Americans were disconnected from

reality and leapt to demonize this class of single mothers. Only Black feminists like Dorothy Roberts and Angela Davis defended them.

ON OTHER ISSUES, Ma sometimes put up a feminist defense. It was early August 1976, the Tuesday before the Saturday my parents were scheduled to wed. Running down the ceremony, Pastor Wilfred Quinby recited the Christian wedding vows for my parents. "Husbands, love your wives, and wives, obey your husbands."

"I'm not obeying him!" Ma interjected. "What!" Pastor Quinby said in shock, turning to look at my father. "What!" Dad said, turning to look at my mother.

"The only man I obeyed was my father, when I was a child," she nearly shouted, staring into Dad's wide eyes. "You are not my father and I'm not a child!"

The clock ticked. Would Dad whip out Bible verses on women's submission and fight for the sexist idea? Would he crawl away and look for another woman, who would submit? Dad chose a different option: the only option that could have yielded their marriage of nearly five decades. He slowly picked up his jaw, popped his eyes back in their sockets, and offered Ma an equitable solution.

"How about: Are you willing to submit one to another?" he asked.

Ma nodded. She liked the sound of "one to another," integrating the Christian concept of submission with feminist equity. My parents wrote their own wedding vows. Pastor Quinby married them as scheduled.

DAD SHOULD NOT have been shocked at Ma's resistance. For some time, Ma had been rethinking Christian sexism. After they wed, Ma attended "consciousness-raising conferences" for Christian women in Queens. What scholar Kimberly Springer calls the

"Black feminist movement" had finally burst through the sexist dams of Christian churches. Black feminists rejected the prevailing Black patriarchal idea that the primary activist role of Black women was submitting to their husbands and producing more Black babies for the "Black nation." Through groups like the Black Women's Alliance (1970) and the National Black Feminist Organization (1973), through Black women's caucuses in Black power and women's liberation groups, Black feminists fought sexism in Black spaces and racism in women's spaces. They developed their own spaces, and a Black feminist consciousness for Black women's liberation, for the liberation of humanity.

Black queer activists, too, had been marginalized after they launched the gay-liberation movement through the Stonewall rebellion in Manhattan in 1969. Braving homophobia in Black spaces and racism in queer spaces, antiracist queer people formed their own spaces. Perhaps the most antiracist queer space of the era may have also been the most antiracist feminist space of the era. In the summer of 1974, a group of Boston Black women separated from the National Black Feminist Organization to form the Combahee River Collective, named for the Combahee River slave raid of 1863 led by Harriet Tubman. They revived the unadulterated freedom politics of General Tubman. In 1977, they shared their views, in a statement drafted by Barbara Smith, Demita Frazier, and Beverly Smith. The Combahee River Collective Statement embodied queer liberation, feminism, and antiracism, like perhaps no other public statement in American history. They did not want Black women to be viewed as inferior or superior to any other group. "To be recognized as human, levelly human, is enough."

"Our politics initially sprang from the shared belief that Black women are inherently valuable," they wrote. "No other ostensibly progressive movement has ever considered our specific oppression as a priority. . . . We realize that the only people who care enough about us to work consistently for our liberation are us." Maria Stewart, America's first feminist known to give a public address to a coed audience, considered and prioritized the specific oppres-

sion of Black women in her daring speeches in the early 1830s in
Boston. So did Sojourner Truth and Frances Harper, before and
after the Civil War. So did Ida B. Wells and Anna Julia Cooper, in
the early 1900s. So did Frances Beal, who audaciously proclaimed
in 1969, "the black woman in America can justly be described as
a 'slave of a slave,'" the victim of the "double jeopardy" of racism
and sexism. This position paper joined an anthology of pieces in
1970 by women like Nikki Giovanni, Audre Lorde, and a young
prodigy in Mississippi named Alice Walker. Editor Toni Cade
Bambara, a Rutgers literary scholar, ensured *The Black Woman*
best reflected "the preoccupations of the contemporary Black
woman in this country," including setting "the record straight on
the matriarch and the evil Black bitch."

But 1991—the year Anita Hill accused U.S. Supreme Court
nominee Clarence Thomas of sexual harassment—proved to be
the pivotal year of Black feminist scholars. They constructed terminology that named the specific oppression facing Black women,
which Black feminists from Maria Stewart to Anna Julia Cooper
to Angela Davis had been identifying for more than a century.
Behind the scenes of what Thomas mind-bogglingly called a
"high-tech lynching" and Black feminists' frontline defense of
Hill, Afro-Dutch scholar Philomena Essed worked on a project
that would help define what was happening. She published her
reflections on in-depth interviews she'd conducted with Black
women in the United States and the Netherlands in *Understanding
Everyday Racism*. "In discussing the experiences of Black women,
is it sexism or is it racism?" Essed asked. "These two concepts narrowly intertwine and combine under certain conditions into one,
hybrid phenomenon. Therefore, it is useful to speak of *gendered
racism*."

· In 1991, UCLA critical race theorist Kimberlé Crenshaw further explored this notion of "intersectionality." That year, she
published "Mapping the Margins: Intersectionality, Identity Politics, and Violence Against Women of Color" in the *Stanford Law
Review*, based on her address at the Third National Conference
on Women of Color and the Law in 1990. "Feminist efforts to

politicize experiences of women and antiracist efforts to politicize experiences of people of color have frequently proceeded as though the issues and experiences they each detail occur on mutually exclusive terrains," Crenshaw theorized. "Although racism and sexism readily intersect in the lives of real people, they seldom do in feminist and antiracist practices."

Racist (and sexist) power distinguishes race-genders, racial (or gender) groups at the intersection of race and gender. Women are a gender. Black people are a race. When we identify Black women, we are identifying a race-gender. A sexist policy produces injustices or inequities between women and men. A racist policy produces injustices or inequities between racial groups. When a policy produces injustices or inequities between race-genders, it is gendered racism, or gender racism for short.

To be antiracist is to reject not only the hierarchy of races but of race-genders. To be feminist is to reject not only the hierarchy of genders but of race-genders. To truly be antiracist is to be feminist. To truly be feminist is to be antiracist. To be antiracist (and feminist) is to level the different race-genders, is to root the inequities between the equal race-genders in the policies of gender racism.

Gender racism was behind the growing number of involuntary sterilizations of Black women by eugenicist physicians— two hundred thousand cases in 1970, rising above seven hundred thousand in 1980. Gender racism produced the current situation of Black women with some collegiate education making just $29 more per week than White women with high school degrees; Black women having to earn advanced degrees before they earn more than White women with bachelor's degrees; and the median wealth of single White women being $81,200

NOTE ON MISOGYNOIR In addition to "gender racism" and "intersectionality," there is a newer and more particular term that I neglected to mention in the hardcover edition: "misogynoir," coined in 2008 by queer Black feminist Moya Bailey. She describes misogynoir as having to do with the "ways that anti-Blackness and misogyny combine to malign Black women in our world."

compared to $1,700 for single Black women. Native women and Black women experience poverty at higher rates than other race-gender groups. Among women, Black and Latinx women still earn the least, while Asian men and White men earn the most among men. Black women are three times more likely to die from pregnancy-related causes than are White women. A college-educated Black woman is three times more likely to lose her baby than a White woman with a high school degree or less. Black women remain nearly twice as likely to be incarcerated as White women.

Gender racism impacts White women and male groups of color, whether they see it or not. White women's resistance to Black feminism and intersectional theory has been self-destructive, preventing resisters from understanding their own oppression. The intersection of racist and sexist ideas, in some cases, degrades White women. For example, sexist notions of "real women" as weak and racist notions of White women as the idealized woman intersect to produce the gender racist idea that the pinnacle of womanhood is the *weak* White woman. This is the gender racist idea that probably helped lead millions of men and women to hate the strong White woman running for president in 2016, Hillary Clinton. Or to give another example, the opposite of the gender racist idea of the unvirtuous hypersexual Black woman is the virtuous *asexual* White woman, a racial construct that has constrained and controlled the White woman's sexuality as it nakedly tainted the Black woman's sexuality as un-rape-able. White men's obsession with accusing Black men of raping White women—and with lynching Black men—was as much about controlling the sexuality of White women as it was about controlling the sexuality of Black men. Racist White patriarchs were re-creating the enslavement era all over again, making it illicit for White women to cohabitate with Black men at the same time as racist White (and Black) men were raping Black women. And the enslavement era remains, amid the hollow cries of race pride drowning out the cries of the sexually assaulted. Gender racist ideas underlie the thinking that when one defends White male abusers like Trump and Brett Kavanaugh one is defending White people; when one defends Black male abusers like Bill Cosby and R. Kelly one is defending Black people.

Male resistance to Black feminism and intersectional theory has been similarly self-destructive, preventing resisters from understanding our specific oppression. The intersection of racist and sexist ideas, in some cases, degrades men of color. Black men reinforce oppressive tropes by reinforcing certain sexist ideas. For example, sexist notions of "real men" as strong and racist notions of Black men as not really men intersect to produce the gender racist idea of the weak Black man, inferior to the pinnacle of manhood, the strong White man.

Sexist notions of men as more naturally dangerous than women (since women are considered naturally fragile, in need of protection) and racist notions of Black people as more dangerous than White people intersect to produce the gender racist idea of the hyperdangerous Black man, more dangerous than the White man, the Black woman, and (the pinnacle of innocence) the White woman. No defense is stronger than the tears of White womanhood, whether innocent or guilty. No prosecution is stronger than the case for inherently guilty Black manhood. These gender racist ideas transform every innocent Black male into a criminal and every White female who harms people into Casey Anthony, the White woman a Florida jury exonerated in 2011, against all evidence, for killing her three-year-old child. White women get away with murder and Black men spend years in prisons for wrongful convictions. After the imprisonment rate of Black men dropped 45 percent between 2000 and 2020, Black men were still approximately six times more likely than White men, twenty-nine times more likely than Black women, and fifty times more likely than White women to be incarcerated. Black men raised in the top 1 percent by millionaires are as likely to be incarcerated as White men raised in households earning $36,000.

. . .

"CONTEMPORARY FEMINIST AND antiracist discourses have failed to consider intersectional identities such as women of color," Kimberlé Crenshaw wrote in 1991. All racial groups are a collection of intersectional identities differentiated by gender, sexuality, class, (dis)ability, ethnicity, skin color, nationality, and culture, among a series of other identifiers. Black women first recognized their own intersectional identity. Black feminists first theorized the intersection of two forms of oppression: sexism and racism. Intersectional theory now gives all of humanity the ability to understand the intersectional oppression of their identities, from impoverished Latinx people to Black men to White women to Native lesbians to transgender Asian people. A theory from and for Black women is a theory for humanity. No wonder Black feminists have been saying from the beginning that when human beings become serious about the freedom of Black women, human beings become serious about the freedom of humanity.

Intersectional Black identities are subjected to what Crenshaw described as the intersection of racism and other forms of bigotry, such as ethnocentrism, colorism, sexism, homophobia, classism, ableism, and transphobia. My journey to being an antiracist first recognized the intersectionality of my ethnic racist ideas, and then my bodily racist ideas, and then my cultural racist ideas, and then my colorist ideas, and then my class racist ideas, and, when I entered graduate school, my gender racist and queer racist ideas.

CHAPTER 15

SEXUALITY

QUEER RACIST IDEA: Any notion that suggests that one race-sexuality is superior or inferior to another race-sexuality in any way, or justifies policies that lead to injustice or inequity between race-sexualities.

QUEER ANTIRACIST IDEA: Any notion that suggests that race-sexualities are equals, or substantiates policies that lead to justice and equity between race-sexualities.

RACIST (AND HOMOPHOBIC) power distinguishes race-sexualities, racial (or sexuality) groups at the intersection of race and sexual orientation. Gay and lesbian people are a sexuality. Latinx people are a race. Latinx gay and lesbian people are a race-sexuality. A homophobic policy produces inequities between heterosexual people and gay and lesbian people. A racist policy produces inequities between racial groups. Queer racism produces and justifies inequities between race-sexualities. Queer racist policies produce a situation where 32 percent of children being raised by Black male same-sex couples live in poverty, compared to 14 percent of children being raised by White male same-sex couples, 13 percent of children raised by Black heterosexuals, and 7 percent of children raised by White heterosexuals. For children being raised by female same-sex couples who live in poverty, the racial disparity is nearly as wide. Black children are four times as likely as White children to be in foster care, and children of Black queer parents are at even greater risk: Black mothers who identify as lesbian or bisexual are about four times more likely than their peers who identify as heterosexual to lose custody of their children to the state. These children of Black queer couples are more likely to live in poverty because their parents are more likely than Black heterosexual and White queer couples to be impoverished.

Homophobia cannot be separated from racism. They've intersected for ages. British physician Havelock Ellis is known for popularizing the term "homosexual." In his first medical treatise on homosexuality, *Sexual Inversion* (1897), he wrote about "the question of sex—with the racial questions that rest on it." He regarded homosexuality as a congenital physiological abnormality, just as he regarded criminality at the time. Ellis adored the father of criminology, Italian physician Cesare Lombroso, who claimed criminals are born, not bred, and that people of color are by nature criminals. In 1890, Ellis published a popular summary of Lombroso's writings.

Ellis spent many years defending against the criminalization of White homosexuality. Following racist scholars, Ellis used comparative anatomy of women's bodies to evidence the biological differences between the sexualities. "As regards the sexual organs it seems possible," Ellis wrote, "to speak more definitively of inverted women than of inverted men." At the time, racist physicians were contrasting the "bound together" clitoris of "Aryan American women" that "goes with higher civilization" and the "free" clitoris "in negresses" that goes with "highly domesticated animals." Homophobic physicians were supposing that "inverted" lesbians "will in practically every instance disclose an abnormally prominent clitoris," wrote New York City prison doctor Perry M. Lichtenstein. Racist ideas suggesting Black people are more hypersexual than White people and homophobic ideas suggesting queer people are more hypersexual than heterosexuals intersect to produce the queer racism of the most hypersexual race-sexuality, the Black queer. Their imagined biological stamp: the abnormally prominent clitoris, which "is particularly so in colored women," Lichtenstein added.

. . . .

WECKEA WAS MY best friend at Temple. We were both brown-skinned with locs and hailed from prideful HBCUs. I usually befriended laid-back and calm people like him. He usually befriended daring and silly people like me. Weckea was as inquisitive a person as I had ever met. He wanted to know everything and damn near did. The only thing he seemed to love as much as a good idea was a good laugh. He was a few years older than me, and it did not take long for me to look up to him intellectually, in the way I looked up to Kaila and Yaba.

We arrived at Temple in the same cohort—Weckea, myself, and another student, Raena. We banded together.

On a rare day when Raena and I ate lunch together without Weckea, the two of us sat outside, near campus, probably delighting in the warm arrival of spring, probably in 2006. We both had food before us. First gossip and small talk and then, out of nowhere: "You know Weckea is gay, right." She barely looked up at me as she said it. Her eyes focused as she gobbled food.

"No, I didn't know that," I said, my voice breaking.

"Well, it's not a big deal he didn't tell you, right?"

"Right." I looked away. Cars honked. People strolled by. An ambulance was coming. For me?

I glanced back at Raena, her chin tucked, eating. Wondering why she'd told me this. I did not see a friendly face of concern as I twitched in my chair. I saw a blankness, if not a face of satisfaction. Was she trying to break up my friendship with Weckea?

Neither of us had much to say after that. Mission accomplished on her part. Weckea's homosexuality made sense, as I thought about it. He had never spoken about dating a woman. When I asked, he deflected. I'd chalked it up to his extreme privacy. He would describe women as pretty or not so pretty but never in a sexual manner, which I chalked up to his conservatism. He was not so conservative after all.

I thought about Black gay men running around having unprotected sex all the time. But Weckea did not seem sex-crazed or reckless. I thought about this hypersexuality and recklessness causing so many Black gay men to contract HIV. I thought wrong. Black gay men are less likely to have condomless sex than White gay men. They are less likely to use drugs like poppers or crystal methamphetamine during sex, which heighten the risk of HIV infections.

I had been around gay Black men before, in FACES, a modeling troupe I'd joined at FAMU. But the gay Black men in the troupe (or, better yet, the ones I thought were gay) had what I thought of as a feminine streak to them: the way they moved, their makeup, the way they struggled to dap me up. I suspected they were gay. Everything about my modeling troupe pinged the homophobia of my friends. My modeling ended up being the only thing my friends joked on more than my orange eyes. But they thought my orange eyes were "gay," too.

I assumed Black gay men performed femininity. I did not know that some gay men, like Weckea, perform masculinity and actually prefer gay men who perform femininity for partners. I did not know (and feminists like Kaila and Yaba were teaching me) about gender being an authentic performance; that the ways women and men traditionally act are not tied to their biology; that men can authentically perform femininity as effectively as women can authentically perform masculinity. Authentically, meaning they are not acting, as the homophobic and even transphobic idea assumes. They are being who they are, like trans men and women are being who they are. I learned this, once and for all, through another close friend at Temple, a butch Black lesbian from Texas. I talked about women with Monica in the way I

NOTE ON "GAYDAR" I deleted "gaydar," a homophobic term that emerged in the 1980s. The concept, of course, relies entirely on (and perpetuates) stereotypes about queer people. Additionally, researchers have found that supposed gaydar is wildly inaccurate. In a chapter where I challenge homophobic ideas, I used terms that carry homophobic ideas. Our intentions, even if we mean well, hardly matter. What matters is what we do. And I must do better.

could not with Weckea. We were drawn to the same women. When we got to joking and relating our romantic experiences, my conversations with Monica did not sound too different from my conversations with my heterosexual male friends at FAMU.

MY MIND TURNED to introspection. Why had Weckea not told me? Why didn't he feel comfortable sharing his sexuality with me? Maybe he sensed my homophobia—in fact, he probably heard it in my rhetoric. He listened intently. He seemed to never forget anything.

Weckea was adept at identifying homophobia and taking the necessary precautions. He must have been protecting himself—and our early friendship—from my homophobia. Now I had a choice: my homophobia or my best friend. I could not have both for long. I chose Weckea and the beginning of our friendship. I chose the beginning of the rest of my lifelong striving against the homophobia of my upbringing, a lifelong striving to be a queer antiracist.

To be a queer antiracist is to equate all the race-sexualities, to strive to eliminate the inequities between the race-sexualities. We cannot be antiracist if we are homophobic or transphobic. We must continue to "affirm that all Black lives matter," as the co-founder of Black Lives Matter, Opal Tometi, once said. Queer people. Straight people. Asexual people. Transgender people. Intersex people. Nonbinary people. Cisgender people. All Black lives include those of impoverished transgender Black women, perhaps the most violated and oppressed of all the Black intersectional groups. The average life expectancy of a transgender woman of color in the Americas is between thirty and thirty-five years. The racial violence they face, the transphobia these women face as they seek to live freely, is unfathomable. I started learning about their freedom fight from the personal stories of transgender activist Janet Mock. But I opened up to their fight on that day I opened to saving my friendship with Weckea.

I am a cisgender Black heterosexual male—"cisgender" mean-

ing my gender identity corresponds to my birth sex, in contrast
to transgender people, whose gender identity does not corre-
spond to their birth sex. To be queer antiracist is to understand
the privileges of my cisgender, of my masculinity, of my hetero-
sexuality, of their intersections. To be queer antiracist is to serve
as an ally to transgender people, to intersex people, to women, to
gender-nonconforming people, to gay people and lesbian people,
to bisexual people, to asexual people, to their intersections, meaning listening, learning, and being led by their equalizing ideas, by
their equalizing policy campaigns, by their power struggle for
equal opportunity and resources. To be queer antiracist is to see
that policies protecting Black transgender women are as critically
important as policies protecting the political ascendancy of queer
White males. To be queer antiracist is to see the new wave of
voter-ID laws, book bans, "Don't Say Gay" bills, and legislation
criminalizing trans children and their supportive parents in Republican states as taking away the rights of our people. To be
queer antiracist is to see homophobia, transphobia, racism, and
queer racism—not the queer person, not the queer space—as the
problem, as abnormal, as unnatural.

THEY SEEMED TO always be there—Yaba and Kaila—sitting
around one of those tables near the entrance of Gladfelter Hall,
sometimes with fellow doctoral students Danielle and Sekhmet. I
usually caught them on a smoke break or lunch break or dinner
break from working together in Gladfelter's computer lab. They
were finishing their doctorates in African American studies, near-
ing the end of a journey I was beginning at Temple.

Whenever Kaila and Yaba were seated there—whenever they
were anywhere—their presence was unmistakable, memorable
and unsettling and inspiring. I could go to war with them at my
side. I learned from them that I am not a defender of Black people if I am not sharply defending Black women, if I am not sharply
defending queer Black people. The two of them exerted their

influence on our department's events. When our department brought in speakers for a public event, they came. When graduate students shared their research at an event, they came. When there was an out-of-town Black studies conference, they came. When they came, let's just say they ensured that when patriarchal ideas arose, when homophobic ideas were put out there, when racist ideas came and intersected, they would come for those ideas like piranhas coming for their daily meal. I watched, stunned, in awe of their intellectual attacks. I call them attacks, but in truth they were defenses, defending Black womanhood and the humanity of queer Black people. They were respectful and measured if the victimizer was respectful and measured with them. But I call them attacks because I felt personally attacked. They were attacking my gender racist ideas about Black women, my queer racist ideas about queer Black people, my gender and queer racist ideas about queer Black women.

I did not want to ever be their prey.

I binge-read every author they mentioned in their public exchanges and in their private exchanges with me. I gobbled up Audre Lorde, E. Patrick Johnson, bell hooks, Joan Morgan, Dwight McBride, Patricia Hill Collins, and Kimberlé Crenshaw like my life depended on it. My life *did* depend on it. I wanted to overcome my gender racist ideas, my queer racist ideas. But I had to be willing to do for Black women and queer Black people what I had been doing for Black men and Black cisgender heterosexuals, which meant first of all learning more—and then defending them like my heroes had.

They were the darkness that scared me. I wanted to run away whenever I came off the elevator, turned the corner, and spotted Yaba and Kaila, whenever I approached the building and they were there. They warmly tossed smiles and greetings as I walked by not fast enough, forcing me to awkwardly toss them back. Sometimes they stopped me in small talk. Over time, they let me join them in long talk, unnerving me the most. It is best to challenge ourselves by dragging ourselves before people who intimidate us with their brilliance and constructive criticism. I didn't think about that. I wanted to run away. They did not let me run away, and I am grateful now because of it.

These women were everything they were not supposed to be, in my patriarchal and homophobic mind, which thought: Queer people are run by sex, not ideas. Queer people are abnormal. Feminists hate men. Feminists want female supremacy. But these Black feminists obviously liked me, a male. They were as ideological as they were sexual as they were normal. They did not speak of women ruling men. They spoke of gender and queer equity and freedom and mutuality and complementarity and power. Their jokes and attacks knew no gender or sexuality. If anything, they were harder on women. They were harder on queer people like Raena. They saw through her long before Weckea and I did.

No one seemed to incite them more than patriarchal women—really, racist patriarchal White women standing behind racist patriarchal White men. I can only imagine what they thought years later, watching Supreme Court Justice Amy Coney Barrett vote to overturn *Roe v. Wade,* or seeing the majority of White women voters persistently support Donald Trump when he was accused of sexual harassment or assault by at least eighteen women, or watching Kayla Moore defend her husband, Alabama's U.S. Senate candidate Roy Moore, who had been accused of pedophilia and sexual assaults. Moore was asked on the campaign trail in 2017 when America was last great. "I think it was great at the time when families were united—even though we had slavery," he said. "Our families were strong, our country had direction." This was long before we had so many women publicly attacking the women saying #MeToo. Patriarchal women, as a term, made no sense to me back then, like the term "homophobic homosexuals." In my mind, only men could be patriarchal, could be sexist. Only cisgender people could be transphobic. Only heterosexuals could be homophobic. The radical Black queer feminist ideas of those two women detached homophobic from heterosexual, detached transphobic from cisgender, detached sexist from men and feminist from women, in the way I later detached racist from White people and antiracist from Black people. They had a problem with homophobia, not with heterosexuals. They had a problem with patriarchy, not with men. Crucially, their going after all homophobes, no matter their sexual identity, showed me that homophobic ideas and policies and power were their fundamental problem. Crucially, their going after all patriarchs, no matter their gender identity, showed me that patriarchal ideas and policies and powers were their fundamental problem. They talked of queer people defending homophobia as powerfully as they talked about heterosexuals building a world for queer love. They talked of women defending sexism as powerfully as men helping to build a feminist world. Maybe they had me in mind. Because they opened that feminist world to me where queer love is wedded to heterosexual love, in harmony. But this world scared me like they scared me. Opened by them, I learned, though—and eventually I wanted to help them create that new world.

I am forever grateful that the Black graduate-student discourse was ruled by queer Black feminists instead of by patriarchal Black male homophobes. They were my first Black feminist role models. They met my homophobic patriarchy and forced me to meet him, too. They forced me to check his ass, as desperate as I was to stay out of the way of their attacks, a desperation that transformed into a curiosity about Black feminism and queer theory itself, a curiosity that transformed into a desire to be a gender antiracist, to be a queer antiracist, to not fail Black people—all Black people.

FAILURE

ACTIVIST: One who has a record of power or policy change.

HE TEMPLE UNIVERSITY classroom started filling. Bodies hugging. Smiles and small talk and catching up. It all annoyed me as I sat, stood, and then sat again at the professor's desk, hoping to begin our Black Student Union (BSU) meeting on time. It was early September 2007. We were laughing and chatting in Philadelphia, but that day, in Louisiana, six teenage lives hung in the balance. We had devised a campaign to help free them. I was prepared to present it in order to secure organizers to execute it. I hardly suspected I was bound to fail.

To understand why racism lives is to understand not only its power but the history of antiracist failure—why people have failed to create antiracist societies. To understand the racial history of failure is to understand failed solutions and strategies. To understand failed solutions and strategies is to understand their cradles: failed racial ideologies.

Incorrect conceptions of race as a social construct (as opposed to a power construct), of racial history as a singular march of racial progress (as opposed to a duel of antiracist and racist progress), of racism as rooted in ignorance and hate (as opposed to powerful self-interest)—all come together to produce solutions bound to fail. Terms and sayings like "I'm not racist" and "race neutral" and "post-racial" and "color-blind" and "only one race, the human race" and "only racists speak about race" and "racism is prejudice plus power" and "Black people can't be racist" and "White people are evil" are bound to fail in identifying and eliminating racist power and policy. Stratagems flouting intersectionality are bound to fail the most degraded racial groups. Civilizing programs will fail since all racial groups are already on the same cultural level. Behavioral-enrichment programs, like mentoring and educational programs, can help individuals but are bound to fail racial groups, which are held back by bad policies, not bad behavior. Healing symptoms instead of changing policies is bound to fail in healing society. Challenging the conjoined twins separately is bound to fail to address economic-racial inequity. Assimilationist integration is bound to fail people of color. All of these ideas are bound to fail as they have consistently failed in the past. But for some reason, their failure doesn't seem to matter: They remain the most popular conceptions and strategies and solutions to combat racism, because they stem from the most popular racial ideologies.

These repetitive failures exact a toll. Racial history does not repeat harmlessly. Instead, its devastation multiplies when generation after generation repeats the same failed strategies and solutions and ideologies, rather than burying past failures in the caskets of past generations.

EARLY WHITE ABOLITIONISTS met regularly at a national convention, thinking the antislavery solution rested in continuing "our parental care" over free Black people, as they stated in 1805. White abolitionists lorded over Black behavior as if on good Black "conduct must, in some measure, depend the liberation of their brethren," as their convention stated in 1804.

The White judge birthed the Black judge. "The further decrease of prejudice, and the amelioration of the condition of

thousands of our brethren who are yet in bondage, greatly depend on our conduct," Samuel Cornish and John Brown Russ-
wurm wrote on March 16, 1827, in one of the opening editorials
of *Freedom's Journal*, the first African American newspaper.

I grew up on this same failed strategy more than one hundred
fifty years later. Generations of Black bodies have been raised by
the judges of "uplift suasion." The judges strap the entire Black
race on the Black body's back, shove the burdened Black body
into White spaces, order the burdened Black body to always act
in an upstanding manner to persuade away White racism, and
punish poor Black conduct with sentences of shame for reinforcing racism, for bringing the race down. I felt the burden my
whole Black life to be perfect before both White people and the
Black people judging whether I am representing the race well.
The judges never let me just be, be myself, be my imperfect self.

IT FELT COOL outside, sometime in the autumn of 2011. Sadiqa
and I had been dating for months. I looked at this Spelman sister
and Georgia peach as a future wife: smitten by her affability as
much as her elegance, by her perceptiveness as much as her easygoing sense of humor; smitten by her love of Black people as
much as her love of healing kids as a pediatrician. She, too, had
been raised in a middle-income Black home by similarly aged
parents who cut their teeth in the movement, who brushed her
teeth in the movement. She, too, had been taught that her climb
up the success ladder uplifted the race. She, too, tried to represent
the race well.

We dined near the window at Buddakan, an Asian fusion restaurant in Old City, Philadelphia. On the opposite wall, a massive
gold statue of Buddha sat on a tiny stage at almost table level,
against a red background that faded into a black center. Eyes
closed. Hands clasped. At peace. Not bothering anyone. Certainly not Sadiqa. But the statue attracted a middle-aged, brown-
haired White guy. Clearly drunk, he climbed onto the tiny stage
and started fondling Buddha before his laughing audience of

drunk friends at a nearby table. I had learned a long time ago to tune out the antics of drunk White people doing things that could get a Black person arrested. Harmless White fun is Black lawlessness.

His loud laughs summoned Sadiqa's look. "Oh, my God!" she said quietly. "What is this guy doing?"

She turned back to her plate, took a bite, and looked up as she swallowed. "At least he's not Black."

I was taken aback but immediately recognized myself—my own thoughts—in Sadiqa's face.

"How would you feel if he was Black?" I asked her, and myself.

"I'd be really embarrassed," she said, speaking for me and for so many of us trapped on the plantation of uplift suasion. "Because we don't need anyone making us look bad."

"In front of White people?" I asked her.

"Yes. It makes them look down on us. Makes them more racist."

We thought on a false continuum, from more racist to less racist to not racist. We believed good Black behavior made White people "less racist," even when our experiences told us it usually did not. But that night, we thought about it together and shared a few critiques of uplift suasion for the first time.

Today, the few critiques would be many. We would critique paternalistic White abolitionists conjuring up uplift suasion. We'd argue against the assumption that poor Black conduct is responsible for White racist ideas, meaning White racist ideas about poor Black conduct are valid. We'd critique the White judge exonerating White people from the responsibility to rid themselves of their own racist ideas; upwardly mobile Black people deflecting responsibility for changing racist policy by imagining they are uplifting the race by uplifting themselves; the near impossibility of perfectly executing uplift suasion, since Black people are humanly imperfect. We'd notice that when racist White people see Black people conducting themselves admirably in public, they see those Black people as extraordinary, meaning not like those ordinarily inferior Black people. We'd remember what history teaches us: that when racist policy knocks Black people down, the judge orders them to uplift themselves, only to be cut down again by racist terror.

Sadiqa and I left the restaurant, but we continued to talk about the uplift-suasion ideology that had been so deeply ingrained in us—to critique it, critique ourselves, and run away from it, toward freedom. All these years later, although the judges can catch us at any moment, I admire Sadiqa's freedom to be Sadiqa. I feel free to move in my imperfections. I represent only myself. If the judges draw conclusions about millions of Black people based on how I act, then they, not I, not Black people, have a problem. They are responsible for their racist ideas; I am not. I am responsible for my racist ideas; they are not. To be antiracist is to let me be me, be myself, be my imperfect self.

ABOLITIONIST WILLIAM LLOYD Garrison did not let Black people be their imperfect selves. "Have you not acquired the esteem, confidence and patronage of the whites, in proportion to your increase in knowledge and moral improvement?" Garrison asked a Black crowd not long after founding *The Liberator* in 1831. Uplift suasion fit his ideology that the best way to "accomplish the great work of national redemption" from slavery was "through the agency of moral power" and truth and reason. Garrison's belief in "moral suasion" and what we can call "educational suasion" also fit his personal upbringing by a pious Baptist mother, his professional upbringing by an editor who believed newspapers are for "instruction," his abolitionist upbringing by moral crusader Benjamin Lundy.

Moral and educational and uplift suasion failed miserably in stopping the astounding growth of slavery in the age of King Cotton before the Civil War. But success, apparently, does not matter when a strategy stems from an ideology. Moral and educational suasion focus on persuading White people, on appealing to their moral conscience through horror and their logical mind through education. But what if racist ideas make people illogical? What if persuading everyday White people is not persuading racist policymakers? What if racist policymakers know about the harmful outcomes of their policies? What if racist policymakers have neither morals nor conscience, let alone moral conscience, to paraphrase Malcolm X? What if no group in history has gained their freedom through appealing to the moral conscience of their oppressors, to paraphrase Assata Shakur? What if economic, political, or cultural self-interest drives racist policymakers, not hateful immorality, not ignorance?

"If I could save the Union without freeing any slave I would do it, and if I could save it by freeing all the slaves I would do that," President Abraham Lincoln wrote on August 20, 1862. "What I do about slavery, and the colored race, I do because I believe it helps to save the Union." On January 1, 1863, Lincoln signed the Emancipation Proclamation as a "necessary war measure." After winning the Civil War, racist Republicans (to distinguish from the less numerous antiracist Republicans) voted to establish the Freedmen's Bureau, reconstruct the South, and extend civil rights and voting privileges to create a loyal Southern Republican base and secure Black people in the South far away from White Northerners, who "want nothing to do with the negroes," as Illinois senator Lyman Trumbull, one of the laws' main sponsors, said.

The "White man's party," as Trumbull identified the Republican Party, grew tired of alienating their racist constituents by militarily defending the Negro from the racist terrorists who knocked Republicans out of Southern power by 1877. Republicans left Black Southerners behind, turning their backs on the outrages of Jim Crow for nearly a century. "Expediency on selfish grounds, and not right with reference to the claims of our common humanity, has controlled our action," Garrison sorrowfully said in an address for the centennial of Independence Day, in 1876.

· · ·

ON JUNE 26, 1934, W.E.B. Du Bois critically assessed the success of educational suasion, as Garrison had critically assessed moral suasion before him: "For many years it was the theory of most Negro leaders . . . that white America did not know of or realize the continuing plight of the Negro." Du Bois later spoke for himself, believing "the ultimate evil was stupidity" early in his career. "Accordingly, for the last two decades, we have striven by book and periodical, by speech and appeal, by various dramatic methods of agitation, to put the essential facts before the American people. Today there can be no doubt that Americans know the facts; and yet they remain for the most part indifferent and unmoved."

Gunnar Myrdal ignored Du Bois's 1934 call for Black people to focus on accruing power instead of persuading White people. The racism problem lay in the "astonishing ignorance" of White Americans, Myrdal advised in *An American Dilemma* in 1944. "There is no doubt, in the writer's opinion, that a great majority of white people in America would be prepared to give the Negro a substantially better deal if they knew the facts."

Popular history tells us that a great majority of White Americans did give the Negro a better deal—the desegregation rulings, Civil Rights Act (1964), and Voting Rights Act (1965)—when they learned the facts. "Gunnar Myrdal had been astonishingly prophetic," according to one captivating history of the civil rights movement. Not entirely. As early as 1946, top State Department official Dean Acheson warned the Truman administration that the "existence of discrimination against minority groups in this country has an adverse effect on our relations" with decolonizing Asian and African and Latin American nations. The Truman administration repeatedly briefed the U.S. Supreme Court on these adverse effects during desegregation cases in the late 1940s and early 1950s, as historian Mary L. Dudziak documents. Not to mention the racist abuse and segregated businesses African diplomats faced in the United States. In 1963, Secretary of State Dean Rusk warned Congress during the consideration of the Civil Rights Act that "in waging this world

struggle we are seriously handicapped by racial or religious discrimination." Seventy-eight percent of White Americans agreed
in a Harris Poll.

Racist power started civil rights legislation out of self-interest.
Racist power stopped out of self-interest when enough African
and Asian and Latin nations were inside the American sphere
of influence, when a rebranded Jim Crow no longer adversely
affected American foreign policy, when Black people started
demanding and gaining what power rarely gives up: power. In
1967, Martin Luther King Jr. admitted, "We've had it wrong and
mixed up in our country, and this has led Negro Americans in
the past to seek their goals through love and moral suasion de-
void of power." But our generation ignores King's words about
the "problem of power, a confrontation between the forces of
power demanding change and the forces of power dedicated to
the preserving of the status quo." The same way King's generation
ignored Du Bois's matured warning. The same way Du Bois's
generation ignored Garrison's matured warnings. The problem
of race has always been at its core the problem of power, not the
problem of immorality or ignorance.

Moral and educational suasion breathes the assumption that
racist minds must be changed before racist policy, ignoring history that says otherwise. Look at the soaring White support for
desegregated schools and neighborhoods decades *after* the policies
changed in the 1950s and 1960s. Look at the soaring White support for interracial marriage decades *after* the policy changed in
1967. Look at the soaring support for Obamacare *after* its passage
in 2010. Racist policymakers drum up fear of antiracist policies
through racist ideas, knowing if the policies are implemented, the
fears they circulate will not come to pass. Once the fears do not
come to pass, people will let down their guards as they enjoy the
benefits. Once they clearly benefit, most Americans will support
and become the defenders of the antiracist policies they once
feared.

To fight for mental and moral changes *after* policy is changed
means fighting alongside growing benefits and the dissipation of

fears, making it possible for antiracist power to succeed. To fight for mental and moral change as a *prerequisite* for policy change is to fight against growing fears and apathy, making it almost impossible for antiracist power to succeed.

The original problem of racism has not been solved by suasion. Knowledge is only power if knowledge is put to the struggle for power. Changing minds is not a movement. Critiquing racism is not activism. Changing minds is not activism. An activist produces power and policy change. If a person has no record of power or policy change, then that person is not an activist.

AS I WAITED to begin the BSU meeting, I wanted to be an activist. I wanted to flee academia. I wanted to free the Jena 6.

On September 1, 2006, the day after Black students had hung out under the "White tree" at Jena High School, White students hung nooses from its branches. The school's superintendent only suspended the White perpetrators for the "prank," which did nothing to curb the subsequent violence against Black students in the small town of Jena, Louisiana. But days after Black students beat up a White student on December 4, 2006, the Jena 6 were arrested. Jesse Ray Beard, Robert Bailey Jr., Mychal Bell, Carwin Jones, Bryant Purvis, and Theo Shaw were charged with attempted murder and conspiracy to commit murder. "When you are convicted, I will seek the maximum penalty allowed by law," promised district attorney Reed Walters, meaning up to one hundred years in prison.

As I sat at the teacher's desk, I felt Mychal Bell's sentencing hearing on September 20 approaching like the butcher's cleaver. An all-White jury had already found him guilty of a lesser charge, aggravated second-degree battery, lining up his life to be cut by as much as twenty-two years.

A somber energy settled inside the classroom, like the darkness outside. Our goal, BSU officers told each other, was to free the Jena 6. But were we willing to do anything? Were we willing to risk our freedom for their freedom? Not if our primary purpose was making ourselves feel better. We formulate and populate and donate to cultural and behavioral and educational enrichment programs to make ourselves feel better, feeling they are helping racial groups, when they are only helping (or hurting) individuals, when only policy change helps groups.

We arrive at demonstrations excited, as if our favorite musician is playing on the speakers' stage. We convince ourselves we are doing something to solve the problem of racism, when we are really doing something to satisfy our feelings. We go home fulfilled, like we dined at our favorite restaurant. And this fulfillment is fleeting. The problems of inequity and injustice persist. They persistently make us feel bad and guilty. We persistently do something to make ourselves feel better as we convince ourselves we are making society better, as we never make society better.

What if instead of a feelings advocacy we had an outcome advocacy that put equitable outcomes before our guilt and anguish? What if we focused our human and fiscal resources on changing power and policy to actually make society, not just our feelings, better?

I COULD WAIT no longer. I cut off the talking and smiling and began presenting the 106 Campaign to Free the Jena 6. I began with phase one: Mobilize at least 106 students on 106 campuses in the mid-Atlantic to rally locally by the end of September and fundraise for the Jena 6 legal defense fund. I presented phase two: Marshal those 106 students from 106 campuses into car caravans that would converge on Washington, D.C., on October 5, 2007.

I painted the picture. "Wonderfully long lines of dozens of cars packed with students on highways and byways driving toward the nation's capital from all directions, from Pennsylvania, Delaware, Maryland, Virginia, West Virginia, and North Carolina." I stared but did not look into the eyes of my audience. I looked at the beautiful picture forming from my lips. "Thousands of cars with signs in the window—'Free the Jena Six'—honking to drivers passing by, who'd honk loudly back in solidarity (or revulsion)."

"Can you see it?" I asked excitedly a few times.

They could see it. For some, the ugly picture.

"Isn't that illegal, the car caravans?" one woman asked, obviously scared.

"What? No! People take car caravans all the time," I replied.

I spoke on, painting the beautiful, ugly picture. "When the car caravans arrived in D.C., they would park their cars in the middle of Constitution Avenue and join the informal march to the Department of Justice. Thousands of cars would be sitting-in on Constitution Avenue and surrounding streets as we presented our six demands of freedom to the Bush administration. When they came with the tow trucks, we would be ready to flatten truck tires. When police units started protecting the tow trucks, we would come with reinforcements of cars. When they blocked off Constitution Avenue, we would strike another street with our cars. When and if they barricaded all the downtown streets, we would wait them out and ride back into downtown Washington whenever they lifted the barricades. We would refuse to stop the sit-in of cars until the Bush administration leaned on the Louisiana governor to lean on Jena officials to drop the charges against the Jena Six."

"This is illegal. They will throw us in prison," someone rebutted with a look of fear.

I should have stopped but I continued my failure, hardly caring that the more I spoke, the more fear I spread—the more fear I spread, the more I alienated people from the 106 Campaign.

"Damn right we could go to prison!" I shot back, feeling like myself. "But I don't care! We're already in prison. That's what America means: prison."

I used the Malcolm X line out of context. But who cared about context when the shock and awe sounded so radical to my self-identified radical ears? When I lashed out at well-meaning people who showed the normal impulse of fear, who used the incorrect terminology, who asked the incorrect question—oh, did I think I was so radical. When my scorched-earth words sent attendees fleeing at rallies and meetings, when my scorched-earth writings sent readers fleeing, oh, did I think I was so radical. When in fact, if all my words were doing was sounding radical, then those words were not radical at all. What if we measure the radicalism of speech by how radically it transforms open-minded people, by how the speech liberates the power within? What if we measure the conservatism of speech by how intensely it keeps people the same, keeps people enslaved by their ideas and fears, conserving their inequitable society? At a time when I thought I was the most radical, I was the most conservative. I was a failure. I failed to address the fears of my BSU peers.

Then again, fear is kind of like race—a mirage. "Fear is not real. It is a product of our imagination," as a Will Smith character tells his son in one of my favorite movies, *After Earth*. "Do not misunderstand me, danger is very real, but fear is a choice."

We do not have to be fearless like Harriet Tubman to be anti-racist. We have to be courageous to be antiracist. Courage is the strength to do what is right in the face of fear, as the anonymous philosopher tells us. I gain insight into what's right from antiracist ideas. I gain strength from fear. While many people are fearful of what could happen if they resist, I am fearful of what could happen if I don't resist. I am fearful of cowardice. Cowardice is the inability to amass the strength to do what is right in the face of fear. And racist power has been terrorizing cowardice into us for generations.

For segregationists like U.S. senator Ben "Pitchfork" Tillman, President Theodore Roosevelt crossed the color line when he dined with Booker T. Washington on October 16, 1901. "The action of President Roosevelt in entertaining that nigger will necessitate our killing a thousand niggers in the South before they will learn their place again." He was not joking.

On July 8, 1876, a young Tillman had joined the power-hungry White mob that murdered at least seven Black militiamen defending Black power in the Black town of Hamburg, South Carolina. All election year long, Tillman's Red Shirts had helped White supremacists violently snatch control of South Carolina. Tillman wore his involvement in the Hamburg Massacre as a badge of honor when he trooped on lynched heads into South Carolina's governorship in 1890 and the U.S. Senate in 1895. "The purpose of our visit to Hamburg was to strike terror," Tillman said at the Red Shirts reunion in 1909. As racist ideas intend to make us ignorant and hateful, racist terror intends to make us fear.

I WALKED OUT of that classroom building alone. I walked to the train station on the edge of campus, deciding on the long escalator down into the subway station that the BSU officers who voted down the 106 Campaign must be ignorant about racism, kind of like the White people supporting the Jena 6's incarceration. Deciding on the screeching train ride up to North Philadelphia that the ultimate evil was ignorance and the ultimate good was education. Deciding as I lay flat on my couch and looked up at the ceiling mirror that a life of educational suasion would be more impactful than any other life I could choose.

I ran back down the lit path of educational suasion on the very night I failed to persuade my BSU peers. I failed at changing minds (let alone policy). But in all my enlightenment, I did not see myself as the failure. I saw my BSU peers as the failure. I did not look in the mirror at my failure doctrine, the doctrine of failing to make change and deflecting fault.

When we fail to open the closed-minded consumers of racist ideas, we blame their closed-mindedness instead of our foolish decision to waste time reviving closed minds from the dead. When our vicious attacks on open-minded consumers of racist ideas fail to transform them, we blame their hate rather than our impatient and alienating hate of them. When people fail to consume our convoluted antiracist ideas, we blame their ignorance rather than our ignorant lack of clarity. When we transform people and do not show them an avenue of support, we blame their lack of commitment rather than our lack of guidance. When the politician we supported does not change racist policy, we blame the intractability of racism rather than our support of the wrong politician. When we fail to gain support for a protest, we blame the fearful rather than our alienating presentation. When the protest fails, we blame racist power rather than our flawed protest. When our policy does not produce racial equity, we blame the people for not taking advantage of the new opportunity, not our flawed policy solution. The failure doctrine avoids the mirror of self-blame. The failure doctrine begets failure. The failure doctrine begets racism.

What if antiracists constantly self-critiqued our own ideas? What if we blamed our ideologies and methods, studied our ideologies and methods, refined our ideologies and methods again and again until they worked? When will we finally stop making the mistake of doing the same thing repeatedly and expecting a different result? Self-critique allows change. Changing shows flexibility. Antiracist power must be flexible to match the flexibility of racist power, propelled only by the craving for power to shape policy in their unjust interests. Racist power believes in by any means necessary. We, their challengers, typically do not, not even some of those inspired by Malcolm X. We care the most about the moral and ideological and financial purity of our ideologies and strategies and fundraising and leaders and organizations. We care less about bringing resources to people in dire straits, as we say we are purifying ourselves for the people in dire straits, as our purifying keeps the people in dire straits. As we critique the privilege and inaction of racist power, we show our privilege and inaction by critiquing every effective strategy, ultimately justifying our inaction on the comfortable seat of privilege. Anything but flexible, we are too often bound by ideologies that are bound by failed strategies of racial change.

What if we assessed the methods and leaders and organizations by their results of policy change and equity? What if strategies and policy solutions stemmed not from ideologies but from problems? What if antiracists were propelled only by the craving for power to shape policy in their equitable interests?

IN VOTING DOWN the 106 Campaign, the BSU officers crafted a different plan. They did something they did not fear. We loudly marched down North Broad Street and rallied on campus on September 20, 2007. That day, thousands of us thought we were protesting, when we were really demonstrating, from Philadelphia to Jena.

We use the terms "protest" and "demonstration" interchangeably, at our own peril, like we interchangeably use the terms "mobilizing" and "organizing." A protest is organizing people for a prolonged campaign that forces racist power to change a policy. A demonstration is mobilizing people momentarily to publicize a problem. Speakers and placards and posts at marches, rallies, petitions, and viral hashtags demonstrate the problem. Demonstrations are, not surprisingly, a favorite of suasionists. Demonstrations annoy power in the way children crying about something they will never get annoy parents. Unless power cannot economically or politically or professionally afford bad press—as power could not during the Cold War, as power cannot during election season, as power cannot close to bankruptcy—power typically ignores demonstrations.

The most effective demonstrations (like the most effective educational efforts) help people find the antiracist power within. The antiracist power within is the ability to view my own racist ideas in the mirror of my past and present, view my own antiracist ideas in the mirror of my future, view my own racial group as equal to other racial groups, view the world of racial inequity and injustice as abnormal, view my own power to resist and overtake racist power and policy. The most effective demonstrations (like the most effective educational efforts) provide methods for people to give their antiracist power, to give their human and financial resources, channeling attendees and their funds into organizations and protests and power-building and power-seizing campaigns. The fundraising behind the scenes of the Jena 6 demonstrations secured skilled defense attorneys, who, by June 26, 2009, quietly got the charges reduced to simple battery, to guilty pleas, to no additional jail time for the accused. Up to that point, Mychal Bell had been imprisoned after pleading guilty to second-degree battery in December 2007.

As important as finding the antiracist power within and financial support, demonstrations can provide emotional support for ongoing protests. Nighttime rallies in the churches of Montgomery, Alabama, rocking with the courage-locking words of Martin Luther King Jr., sustained those courageous Black women who primarily boycotted the public buses and drained that revenue stream for the city throughout 1956.

The most effective protests create an environment whereby changing the racist policy becomes in power's self-interest, like desegregating businesses because the sit-ins are driving away customers, like increasing wages to restart production, like giving teachers raises to resume schooling, like passing a law to attract a well-organized force of donors or voters. But it is difficult to create that environment, since racist power makes laws that illegalize most protest threats. Organizing and protesting are much harder and more impactful than mobilizing and demonstrating. Seizing power is much harder than protesting power and demonstrating its excesses.

The demonstrations alone had little chance of freeing the Jena 6. A judge denied bail for one of the Jena 6 the day after the demonstrations. The news shocked and alienated some of my BSU peers from activism. After all, when we attend or organize demonstrations thinking they are protests, thinking they can change power and policy, and see no change happening, it is hard not to become cynical. It is hard not to think the Goliath of racism can never be defeated. It is hard to think of our strategies and solutions and ideologies and feelings as the true failures. It is hard to think we actually have all the tools for success.

SUCCESS

INANCE SCHOLAR BOYCE Watkins lectured on racism as a disease. I agonized over this conception. Not foundational enough, eternal enough, revolutionary enough on this eleventh evening of Black History Month in 2010. When the question-and-answer period arrived, I tossed up my arm from the back row, as Caridad smiled.

Caridad and I had been whispering for most of the lecture. For once, I felt confidence tingling in my head. Days before, Professor Asante had hooded me with my doctoral degree at Temple's commencement. The teen who hated school had finished graduate school in 2010, had committed himself to school for life.

Caridad was probably the one who ushered me to the lecture at SUNY Oneonta, our state college in the town of Oneonta, in upstate New York. Forgive me for calling Oneonta a town. Rural White people from surrounding areas labeled Oneonta "the city."

At Oneonta, Whiteness surrounded me like clouds from a plane's window, which didn't mean I found no White colleagues who were genial and caring. But it was Caridad, and all her

Puerto Rican feminist and antiracist ideas, who took me by the arm when I arrived as a dissertation fellow in 2008 and brought me closer when I stayed and joined the faculty in 2009.

We were bound to become as close as our chairs. I filled the Black history post left vacant by Caridad's husband of eighteen years, Ralph. Metastatic cancer had taken Ralph's Black body in 2007. She probably could not look at me without seeing me standing in Ralph's shoes.

Her husband lost his fight to cancer but Caridad's life as an Afro-Latinx woman had brought its own fights—for peace, to be still. But she was a fighter, tireless and durable, as antiracists must be to succeed.

SUCCESS. THE DARK road we fear. Where antiracist power and policy predominate. Where justice lives. Where equal opportunities and thus outcomes exist between the equal groups. Where people blame policy, not people, for societal problems. Where nearly everyone has more than they have today. Where racist power lives on the margins, like antiracist power does today. Where antiracist ideas are our common sense, like racist ideas are today.

Neither failure nor success is written. The story of our generation will be based on what we are willing to do. Are we willing to endure the grueling fight against racist power and policy? Are we willing to transform the antiracist power we gather within us to antiracist power in our society?

Caridad was willing, which strengthened my will. Caridad understood that even as her students struggled with racist and gender racist and queer racist and class racist ideas, they also had within them the capacity to learn and change. She did not free the antiracist power within them with ideological attacks. Her classes were more like firm hugs tailored to students' experiences, compelling self-reflection. She took her Black and Afro-Latinx students—who were fighting their own anti-African cultural conditioning—to Ghana each year, where they found themselves eagerly immersed in their African ancestry by the trip's end.

Meanwhile, I fought to survive at the intersections. The impulses of my bigoted past constantly threatened to take me back to the plantation of racist power. Caridad extended the arms of Kaila, Yaba, and Weckea around me, ensuring I did not revert to my old thinking when I left Temple.

"INSTEAD OF DESCRIBING racism as a disease, don't you think racism is more like an organ?" I asked the lecturer. "Isn't racism essential for America to function? Isn't the system of racism essential for America to live?"

All my leading questions did not bait Boyce Watkins into a defense of his disease conception. Too bad. I wanted to engage him. I was not much of an intellectual. I closed myself off to new ideas that did not *feel* good. Meaning I shopped for conceptions of racism that fit my ideology and self-identity.

Asking antiracist folks to change their perspective on racism can be as destabilizing as asking racist folks to change their perspective on the races. Antiracist folks can be as doctrinaire in their view of racism as racist folks can be in their view of not-racism. How can antiracist people ask racist people to open their minds and change when we are sometimes closed-minded and unwilling to change? I ignored my own hypocrisy, as people customarily do when it means giving up what they hold dear. Giving up my conception of racism meant giving up my view of the world and myself. I would not do that without a fight. I would lash out at anyone who "attacked" me with new ideas, unless I feared and respected them like I feared and respected Kaila and Yaba.

I DERIVED MY perspective on racism from a book I first read in graduate school. When Joe Biden and other Democratic candidates spoke of "institutional racism" on the presidential campaign trail in 2019 and 2020, when activists took to the streets after the murder of George Floyd and spoke of "institutional racism," they were using, whether they realized it or not, a formulation coined in 1967 by Black Power activist Kwame Ture and political scientist Charles Hamilton in *Black Power: The Politics of Liberation in America*.

"Racism is both overt and covert," Ture and Hamilton explained. "It takes two, closely related forms: individual whites acting against individual blacks, and acts by the total white community against the black community. We call these individual racism and institutional racism. The first consists of overt acts by individuals. . . . The second type is less overt, far more subtle, less identifiable in terms of *specific* individuals committing the acts."

But I've since realized that "individual racism" is a contradiction in terms. An individual can challenge racism as an antiracist. An individual can express racist ideas, can support racist policies. An individual can be racist. But an individual cannot engage in racism; racism is structural, institutional, and systemic.

Even still, Ture and Hamilton distinguished the "individual" and "overt" racism of "white terrorists" who bomb a Black church and kill Black children from the "institutional" and "covert" racism of "when in that same city—Birmingham, Alabama—five hundred black babies die each year because of the lack of proper food, shelter and medical facilities."

It is, as I thought upon first read, the gloomy system keeping us down and dead. The system's acts are covert, just as the racist ideas of the people are implicit. I could not wrap my head around the system or precisely define it, but I knew the system was there, like the polluted air in our atmosphere, poisoning Black people to the benefit of White people.

But what if the atmosphere of racism has been polluting most White people, too? And what if racism has been working in the opposite way for a handful of Black individuals, who find the fresh air of wealth and power in racist atmospheres? Framing institutional racism as acts by the "total White community against the total Black community" accounts for the ways White people benefit from racist policies when compared to their Black peers. (White impoverished people benefit more than Black impoverished people. White women benefit more than Black women.

White gay people benefit more than Black gay people.) But this framing of White people versus Black people does *not* take into account that most White people would benefit more from antiracism than racism. This framing of White people versus Black people does not take into account that all White people do not benefit equally from racism. It does not take into account how rich White people benefit more from racist policies than impoverished and middle-income White people. It does not take into account that Black people are not harmed equally by racism or that some Black individuals champion White supremacy to boost their own wealth and power.

But I did not care. I thought I had it all figured out. I thought of racism as an inanimate, invisible, immortal system, not as a living, recognizable, mortal disease of cancer cells that we could identify and treat and kill. At times, I thought White people covertly operated the system, fixed it to benefit the total White community at the expense of the total Black community.

The construct of covert institutional racism opens American eyes to racism and, ironically, closes them, too. Separating the overt individual from the covert institutional veils the specific policy choices that cause racial injustices and inequities, policies made by specific people. Covering up the specific policies and policymakers prevents us from identifying and replacing the specific policies and policymakers. We become unconscious to racist policymakers and policies as we lash out angrily at the abstract bogeyman of "the system."

The perpetrators behind the five hundred Black babies dying each year in Birmingham "because of the lack of proper food, shelter and medical facilities" were no less overt than the "white terrorists" who killed four Black girls in a Birmingham church in 1963. In the way investigators can figure out exactly who those church bombers were, antiracist researchers can figure out exactly what policies caused five hundred Black babies to die each year and exactly who put those policies in place. In the way people have learned to see racist abuse coming out of the mouths of racist individuals, people can learn to see racial inequities emerging from racist policies. All forms of racism are overt if our antiracist eyes are open to seeing racist policy in racial inequity.

But we do not see. Our eyes have been closed by racist ideas and the unacknowledged bond between the institutional antiracist and the post-racialist. They bond on the idea that institutional racism is often unseen and unseeable. Because it is covert, the institutional antiracist says. Because it hardly exists, the post-racialist says.

A similar bond exists between implicit bias and post-racialism. They bond on the idea that racist ideas are buried in the mind. Because they are implicit and unconscious, implicit bias says. Because they are dead, post-racialism says.

TURE AND HAMILTON could not have foreseen how their concepts of overt and covert racism turned racism into something hidden and unknowable. Ture and Hamilton were understandably focused on distinguishing the individual from the institutional. They were reacting to the same moderate and liberal and assimilationist and Northern forces that all these years later still reduce racism to the individual acts of White Klansmen and Jim Crow Southerners and MAGA Republicans and N-word users and White supremacist shooters. " 'Respectable' individuals can absolve themselves from individual blame: *they* would never plant a bomb in a church; *they* would never stone a black family," Ture and Hamilton wrote. "But they continue to support political officials and institutions that would and do perpetuate institutionally racist policies."

The term "institutionally racist policies" is more concrete than "institutional racism." The term "racist policies" is more concrete than "institutionally racist policies," since "institutional" and "policies" are redundant: Policies are institutional. But I still occasionally use the terms "institutional racism" and "systemic racism" and "structural racism" and "overt" and "covert." They are like my first language of racism. But when we realize old words do not exactly and clearly convey what we are trying to describe,

244 • HOW TO BE AN ANTIRACIST

we should turn to new words. I struggle to concretely explain what "institutional racism" means to the Middle Eastern small businessman, the Black service worker, the White teacher, the Latinx nurse, the Asian factory worker, and the Native store clerk who do not take the courses on racism, do not read the books on racism, do not go to the lectures on racism, do not watch the specials on racism, do not listen to the podcasts on racism, do not attend the rallies against racism.

I try to keep everyday people in mind when I use "racist policies" instead of "institutional racism."

Policymakers and policies make societies and institutions, not the other way around. The United States is a racist nation because its policymakers and policies have been racist from the beginning. The conviction that racist policymakers can be overtaken, and racist policies can be changed, and the racist minds of their victims can be changed, is disputed only by those invested in preserving racist policymakers, policies, and habits of thinking.

Racism has always been terminal *and* curable. Racism has always been recognizable and mortal.

THE RAIN FELL on his gray hooded sweatshirt. It was February 26, 2012, a boring Sunday evening. I looked forward to my first book, on Black student activism in the late 1960s, being published in two weeks. The hooded teen looked forward to enjoying the watermelon juice and Skittles he'd purchased from a nearby 7-Eleven. The seventeen-year-old was easygoing, laid-back, like his strut. He adored LeBron James, hip-hop, and *South Park,* and dreamed of one day piloting airplanes.

Over six feet tall and lanky, Trayvon Martin ambled back in the rain to the Retreat at Twin Lakes. His father, Tracy Martin, had been dating a woman who lived in the gated community in Sanford, a suburb of Orlando, Florida. Tracy had brought along his son to talk to him, to refocus his mind on attending college like his older brother. Trayvon had just been suspended for carrying a bag with a trace of marijuana at his Miami high school.

While suburban White teenage boys partied and drank and drove and smoked and snorted and assaulted to a chorus of "boys will be boys," urban Black boys faced zero tolerance in a policed state.

Martin dodged puddles on his slow stroll home. He called his girlfriend. He talked and walked through the front gate (or took a shortcut) into the cluster of sandy-colored two-story town-houses. As in many neighborhoods during the Great Recession, investors had been buying foreclosed properties and renting them out. With renters came unfamiliar faces, transient faces, and racist residents who connected the presence of Black teenagers with the "rash" of seven burglaries in 2011. They promptly organized a neighborhood-watch group.

The watch-group organizer was born a year after me, to a White Vietnam veteran and a Peruvian immigrant. Raised not far from where my family moved to in Manassas, Virginia, George Zimmerman moved to Florida as I did, after graduating high school. His assault charges and domestic-violence accusations altered his early plans to be a police officer. But nothing altered his conviction that the Black body—and not his own—was the danger in his midst.

Zimmerman decided to run an errand. He hopped in his truck, his licensed 9-millimeter handgun tucked in a holster in his waistband. He drove. He noticed a hooded Black teenager walking through the complex. He dialed 911. The Black body's presence, a crime.

I DID NOT plan for my second book to be a history of racist ideas, as Zimmerman zeroed in on what could have been any Black male body, as he zeroed in on the teenager President Obama thought "could have been my son." After my first book, on the Black Campus Movement, I planned to research the student origins of Black studies in the 1960s. Then I realized that Black students were demanding Black studies because they considered all the existing disciplines to be racist. That the liberal scholars dominating those disciplines were refusing to identify their assimilationist ideas as racist. That they were identifying as "not-racist," like the segregationists they were calling racist. That Black students were calling them both racist, redefining racist ideas. I wanted to write a long history using Black students' redefinition of racist ideas. But the daunting task scared me, like Zimmerman's glare scared Martin.

Martin called a friend and told his friend he was being followed. He picked up the pace. "Hey, we've had some break-ins in my neighborhood," Zimmerman told the 911 dispatcher. "And there's a real suspicious guy. . . . This guy looks like he's up to no good, or he's on drugs or something. . . . A dark hoodie, like a gray hoodie." He asked how long it would take for an officer to get there, because "these assholes, they always get away."

Martin ran. Zimmerman leapt out of his car in pursuit, gun at his waist, phone in hand. The dispatcher told him to stop. Zimmerman ended the call and caught up to Martin, several minutes after 7:00 P.M. Only one person living knows exactly what happened next: Zimmerman, probably fighting to apprehend the purported criminal. Martin probably fighting off the actual aggressor for his life. Zimmerman squeezing the trigger and ending Martin's life. Claiming self-defense to save his own life. A jury agreeing, on July 13, 2013.

HEARTBROKEN, ALICIA GARZA typed "Black Lives Matter" into the mourning nights, into the Black caskets piling up before her as people shouted all those names from Trayvon Martin to Michael Brown to Sandra Bland to Korryn Gaines. The deaths and accusations and denials and demonstrations and deaths—it all gave me the strength each day to research for *Stamped from the Beginning.*

By the summer of 2012, I was finding and tagging every racist idea I could find from history. Racist ideas piled up before me like trash at a landfill. Tens of thousands of pages of Black people being trashed as natural or nurtured beasts, devils, animals, rapists, slaves, criminals, kids, predators, brutes, idiots, prostitutes, cheats, and dependents. More than five hundred years of toxic ideas on the Black body. Day after week, week after month, month after year, oftentimes twelve hours a day for three horrifically long years, I waded through this trash, consumed this trash, absorbed its toxicity, before I released a tiny portion of this trash onto the page.

All that trash, ironically, cleansed my mind if it did not cleanse my gut. While collecting this trash, I realized I had been unwittingly doing so my whole life. Some I had tossed away after facing myself in the mirror. Some trash remained. Like the dirty bags or traces of "them niggers" and "White people are devils" and "servile Asians" and "terrorist Middle Easterners" and "dangerous Black neighborhoods" and "weak Natives" and "angry Black women" and "Latinx invaders" and "irresponsible Black mothers" and "deadbeat Black fathers." A mission to uncover and critique America's life of racist ideas turned into a mission to uncover and critique my life of racist ideas, which turned into a lifelong mission to be antiracist.

It happens for me in successive steps, these steps to be an antiracist.

I stop using the "I'm not a racist" or "I can't be racist" defense of denial.

I define the term racist (someone who is expressing an idea of racial hierarchy, or through actions or inaction is supporting a policy that leads to racial inequity or injustice).

I acknowledge the racist policies I support and racist ideas I express.

I accept their source (my upbringing inside a nation making us racist).

I define the term antiracist (someone who is expressing an idea of racial equality, or is actively supporting a policy that leads to racial equity or justice).

I struggle for antiracist power and policy in my spaces. (Seizing a policymaking position. Joining an antiracist organization or protest. Publicly donating my time or privately donating my funds to antiracist policymakers, organizations, and protests fixated on changing power and policy.)

I struggle to remain at the antiracist intersections where racism is mixed with other bigotries. (Eliminating racial distinctions in biology and behavior. Equalizing distinctions in ethnicities, bodies, cultures, colors, classes, spaces, genders, and sexualities.)

I struggle to think with antiracist ideas. (Seeing racist policy in racial injustice and inequity. Leveling group differences. Not being fooled into generalizing individual negativity. Not being fooled by misleading statistics or theories that blame people for racial injustice or inequity.)

Racist ideas fooled me nearly my whole life. I refused to allow racist ideas to continue making a fool out of me, a chump out of me, a slave out of me. I realized there is nothing wrong with any of the racial groups and everything wrong with individuals like me who think there is something wrong with any of the racial groups. It felt so good to cleanse my mind.

But I did not cleanse my body. I kept most of the toxic trash in my gut between 2012 and 2015. Did not talk about most of it. Tried to laugh it off. Did not address the pain of feeling the racist ideas butchering my Black body for centuries. But how could I worry about my body as I stared at police officers butchering the Black body almost every week on my cellphone? How could I worry about my body when racist people blamed the dead, when the dead's loved ones cried and raged and numbed?

How could I worry about my suffering while Sadiqa suffered?

CHAPTER 18

SURVIVAL

ADIQA AND I rarely sat on the rounded cream sofa in our new home in Providence. But our nerves brought us into the living room on this day in late August 2013.

We'd moved in weeks before as newlyweds. We eloped and changed our last names together months before, in a picturesque affair captured in *Essence*'s "Bridal Bliss" column. Sadiqa's gold dress and red accessories and cowrie-shell adornments and regal aura sitting on her throne of a peninsula beach as the waves bowed under the colorful sunset were all so sublime.

Still high from the pictures, we were crashing down now. We held hands, waiting for the phone call from the radiologist who performed the ultrasound and biopsy. A week prior, Sadiqa told me about the lump. She did not think much of it, probably knowing that 96 percent of women diagnosed with breast cancer are over forty years old. She was thirty-four. But she obliged my requests to see a doctor that day. The phone rang. We jumped as if we were watching a horror flick. On speakerphone, the doctor said Sadiqa had invasive breast cancer.

Minutes later, we were upstairs. Sadiqa could not do it. I had to call and tell a mother who had lost a daughter that her living daughter had cancer. I stood in our guest room as her mother let out a wail, as Sadiqa wailed in our bedroom, as I wailed in my mind.

The wailing soon stopped, if the worry encircling and suffocating my wife did not. Sadiqa surveyed the fight ahead. Surgery to remove the lump. Chemotherapy to prevent a recurrence. Close monitoring to notice and treat any recurrence.

Sadiqa had time before surgery. We decided to freeze embryos in case the chemotherapy harmed her ovaries. The process dangerously overstimulated her ovaries, filling her abdomen with fluid, causing a blood clot. We slept in the hospital for a week as she recovered. All before her cancer fight.

The blood clot made doing surgery first too dangerous. Chemotherapy came first, which meant three months of anguish. She was a foodie who couldn't really taste her food. She had to push through chronic fatigue to exercise. She'd just completed twelve years of medical training, but now instead of seeing patients, she'd become one herself. It was like training hard for a marathon and getting sick steps into the race. But she kept running: through chemotherapy, through three surgeries, through another year of less toxic chemotherapy. And she survived.

I HAD TROUBLE separating Sadiqa's cancer from the racism I studied. The two consumed my life over the final months of 2013 and during the better part of 2014 and 2015. Months after Sadiqa survived stage-2 breast cancer, Ma was diagnosed with stage-1 breast cancer. She endured radiation and a lumpectomy in 2015. Those years were all about caretaking Sadiqa, helping Dad caretake Ma, and—when they were sleeping or enjoying company or desiring alone time—retreating from the pain of their cancer into the stack of racist ideas I'd collected.

Over time, the source of racist ideas became obvious, but I had trouble acknowledging it. The source did not fit my conception of racism, my racial ideology, my racial identity. I became a college professor to educate away racist ideas, seeing ignorance as the source of racist ideas, seeing racist ideas as the source of racist policies, seeing mental change as the principal solution, seeing myself, an educator, as the primary solver.

Watching Sadiqa's courage to break down her body to rebuild her body inspired me to accept the source of racist ideas I found while researching their entire history—even though it upended my previous way of thinking. My research kept pointing me to the same answer: The source of racist ideas was not ignorance and hate, but self-interest.

The history of racism is the history of powerful policymakers erecting racist policies out of self-interest, then producing racist ideas to defend and rationalize the inequitable effects of their policies, while everyday people consume those racist ideas, which in turn bleeds ignorance and hate. Treating ignorance and hate and expecting racism to shrink suddenly seemed like treating a cancer patient's symptoms and expecting the tumors to shrink. The body politic might feel better momentarily from the treatment—from trying to eradicate hate and ignorance—but as long as the underlying cause remains, the tumors grow, the symptoms return, and injustices spread like cancer cells, threatening the life of the body politic. Educational and moral suasion is not only a failed strategy. It is a fatal strategy.

THIS MESSAGE OF focusing on policy change over mental change was written in my next book, *Stamped from the Beginning*. After the book came out, I took this message on the road. I talked about racist policies leading to racist ideas, not the other way around, as we have commonly thought. I talked about eliminating racist policies if we ever hope to eliminate racist ideas. I talked and talked, unaware of my new hypocrisy, which readers and attendees picked up on. "What are *you* doing to change policy?" they kept asking me in public and private.

I started questioning myself. What am I doing to change policy? How can I genuinely urge people to focus on changing policy if I am not focused on changing policy? Once again, I had to confront and abandon a cherished idea.

I did not need to forsake antiracist research and education. I needed to forsake my orientation to antiracist research and education. I had to forsake the suasionist bred into me, of researching and educating for the sake of changing minds. I had to start researching and educating to change policy. The former strategy produces a public scholar. The latter produces public scholarship.

EVENTUALLY, I FOUND myself at Boston University, founding and directing the Center for Antiracist Research. My research in the history of racism and antiracism revealed that research, policy, narrative, and advocacy had been crucial in successfully replacing racist policy with antiracist policy.

We envisioned a center organized around connected offices of research, policy, narrative, and advocacy. Academics, professionals, and students in each of these four pillars would focus on the most critical and seemingly intractable racial inequities. The Center would research the racist policies causing racial inequity, innovate antiracist policy correctives, narrate the research and policy correctives, and help advocate for campaigns of change that work with antiracist power in locales to institute policy correctives.

THIS BU CENTER for Antiracist Research would model some of the steps we can all take to eliminate racial injustice and inequity in our spaces.

> *Admit racial injustice and inequity are problems of bad policy, not bad people.*
> *Identify racial injustice and inequity in all their intersections and manifestations.*
> *Investigate and uncover the racist policies causing racial injustice or inequity.*

Formulate or find antiracist policy that can eliminate racial injustice or inequity.

Figure out who or what group has the power to institute antiracist policy.

Disseminate and educate about the uncovered racist policy and antiracist policy correctives.

Work with sympathetic antiracist policymakers to institute the antiracist policy.

Deploy antiracist power to compel or drive from power the unsympathetic racist policymakers in order to institute the antiracist policy.

Monitor closely to ensure the antiracist policy reduces and eliminates racial injustice or inequity.

When policies fail, do not blame the people harmed by the racial injustice. Start over and seek out new and more effective antiracist treatments until they work.

Monitor closely to prevent new racist policies from being instituted.

On the September night I unveiled the vision for what years later became the Boston University Center for Antiracist Research, racist terror unveiled its vision, too. After my presentation, during my late-night class at American University, where I taught at the time, an unidentified, middle-aged White male, dressed in construction gear, posted copies of Confederate flags with cotton balls inside several buildings. He posted them on the bulletin boards outside my classroom. The timing did not seem coincidental. I ignored my fears and pressed on during the final months of 2017. This wasn't the only thing I put out of my mind. I also ignored my weight loss and pressed on. It became annoying going in and out of bathrooms only to produce nothing, only to still feel like I needed to go minutes later. But I felt I had more important matters to worry about. After all, White supremacists were running and terrorizing the United States and their power was spreading across the Western world.

I did not have a rejuvenating break during Thanksgiving. I was bedridden. The throwing up started and stopped after the weekend. The bloody diarrhea did not. It all became worse. By

Christmas, things had become acute. I obliged when Sadiqa urged me to get myself checked out.

Neither the nurse practitioner nor Sadiqa thought it was anything serious. I was thirty-five, about half the median age for the worst possibility, colon cancer. I did not exhibit any of the risk factors for colon cancer, since I exercised, rarely drank, never smoked, and had been a vegan since Sadiqa and I made the change to help prevent a recurrence of her cancer. We scheduled a precautionary colonoscopy for January 10, 2018.

I WAS GROGGY from the anesthesia early that morning. Cleaning out my colon had been an all-night affair. Sadiqa helped me put on my clothes in the small and dreary consultation room. No windows or striking colors or decorations, only pictures of the GI tract hanging on the walls. The Black woman doctor who'd performed the colonoscopy entered the room with a serious look on her face.

"I saw something abnormal," she said, sitting down. "I saw a mass in the sigmoid colon. It is large and friable, and it is bleeding." I looked at her in confusion, not knowing what she meant. Sadiqa looked at her in shock, knowing exactly what she meant.

She said she could not get her scope past the mass. It was obstructing the colon. "It is most likely cancerous," she said.

She paused as my confusion converted into shock. I checked out of myself. Sadiqa had to speak for me, really listen for me. The doctor told me to get blood work that day and get my body scanned the next day to confirm the cancer. I did not know what to think or feel. And so I did not feel or think anything other than shock.

At one point, several minutes later, perhaps as someone drained me of blood, I thought about Professor Mazama. About when I told her Sadiqa's diagnosis and asked, "Why her?"

"Why not her?" Professor Mazama responded.

Why not me?

I thought of Sadiqa's and Ma's and Dad's cancer fights. *Why not me?* They survived. *Why shouldn't I be the one to die?*

WE LEFT THE medical office in downtown Washington and headed for Busboys and Poets to meet Ma for breakfast. We sat down at the table. Ma had been waiting for a half hour. She asked why it took so long. I was still silent, looking down, up, away from anyone's eyes. Sadiqa told Ma about the mass. That it was probably cancer. "Okay, if it is, we will deal with it," Ma said. I looked up into her eyes, holding back tears. "We will deal with it," she said again. I knew she was serious. "Yes, we will," Sadiqa said, snatching my eyes. *Yes, we will,* I said to myself, absorbing their courage.

That night, I received more courage, when Sadiqa and I assumed we'd caught the cancer early. Probably stage 1 or 2. Perhaps 3. Not stage 4. About 86 percent of people diagnosed with stage-4 colon cancer die within five years.

The next day, they confirmed it. I had metastatic colon cancer. Stage 4. *Maybe we won't be able to deal with it.*

OUR WORLD IS suffering from metastatic cancer. Stage 4. Racism has spread to nearly every part of the body politic, intersecting with bigotry of all kinds, justifying all kinds of injustices by victim blaming; heightening exploitation and misplaced hate; spurring mass shootings, arms races, and demagogues who polarize nations; shutting down essential organs of democracy; and threatening the life of human society with inequality, pandemics, nuclear war, and climate change. In the United States, the metastatic cancer has been spreading, contracting, and threatening to kill the American body as it nearly did before its birth, as it nearly did during its Civil War. But how many people stare inside the body of their nations' racial inequities, their neighborhoods' racial inequities, their occupations' racial inequities, their institutions' racial inequities, and flatly deny that their policies are racist? They flatly deny that racial inequity is the signpost of racist policy. They flatly deny the racist policy as they use racist ideas to justify the racial inequity. They flatly deny the cancer of racism as the cancer cells spread and literally threaten their own lives and the lives of the people and spaces and places they hold dear. The popular conception of denial—like the popular strategy of suasion—is fatal.

I HAD BEEN thinking all week about denial, before the diagnosis, after the diagnosis. I still could not separate racism and cancer. I sat in the waiting rooms, between medical meetings, tests, and procedures, writing an essay arguing that the heartbeat of racism is denial, the heartbeat of antiracism is confession. It appeared in *The New York Times* on Sunday, January 14, 2018, three days after my diagnosis. But my writing on the denial of racism did not stop me from denying the severity of my cancer. I could not confess I was likely to die. Then again, I did not lash out at the doctors who diagnosed my cancer in the way deniers often lash out at the experts who describe them as racist.

I had been privately making sense of racism through cancer since Sadiqa's diagnosis. Except now I started making sense out of my cancer through my new conception of racism. Denying my ability to succeed in my cancer fight did not differ from those denying our ability to succeed in the antiracism fight. Denial is much easier than admission, than confession.

I have cancer. The most serious stage. Cancer is likely to kill me. I can survive cancer against all odds.

My society has racism. The most serious stage. Racism is likely to kill my society. My society can survive racism against all odds.

I prepared myself to fight. I looked past what could harm me in the fight to see all that could bring me joy if I survived. Dancing through life with my surviving and thriving partner. Watching my nearly two-year-old Black girl grow into a phenomenal person. Growing myself into a better self through the love of my constructive family and friends and mentors I know and do not know. Engaging the open-minded readers of *Stamped from the Beginning*. Building what later became the Boston University Center for Antiracist Research into an intellectual factory for racial equity and justice. Witnessing my beloved New York Knicks finally win an NBA championship. Writing for *The Atlantic,* in the same pages as W.E.B. Du Bois. Finishing this book and sharing it with the world.

I looked at the antiracist progress coming in my lifetime, the antiracist society coming in my granddaughter's lifetime, our great-grandchildren refusing to return to the racist time when all the victims of all forms of bigotries that feed and are fed by racism had far less resources, far less of an opportunity to be one with their humanity, to be one with human difference, to be one with our shared humanity.

MY TREATMENT PLAN took shape like battle plans. Six months of chemotherapy. If my tumors shrank, the chance for surgery. The chance of removing the rest of the tumors. The chance at life if there was not a recurrence. A long shot. But a chance.

On Mondays, every three weeks, beginning in late January 2018, I received chemo injections and started taking two weeks of chemo pills. By Tuesdays, I already felt like I had been jumped by Smurf and his boys. Could barely climb out of bed. Could barely write this book. Could barely eat and drink. But I pushed myself to get out of bed, to write, to stay hydrated, because when I did not exercise my body and mind, when I did not consume enough protein and thoughts and fluids, I could feel the toxicity levels rising in my body, exacerbating all the symptoms.

To keep up with my life, I had to go outside into the bitter cold of winter, not merely to the gym but to meetings, to speaking engagements, to life. The chemo made me hypersensitive to cold. Thirty degrees outside felt like negative ten degrees inside me. Whenever I breathed in cold air, it hurt my lungs. Whenever I drank ice-cold fluids, it hurt my throat. Whenever I touched anything cold, it hurt my fingers.

Instead of wallowing in the chronic discomfort or asking the doctor to ease the chemo, I found ways to make myself more comfortable. Pain is usually essential to healing. When it comes to healing America of racism, we want to heal America without pain, but without pain, there is no progress.

MY TUMORS SHRANK enough for me to go on the surgical table by the end of the summer of 2018. Surgeons removed what was left and sewed me back together. Pathologists dissected what they took out and did not find any cancer cells. The six months of chemotherapy had obliterated, apparently, all the cancer. My doctors were as shocked as I had been when I was diagnosed. I had a good chance to land in the 14 percent of people who survived stage-4 colon cancer.

WE CAN SURVIVE metastatic racism. Forgive me. I cannot separate the two, and no longer try. What if humanity connected the two? Not just the number of people of all races who would not die each year from cancer if we launched a war against cancer instead of against bodies of color. Not just the better prevention and treatment options doctors would have if we diverted to cancer care and research a portion of the trillions of tax dollars we spend on cutting taxes for the rich, imprisoning people, surveilling people, bombing people, and putting troops in harm's way.

What if we treated racism in the way we treat cancer? What has historically been effective at combatting racism is analogous to what has been effective at combatting cancer. I am talking about the treatment methods that gave me a chance at life, that give millions of cancer fighters and survivors like me, like you, like our loved ones, a chance at life. The treatment methods that gave millions of our relatives and friends and idols who did not survive cancer a chance at a few more days, months, years of life. What if humans connected the treatment plans?

Saturate the body politic with the chemotherapy or immunotherapy of antiracist policies that shrink the tumors of racial injustice, that kill undetectable cancer cells. Remove any remaining racist policies, the way surgeons remove the tumors. Ensure there are clear margins, meaning no cancer cells of injustice left in the body politic, only the healthy cells of justice. Encourage the consumption of healthy foods for thought and the regular exercising of antiracist ideas, to reduce the likelihood of a recurrence. Monitor the body politic closely, especially where the tumors of racial injustice previously existed. Detect and treat a recurrence early, before it can grow and threaten the body politic.

But before we can treat, we must believe. Believe all is not lost for you and me and our society. Believe in the possibility that we can strive to be antiracist from this day forward. Believe in the possibility that we can transform our societies to be antiracist from this day forward. Racist power is not godly. Racist policies are not indestructible. Racial injustices and inequities are not inevitable. Racist ideas are not natural to the human mind.

Race and racism are power constructs of the modern world. For roughly two hundred thousand years, before race and racism were constructed in the fifteenth century, humans saw color but did not group the colors into continental races, did not commonly attach negative and positive characteristics to those colors and rank the races to justify racial inequity, to reinforce racist power and policy. Racism is not even six hundred years old. It's a cancer that we've caught early.

But racism is one of the fastest-spreading and most fatal cancers humanity has ever known. It is hard to find a place where its cancer cells are not dividing and multiplying. There is nothing I see in our world today, in our history, giving me hope that one day antiracists will win the fight, that one day the flag of antiracism will fly over a world of justice and equity for all. What gives me hope is a simple truism. Once we lose hope, we are guaranteed to lose. But if we ignore the odds and fight to create an antiracist world, then we give humanity a chance to one day survive, a chance to live in communion, a chance to be forever free.

ACKNOWLEDGMENTS

It was the people who kept asking the question that framed this book. People in audiences, in private conversations, in emails, on phone calls, on social media—the people urged me to write this book by asking again and again how they could be antiracist. I would like to first acknowledge and thank the people—the many people I know, and more I do not know—who trusted in me to deliver an answer.

I want to thank Ayesha Pande, my literary agent and friend, for encouraging the book idea when I relayed it to you in 2016. I am forever appreciative of your indelible confidence, support, and stewardship through this process from idea to book.

I would like to acknowledge Chris Jackson, my book editor, for your editorial wisdom and constructive vision. This book was quite difficult to wrap my head around and write—the chrono-logical personal narrative interspersed with a series of connected chapter themes that build on each other like a stepladder to being antiracist. And so I am filled with gratitude for your patience and clear-eyed conceptual tools that helped in this book's construc-tion. And to the whole One World squad: thank you, especially you, Nicole. I must also acknowledge all the great folks in production, sales, marketing, and publicity at Random House, especially Maria, Stacey, and Ayelet. I know how crucial you are in getting these pages into hands, and I can't thank you enough.

I could not have produced and revised this book without the memories of its characters, especially my father, who has an almost perfect memory, and of course Ma, and Sadiqa, Kaila, Yaba, Clarence, and Weckea, another person whose memory is flawless. And so thank you. I could not have produced and revised this book without the tremendous amount of scholarship and reporting on racism and antiracism. And so thank you to all those researchers and theorists and journalists.

I could not have produced this book without my health. And so thank you to all the medical providers who armed me during my cancer fight.

A horde of people throughout my life, knowingly and unknowingly, with good intentions and bad intentions, put up mirrors that forced me to self-reflect. I must thank all these people, many of whom are in this book. I want to express my gratitude to all those who assisted me during my journey through academia, from my professors, like Drs. Jackson, Asante, and Mazama, to my colleagues and mentors at colleges and universities where I was employed. I most especially want to thank the dream of a team: Adeline Gutierrez Nunez, Tami Nguyen, Heather Sanford, and Hunter Moyler.

Thank you to all my friends and relatives, especially my parents and brothers. As you know, this book would have been impossible without you and your love.

Finally, I want to thank faith, my daughter, Imani. One day, you will learn how critical you were to the life of this book. And excuse me while I give another shout-out to my rock, partner, and best friend, who has given so much to me and meant so much to me and humanity, Sadiqa.

NOTES

My Racist Introduction

5 **acquired his nickname, "Stonewall"** National Park Service, "Stonewall Jackson Monument: Manassas National Battlefield Park," www.nps.gov /places/000/stonewall-jackson-monument.htm.

7 **Note on Martin and Malcolm: "A riot is the language of the unheard"** "MLK: A Riot Is the Language of the Unheard," *60 Minutes Overtime,* August 25, 2013, www.cbsnews.com/news/mlk-a-riot-is-the-language-of-the -unheard/.

9 **"Laziness is a trait in Blacks"** John R. O'Donnell, *Trumped!: The Inside Story of the Real Donald Trump—His Cunning Rise and Spectacular Fall* (New York: Simon & Schuster, 1991). O'Donnell is the former president of Trump Plaza Hotel and Casino in Atlantic City. In his memoir, he quoted Trump's criticism of a Black accountant. Here is the full quote: "Black guys counting my money! I hate it. The only kind of people I want counting my money are short guys that wear yarmulkes every day. . . . I think that the guy is lazy. And it's probably not his fault, because laziness is a trait in blacks. It really is, I believe that. It's not anything they can control." Trump at first denied he said this, but later told a *Playboy* reporter, "The stuff O'Donnell wrote about me is probably true." See Mark Bowden, "The Art of the Donald: The Trumpster Stages the Comeback of a Lifetime," *Playboy,* May 1997.

9 **as mostly criminals and rapists** " 'Drug Dealers, Criminals, Rapists': What Trump Thinks of Mexicans," BBC, August 31, 2016, www.bbc.com /news/av/world-us-canada-37230916/drug-dealers-criminals-rapists-what -trump-thinks-of-mexicans.

9 **"a total and complete shutdown of Muslims entering the United States"** This promise came from a Trump campaign statement released on December 7, 2015. For the full statement, see Jessica Estepa, "'Preventing Muslim Immigration' Statement Disappears from Trump's Campaign Site," *USA Today,* May 8, 2017, www.usatoday.com/story/news/politics /onpolitics/2017/05/08/preventing-muslim-immigration-statement -disappears-donald-trump-campaign-site/101436780/.

9 **he routinely called his Black critics "stupid"** For a collection of his statements, see David Nakamura, "Trump's Insults Toward Black Reporters, Candidates Echo 'Historic Playbooks' Used Against African Americans, Critics Say," *The Washington Post,* November 9, 2018, www.washingtonpost.com /politics/trumps-insults-toward-black-reporters-candidates-echo-historic -playbooks-used-against-african-americans/2018/11/09/74653438-e440 -11e8-b759-3d88a5ce9e19_story.html.

10 **"all have AIDS"** See Michael D. Shear, "Out of Chaos, Trump Reshapes Immigration," *The Boston Globe,* December 23, 2017, www.bostonglobe .com/news/nation/2017/12/23/out-chaos-trump-reshapes-immigration /b1zNkTCRCCnH28q8SUh3JM/story.html?event=event12.

10 **"very fine people"** See Rosie Gray, "Trump Defends White-Nationalist Protesters: 'Some Very Fine People on Both Sides,'" *The Atlantic,* August 15, 2017, www.theatlantic.com/politics/archive/2017/08/trump -defends-white-nationalist-protesters-some-very-fine-people-on-both -sides/537012/.

10 **"that you have ever interviewed"** See Anne Gearan, "Trump Says 'I'm Not a Racist' and Denies 'Shithole Countries' Remark," *The Washington Post,* January 14, 2018, www.washingtonpost.com/news/post-politics/wp /2018/01/14/trump-says-im-not-a-racist-and-denies-shithole-countries -remark/.

10 **"you've ever met"** See Eugene Scott, "Donald Trump: I'm 'the Least Racist Person,'" CNN, September 15, 2016, www.cnn.com/2016/09/15 /politics/donald-trump-election-2016-racism/index.html.

10 **"you've ever encountered"** See Mark Fisher, "Donald Trump: 'I Am the Least Racist Person,'" *The Washington Post,* June 10, 2016, www .washingtonpost.com/politics/donald-trump-i-am-the-least-racist-person /2016/06/10/eac7874c-2f3a-11e6-9de3-6e6e7a14000c_story.html.

10 **Denial is the heartbeat of being racist** For more on this idea, see Ibram X. Kendi, "The Heartbeat of Racism Is Denial," *The New York Times,* January 13, 2018, www.nytimes.com/2018/01/13/opinion/sunday/heartbeat -of-racism-denial.html. The article also appeared in the Sunday print edition the following day.

10 **"'Racist' isn't a descriptive word"** For Richard Spencer's full quote, see Tristan Scott, "Who Is Richard Spencer?" *Flathead Beacon,* November 26, 2014, www.flatheadbeacon.com/2014/11/26/richard-spencer/.

11 not the equivalent of a "slur" Ibid.

11 **"Our Constitution is color-blind"** For Justice Harlan's full dissent, see "Separate but Equal," in *Great Decisions of the U.S. Supreme Court*, eds. Maureen Harrison and Steve Gilbert (New York: Barnes & Noble Books, 2003), 46–58. For Harlan's quotes on the Constitution and the "white race," see 53.

Chapter 1: Definitions

16 **Skinner was growing famous** For explanatory pieces on Skinner's life and influence and role in Urbana '70, see James Earl Massey, "The Unrepeatable Tom Skinner," *Christianity Today*, September 12, 1994, www.christianitytoday.com/ct/1994/september12/4ta011.html; and Edward Gilbreath, "A Prophet Out of Harlem," *Christianity Today*, September 16, 1996, www.christianitytoday.com/ct/1996/september16/6ta036.html.

16 **third and fourth books** Tom Skinner, *How Black Is the Gospel?* (Philadelphia: Lippincott, 1970); and Tom Skinner, *Words of Revolution: A Call to Involvement in the Real Revolution* (Grand Rapids, MI: Zondervan, 1970).

17 **"The Black Aesthetic"** For the lessons Addison Gayle shared in this course, see his landmark book, *The Black Aesthetic* (Garden City, NY: Doubleday, 1971).

17 **Larry read James Baldwin's** *The Fire Next Time* (New York: Dial, 1963); Richard Wright, *Native Son* (New York: Harper, 1940); Amiri Baraka (LeRoi Jones), *Dutchman and the Slave: Two Plays* (New York: William Morrow, 1964); and Sam Greeley, *The Spook Who Sat by the Door* (New York: Baron, 1969).

17 **Soul Liberation launched into their popular anthem** For a remembrance of this evening with Soul Liberation playing and Tom Skinner preaching that is consistent with my parents' memories, see Edward Gilbreath, *Reconciliation Blues: A Black Evangelical's Inside View of White Christianity* (Downers Grove, IL: InterVarsity Press, 2006), 66–69.

17 **When the music ended, it was time: Tom Skinner** For the audio and text of Tom Skinner's sermon at Urbana '70, entitled "The U.S. Racial Crisis and World Evangelism," see urbana.org/message/us-racial-crisis-and-world-evangelism.

18 **saved into Black liberation theology** For a good book on the philosophy of Black theology, see James H. Cone, *Risks of Faith: The Emergence of a Black Theology of Liberation, 1968–1998* (Boston: Beacon Press, 2000).

18 **churchless church of the Black Power movement** For an overview of Black Power, see Peniel E. Joseph, *Waiting 'Til the Midnight Hour: A Narrative History of Black Power in America* (New York: Henry Holt, 2006).

19 *Black Theology & Black Power* James H. Cone, *Black Theology & Black Power* (New York: Seabury, 1969).

19 *A Black Theology of Liberation* James H. Cone, *A Black Theology of Liberation* (Philadelphia: Lippincott, 1970).

20 **The houselessness rate in 2022** National Alliance to End Homelessness, "Counts and Rates by Race/Ethnicity, 2020: Rate Per 10,000," *State of Homelessness: 2022 Edition,* endhomelessness.org/homelessness-in-america /homelessness-statistics/state-of-homelessness/.

22 **commandeered the term "racial discrimination"** Southern segregationists cried "discrimination" in their opposition to civil rights legislation in the 1960s. For example, Sen. Sam Ervin (D-NC), objecting to the Civil Rights Act of 1968, asked, "How can we abolish discrimination on the basis of race by passing a law which only applies where race is concerned and which does discriminate against certain victims of crime simply upon the basis of either the race of the victim of the crime or the race of the person who commits the crime upon him?" U.S Congress, *Congressional Record,* 90th Cong., 2nd sess., Vol. 114, Pt. 1, January 18, 1968, 331.

22 **how positive discrimination is sometimes defined** See Government Equalities Office, *Equality Act of 2010: What Do I Need to Know? A Quick Start Guide to Using Positive Action in Recruitment and Promotion,* January 2011, assets.publishing.service.gov.uk/government/uploads/system/uploads /attachment_data/file/85014/positive-action-recruitment.pdf.

22 **another way positive discrimination is defined** Australian Human Rights Commission, "Positive Discrimination," humanrights.gov.au/quick-guide /12078.

23 **officials in the United States** Abby Goodnough and Jan Hoffman, "Front-line Workers and People Over 74 Should Get Shots Next, C.D.C. Panel Says," *The New York Times,* January 14, 2021, www.nytimes.com/2020/12 /20/health/covid-vaccine-first-elderly-workers.html.

23 **and in many countries around the world** See "Why Some Nations Have Deadlier Outbreaks with the Same Covid-19 Vaccines," *The Straits Times,* October 13, 2021, www.straitstimes.com/world/why-some-nations -have-deadlier-outbreaks-with-the-same-covid-19-vaccines; Organisation for Economic Co-operation and Development (OECD), "Access to COVID-19 Vaccines: Global Approaches in a Global Crisis," March 18, 2021, www .oecd.org/coronavirus/policy-responses/access-to-covid-19-vaccines-global -approaches-in-a-global-crisis-c6a18370/; and World Health Organization, "172 Countries and Multiple Candidate Vaccines Engaged in COVID-19 Vaccine Global Access Facility," August 24, 2020, www.who.int/news/item /24-08-2020-172-countries-and-multiple-candidate-vaccines-engaged-in -covid-19-vaccine-global-access-facility.

23 **research has shown saved lives** Joshua R. Goldstein, Thomas Cassidy, and Kenneth W. Wachter, "Vaccinating the Oldest Against COVID-19 Saves Both the Most Lives and Most Years of Life," *PNAS* 118, no. 11, doi.org/10 .1073/pnas.2026322118.

23 **refused to engage in positive antiracist discrimination** Ahead of the December 2020 vote on the recommended priority groups for the CDC vaccine

strategy, Dr. Jose R. Romero, the chair of the Advisory Committee on Immunization Practices (ACIP), said, "We have never targeted a specific ethnic nor racial group for receipt of the vaccine. Our decisions, recommendations better said, for the groups that are priority take into account the burden of disease within those groups. And within those groups, White, Caucasian individuals predominate." CDC, "December 20, 2020 ACIP Meeting—ACIP Vote," December 30, 2020, www.youtube.com/watch?v=pPElO2dBqmU.

23 **policymakers . . . are disproportionately elderly** See Veronica Magan, "How Old Is the 117th Congress?" *FiscalNote,* February 2, 2021, fiscalnote .com/blog/how-old-is-the-117th-congress.

23 **elderly people vote at disproportionately high rates** Emily Brandon, "Why Older Citizens Are More Likely to Vote," *U.S. News & World Report,* October 5, 2020, money.usnews.com/money/retirement/aging/articles/why -older-citizens-are-more-likely-to-vote.

23 **elderly people are disproportionately White** "Only 10% of all the people who were members of racial and ethnic minority populations were age 65 and older in 2019 compared to 21% of the non-Hispanic white population." Administration on Aging, Administration for Community Living, U.S. Department of Health and Human Services, *2020 Profile of Older Americans,* May 2021, 7, acl.gov/sites/default/files/Aging%20and%20Disability%20in %20America/2020ProfileOlderAmericans.Final_.pdf.

23 **The most common age** Katherine Schaeffer, "The Most Common Age Among Whites in U.S. is 58—More Than Double That of Racial and Ethnic Minorities," Pew Research Center, July 30, 2019, www.pewresearch .org/fact-tank/2019/07/30/most-common-age-among-us-racial-ethnic -groups/.

24 **"You do not take a person who"** For a transcript of President Johnson's speech at Howard, see Lyndon B. Johnson, "Commencement Address at Howard University," June 4, 1965, *American Presidency Project,* UC Santa Barbara, www.presidency.ucsb.edu/documents/commencement-address-how ard-university-fulfill-these-rights.

25 **"In order to get beyond racism"** For his full dissent, see Harry Blackmun, Dissenting Opinion, *Regents of the Univ. of Cal. v. Bakke, 1978,* C-SPAN Landmark Cases, landmarkcases.c-span.org/Case/27/Regents-Univ-Cal-v -Bakke.

25 **"reverse discrimination"** Conservative columnist James J. Kilpatrick coined the term "reverse discrimination" in 1974. Kilpatrick, like many subsequent users of this term, invoked "reverse discrimination" in an attack on affirmative action policies. See Kilpatrick, "The DeFunis Syndrome," *Nation's Business,* June 1974, 13–14, archive.org/details/Nations-Business-1974-06 /page/n17/mode/2up.

25 **A racist idea is** See Ibram X. Kendi, *Stamped from the Beginning: The Definitive History of Racist Ideas in America* (New York: Nation Books, 2016).

25 **"The blacks, whether originally a distinct race"** Thomas Jefferson, *Notes on the State of Virginia* (1785; Boston: Lilly and Wait, 1832), 150.

26 **Great Migration** The Great Migration refers to the six million Black people who left the South for the North and West between 1915 and 1970. For the best book on the Great Migration, see Isabel Wilkerson, *The Warmth of Other Suns: The Epic Story of America's Great Migration* (New York: Vintage Books, 2010).

26 **non-White Global South is being victimized** See "Climate Change Will Hit Poor Countries Hardest, Study Shows," *The Guardian,* September 27, 2013, www.theguardian.com/global-development/2013/sep/27/climate-change-poor-countries-ipcc; and Jeremy Williams, "Why Climate Change Is Inherently Racist," BBC, January 26, 2022, www.bbc.com/future/article/20220125-why-climate-change-is-inherently-racist.

26 **Droughts and food scarcity** See European Commission Joint Research Centre, "Drought Lowers Food Production in Parts of Southern, Eastern, and Northern Africa," March 8, 2022, joint-research-centre.ec.europa.eu/jrc-news/drought-lowers-food-production-parts-southern-eastern-and-northern-africa-2022-03-08_en.

27 **nearly one-fifth of the world's undernourished population** Southern and Eastern Africa are home to 17.2 percent of the world's undernourished population. Food and Agriculture Organization of the United Nations, *The State of Food Security and Nutrition in the World, 2021,* 11, www.fao.org/documents/card/en/c/cb4474en.

27 **Note on "undernourished": I wrongly used the term "malnourished"** For more on the distinction between undernutrition and malnutrition, see World Health Organization, "Malnutrition," June 9, 2021, www.who.int/news-room/fact-sheets/detail/malnutrition.

27 **higher lead poisoning rates than Flint, Michigan** See M. B. Pell and Joshua Schneyer, "Reuters Finds 3,810 U.S. Areas with Lead Poisoning Double Flint's," Reuters, November 14, 2017, www.reuters.com/article/us-usa-lead-map/reuters-finds-3810-u-s-areas-with-lead-poisoning-double-flints-idUSKBN1DE1H2.

27 **Alzheimer's, a disease more prevalent among African Americans** Black Americans age seventy and older are twice as likely as their White peers to have Alzheimer's or another type of dementia. See Alzheimer's Association, "Black Americans and Alzheimer's," www.alz.org/help-support/resources/black-americans-and-alzheimers. For an excellent essay on African Americans and Alzheimer's, see Marita Golden, "African Americans Are More Likely Than Whites to Develop Alzheimer's. Why?" *The Washington Post Magazine,* June 1, 2017, www.washingtonpost.com/lifestyle/magazine/why-are-african-americans-so-much-more-likely-than-whites-to-develop-alzheimers/2017/05/31/9bfbcccc-3132-11e7-8674-437ddb6e813e_story.html.

27 **four additional years—and five additional years** See Centers for Disease Control and Prevention (CDC), National Center for Health Statistics, "Life Expectancy in the U.S. Declined a Year and Half in 2020," news release, July 21, 2021, www.cdc.gov/nchs/pressroom/nchs_press_releases/2021 /202107.htm.

27 **Black infants die at twice the rate of White infants** See CDC, "Infant Mortality," September 8, 2021, www.cdc.gov/reproductivehealth /maternalinfanthealth/infantmortality.htm.

27 **African Americans are 33 percent more likely to die of cancer** "Compared with White people, the risk of death after adjusting for sex, age, and stage at diagnosis is 33% higher in Black people." See Rebecca L. Siegel, Kimberly D. Miller, and Ahmedin Jemal, "Cancer Statistics, 2022," *CA: A Cancer Journal for Clinicians* 72, no. 1 (January/February 2022), doi.org/10 .3322/caac.21708.

28 **prostate cancer, which kills twice as many Black men** National Cancer Institute, "Cancer Disparities," March 28, 2022, www.cancer.gov/about -cancer/understanding/disparities.

28 **Breast cancer disproportionately kills** Black women are 41 percent more likely than White women to die of breast cancer. See Angela N. Giaquinto, Kimberly D. Miller, Ann Goding Sauer, Ahmedin Jemal, and Rebecca L. Siegel, "Cancer Statistics for African American/Black People 2022," *CA: A Cancer Journal for Clinicians* 72, no. 3 (May/June 2022), doi.org/10.3322 /caac.21718.

28 **Three million African Americans and four million Latinx Americans secured health insurance** Namrata Uberoi, Kenneth Finegold, and Emily Gee, "Health Insurance Coverage and the Affordable Care Act, 2010–2016," ASPE Issue Brief, Department of Health & Human Services, March 3, 2016, aspe.hhs.gov/system/files/pdf/187551/ACA2010-2016.pdf.

28 **28.5 million Americans remained uninsured** "Since Obamacare Became Law, 20 Million More Americans Have Gained Health Insurance," *Fortune,* November 15, 2018, fortune.com/2018/11/15/obamacare-americans-with -health-insurance-uninsured/.

28 **a number that has risen to 31.6 million** Amy E. Cha and Robin A. Cohen, "Demographic Variation in Health Insurance Coverage: United States, 2020," National Health Statistics Reports, no. 169, February 11, 2022, www.cdc.gov/nchs/data/nhsr/nhsr169.pdf.

28 **Congress repealed the individual mandate in 2017** For the ramifications of the repeal, see Dylan Scott and Sarah Kliff, "Republicans Have Finally Repealed a Crucial Piece of Obamacare," *Vox,* December 20, 2017, www.vox.com/policy-and-politics/2017/11/14/16651698/obamacare -individual-mandate-republican-tax-bill.

28 **Racist voting policy has evolved** For studies on voter suppression, see Carol Anderson, *One Person, No Vote: How Voter Suppression Is Destroying*

Our Democracy (New York: Bloomsbury, 2018); Allan J. Lichtman, *The Embattled Vote in America: From the Founding to the Present* (Cambridge, MA: Harvard University Press, 2018); and Ari Berman, *Give Us the Ballot: The Modern Struggle for Voting Rights in America* (New York: Farrar, Straus & Giroux, 2015). For a blueprint on how to combat voter suppression, see Stacey Abrams, *Our Time Is Now: Power, Purpose, and the Fight for a Fair America* (New York: Henry Holt, 2020).

28 **"target African Americans with almost surgical precision"** Christopher Ingraham, "The 'Smoking Gun' Proving North Carolina Republicans Tried to Disenfranchise Black Voters," *The Washington Post,* July 29, 2016, www.washingtonpost.com/news/wonk/wp/2016/07/29/the-smoking -gun-proving-north-carolina-republicans-tried-to-disenfranchise-black -voters/.

28 **Wisconsin's strict voter-ID law suppressed** Ari Berman, "Wisconsin's Voter-ID Law Suppressed 200,000 Votes in 2016 (Trump Won by 22,748)," *The Nation,* May 9, 2017, www.thenation.com/article/wisconsins-voter-id -law-suppressed-200000-votes-trump-won-by-23000/.

28 **more than 440 voter suppression bills in 49 states that year** "Voting Laws Roundup: December 2021," Brennan Center for Justice, January 12, 2022, www.brennancenter.org/our-work/research-reports/voting-laws-roundup -december-2021.

28 **the court upheld Arizona laws** Nina Totenberg, "The Supreme Court Deals a New Blow to Voting Rights, Upholding Arizona Restrictions," NPR, July 1, 2021, www.npr.org/2021/07/01/998758022/the-supreme-court-up held-upholds-arizona-measures-that-restrict-voting.

29 **"We have all been programmed"** Audre Lorde, "Age, Race, Class, and Sex: Women Redefining Difference," in *Sister Outsider: Essays and Speeches* (Freedom, CA: Crossing Press, 1984), 115.

Chapter 2: Dueling Consciousness

31 **"We can put drug abuse on the run"** Ronald Reagan, "Remarks on Signing Executive Order 12368, Concerning Federal Drug Abuse Policy Functions," June 24, 1982, Ronald Reagan Presidential Library & Museum, www.reaganlibrary.gov/archives/speech/remarks-signing-executive-order -12368-concerning-federal-drug-abuse-policy.

31 **American prison population to quadruple** See Fox Butterfield, "Study Finds Big Increase in Black Men as Inmates Since 1980," *The New York Times,* August 28, 2002, www.nytimes.com/2002/08/28/us/study-finds -big-increase-in-black-men-as-inmates-since-1980.html.

31 **more people were incarcerated for drugs** Jonathan Rothwell, "Drug Offenders in American Prisons: The Critical Distinction Between Stock and Flow," Brookings, November 25, 2015, www.brookings.edu/blog/social

-mobility-memos/2015/11/25/drug-offenders-in-american-prisons-the
-critical-distinction-between-stock-and-flow/.

31 **White Americans are more likely than Black and Latinx Americans
to sell drugs** Keegan Hamilton, "The War on Drugs Remains as Racist
as Ever, Statistics Show," *Vice,* March 14, 2017, www.vice.com/en/article
/7xwybd/the-war-on-drugs-remains-as-racist-as-ever-statistics-show.

31 **these groups consume drugs at similar rates** Ibid.; and Center for Behavioral Health Statistics and Quality, *Racial/Ethnic Differences in Substance
Use, Substance Use Disorders, and Substance Use Treatment Utilization among
People Aged 12 or Older (2015–2019)* (Rockville, MD: Substance Abuse
and Mental Health Services Administration, 2021),13, www.samhsa.gov
/data/sites/default/files/reports/rpt35326/2021NSDUHSUChartbook102
221B.pdf.

31 **Black Americans convicted of nonviolent drug-related activities remain
in prisons** U.S. Department of Justice, Bureau of Justice Statistics, *Compen-
dium of Federal Justice Statistics, 2003,* 112 (Table 7.16) (2003), bjs.ojp.usdoj
.gov/content/pub/pdf/cfjs03.pdf.

31 **Black and Latinx Americans were still grossly overrepresented** These
findings, based on data from 2016 and included in the original hardcover
edition, remained true in a 2020 analysis of data from 2018. John Gramlich, "Black Imprisonment Rate in the U.S. Has Fallen by a Third Since
2006," Pew Research Center, May 6, 2020, www.pewresearch.org/fact
-tank/2020/05/06/share-of-black-white-hispanic-americans-in-prison
-2018-vs-2006/.

31 **historian Elizabeth Hinton recounts** Elizabeth Hinton, *From the War on
Poverty to the War on Crime: The Making of Mass Incarceration in America* (Cambridge, MA: Harvard University Press, 2016).

31 **"the year when this country began a thorough"** Lyndon B. Johnson
quoted by Elizabeth Hinton, "Why We Should Reconsider the War on
Crime," *Time,* March 20, 2015, time.com/3746059/war-on-crime-history/.

32 **Nixon announced his war on drugs in 1971** "President Nixon De-
clares Drug Abuse 'Public Enemy Number One,'" June 17, 1971, Richard Nixon Foundation, www.youtube.com/watch?v=y8TGLLQlD9M&ab
_channel=RichardNixonFoundation.

32 **"We could arrest their leaders"** John Ehrlichman quoted in Dan Baum,
"Legalize It All: How to Win the War on Drugs," *Harper's,* April 2016, harp
ers.org/archive/2016/04/legalize-it-all/.

32 **"the hard won gains of the civil rights movement"** *Washington Afro-
American* quoted in James Forman Jr., *Locking Up Our Own: Crime and
Punishment in Black America* (New York: Farrar, Straus & Giroux, 2017),
126–27.

32 **calling for and largely receiving** By the early 1990s, Black Americans'

"calls for tough sentencing and police protection were paired with calls for full employment, quality education and drug treatment, and criticism of police brutality." See Elizabeth Hinton, Julilly Kohler-Hausmann, and Vesla M. Weaver, "Did Blacks Really Endorse the 1994 Crime Bill?" *The New York Times,* April 13, 2016, www.nytimes.com/2016/04/13/opinion/did-blacks-really-endorse-the-1994-crime-bill.html.

33 **"remedy . . . is not as simple"** Eleanor Holmes Norton, "Restoring the Traditional Black Family," *The New York Times,* June 2, 1985, www.nytimes.com/1985/06/02/magazine/restoring-the-traditional-black-family.html.

33 **which were chopping the ladder** See William Greider, "What Reagan Has Done to America," *Rolling Stone,* December 23, 1982, www.rollingstone.com/culture/culture-news/what-reagan-has-done-to-america-79233/.

33 **The Reagan Revolution was just that** For a comprehensive overview of the racial and economic effects of Reagan's policies, including the statistics cited in this paragraph, see Manning Marable, *Race, Reform, and Rebellion: The Second Reconstruction and Beyond in Black America, 1945–2006,* 3rd ed. (Jackson: University Press of Mississippi, 2007).

35 **defined by its disproportionate White majority** While the middle class has grown more diverse since the 1980s, White people remain disproportionately represented, especially in the wealthiest brackets of the middle class. See Christopher Pulliam, Richard V. Reeves, and Ariel Gelrud Shiro, "The Middle Class Is Already Racially Diverse," Brookings, October 30, 2020, www.brookings.edu/blog/up-front/2020/10/30/the-middle-class-is-already-racially-diverse/.

35 **"It is a peculiar sensation, this double-consciousness"** For this and the following quotes, see W.E.B. Du Bois, *The Souls of Black Folk: Essays and Sketches* (Chicago: A. C. McClurg & Co., 1903), 3–4.

35 **"escape into the mass of Americans"** W.E.B. Du Bois, "On Being Ashamed of Oneself: An Essay on Race Pride," *The Crisis* 40, no. 9 (September 1933), 199.

36 **"relic of barbarism" . . . "the low social level of the mass of the race"** Du Bois, *The Souls of Black Folk,* 53.

36 **"Do Americans ever stop to reflect"** W.E.B. Du Bois, "The Talented Tenth," in *The Negro Problem: A Series of Articles by Representative American Negroes of To-Day* (New York: James Pott & Company, 1903).

37 **the human trader** I've changed references to "the slave trade" to "the human trade" in order to avoid repeating the violent abstraction that perpetuated this system. "Human trade" calls our attention to the horrors of the transport and sale of human beings. On this point, I take inspiration from Nikole Hannah-Jones, "Democracy," in *The 1619 Project: A New Origin Story,* eds. Nikole Hannah-Jones, Caitlin Roper, Ilena Silverman, and Jake Silverstein (New York: One World, 2021), 7–36.

37 **Assimilationist ideas and segregationist ideas** For more, see Ibram X. Kendi, *Stamped from the Beginning: The Definitive History of Racist Ideas in America* (New York: Nation Books, 2016).

38 **Trump's descriptor for Latinx immigrants** See Gregory Korte and Alan Gomez, "Trump Ramps Up Rhetoric on Undocumented Immigrants: 'These Aren't People. These Are Animals,'" *USA Today,* May 16, 2018, www.usatoday.com/story/news/politics/2018/05/16/trump-immigrants -animals-mexico-democrats-sanctuary-cities/617252002/.

38 **"I am apt to suspect the negroes"** See Andrew Valls, "'A Lousy Empiri-cal Scientist,' Reconsidering Hume's Racism," in *Race and Racism in Modern Philosophy,* ed. Andrew Valls (Ithaca, NY: Cornell University Press, 2005), 128–29.

38 **"all men are created equal"** "Declaration of Independence: A Transcription," National Archives, www.archives.gov/founding-docs/declaration-transcript.

38 **"It would be hazardous to affirm that"** Thomas Jefferson to Marquis de Chastellux, June 7, 1785, *Founders Online,* National Archives, founders .archives.gov/documents/Jefferson/01-08-02-0145.

39 **"history of the American Negro is the history of this strife"** Du Bois, *The Souls of Black Folk,* 4.

39 **"by white men for white men"** Jefferson Davis, *Congressional Globe,* 36th Cong., 1st Sess., April 12, 1860, 1682. Davis, then a senator, proclaimed, "This Government was not founded by negroes nor for negroes, but by white men for white men."

39 **"become assimilated into American culture"** Gunnar Myrdal, *An Ameri-can Dilemma: The Negro Problem and Modern Democracy* (New York: Harper & Brothers, 1944), 2:929.

Chapter 3: Power

41 **White New Yorkers were separating their children** For a few good books on what White people in New York and across the nation were doing, see Matthew F. Delmont, *Why Busing Failed: Race, Media, and the National Resis-tance to School Desegregation* (Berkeley: University of California Press, 2016); Jonathan Kozol, *The Shame of the Nation: The Restoration of Apartheid School-ing in America* (New York: Three Rivers Press, 2005); and Kevin M. Kruse, *White Flight: Atlanta and the Making of Modern Conservatism* (Princeton, NJ: Princeton University Press, 2007).

42 **Black parents did not mind paying** For some of the early research on this issue, see Diana T. Slaughter and Barbara Schneider, "Parental Goals and Black Student Achievement in Urban Private Elementary Schools: A Syn-opsis of Preliminary Research Findings," *The Journal of Intergroup Relations* 13, no. 1 (1985), 24–33; and Diana T. Slaughter and Barbara Schneider, *Newcomers: Blacks in Private Schools* (Evanston, IL: Northwestern Univer-

sity School of Education, 1986). In 2022, the National Center for Education Statistics reported that 4.7 million K–12 students were enrolled in private elementary and secondary schools in the United States. Students included 15 percent of Pacific Islander children; 12 percent of White children; 10 percent of Asian children; 10 percent of mixed race children; 6 percent of Black children; 5 percent of American Indian/Alaska Native children; and 4 percent of Latinx children. See National Center for Education Statistics, "Private School Enrollment," *Condition of Education*, 2022, U.S. Department of Education, Institute of Education Science, nces.ed.gov/programs/coe /indicator/cgc/private-school-enrollment.

43 **Note on kids and race: precisely how early it comes for us** For these research findings and other insights from experts in various disciplines, see Ibram X. Kendi, *How to Raise an Antiracist* (New York: One World, 2022).

45 **the first character in the history of racist power** Ibram X. Kendi, *Stamped from the Beginning: The Definitive History of Racist Ideas in America* (New York: Nation Books, 2016), 22–25.

46 **circumvent Islamic human traders** For more on this history, see Robert C. Davis, *Christian Slaves, Muslim Masters: White Slavery in the Mediterranean, the Barbary Coast, and Italy, 1500–1800* (New York: Palgrave Macmillan, 2003); Matt Lang, *Trans-Saharan Trade Routes* (New York: Cavendish, 2018); and John Wright, *The Trans-Saharan Slave Trade* (New York: Routledge, 2007).

46 **feared "black" hole of Cape Bojador** Martin Meredith, *The Fortunes of Africa: A 5000-Year History of Wealth, Greed, and Endeavor* (New York: PublicAffairs, 2014), 93–94; Gomes Eanes de Zurara, *The Chronicle of the Discovery and Conquest of Guinea*, 2 vols. (London: Hakluyt Society, 1896).

46 **"white enough, fair to look upon, and well proportioned"** Zurara, *The Chronicle of the Discovery and Conquest of Guinea*, 1: 82.

46 **first used the term "race" in a 1481 hunting poem** Jacques de Brézé, "La chasse du sénéchal de Normandie," in *Le Livre de la Chasse du Grand Seneschal de Normandye et Les Dits du Bon Chien Souillard* [by J. de Brézé](1481; Paris: Augustine Aubry, 1858), 21.

46 **same diplomat who brought the addictive tobacco plant** The botanical name for tobacco, *Nicotiana tabacum*, honors Nicot. See "M. Nicot Was Nicotine's Godfather," *San Francisco Call*, May 7, 1910, cdnc.ucr.edu /?a=d&d=SFC19100507.2.25&e=-------en--20--1--txt-txIN--------1.

46 **formally defined race for the first time** Kendi, *Stamped from the Beginning*, 36.

46 **"Race . . . means descent"** See Aimar de Ranconnet and Jean Nicot, *Trésor de la langue française* (Paris: David Douceur, 1606), 533.

47 **"like beasts, without any custom of reasonable beings"** Zurara, *The Chronicle of the Discovery and Conquest of Guinea*, 1: 85-86.

47 *negros da terra* See Mieko Nishida, *Slavery & Identity: Ethnicity, Gender, and*

Race in Salvador, Brazil, 1808–1888 (Bloomington: Indiana University Press, 2003), 13.

47 **"strong for work, the opposite of the natives"** Zuazo quoted in David M. Traboulay, *Columbus and Las Casas: The Conquest and Christianization of America, 1492–1566* (Lanham, MD: University Press of America, 1994), 58.

47 **Linnaeus locked in the racial hierarchy** Linnaeus published the first edition of *Systema Naturae* in 1735 but did not classify human beings until the tenth edition, released in 1758. See Dorothy Roberts, *Fatal Invention: How Science, Politics, and Big Business Re-Create Race in the Twenty-First Century* (New York: New Press, 2011), 29–30.

47 **Linnaeus positioned** For these quotes from *Systema Naturae*, see Roberts, *Fatal Invention*, 29–30.

48 **927 enslaved Africans landed in Portugal** Zurara, *The Chronicle of the Discovery and Conquest of Guinea*, 1: xxi.

48 **Prince Henry's royal fifth (*quinto*)** The very first Portuguese expedition beyond Cape Bojador dedicated solely to mass enslaving, organized in 1444, required a commitment to surrender one-fifth of all captured Africans to Prince Henry. See Peter Russell, *Prince Henry "the Navigator": A Life* (New Haven, CT: Yale University Press, 2000), 239–40.

48 **"to the great praise of his memory"** Zurara, *The Chronicle of the Discovery and Conquest of Guinea*, 1: xii.

48 **"than from all the taxes levied on the entire kingdom"** *The Travels of Leo of Rozmital, 1465–1467,* trans. and ed. Malcolm Letts (1957; Farnham, UK: Ashgate Publishing, 2010), 107.

Chapter 4: Biology

51 **BIOLOGICAL RACIST IDEA** The definition in the hardcover edition originally read, BIOLOGICAL RACIST: One who is expressing the idea that the races are meaningfully different in their biology and that these differences create a hierarchy of value.

51 **BIOLOGICAL ANTIRACIST IDEA** The definition in the hardcover edition originally read, BIOLOGICAL ANTIRACIST: One who is expressing the idea that the races are meaningfully the same in their biology and there are no genetic racial differences.

52 **Black students were twice as likely as White students to be suspended** See Renee Ryberg, Sarah Her, Deborah Temkin, and Kristen Harper, "Despite Reductions Since 2011–12, Black Students and Students with Disabilities Remain More Likely to Experience Suspension," Child Trends, August 9, 2021, www.childtrends.org/publications/despite-reductions-black-students-and-students-with-disabilities-remain-more-likely-to-experience-suspension.

52 **The suspension rate of Black students** U.S. Department of Education, Office for Civil Rights, *An Overview of Exclusionary Discipline Practices in*

Public Schools for the 2017–18 School Year, June 2021, www2.ed.gov/about/offices/list/ocr/docs/crdc-exclusionary-school-discipline.pdf.

53 **"microaggression," a term coined by eminent Harvard psychiatrist Chester Pierce** Chester Pierce, "Offensive Mechanism," in *The Black Seventies,* ed. Floyd B. Barbour (Boston: Porter Sargent, 1970), 280.

53 **"brief, everyday exchanges that send denigrating messages"** Derald Wing Sue, *Microaggressions in Everyday Life: Race, Gender, and Sexual Orientation* (Hoboken, NJ: John Wiley & Sons, 2010), 24.

53 **the so-called post-racial era** For more, see Ibram X. Kendi, "Our New Postracial Myth," *The Atlantic,* June 22, 2021, www.theatlantic.com/ideas/archive/2021/06/our-new-postracial-myth/619261/.

54 **its effects on people** See Joanne Lewsley, "What Are the Effects of Racism on Health and Mental Health?" *Medical News Today,* July 28, 2020, www.medicalnewstoday.com/articles/effects-of-racism; and Laurie Fickman, "Racial Discrimination Linked to Suicide," University of Houston, news release, August 3, 2020, www.uh.edu/news-events/stories/august-2020/08032020-rheeda-walker-racism-and-suicide-african-americans.php.

55 **The Black child is ill-treated like an adult** Research shows that adults perceive Black boys and girls as less innocent and more adultlike than their White peers. This racist and gendered categorization stems from what experts call "adultification." "Adultification is a form of dehumanization,™ robbing Black children of the very essence of what makes childhood distinct from all other developmental periods: innocence. Adultification contributes to a false narrative that Black youths' transgressions are intentional and malicious." See Rebecca Epstein, Jamilia J. Blake, and Thalia González, *Girlhood Interrupted: The Erasure of Black Girls' Childhood* (Washington, D.C.: Georgetown Law Center on Poverty and Inequality, August 2017), 1–2, 6.

56 **"more natural physical ability"** John Hoberman, *Darwin's Athletes: How Sport Has Damaged Black America and Preserved the Myth of Race* (New York: Houghton Mifflin, 1997), 146.

56 **"one drop of Negro blood makes a Negro"** Thomas Dixon, *The Leopard's Spots: A Romance of the White Man's Burden, 1865–1900* (New York: Doubleday, 1902), 242.

56 **"if blacks have certain inherited abilities"** Dinesh D'Souza, *The End of Racism: Principles for a Multiracial Society* (New York: Free Press, 1995), 440–41.

57 **"large size of the negro's penis"** William Lee Howard, "The Negro as a Distinct Ethnic Factor in Civilization," *Medicine* 9 (June 1903), 423–26.

57 **"I've bounced this off a number of colleagues"** See Alex Beasley, "Black Hypertension Theory Criticized: Doctor Says Slavery Conditions May Be Behind Problem," *Orlando Sentinel,* January 21, 1988, www.orlandosentinel.com/news/os-xpm-1988-01-21-0010200256-story.html.

57 **slavery/hypertension thesis received the red-carpet treatment** Clarence

Grim and Thomas W. Wilson, two of the principal authors of the slavery/hypertension thesis, published an article in *Hypertension* in October 1991. By the middle of the month, *Science News,* the *Journal of the American Medical Association,* and *Natural History* had reported on the article. In December 1992, Philip D. Curtin, a historian of Africa and the Atlantic human trade, invoked historical evidence to debunk Grim and Wilson's hypothesis. Curtin concluded, "The mortality during the slave trade was not from salt-depleting causes. . . . No evidence has been advanced that a dietary trauma experienced by 80% of one's ancestors over a period of less than 1 year, 220 years ago, could bring about a genetic change lasting to the present. Yet these hypotheses were published in the serious medical press and picked up by popular medical literature late in 1991 as though they were possibly true. Perhaps we should try harder to close the gap between scientific and historical narrative." See Philip D. Curtin, "The Slavery Hypothesis for Hypertension among African Americans: The Historical Evidence," *American Journal of Public Health* 82, no. 12 (December 1992), 1681–86, www.ncbi.nlm.nih .gov/pmc/articles/PMC1694537/?page=1.

57 **"The people who were scattered over the earth"** Genesis 9:18–27.

58 **"all his posteritie after him"** See George Best, *A True Discourse of the Late Voyages of Discoverie* (1578), in Richard Hakluyt, *The Principal Navigations Voyages Traffiques & Discoveries of the English Nation Made by Sea or Over-land to the Remote and Farthest Distant Quarters of the Earth at any time within the compasse of these 1600 Yeeres* (Glasgow: James MacLehose and Sons, 1903–1905), 7: 263–64.

58 **descending from "a different Adam"** See Justin E. H. Smith, *Nature, Human Nature & Human Difference: Race in Early Modern Philosophy* (Princeton, NJ: Princeton University Press, 2015), 92–113.

58 **released** *Men Before Adam* Isaac de La Peyrère, *Men Before Adam* (London, 1656).

58 **threw him in prison and ordered his books burned** David Rice McKee, "Isaac de la Peyrère, a Precursor of Eighteenth-Century Critical Deists," *PMLA* 59, no. 2 (June 1944), 457–58.

58 **"race of Men, not derivable from Adam"** Morgan Godwyn, *The Negro's and Indian's Advocate* (London, 1680), 15–16. Godwyn, an Anglican minister, traveled to Virginia and Barbados between 1665 and 1680. He recorded the beliefs enslavers used to justify their enslaving. Godwyn advocated for enslaved people to be converted to Christianity, in part because he believed it would make them less likely to resist their bondage. See Derek Hughes, ed., *Versions of Blackness: Key Texts on Slavery from the Seventeenth Century* (New York: Cambridge University Press, 2007), 344.

58 **debate climaxed in the 1770s** See, for example, arguments advanced around this time by Immanuel Kant and David Hume, two of the most central Enlightenment thinkers. In 1775, German philosopher Kant de-

fended monogenesis in his essay "On the Different Races of Men," arguing that all human beings descended from a single "stem species." Hume, on the other hand, demonstrated support for polygenesis. The 1777 posthumous edition of the Scottish philosopher's *Essays, Moral, Political and Literary* (published in 1753 with the footnote quoted in Chapter Two) included a revision that limited racial inferiority to Black people. Enslavers like Edward Long—who authored the influential proslavery treatise *The History of Jamaica* in 1774—seized on Hume's polygenetic ideas to defend the institution from the transatlantic antislavery movement. See Bernard Boxill, "Kantian Racism and Kantian Teleology," in *The Oxford Handbook of Philosophy and Race,* ed. Naomi Zack (New York: Oxford University Press, 2017), doi .org/10.1093/oxfordhb/9780190236953.013.46; Aaron Garrett and Silvia Sebastiana, "David Hume on Race," Ibid., doi.org/10.1093/oxfordhb /9780190236953.013.43; and Suman Seth, "Materialism, Slavery, and *The History of Jamaica,*" *Isis* 105, no. 4 (December 2014), 765, www.journals .uchicago.edu/doi/epdf/10.1086/679423.

58 **seemingly came down on the side of monogenesis. Still, he expressed** "Race," in *The Bloomsbury Encyclopedia of the American Enlightenment,* ed. Mark G. Spencer (New York: Bloomsbury, 2015), 1:863; and Thomas Jefferson, *Notes on the State of Virginia* (1785; Boston: Lilly and Wait, 1832), 65, 150.

58 **Samuel Morton and Louis Agassiz** In *Crania Americana* (1839) and *Crania Aegyptiaca* (1844), Morton measured the skulls of Native Americans and ancient Egyptians, respectively, to create a racial hierarchy that alleged polygenesis and white supremacy. Morton heavily influenced Agassiz. In a letter to his mother after visiting Morton in December 1846, Agassiz wrote: "That collection [Morton's collection of skulls in Philadelphia] alone was worth the trip to America. . . . As much as I try to feel pity at the sight of this degraded and degenerate race, as much as their fate fills me with compassion in thinking of them as really men, it is impossible for me to repress the feeling that they are not of the same blood as us." Later that month, Agassiz delivered a lecture at Boston's Lowell Institute in which he argued that Black people had a different origin than White people. See Louis Menand, "Morton, Agassiz, and the Origins of Scientific Racism in the United States," *Journal of Blacks in Higher Education,* no. 34 (Winter 2001 /2002), 110–13.

59 **"each species has been independently created"** Charles Darwin, *On the Origin of Species* (London: John Murray, 1859), 6.

59 **another method to biologically distinguish and rank the races** For example, British intellectual Herbert Spencer coined the term "survival of the fittest," which, he explained, was "that which Mr. Darwin has called 'natural selection, or the preservation of favoured races in the struggle for life.'" Spencer's concept of "survival of the fittest" inspired social Darwinism and eugenics. See Herbert Spencer, *The Principles of Biology*

(London: Williams and Norgate, 1864), 1: 444–45; and Erna Kurbegovic, "Spencer, Herbert," Eugenics Archive, eugenicsarchive.ca/discover/tree /5233b47c5c2ec5000000007e#:~:text=Spencer%20is%20best%20known %20for,in%20social%20Darwinism%20and%20eugenics.

59 **who founded American sociology** See American Sociological Association, "Albion Woodbury Small," www.asanet.org/about/governance-and -leadership/council/presidents/albion-w-small.

59 **"the second fate is often predicted for the negroes"** Albion W. Small and George E. Vincent, *An Introduction to the Study of Society* (New York: American Book Company, 1894), 179.

59 **policies encouraging reproduction among those considered to have superior genes** For excellent histories of the eugenics movement in the United States, see Wendy Kline, *Building a Better Race: Gender, Sexuality, and Eugenics from the Turn of the Century to the Baby Boom* (Berkeley: University of California Press, 2001) and Alexandra Minna Stern, *Eugenic Nation: Faults and Frontiers of Better Breeding in Modern America* (Berkeley: University of California Press, 2005).

59 **eugenics-driven policies of Nazi Germany** See James Q. Whitman, *Hitler's American Model: The United States and the Making of Nazi Race Law* (Princeton, NJ: Princeton University Press, 2017).

60 **"spread out a magnificent map"** "Remarks Made by the President . . . on the Completion of the First Survey of the Entire Human Genome Project," The White House, Office of the Press Secretary, National Human Genome Research Institute, June 26, 2000, www.genome.gov/10001356/june-2000 -white-house-event and "Reading the Book of Life; White House Remarks on Decoding of Genome," *The New York Times,* June 27, 2000, www .nytimes.com/2000/06/27/science/reading-the-book-of-life-white-house -remarks-on-decoding-of-genome.html.

60 **"Scientists planning the next phase of the human genome project"** Nicholas Wade, "For Genome Mappers, the Tricky Terrain of Race Requires Some Careful Navigating," *The New York Times,* July 20, 2001, www .nytimes.com/2001/07/20/us/for-genome-mappers-the-tricky-terrain-of -race-requires-some-careful-navigating.html.

60 **"there is a genetic component to human social behavior"** Nicholas Wade, *A Troublesome Inheritance: Genes, Race and Human History* (New York: Penguin Press, 2014), 242.

60 **"People are born with ancestry"** Jones quoted in Dorothy Roberts, *Fatal Invention: How Science, Politics, and Big Business Re-Create Race in the Twenty-First Century* (New York: New Press, 2011), 63.

61 **more genetic diversity between populations** Roberts, *Fatal Invention,* 51–53.

61 **"the mapping of the human genome concluded"** Ken Ham, "There Is Only One Race—the Human Race," *The Cincinnati Enquirer,* Septem-

ber 4, 2017, www.cincinnati.com/story/opinion/contributors/2017/09/04
/there-only-one-race-human-race/607985001/. Also see Ken Ham and A.
Charles Ware, *One Race One Blood: A Biblical Answer to Racism* (Green Forest,
AR: Master Books, 2010).

Chapter 5: Ethnicity

64 **ETHNIC RACIST IDEA** The definition in the hardcover edition was
for ETHNIC RACISM, which I now define as: A powerful collection of
inequitable and unjust policies that lead to injustice and inequity between
racialized ethnic groups and are substantiated by ideas of racial hierarchy
about racialized ethnic groups.

64 **ETHNIC ANTIRACIST IDEA** The definition in the hardcover edition
was for ETHNIC ANTIRACISM, which I now define as: A powerful collection of equitable and just policies that lead to justice and equity between
racialized ethnic groups and are substantiated by ideas of racial equality
about racialized ethnic groups.

65 **Million Man–marched in Washington, D.C.** An estimated 870,000 people, mostly Black men, attended the Million Man March, a figure that far
surpassed the 250,000 attendees of the March on Washington in 1963. The
event, held on October 16, 1995, featured twelve hours of speeches, including addresses by civil rights icons such as Rosa Parks, Maya Angelou,
Rev. Benjamin Chavis, and Rev. Al Sharpton. The Nation of Islam organized the march as a national "holy day of atonement and reconciliation." They called on Black men to take responsibility to be present in
their children's lives and reject drug use and crime. Though many Black
men attended to protest racism and its impact on housing, employment,
and other everyday concerns, the organizers' language of racial uplift re-
peated assimilationist racist ideas. See Michael A. Fletcher and Hamil R.
Harris, "Million Man March Gets Another Head Count," *The Washington
Post*, October 25, 1995, www.washingtonpost.com/archive/local/1995/10
/25/million-man-march-gets-another-head-count/4a55d01a-0423-4a32
-8e0b-8fbbe91070e3/; Michael Janofsky, "The March on Washington: The
Overview," *The New York Times*, October 16, 1995, www.nytimes.com
/1995/10/16/us/march-washington-overview-debate-march-farrakhan
-persists-black-men-converge.html; and Leah Asmelash, "A Look Back at
the Million Man March, 25 Years Later," CNN, October 16, 2020, www
.cnn.com/2020/10/16/us/million-man-march-25-year-trnd/index.html.

66 **Korean storekeeper who killed fifteen-year-old Latasha Harlins** See
Brenda E. Stevenson, *The Contested Murder of Latasha Harlins: Justice, Gender,
and the Origins of the LA Riots* (2012, New York: Oxford University Press,
2015).

66 **Haitian immigrant named Abner Louima** See Dan Barry, "Officer
Charged in Man's Torture at Station House," *The New York Times*, August 14,

1997, www.nytimes.com/1997/08/14/nyregion/officer-charged-in-man-s
-torture-at-station-house.html; and Jim O'Grady and Beth Fertig, "Twenty
Years Later: The Police Assault on Abner Louima and What It Means,"
WNYC News, August 9, 2017, www.wnyc.org/story/twenty-years-later
-look-back-nypd-assault-abner-louima-and-what-it-means-today/.

66 **forty-one bullets at the body of Amadou Diallo** See Beth Roy, *41
Shots . . . and Counting: What Amadou Diallo's Story Teaches Us About Policing, Race and Justice* (Syracuse, NY: Syracuse University Press, 2009).

67 **Congolese as "magnificent blacks"** Quoted in Hugh Thomas, *The Slave
Trade: The Story of the Atlantic Slave Trade, 1440–1870* (New York: Simon &
Schuster, 2013), 399.

67 **from Senegambia "the best slaves"** Ibid.

67 **"the best and most faithful of our slaves"** Christopher Codrington
quoted in Ibid., 400.

67 **nearly twice as much as captives from Angola** Ibid., 402.

67 **Angolans were traded more** Ibid., 401.

67 **captives hauled into Jamestown, Virginia, in August 1619** See Nikole
Hannah-Jones, "Our Democracy's Founding Ideals Were False When They
Were Written. Black Americans Have Fought to Make Them True," *The
New York Times Magazine,* August 14, 2019, www.nytimes.com/interactive
/2019/08/14/magazine/black-history-american-democracy.html.

67 **"The Negroes from the Gold Coast, Popa, and Whydah"** Quoted in
Thomas, *The Slave Trade,* 401.

68 **"African chiefs were the ones waging war on each other"** President
Yoweri Museveni quoted in "Clinton Starts African Tour," BBC News,
March 23, 1998, news.bbc.co.uk/2/hi/africa/68483.stm.

68 **did not believe they were selling their own people** Historian John K.
Thornton explains, "The fact that military enslavement was by far the most
significant method is important, for it means that rulers were not, for the
most part, selling their own subjects but people whom they, at least, regarded as aliens." Thornton, *Africa and Africans in the Making of the Atlantic World, 1400–1800,* 2nd ed. (New York: Cambridge University Press,
1998), 99.

68 **Taken together, these bills** See D'vera Cohn, "How U.S. Immigration
Laws and Rules Have Changed Through History," Pew Research Center,
September 30, 2015, www.pewresearch.org/fact-tank/2015/09/30/how-u
-s-immigration-laws-and-rules-have-changed-through-history/.

68 **Between 1980 and 2000, the Latinx immigrant population ballooned**
See Antonio Flores, "2015, Hispanic Population in the United States Statistical Portrait," Pew Research Center, September 18, 2017, www.pewhispanic
.org/2017/09/18/facts-on-u-s-latinos/.

68 **As of 2022, Black immigrants account for 10 percent** Black immigrants
comprise a larger share of the total Black population in the United States

than they did at the time of the first edition's release. I've provided the most recent data here. The original text stated: "As of 2015, Black immigrants accounted for 8.7 percent of the nation's Black population, nearly triple their share in 1980." For the more recent statistics cited in this edition, see Christine Tamir, "Key Findings about Black Immigrants in the U.S.," Pew Research Center, January 27, 2022, www.pewresearch.org/fact-tank/2022 /01/27/key-findings-about-black-immigrants-in-the-u-s/.

69 **West Indian immigrants in the 1990s tended** See Mary C. Waters, "The Role of Lineage in Identity Formation Among Black Americans," *Qualitative Sociology* 14, no. 1 (March 1991), 57–76. Waters later drew on such interviews in her book *Black Identities: West Indian Immigrant Dreams and Realities* (Cambridge, MA: Harvard University Press, 1999).

69 **African Americans tended to categorize West Indians** Ibid.

70 **1882 Chinese Exclusion Act** For anti-Asian immigration violence and policies, see Beth Lew-Williams, *The Chinese Must Go: Violence, Exclusion, and the Making of the Alien in America* (Cambridge, MA: Harvard University Press, 2018); and Erika Lee, *The Making of Asian America: A History* (New York: Simon & Schuster, 2015).

70 **"America must be kept American," President Calvin Coolidge said** Coolidge quoted in David J. Goldberg, *Discontented America: The United States in the 1920s* (Baltimore: Johns Hopkins University Press, 1999), 163.

70 **in the case of Mexican Americans, be forcibly repatriated** For literature on Mexican repatriations, see Francisco E. Balderrama and Raymond Rodríguez, *Decade of Betrayal: Mexican Repatriation in the 1930s* (Albuquerque: University of New Mexico Press, 2006); and Alex Wagner, "America's Forgotten History of Illegal Deportations," *The Atlantic,* March 6, 2017, www.theatlantic.com/politics/archive/2017/03/americas-brutal-forgotten -history-of-illegal-deportations/517971/.

70 **proclaimed Maine Representative Ira Hersey** Hersey quoted in Benjamin B. Ringer, *We the People and Others: Duality and America's Treatment of Its Racial Minorities* (New York: Routledge, 1983), 801–2.

70 **"When the numbers reached about this high in 1924"** "The American People Are Angry Alright . . . at the Politicians," Steve Bannon interviews Jeff Sessions, SiriusXM, October 4, 2015, soundcloud.com/siriusxm-news -issues/the-american-people-are-angry.

70 **policies geared toward making America White again** For an overview and analysis of the 472 executive actions affecting immigration policy completed during the Trump administration, see Jessica Bolter, Emma Israel, and Sarah Pierce, *Four Years of Profound Change: Immigration Policy during the Trump Presidency* (Washington, D.C.: Migration Policy Institute, 2022), www.migrationpolicy.org/research/four-years-change-immigration-trump.

70 **"We should have more people from places like Norway"** Trump quoted in Sarah Ruiz-Grossman, "People on Twitter Tell Trump No One in Nor-

way Wants to Come to His 'Shithole Country,'" *HuffPost*, January 11, 2018, www.huffpost.com/entry/trump-shithole-countries-norway_us_5a58199 ce4b0720dc4c5b6dc.

71 **Anglo-Saxons terrorizing Irish Catholics and Jews** See Erika Lee, *America for Americans: A History of Xenophobia in the United States* (New York: Basic Books, 2019); and Peter Gottschalk, *American Heretics: Catholics, Jews, Muslims and the History of Religious Intolerance* (New York: Palgrave Macmillan, 2013).

71 **Cuban immigrants being privileged over Mexican immigrants** See Brittany Blizzard and Jeanne Batalova, "Cuban Immigrants in the United States," Migration Policy Institute, June 11, 2020, www.migrationpolicy.org /article/cuban-immigrants-united-states-2018.

71 **model-minority construction** See Ellen D. Wu, *The Color of Success: Asian Americans and the Origins of the Model Minority* (Princeton, NJ: Princeton University Press, 2013).

71 **"Five Civilized Tribes" of Native Americans** See Roxanne Dunbar-Ortiz, *An Indigenous Peoples' History of the United States: ReVisioning American History* (Boston: Beacon Press, 2014) and Grant Foreman, *Indian Removal: The Emigration of the Five Civilized Tribes of Indians* (1932; Norman: University of Oklahoma Press, 1972).

72 **receive welfare at similar rates** See Table 19 in U.S. Department of Health & Human Services, Office of Family Assistance, *Characteristics and Financial Circumstances of TANF Recipients, Fiscal Year 2019,* November 5, 2020, www.acf.hhs.gov/ofa/data/characteristics-and-financial-circumstances-tanf -recipients-fiscal-year-2019.

72 **states with larger Black populations tend to offer the lowest welfare benefits** Ali Safawi and Cindy Reyes, "States Must Continue Recent Momentum to Further Improve TANF Benefit Levels," Center on Budget and Policy Priorities, December 2, 2021, www.cbpp.org/research/family -income-support/states-must-continue-recent-momentum-to-further -improve-tanf-benefit.

74 **African Americans commonly degrading Africans as "barbaric"** For examples of these ideas, see Ibram X. Kendi, *Stamped from the Beginning: The Definitive History of Racist Ideas in America* (New York: Nation Books, 2016), 157, 200.

74 **calling West Indians in 1920s Harlem "monkey chasers"** See Marcy S. Sacks, *Before Harlem: The Black Experience in New York City Before World War I* (Philadelphia: University of Pennsylvania Press, 2006), 29.

75 **the median family income of African Americans** See Monica Anderson, "Chapter 1: Statistical Portrait of the U.S. Black Immigrant Population," Pew Research Center, April 9, 2015, www.pewsocialtrends.org /2015/04/09/chapter-1-statistical-portrait-of-the-u-s-black-immigrant -population/.

75 **"more entrepreneurial than native-born blacks"** "Black Like Me," *The Economist,* May 11, 1996.

76 **Black immigrants . . . earn college degrees** The original edition stated that Black immigrants were, on average, the most educated group of immigrants in the United States. Now 31 percent of Black immigrants ages twenty-five and older have a bachelor's degree or higher, compared to 33 percent of the overall immigrant population. Christine Tamir and Monica Anderson, "3. A Growing Share of Black Immigrants Have a College Degree or Higher," Pew Research Center, January 20, 2022, www.pewresearch.org/race-ethnicity/2022/01/20/a-growing-share-of-black-immigrants-have-a-college-degree-or-higher/ and "5. Household Income, Poverty Status and Home Ownership among Black Immigrants," Pew Research Center, www.pewresearch.org/race-ethnicity/2022/01/20/household-income-poverty-status-and-home-ownership-among-black-immigrants/.

76 **earn lower wages than similarly trained non-Black immigrants** In 2019, the median household income ($57,200) for Black immigrants was nearly $6,000 less than the median household income ($63,000) for the U.S. immigrant population. See Tamir and Anderson, "5. Household Income, Poverty Status and Home Ownership Among Black Immigrants."

76 **the highest unemployment rate of any immigrant group** Among the foreign-born population in 2021, Blacks had the highest unemployment rate (7.1 percent), followed by Hispanics (5.7 percent), Whites (5.2 percent), and Asians (4.9 percent), and See U.S. Bureau of Labor Statistics, "Labor Force Characteristics of Foreign-Born Workers Summary," news release, May 18, 2022, www.bls.gov/news.release/forbrn.nr0.htm.

76 **"immigrant self-selection"** Suzanne Model, *West Indian Immigrants: A Black Success Story?* (New York: Russell Sage Foundation, 2008), 56–59.

76 **the "migrant advantage"** Isabel Wilkerson, *The Warmth of Other Suns: The Epic Story of America's Great Migration* (New York: Vintage Books, 2010), 264–65.

76 **"West Indians are not a black success story"** Model, *West Indian Immigrants,* 3.

77 **Rosemary Traoré found in a study** Rosemary L. Traoré, "African Students in America: Reconstructing New Meanings of 'African American' in Urban Education," *Intercultural Education* 14, no. 3 (2003), 244.

Chapter 6: Body

78 **BODILY RACIST IDEA** The definition in the hardcover edition originally read, BODILY RACIST: One who is perceiving certain racialized bodies as more animal-like and violent than others.

78 **BODILY ANTIRACIST IDEA** The definition in the hardcover edition originally read, BODILY ANTIRACIST: One who is humanizing, deracializing, and individualizing nonviolent and violent behavior.

78 **the kids of working-class White families** For a good study on the transformation in New York City, see Walter Thabit, *How East New York Became a Ghetto* (New York: New York University Press, 2003).

79 **"Blacks must understand and acknowledge"** "Transcript of President Clinton's Speech on Race Relations," October 16, 1995, CNN, October 17, 1995, www.cnn.com/US/9510/megamarch/10-16/update /transcript.html.

79 **the Black body was as devilish as any people** John Smith, "Advertisements: Or, The Path-way to Experience to Erect a Plantation," in *Capt. John Smith, Works, 1608–1631*, ed. Edward Arber (Birmingham, UK: E. Arber, 1884), 955.

79 **"make yourself infinitely Blacker than you are already"** See Cotton Mather, *A Good Master Well Served* (Boston: B. Green, and J. Allen, 1696), 53.

79 **"the Cruel dispositions of those Creatures"** Drysdale quoted in Mary Miley Theobald, "Slave Conspiracies in Colonial Virginia," *Colonial Williamsburg Journal* (Winter 2005–2006), research.colonialwilliamsburg.org /Foundation/journal/Winter05-06/conspiracy.cfm.

79 **federal "appropriations for protecting . . . against ruthless savages"** "A Declaration of the Causes Which Impel the State of Texas to Secede from the Federal Union," February 2, 1861, Texas State Library and Archives Commission, www.tsl.texas.gov/ref/abouttx/secession/2feb1861.html.

79 **"The poor African has become a fiend"** Tillman quoted in Albert Bushnell Hart, *The Southern South* (New York: D. Appleton and Company, 1912), 93.

79 **"large . . . criminal display of the violence among minority groups"** Marvin E. Wolfgang and Franco Ferracuti, *The Subculture of Violence: Toward an Integrated Theory in Criminology* (1967; New York: Routledge, 2001), 264.

80 **"The core criminal-justice population is the black underclass"** Heather Mac Donald, *The War on Cops: How the New Attack on Law and Order Makes Everyone Less Safe* (New York: Encounter Books, 2016), 233.

80 **Americans today see the Black body** John Paul Wilson, Kurt Hugenberg, and Nicholas O. Rule, "Racial Bias in Judgments of Physical Size and Formidability: From Size to Threat," *Journal of Personality and Social Psychology* 113, no. 1 (July 2017), 59–80, www.apa.org/pubs/journals/releases/psp -pspi0000092.pdf.

80 **lynched by the thousands** The Equal Justice Initiative estimated that approximately 6,500 Black people were lynched in the United States between 1865 and 1950. See Equal Justice Initiative, "Reconstruction in America: Racial Violence after the Civil War," 2020, eji.org/reports/reconstruction -in-america-overview/.

81 **I considered joining the Zulu Nation** I did not identify the Zulu Nation as a gang then; neither did its members. Here is an article on the debate over the

term as well as what the Zulu Nation was facing in the mid-1990s in NYC: Adam Nossiter, "Hip-Hop Club (Gang?) Is Banned in the Bronx; Cultural Questions About Zulu Nation," *The New York Times,* October 4, 1995, www.nytimes.com/1995/10/04/nyregion/hip-hop-club-gang-is-banned -in-the-bronx-cultural-questions-about-zulu-nation.html.

82 **comprise 13 percent of the U.S. population** U.S. Census Bureau, "Quick Facts: United States," www.census.gov/quickfacts/fact/table/US /PST045221.

82 **Black bodies accounted for 26 percent** (Numbers rounded to the nearest whole percent.) The first edition included data from 2015, 2016, 2017, and 2018. Unarmed Black people are now, on average, even more likely, compared to unarmed White people, to be killed by police officers than at the time of publication in 2019. See the *Washington Post* database on police shootings, which is updated regularly, www.washingtonpost.com/graphics /investigations/police-shootings-database/.

82 **the largest series of demonstrations in U.S. history** Larry Buchanan, Quoctrung Bui, and Jugal K. Patel, "Black Lives Matter May Be the Largest Movement in U.S. History," *The New York Times,* July 3, 2020, www .nytimes.com/interactive/2020/07/03/us/george-floyd-protests-crowd -size.html.

82 **more than three times as likely to be killed** See "Fatal Police Shootings of Unarmed Black People in US More Than 3 Times as High as in Whites," *BMJ* (*British Medical Journal*), October 27, 2020, www.bmj.com/company /newsroom/fatal-police-shootings-of-unarmed-black-people-in-us-more -than-3-times-as-high-as-in-whites/.

83 **Republicans called those items "welfare for criminals"** See Elizabeth Hinton, Julilly Kohler-Hausmann, and Vesla M. Weaver, "Did Blacks Really Endorse the 1994 Crime Bill?" *The New York Times,* April 13, 2016, www .nytimes.com/2016/04/13/opinion/did-blacks-really-endorse-the-1994 -crime-bill.html; and U.S. Congress, *Congressional Record,* 103rd Cong., 2nd Sess., Vol. 140, Pt. 15, August 11, 1994, 21520. Christopher Cox (R-CA) was the congressman who referred to portions of the proposed bill as "welfare for criminals."

83 **Twenty-six of the thirty-eight voting members** Hinton, Kohler-Hausmann, and Weaver, "Did Blacks Really Endorse the 1994 Crime Bill?"

83 **their fear for my Black body—and of it** See James Forman Jr., *Locking Up Our Own: Crime and Punishment in Black America* (New York: Farrar, Straus & Giroux, 2017).

83 **eligible, when I turned thirteen in 1995, to be tried as an adult** For overviews of the 1994 Crime Bill and its impacts, see Lauren-Brooke Eisen, "The 1994 Crime Bill and Beyond: How Federal Funding Shapes the Criminal Justice System," Brennan Center for Justice, September 9, 2019, www.brennancenter.org/our-work/analysis-opinion/1994-crime-bill-and

-beyond-how-federal-funding-shapes-criminal-justice; and Ranya Shannon, "3 Ways the 1994 Crime Bill Continues to Hurt Communities of Color," Center for American Progress, May 10, 2019, www.americanprogress .org/article/3-ways-1994-crime-bill-continues-hurt-communities-color/.

83 **"put politics and party above law and order"** Ann Devroy, "Crime Bill Is Signed with Flourish," *The Washington Post*, September 14, 1994, www .washingtonpost.com/archive/politics/1994/09/14/crime-bill-is-signed -with-flourish/650b1c2f-e306-4c00-9c6f-80bc9cc57e55/.

84 **the most expensive crime bill in U.S. history** Kenneth J. Cooper, "House Passes $30 Billion Crime Bill, 235 to 195," *The Washington Post*, August 22, 1994, www.washingtonpost.com/archive/politics/1994/08/22 /house-passes-30-billion-crime-bill-235-to-195/c1780662-ae99-42b3-a698 -21b270d46a52/.

84 **John J. DiIulio Jr. warned of the "coming of the super-predators"** John DiIulio, "The Coming of the Super-Predators," *The Weekly Standard*, November 27, 1995, www.washingtonexaminer.com/weekly-standard/the -coming-of-the-super-predators.

84 **later said he regretted using the term** Elizabeth Becker, "As Ex-Theorist on Young 'Superpredators,' Bush Aide Has Regrets," *The New York Times*, February 9, 2001, www.nytimes.com/2001/02/09/us/as-ex-theorist-on -young-superpredators-bush-aide-has-regrets.html.

84 **"teenagers and adults who are themselves deviant, delinquent or criminal"** William J. Bennett, John J. DiIulio, Jr., and John P. Walters, *Body Count: Moral Poverty . . . and How to Win America's War against Crime and Drugs* (New York: Simon & Schuster, 1996), 27–28.

85 **Violence had already begun its dramatic decline** Violence "more than doubled" between the late 1960s and early 1990s, peaking in 1991 before "beginning a long-term decline." In fact, violence was decreasing prior to the passage of the 1994 Crime Bill. The homicide rate "followed a similar pattern." See Rashawn Ray and William A. Galston, "Did the 1994 Crime Bill Cause Mass Incarceration," Brookings, August 28, 2020, www.brook ings.edu/blog/fixgov/2020/08/28/did-the-1994-crime-bill-cause-mass -incarceration/; and Disaster Center, "United States Population and Number of Crimes, 1960–2019," www.disastercenter.com/crime/uscrime.htm.

85 **Note on "violence" and "crime":** I've learned from abolitionist writers Mariame Kaba, *We Do This 'Til We Free Us: Abolitionist Organizing and Transforming Justice* (Chicago: Haymarket Books, 2021); and Derecka Purnell, *Becoming Abolitionists: Police, Protests, and the Pursuit of Freedom* (New York: Astra House, 2021).

85 **Note on "violence" and "crime": the more severe violence that policy choices inflict on whole communities** See "Pressley, Advocates Re-Introduce People's Justice Guarantee to Transform Criminal Legal System," Congresswoman Ayanna Pressley, March 11, 2021, pressley.house

.gov/2021/03/11/pressley-advocates-re-introduce-people-s-justice-guar
antee-transform-criminal/.

85 **Note on "violence" and "crime": alcohol use is more harmful to the
body** For an accessible overview of peer-reviewed research on this topic, see
Erin Brodwin, "We Took a Scientific Look at Whether Weed or Alcohol Is
Worse for You—and There Appears to be a Winner," *Business Insider,* August 28, 2018, www.businessinsider.com/alcohol-marijuana-which-worse
-health-2017-11.

85 **Note on "violence" and "crime": the easy availability of guns—which
has been proven to spur gun violence** Emma Tucker and Priya Krish-
nakumar, "States with Weaker Gun Laws Have Higher Rates of Firearm
Related Homicides and Suicides, Study Finds," CNN, May 27, 2022, www
.cnn.com/2022/01/20/us/everytown-weak-gun-laws-high-gun-deaths
-study/index.html.

85 **Homicides had dropped** Disaster Center, "United States Population and
Number of Crimes, 1960–2019."

85 **intense crack-market competition and unregulated gun trafficking
spiked the rate** For an early and influential (if problematic) study of this
phenomenon, see Alfred Blumstein and Daniel Cork, "Linking Gun Availability to Youth Gun Violence," *Law and Contemporary Problems* 59, no. 1
(December 1996), 5–24, scholarship.law.duke.edu/cgi/viewcontent.cgi?htt
psredir=1&article=4309&context=lcp.

87 **In 1993, near the height of urban violence** Detis T. Duhart, "Urban,
Suburban, and Rural Victimization, 1993–98," Bureau of Justice Statistics
Special Report, National Crime Victimization Survey, U.S. Department of
Justice, October 2000, 3, www.bjs.gov/content/pub/pdf/usrv98.pdf.

87 **In 2020, for every thousand urban residents** Violence in urban areas
has declined further since the hardcover publication of *How to Be an Antiracist.* The original text read, "In 2016, for every thousand urban residents, about thirty, or 3 percent, reported being victims of violent crimes."
For data referenced in this edition, see Rachel E. Morgan and Alexandra
Thompson, "Criminal Victimization, 2020," Bureau of Justice Statistics,
U.S. Department of Justice, October 2021, 10, www.bjs.ojp.gov/sites/g
/files/xyckuh236/files/media/document/cv20.pdf.

87 **more than half of violent incidents in 2020 went unreported** Statisti-
cians found that only "about 40 percent" of violent incidents were reported
to police in 2020. Ibid., 1.

87 **being around violence can create adverse effects** See U.S. Department of Health and Human Services, Office of Disease Prevention and
Health Promotion, "Crime and Violence," Healthy People 2030, health
.gov/healthypeople/priority-areas/social-determinants-health/literature
-summaries/crime-and-violence.

88 **more dangerous than "war zones"** Jenna Johnson, "Donald Trump to

African American and Hispanic Voters: 'What Do You Have to Lose?'" *The Washington Post,* August 22, 2016, www.washingtonpost.com/news /post-politics/wp/2016/08/22/donald-trump-to-african-american-and -hispanic-voters-what-do-you-have-to-lose/.

88 **Note on the criminal punishment system: As abolitionists have pointed out** See, for example, Mariame Kaba, *We Do This 'Til We Free Us.*

89 **A study that used National Longitudinal Survey of Youth data** Delbert S. Elliott, "Longitudinal Research in Criminology: Promise and Practice," paper presented at the NATO Conference on Cross-National Longitudinal Research on Criminal Behavior, July 19–25, 1992, Frankfurt, Germany.

89 **as the Urban Institute stated** Austin Nicholas, Josh Mitchell, and Stephan Lindner, *Consequences of Long-Term Unemployment* (Washington, D.C.: Urban Institute, 2013), 1.

89 **the 2.5 percentage-point decrease in unemployment between 1992 and 1997** Steven Raphael and Rudolf Winter-Ebmer, "Identifying the Effect of Unemployment on Crime," *Journal of Law & Economics* 44, no. 1 (April 2001), 281.

89 **Sociologist Karen F. Parker strongly linked** Tanvi Misra, "How Black-Owned Businesses Help Reduce Youth Violence," CityLab | Economy, Bloomberg, March 16, 2015, www.bloomberg.com/news/articles/2015-03 -16/a-new-study-finds-that-black-entrepreneurship-helps-decrease-youth -crime-in-african-american-communities.

89 **43 percent reduction in violence-related arrests for Black youths** Alexia Elejalde-Ruiz, "Nearly Half of Young Black Men in Chicago Out of Work, Out of School: Report," *Chicago Tribune,* January 25, 2016, www .chicagotribune.com/ct-youth-unemployment-urban-league-0126-biz -20160124-story.html.

89 **Black neighborhoods do not all have similar levels** "Variations in levels of violent crime are linked to complex characteristics of neighborhoods, including disadvantage, segregation, land use, social control, social capital, and social trust, as well as the characteristics of nearby neighborhoods." See HUD USER, "Neighborhoods and Violent Crime," *Evidence Matters,* Summer 2016, www.huduser.gov/portal/periodicals/em/summer16/highlight2 .html.

90 **the highest rates of unemployment of any demographic group** In the first quarter of 2022, Black teenagers aged eighteen and nineteen had the highest unemployment rates in the country at 21.6 percent. See U.S. Bureau of Labor Statistics, "Labor Force Statistics from the Current Population Survey," April 1, 2022, www.bls.gov/web/empsit/cpsee_e16.htm. For a graphical representation of Black youths' unemployment rates over time, see U.S. Bureau of Labor Statistics, "Unemployment Rate—16–19 Yrs., Black or African American," retrieved from FRED, Federal Reserve Bank of St. Louis, fred.stlouisfed.org/series/LNS14000018.

Chapter 7: Culture

92 **CULTURAL RACIST IDEA** The definition in the hardcover edition was for CULTURAL RACIST, which I now define as: One who is creating a cultural standard and imposing a cultural hierarchy among racialized ethnic groups.

92 **CULTURAL ANTIRACIST IDEA** The definition in the hardcover edition was for CULTURAL ANTIRACIST, which I now define as: One who is rejecting cultural standards and equalizing cultural differences among racialized ethnic groups.

93 **a term coined by psychologist Robert Williams in 1973** Robert L. Williams, *History of the Association of Black Psychologists: Profiles of Outstanding Black Psychologists* (Bloomington, IN: AuthorHouse, 2008), 80. See also Robert L. Williams, ed., *Ebonics: The True Language of Black Folks* (St. Louis, MO: Institute of Black Studies, 1975).

93 **"the legitimacy and richness" of Ebonics as a language** "Oakland School Board Resolution on Ebonics (Original Version)," *Journal of English Linguistics* 26, no. 2 (June 1998), 170–79; doi.org/10.1177/007542429802600207.

94 **Jesse Jackson at first called it "an unacceptable surrender"** Neil A. Lewis, "Black English Is Not a Second Language, Jackson says," *The New York Times,* December 23, 1996, www.nytimes.com/1996/12/23/us/black -english-is-not-a-second-language-jackson-says.html.

94 **African American Ebonics, Jamaican Patois, Haitian Creole, Brazilian Calunga, and Cubano** See John Baugh, *Out of the Mouths of Slaves: African American Language and Educational Malpractice* (Austin: University of Texas Press, 1999); Barbara Lalla and Jean D'Costa, *Language in Exile: Three Hundred Years of Jamaican Creole* (Tuscaloosa: University of Alabama Press, 1990); Arthur K. Spears and Carole M. Berotte Joseph, eds., *The Haitian Creole Language: History, Structure, Use, and Education* (Lanham, MD: Lexington Books, 2010); Steven Byrd, *Calunga and the Legacy of an African Language in Brazil* (Albuquerque: University of New Mexico Press, 2012); and John M. Lipski, *A History of Afro-Hispanic Language: Five Centuries, Five Continents* (Cambridge, UK: Cambridge University Press, 2005).

94 **modern English had grown from Latin, Greek, and Germanic roots** See Albert C. Baugh and Thomas Cable, *A History of the English Language*, 5th ed. (London: Routledge, 2002); and Tamara M. Green, *The Greek & Latin Roots of English*, 3rd ed. (Lanham, MD: Rowman & Littlefield, 2003).

94 **"In practically all its divergences"** Gunnar Myrdal, *An American Dilemma: The Negro Problem and Modern Democracy* (New York: Harper & Brothers, 1944), 2:928.

94 **the "bible" of the civil rights movement** Roy Wilkins, executive director of the NAACP, wrote that Myrdal's study "would be used more or less as a Bible for Americans to guide them in their treatment of the Negro." Wilkins quoted in Walter A. Jackson, *Gunnar Myrdal and American's Conscience: Social*

Engineering and Racial Liberalism, 1938–1987 (Chapel Hill: University of North Carolina Press, 1994), 113.

95 **"It is to the advantage of American Negroes"** Myrdal, *An American Dilemma*, 2:929.

95 **as President Theodore Roosevelt said in 1905** Theodore Roosevelt, "At the Lincoln Dinner of the Republican Club, New York, February 13, 1905," in *A Compilation of the Messages and Speeches of Theodore Roosevelt, 1901–1905,* ed. Alfred Henry Lewis (New York: Bureau of National Literature and Art, 1906), 1:562.

95 **the first formal Black intellectual society** "American Negro Academy (ANA)," Encyclopedia.com, www.encyclopedia.com/history/encyclopedias-almanacs-transcripts-and-maps/american-negro-academy-ana.

95 **those racist Americans who classed Africans as fundamentally imitative** For example, see Lothrop Stoddard, *The Rising Tide of Color Against White World-Supremacy* (New York: Charles Scribner's Sons, 1921), 100–101. Stoddard seethed, "The negro is a facile, even eager, imitator; but there he stops."

95 **"This quality of imitation has been the grand preservative"** Alexander Crummell, "The Destined Superiority of the Negro," in *Civilization & Black Progress: Selected Writings of Alexander Crummell on the South,* ed. J. R. Oldfield (Charlottesville: University of Virginia Press, 1995), 51.

96 **Jason Riley . . . did not see us or our disciples** Jason L. Riley, *Please Stop Helping Us: How Liberals Make It Harder for Blacks to Succeed* (New York: Encounter Books, 2015), 51.

96 **"If blacks can close the civilization gap"** Dinesh D'Souza, *The End of Racism: Principles for a Multiracial Society* (New York: Free Press, 1995), 527.

97 **"outward physical manifestations of culture"** Linda James Myers, "The Deep Structure of Culture: Relevance of Traditional African Culture in Contemporary Life," in *Afrocentric Visions: Studies in Culture and Communication,* ed. Janice D. Hamlet (Thousand Oaks, CA: SAGE, 1998), 4.

97 **"North American negroes . . . in culture and language"** Franz Boas, *The Mind of Primitive Man* (New York: Macmillan, 1911), 127–28.

97 **"It is very difficult to find in the South today"** Robert Park, "The Conflict and Fusion of Cultures with Special Reference to the Negro," *Journal of Negro History* 4, no. 2 (April 1919), 116.

97 **"Stripped of his cultural heritage"** E. Franklin Frazier, *The Negro Family in the United States* (1939; Chicago: University of Chicago Press, 1940), 41.

97 **"the Negro is only an American . . . no values and culture to guard and protect"** Nathan Glazer, "The Negroes," in Nathan Glazer and Daniel Patrick Moynihan, *Beyond the Melting Pot: The Negroes, Puerto Ricans, Jews, Italians, and Irish of New York City* (Cambridge, MA: MIT Press, 1963), 53.

97 **"we are not Africans," Bill Cosby told the NAACP** Adam Serwer, "Bill Cosby's Famous 'Pound Cake' Speech, Annotated," *BuzzFeed,* July 9,

2015, www.buzzfeednews.com/article/adamserwer/bill-cosby-pound-for -pound.

97 **African cultures had been overwhelmed** See Boas, *The Mind of Primitive Man.*

98 **"the deep structure of culture"** See Wade Nobles, "Extended Self: Rethinking the So-called Negro Self of Concept," in *Black Psychology,* ed. Reginald L. Jones, 3rd ed. (Berkeley, CA: Cobb & Henry, 1991), 295–302.

98 **Western "outward" forms "while retaining inner [African] values"** Melville J. Herskovits, *The Myth of the Negro Past* (New York: Harper & Brothers Publishers, 1941), 298.

99 **Hip-hop has had the most sophisticated vocabulary** Varun Jewalikar and Federica Fragapane, "Hip Hop Has the Largest Average Vocabulary Size Followed by Heavy Metal," *Musixmatch,* December 3, 2015, lab.musixmatch .com/vocabulary_genres/.

99 **"rap retards black success"** John H. McWhorter, "How Hip-Hop Holds Blacks Back," *City Journal,* Summer 2003, www.city-journal.org/html/how -hip-hop-holds-blacks-back-12442.html.

99 **"You can't listen to all that language and filth"** See Patrick Rogers, "Gunning for Gangstas," *People,* June 26, 1995, people.com/archive/gun ning-for-gangstas-vol-43-no-25/.

100 **Nathan Glazer, who lamented** Nathan Glazer, *We Are All Multiculturalists Now* (Cambridge, MA: Harvard University Press, 1997).

101 **"That every practice and sentiment is barbarous"** James Beattie, *An Essay on the Nature and Immutability of Truth; In Opposition to Sophistry and Scepticism* (Edinburgh: A. Kincaid & J. Bell, 1770), 483.

102 **In the fable** "Townsend Version (The Man and the Lion)," in "The Lion and the Statue," *Fables of Aesop,* fablesofaesop.com/the-lion-and-the-statue .html.

102 **"All cultures must be judged in relation to their own history"** Ashley Montagu, *Man's Most Dangerous Myth: The Fallacy of Race,* 2nd ed. (New York: Columbia University Press, 1945), 150.

Chapter 8: Behavior

103 **BEHAVIORAL RACIST IDEA** The definition in the hardcover edition originally read, BEHAVIORAL RACIST: One who is making individuals responsible for the perceived behavior of racial groups and making racial groups responsible for the behavior of individuals.

103 **BEHAVIORAL ANTIRACIST IDEA** The definition in the hardcover edition originally read, BEHAVIORAL ANTIRACIST: One who is making racial group behavior fictional and individual behavior real.

103 **As legal scholar James Forman Jr. documents** James Forman Jr., *Locking Up Our Own: Crime and Punishment in Black America* (New York: Farrar, Straus & Giroux, 2017), 185–216.

103 **"Did Martin Luther King successfully fight"** Eric Holder quoted in Paul Duggan, "D.C. Residents Urged to Care, Join War on Guns," *The Washington Post,* January 14, 1995, www.washingtonpost.com/archive/local/1995 /01/14/dc-residents-urged-to-care-join-war-on-guns/0b36f1f3-27ac -4685-8fb6-3eda372e93ac/.

104 **"You are costing everybody's freedom," Jesse Jackson told** Jesse Jackson quoted in Forman, *Locking Up Our Own*, 195.

104 **The so-called "first Black president"** See Toni Morrison, "Comment," *The New Yorker,* September 27, 1998, www.newyorker.com/magazine/1998 /10/05/comment-6543; and Ta-Nehisi Coates, "It Was No Compliment to Call Bill Clinton 'The First Black President,'" *The Atlantic,* August 27, 2015, www.theatlantic.com/politics/archive/2015/08/toni-morrison-wasnt -giving-bill-clinton-a-compliment/626928/.

104 **"It isn't racist for Whites to say"** "Transcript of President Clinton's Speech on Race Relations," October 16, 1995, CNN, October 17, 1995, www.cnn .com/US/9510/megamarch/10-16/clinton/update/transcript.html.

104 **Black people needed to stop playing "race cards"** Peter Collier and David Horowitz, eds., *The Race Card: White Guilt, Black Resentment, and the Assault on Truth and Justice* (Rocklin, CA: Prima, 1997), viii.

104 **disinterested, racist teachers** Theresa Glennon, "Looking for Air: Excavating Destructive Educational and Racial Policies to Build Successful School Communities," in *Justice for Kids: Keeping Kids Out of the Juvenile Justice System,* ed. Nancy E. Dowd (New York: New York University Press, 2011), 112.

104 **overcrowded schools** While I was in high school, the National Center for Education Statistics highlighted glaring racial disparities in school overcrowding, observing, "Schools with more than 50 percent minority enrollment were more likely to report being severely overcrowded than were schools with 21 to 50 percent minority enrollment and those with 5 percent or less minority enrollment (15 percent versus 6 percent and 4 percent, respectively)." National Center for Education Statistics, "Condition of America's Public School Facilities: 1999," nces.ed.gov/surveys/frss/publications /2000032/index.asp?sectionid=8.

104 **daily racist attacks that fell on young Black boys and girls** These attacks continued into the so-called post-racial era. A study conducted in 2020 reported that Black adolescents average more than five experiences of racism each day. See Devin English, Sharon F. Lambert, Brendesha M. Tynes, Lisa Bowleg, Maria Cecilia Zea, and Lionel C. Howard, "Daily Multidimensional Racial Discrimination among Black U.S. American Adolescents," *Journal of Applied Developmental Psychology* 66 (January–February 2020), doi .org/10.1016/j.appdev.2019.101068.

106 **Note on behavioral racist ideas: racist theorists spoke about specific racial groups** See Ibram X. Kendi, *Stamped from the Beginning: The Definitive History of Racist Ideas in America* (New York: Nation Books, 2016).

106 **Note on behavioral racist ideas: pointed to irresponsible personal behaviors** For critiques of this line of attack, see Keeanga-Yamahtta Taylor, "The Black Plague," *The New Yorker,* April 16, 2020, www.newyorker.com /news/our-columnists/the-black-plague; and Ibram X. Kendi, "Why Don't We Know Who the Coronavirus Victims Are?" *The Atlantic,* April 1, 2020, www.theatlantic.com/ideas/archive/2020/04/stop-looking-away-race -covid-19-victims/609250/.

106 **The same behavioral racist ideas drove many of the Trump voters** See Kenrya Rankin, "Poll: Trump Supporters More Likely to View Black People as 'Violent' and 'Lazy,'" *Colorlines,* July 1, 2016, www.colorlines.com /articles/poll-trump-supporters-more-likely-view-black-people-violent -and-lazy; and Tom Jacobs, "Research Finds That Racism, Sexism, and Status Fears Drove Trump Voters," *Pacific Standard,* April 24, 2018, psmag.com /news/research-finds-that-racism-sexism-and-status-fears-drove-trump -voters.

106 **"America's Black community . . . has turned America's major cities"** See Eli Rosenberg, "Homeland Security Official Resigns After Comments Linking Blacks to 'Laziness' and 'Promiscuity' Come to Light," *The Washington Post,* November 17, 2017, www.washingtonpost.com/news/powerpost /wp/2017/11/16/republican-appointee-resigns-from-the-dhs-after-past -comments-about-blacks-muslims-come-to-light/.

106 **"obvious for decades that the real culprit is black behavior"** Jason L. Riley, *Please Stop Helping Us: How Liberals Make It Harder for Blacks to Succeed* (New York: Encounter Books, 2015), 4.

107 **"had improved greatly in every respect"** John C. Calhoun quoted in B. Ricardo Brown, *Until Darwin, Science, Human Variety and the Origins of Race* (New York: Routledge, 2016), 72.

107 **Freed Black people "cut off" "from the spirit of White society"** Philip A. Bruce, *The Plantation Negro as a Freeman: Observations on His Character, Condition, and Prospects in Virginia* (New York: G. P. Putnam's Sons, 1889), 48, 242, 53, 129, 16, 42–43, 212, 3–4.

108 **"All the vices which are charged upon the Negroes"** Benjamin Rush, *An Address to the Inhabitants of the British Settlements in America, Upon Slave-Keeping* (Boston: John Boyles, 1773), 2–3.

108 **first White antislavery society** Rush was one of the primary organizers, in 1774, of the Pennsylvania Society for Promoting the Abolition of Slavery, and the Relief of Free Negroes Unlawfully Held in Bondage. Donald J. D'Elia, "Dr. Benjamin Rush and the Negro," *Journal of the History of Ideas* 30, no. 3 (July–September 1969), 413–22.

108 **Garrison stated that slavery "degraded" Black people** William Lloyd Garrison, "Preface," in Frederick Douglass, *Narrative of the Life of Frederick Douglass, an American Slave* (1845; Boston: Anti-Slavery Office, 1849), vii.

108 **"the first and greatest step toward the settlement"** W.E.B. Du Bois,

"The Conversation of Races," in *W.E.B. Du Bois: A Reader,* ed. David Levering Lewis (New York: Henry Holt, 1995), 20–27.

108 **Jim Crow historian's framing of slavery** See Bruce, *The Plantation Negro as a Freeman.*

108 **Black "infighting," materialism, poor parenting, colorism, defeatism, rage** See Joy DeGruy, *Post Traumatic Slave Syndrome: America's Legacy of Enduring Injury and Healing* (Portland, OR: Uptone Press, 2005).

109 **PTSD rates ranged from 13.5 to 30 percent** Miriam Reisman, "PTSD Treatment for Veterans: What's Working, What's New, and What's Next," *Pharmacy and Therapeutics* 41, no. 10 (2016), 623–34.

109 **the first generation of emancipated Black people** The field-defining work on this era is Eric Foner, *Reconstruction: America's Unfinished Revolution, 1863–1877* (New York: Harper & Row, 1988).

109 **"There is not one personality trait of the Negro"** Abram Kardiner and Lionel Ovesey, *The Mark of Oppression: A Psychosocial Study of the American Negro* (New York: W. W. Norton, 1951), 81, 89, 290.

110 **all of twenty-five subjects** Ibid., xv.

111 **The so-called Nation's Report Card told Americans** For this data in the Nation's Report Card, visit the NAEP Data Explorer at www.nationsreportcard.gov/ndecore/landing.

111 **By 2019, the scoring gaps** Ibid. In 2019, Asian and Pacific Islander fourth-graders scored thirty-six points, White fourth-graders scored twenty-five points, and Latinx fourth-graders scored seven points higher than Black fourth-graders on the standardized math tests. This data has been updated since the first edition.

111 **The racial "achievement gap" in reading** Ibid. The racial "achievement gap" in reading between White and Black fourth-graders decreased by six points between 1992 and 2019 (a thirty-two-point difference in 1992 compared to a twenty-six-point difference in 2019). The gap widened between White and Black twelfth-graders by eight points (a twenty-four-point difference in 1992 compared to a thirty-two-point difference in 2019). This data has been updated since the first edition.

111 **Among students who graduated high school in 2019** The differential between Black and Native students was twenty-one points. See Greta Anderson, "More SAT Test Takers but Lower Scores," *Inside Higher Ed,* September 24, 2019, www.insidehighered.com/admissions/article/2019/09/24/minority-and-first-generation-sat-scores-fall-behind.

111 **the U.S. test-prep and private tutoring industry** The first edition shared the estimated worth calculated by Global Industry Analysts, Inc., which stated that the industry was worth $12 billion in 2014 and projected to reach $17.5 billion in 2020. The COVID-19 pandemic and the societal turn to remote learning contributed to expansion that shattered experts' expectations. See "Global Private Tutoring Market to Reach $201.8 Billion

by 2026," Cision PR Newswire, March 24, 2022, www.prnewswire.com
/news-releases/global-private-tutoring-market-to-reach-201-8-billion
-by-2026--301507676.html.

112 **concentrated in Asian and White communities** Researchers recently examined geocoded data from 1997 to 2016 pertaining to U.S. private tutoring center locations. They found, "the number and growth of private
tutoring centers is heavily concentrated in geographic areas with high income and parental education. Nearly half of tutoring centers are in areas in
the top quintile of income. . . . Even conditional on income and parental
education, private tutoring centers tend to locate in areas with many immigrant and Asian-American families." See Edward Kim, Joshua Goodman,
and Martin R. West, "Kumon In: The Recent, Rapid Rise of Private Tutoring Centers" (EdWorkingPaper 21-367), 2021, www.edworkingpapers
.com/sites/default/files/ai21-367.pdf (courtesy of the Annenberg Institute
at Brown University).

113 **the so-called "attribution effect"** Mark Sherman, "Why We Don't Give
Each Other a Break," *Psychology Today,* June 20, 2014, www.psychologytoday
.com/us/blog/real-men-dont-write-blogs/201406/why-we-dont-give
-each-other-break.

114 **a half cousin of Charles Darwin** See Raymond E. Fancher, "Scientific
Cousins: The Relationship between Charles Darwin and Francis Galton,"
American Psychologist, 64, no. 2 (February–March 2009), 84–92.

114 **"average intellectual standard of the negro race is some two grades
below our own"** Francis Galton, *Hereditary Genius: An Inquiry into Its Laws
and Consequences* (London: MacMillan and Co, 1869), 338.

114 **France's Alfred Binet and Theodore Simon succeeded** See Margaret B.
White and Alfred E. Hall, "An Overview of Intelligence Testing," *Educational Horizons* 58, no. 4 (Summer 1980), 210–16.

114 **"enormously significant racial differences in general intelligence"** Lewis
M. Terman, *The Measurement of Intelligence: An Explanation of and a Complete
Guide for the Use of the Stanford Revision and Extension of The Binet-Simon
Intelligence Scale* (Boston: Houghton Mifflin, 1916), 92.

114 **1.7 million U.S. soldiers during World War I** Dorothy Roberts, *Killing
the Black Body: Race, Reproduction, and the Meaning of Liberty* (New York:
Pantheon, 1997), 63.

114 **Brigham presented the soldiers' racial scoring gap** See Carl C. Brigham,
A Study of American Intelligence (Princeton, NJ: Princeton University Press,
1923).

114 **created the Scholastic Aptitude Test, or SAT, in 1926** Bruce G. Ham-
mond, "The SAT and Systemic Racism," *Inside Higher Ed,* August 17,
2020, www.insidehighered.com/admissions/views/2020/08/17/history-sat
-reflects-systemic-racism-opinion.

114 Physicist William Shockley and psychologist Arthur Jensen carried these eugenic ideas See Stephen Jay Gould, *The Mismeasure of Man,* rev. ed. (New York: W. W. Norton, 1996), 368–69, 30.

114 genetic explanations . . . had largely been discredited See Carl N. Degler, *In Search of Human Nature: The Decline and Revival of Darwinism in American Social Thought* (New York: Oxford University Press, 1991).

115 "both genes and the environment have something to do with racial differences" Richard J. Herrnstein and Charles Murray, *The Bell Curve: Intelligence and Class Structure in American Life* (New York: Free Press, 1994), 311.

115 further enlarged the role of standardized testing See Alyson Klein, "No Child Left Behind: An Overview," *EdWeek,* April 10, 2015, www.edweek.org/policy-politics/no-child-left-behind-an-overview/2015/04; and Claudio Sanchez and Cory Turner, "Obama's Impact on America's Schools," NPR, January 13, 2017, www.npr.org/sections/ed/2017/01/13/500421608/obamas-impact-on-americas-schools.

115 banged the drum of the "achievement gap" See Klein, "No Child Left Behind."

115 districts with a higher proportion of White students receive Since the first edition, EdBuild, a nonprofit organization focused on school funding, completed a nationwide study that provided these figures. See EdBuild, "Nonwhite School Districts Get $23 Billion Less Than White Districts Despite Serving the Same Number of Students," February 2019, edbuild.org/content/23-billion.

115 lack basic supplies, basic textbooks, healthy food, and water Take, for example, the chronic underfunding of Black schools in Mississippi. See Lorelei Laird, "Lawsuit Alleges Mississippi Deprives Black Children of Equal Educational Opportunities," *ABA Journal,* May 23, 2017, www.abajournal.com/news/article/lawsuit_alleges_mississippi_deprives_black_children_of_equal_educational_op.

116 "We must no longer be ashamed of being black" Martin Luther King Jr., "Where Do We Go from Here?" August 16, 1967, The Martin Luther King, Jr. Research and Education Institute, Stanford University, kinginstitute.stanford.edu/where-do-we-go-here.

118 named it College of the Year in 1997 "Time Survey Names Florida A&M 'College of the Year,'" CNN, August 24, 1997, www.cnn.com/US/9708/24/top.colleges/.

118 Florida A&M had outpaced Harvard See "FAMU Ties Harvard in Recruitment of National Achievement Scholars," *Diverse: Issues in Higher Education,* January 31, 2001, www.diverseeducation.com/recruitment-retention/article/15077445/famu-ties-harvard-in-recruitment-of-national-achievement-scholars.

Chapter 9: Color

119 **COLORIST IDEA** The definition in the hardcover edition was for COLORISM, which I now define as: A powerful collection of inequitable and unjust policies that lead to injustice and inequities between Light people and Dark people, supported by ideas of racial hierarchy about Light and Dark people.

119 **COLOR ANTIRACIST IDEA** The definition in the hardcover edition was for COLOR ANTIRACISM, which I now define as: A powerful collection of equitable and just policies that lead to equity between Light people and Dark people, supported by ideas of racial equality about Light and Dark people.

119 **"the best college marching band in the country"** For this quote and a history, see Curtis Inabinett Jr., *The Legendary Florida A&M University Marching Band: The History of "The Hundred"* (New York: Page Publishing, 2016).

120 **an eye color that is rare for anyone** Only about 5 percent of the world population, and 18 percent of the U.S. population, have hazel eyes. See Amanda Barrell, "Eye Color Percentages around the World," *Medical News Today,* November 25, 2020, www.medicalnewstoday.com/articles/eye-color -percentage.

121 **the explanation of most buyers** For a study on women who use such skin-bleaching products, see Kathryn Harper and Becky L. Choma, "Internalised White Ideal, Skin Tone Surveillance, and Hair Surveillance Predict Skin and Hair Dissatisfaction and Skin Bleaching among African American and Indian Women," *Sex Roles* 80 (June 2019), 735–74.

121 **"white beauty repackaged with dark hair"** Margaret L. Hunter, *Race, Gender, and the Politics of Skin Tone* (New York: Routledge, 2005), 57.

121 **"colorism," a term coined by novelist Alice Walker** Walker defined colorism as "prejudicial or preferential treatment of same-race people based solely on their color." Walker, *In Search of Our Mothers' Gardens: Womanist Prose* (San Diego, CA: Harcourt Brace & Company, 1983), 290.

122 **relegate them to minority status** According to the 2020 census, between 2010 and 2020, the absolute number of White people in the United States decreased for the first time since 1790, the year of the first census. See Tara Bahrampour and Ted Mellnik, "Census Data Shows Widening Diversity; Number of White People Falls for First Time," *The Washington Post,* August 12, 2021, www.washingtonpost.com/dc-md-va/2021/08/12/census -data-race-ethnicity-neighborhoods/; and William H. Frey, "The US Will Become 'Minority White' in 2045, Census Projects," Brookings, March 14, 2018, brook.gs/2FGHmHa.

122 **the biracial key to racial harmony** See, for example, Moises Velasquez-Manoff, "What Biracial People Know," *The New York Times,* March 4, 2017, www.nytimes.com/2017/03/04/opinion/sunday/what-biracial-people -know.html.

122 **"skin color paradox"** Jennifer L. Hochschild and Vesla Weaver, "The Skin Color Paradox and the American Racial Order," *Social Forces* 86, no. 2 (December 2007), 643–70.

122 **White children attribute positivity to lighter skin** "Study: White and Black Children Biased Toward Lighter Skin," CNN, May 14, 2010, cnn.com/2010/US/05/13/doll.study/index.html.

122 **White people usually favor lighter-skinned politicians** In a survey of more than two thousand White adults, political scientist Vesla Weaver observed "a clear favoritism for the light-skinned black candidate when race is controlled, regardless of platform, gender, and partisanship." See Weaver, "The Electoral Consequences of Skin Color: The 'Hidden' Side of Race in Politics," *Political Behavior* 34, no. 1 (March 2012), 186–87.

122 **disproportionately at risk of hypertension** Elizabeth A. Adams, Beth E. Kurtz-Costes, and Adam J. Hoffman, "Skin Tone Bias among African Americans: Antecedents and Consequences across the Life Span," *Developmental Review* 40 (2016), 109.

122 **significantly lower GPAs than Light students** Maxine S. Thompson and Steve McDonald, "Race, Skin Tone, and Educational Achievement," *Sociological Perspectives* 59, no. 1 (Spring 2016), 91–111.

122 **racist Americans have higher expectations for Light students** Ebony O. McGree, Adam Alvarez, and H. Richard Milner, "Colorism as a Salient Space for Understanding in Teacher Preparation," *Theory into Practice* 55, no. 1 (2016), 74.

123 **remember educated Black men as Light-skinned** Avi Ben-Zeev, Tara C. Dennehy, Robin I. Goodrich, Branden S. Kolarik, and Mark W. Geisler, "When an 'Educated' Black Man Becomes Lighter in the Mind's Eye: Evidence for a Skin Tone Memory Bias," *SAGE Open* 4, no. 1 (January 2014), 1–9, journals.sagepub.com/doi/full/10.1177/2158244013516770.

123 **employers prefer Light Black men** Matthew S. Harrison and Kecia M. Thomas, "The Hidden Prejudice in Selection: A Research Investigation on Skin Color Bias," *Journal of Applied Social Psychology* 39, no. 1 (January 2009), 134–68.

123 **Dark Filipino men have lower income than their lighter peers** Lisa Kiang and David T. Takeuchi, "Phenotypic Bias and Ethnic Identity in Filipino Americans," *Social Science Quarterly* 90, no. 2 (June 2009), 428–45.

123 **Dark immigrants to the United States . . . tend to have less wealth and income** Angela R. Dixon and Edward E. Telles, "Skin Color and Colorism: Global Research, Concepts, and Measurement," *Annual Review of Sociology* 43, no. 1 (July 2017), 408.

123 **Light Latinas receive higher wages** Maria Cristina Morales, "Ethnic-Controlled Economy or Segregation? Exploring Inequality in Latina/o Co-Ethnic Jobsites," *Sociological Forum* 24, no. 3 (September 2009), 601–4.

123 **Dark Latinx people are more likely to be employed at ethnically ho-**

mogeneous jobsites Maria Cristina Morales, "The Ethnic Niche as an Economic Pathway for the Dark Skinned: Labor Market Incorporation of Latina/o Workers," *Hispanic Journal of Behavioral Sciences* 30, no. 3 (August 2008), 280–98.

123 **Dark sons and Light daughters receive higher-quality** Antoinette M. Landor, Leslie Gordon Simons, Ronald L. Simons, et al., "Exploring the Impact of Skin Tone on Family Dynamics and Race-Related Outcomes," *Journal of Family Psychology* 27, no. 5 (2013), 817–26, doi.org/10.1037/a00 33883.

123 **Skin color influences perceptions of attractiveness** Mark E. Hill, "Skin Color and the Perception of Attractiveness Among African Americans: Does Gender Make a Difference?" *Social Psychology Quarterly* 65, no. 1 (March 2002), 77–91. See J. Camille Hall, "No Longer Invisible: Understanding the Psychosocial Impact of Skin Color Stratification in the Lives of African American Women," *Health & Social Work* 42, no. 2 (May 2017), 71–78 on colorism as a source of psychological distress for Black women.

123 **As skin tone lightens, levels of self-esteem among Black women rise** Adams, Kurtz-Costes, and Hoffman, "Skin Tone Bias Among African Americans," 107.

123 **Dark Black women receive the harshest prison sentences** Jill Viglione, Lance Hannon, and Robert DeFina, "The Impact of Light Skin on Prison Time for Black Female Offenders," *The Social Science Journal* 48 (2011), 250–58. Sociologist Ellis P. Monk studied the impact of colorism on the likelihood of arrest and incarceration. He observed, "the darkest-skinned African Americans . . . have 121% higher odds of ever having been arrested compared to the lightest-skinned respondents" and "103% higher odds of having been incarcerated." See Monk, "The Color of Punishment: African Americans, Skin Tone, and the Criminal Justice System," *Ethnic and Racial Studies* 42, no. 10 (2019), 1593–1612.

123 **White men with African facial features who are convicted of felonies receive harsher sentences** Ryan D. King and Brian D. Johnson, "A Punishing Look: Skin Tone and Afrocentric Features in the Halls of Justice," *American Journal of Sociology* 122, no. 1 (July 2016), 90–124.

123 **Dark female students are nearly twice as likely to be suspended** Jamilia J. Blake, Verna M. Keith, Wen Luo, Huong Le, and Phia Salter, "The Role of Colorism in Explaining African American Females' Suspension Risk," *School Psychology Quarterly* 32, no. 1 (March 2017), 126, doi.org/10.1037 /spq0000173.

123 **can be almost as wide as inequities between Black and White Americans** For example, in one study on the interracial and intraracial wage gap, researchers identified "a significant wage gap between white workers and black workers who are not light-skinned and a smaller, and statistically insignificant, difference in the wage level of white and light-complexioned

black workers." See Arthur H. Goldsmith, Darrick Hamilton, and William Darity Jr., "From Dark to Light: Skin Color and Wages among African-Americans," *The Journal of Human Resources* 42, no. 4 (Fall 2007), 701–38.

124 **Even Dark gay men heard it** Donovan Thompson, " 'I Don't Normally Date Dark-Skin Men': Colorism in the Black Gay Community," *Huffington Post*, April 9, 2014, www.huffingtonpost.com/entry/i-dont-normally-date-dark_b_5113166.html.

125 **"You're never Black enough"** Lisa Capretto, "Colorism: Light-Skinned African-American Women Explain the Discrimination They Face," *Huffington Post*, January 13, 2014, www.huffingtonpost.com/entry/colorism-discrimination-iyanla-vanzant_n_4588825.html.

125 **their struggle to integrate with Dark people** Lynn Okura, "Light-Skinned Black Women on the Pain of Not Feeling 'Black Enough,' " *Huffington Post*, January 22, 2015, www.huffingtonpost.com/entry/light-girls-not-black-enough_n_6519488.html.

125 **the one-drop rule** See Yaba Blay, "How the 'One Drop Rule' Became a Tool of White Supremacy," *Literary Hub*, February 22, 2021, lithub.com/how-the-one-drop-rule-became-a-tool-of-white-supremacy/.

126 **"that the Negro's . . . do entertain as high thoughts"** Morgan Godwyn, *The Negro's and Indian's Advocate* (London, 1680), 21.

126 **African people must accept the "correct conception" of beauty** Johann Joachim Winckelmann, *History of the Art of Antiquity*, trans. Harry Francis Mallgrave (1746; Los Angeles: Getty Research Institute, 2006), 192–95.

126 **Enslavers more often worked Light people in the house** William L. Andrews, *Slavery and Class in the American South: A Generation of Slave Narrative Testimony, 1840–1865* (New York: Oxford University Press, 2019), 102.

126 **"Ferocity and stupidity are the characteristics of those tribes"** John Ramsay McCulloch, *A Dictionary, Geographical, Statistical, and Historical of the Various Countries, Places, and Principal Natural Objects in the World* (London: Longman, Orme, Brown, Green, and Longmans, 1841), 1:33.

127 **spoke before the White men who wrote the U.S. Constitution** Members of the American Philosophical Society included its founder, Benjamin Franklin, as well as James Madison, James Wilson, and other attendees of the Constitutional Convention. See *List of the Members of the American Philosophical Society* (Philadelphia: The Society, 1890), 3–17.

127 **Smith's racist light** See Samuel Stanhope Smith, *An Essay on the Causes of the Variety of Complexion and Figure in the Human Species* (Philadelphia: Robert Aitken, 1787), 57–58, 32.

127 **"The hair of the white man is *more perfect*"** Emphasis in original. Peter A. Browne, "The Classification of Mankind, by the Hair and Wool of Their Heads . . . ," in *Negro-Mania: Being an Examination of the Falsely Assumed Equality of the Various Races of Men*, ed. John Campbell (Philadelphia: Campbell & Power, 1851), 339–64.

127 **"a degenerate, unnatural offspring"** J. C. Nott, "The Mulatto a Hybrid—Probable Extermination of the Two Races if the Whites and Blacks Are Allowed to Intermarry," *Boston Medical and Surgical Journal* 29, no. 2 (August 1843), 31.

127 **private racist ideas, which typically described Light women as smarter** See Walter Johnson, *Soul by Soul: Life Inside the Antebellum Slave Market* (Cambridge, MA: Harvard University Press, 1999), 150–56.

127 **Enslavers paid much more for enslaved Light females** Ibid.

127 **men cast these "yaller gals" and "Jezebels"** See Melissa Harris-Perry, *Sister Citizen: Shame, Stereotypes, and Black Women in America* (New Haven, CT: Yale University Press, 2011); and Dorothy Sterling, ed., *We Are Your Sisters: Black Women in the Nineteenth Century* (New York: W. W. Norton & Company, 1984), 27–28.

127 **"tragic mulattoes"** For an explanation of the "tragic mulatto" myth and its deployment in popular culture, see David Pilgrim, "The Tragic Mulatto Myth," Jim Crow Museum, Ferris State University, November 2000, www.ferris.edu/HTMLS/news/jimcrow/mulatto/homepage.htm.

127 **"of fine European features and a high, indomitable spirit"** Harriet Beecher Stowe, *Uncle Tom's Cabin* (London: George Routledge & Co., 1852), 123.

127 **"Sons of White fathers"** Ibid., 293.

127 **"more likely to enlist themselves under the banners of the whites"** Edwin C. Holland, *A Refutation of the Calumnies Circulated Against the Southern and Western States Respecting the Institution and Existence of Slavery Among Them* (Charleston, SC: A. E. Miller, 1822), 84.

127 **Maybe Holland had the Brown Fellowship Society** Thomas C. Holt, *Black over White: Negro Political Leadership in South Carolina During Reconstruction* (Urbana: University of Illinois Press, 1977), 65–67.

128 **White and Light only barbershops** See Haynes Johnson, *Dusk at the Mountain* (Garden City, NY: Doubleday, 1963); and Chris Myers Asch and George Derek Musgrove, *Chocolate City: A History of Race and Democracy in the Nation's Capital* (Chapel Hill: University of North Carolina Press, 2017).

128 **After slavery, Light people were wealthier** See Taunya Lovell Banks, "A Darker Shade of Pale Revisited: Disaggregated Blackness and Colorism in the 'Post-Racial' Obama Era," in *Color Matters: Skin Tone Bias and the Myth of a Post-Racial America,* ed. Kimberly Jade Norwood (New York: Routledge, 2014), 100–102.

128 **dozens of cities had "Blue Vein" societies** Willard B. Gatewood, *Aristocrats of Color: The Black Elite, 1880–1920* (Bloomington: Indiana University Press, 1990), 157–61.

128 **"not white enough to show blue veins"** Charles W. Chesnutt, "The Wife of His Youth," *The Atlantic Monthly,* July 1898, www.theatlantic.com/magazine/archive/1898/07/the-wife-of-his-youth/306658/.

128 **Light people reproduced the paper-bag test, pencil test, door test, and comb test** Kathy Russell, Midge Wilson, and Ronald Hall, *The Color Complex: The Politics of Skin Color Among African Americans* (New York: Anchor Books, 1993), 27.

128 **deemed constitutional "equal but separate accommodations"** *Plessy v. Ferguson*, 163 U.S. 537 (1896), available courtesy of Cornell Law School's Legal Information Institute, www.law.cornell.edu/supremecourt/text/163 /537.

128 **hailed from a proud Light community in New Orleans** Blair L. M. Kelley, "*Plessy* and Early Challenges to the Doctrine of 'Separate, but Equal,'" in *From the Grassroots to the Supreme Court: Brown v. Board of Education and American Democracy,* ed. Peter F. Lau (Durham, NC: Duke University Press, 2004), 23.

128 **Carroll considered the interracial intercourse** See Charles Carroll, *"The Negro a Beast"; Or, "In the Image of God"* (St. Louis, MO: American Book and Bible House, 1900), 292–96.

128 **framing Dark people as committing "more horrible crimes"** George T. Winston, "The Relation of the Whites to the Negroes," *Annals of the American Academy of Political and Social Science* 18 (July 1901), 108–9.

128 **declaring that biracial people were responsible** Edward Byron Reuter claimed, "In all other countries where a mulatto group exists alongside a group of unmixed blood, there seems to be a preponderance of mulattoes among the gifted individuals of the race. . . . The mixed-bloods in every racial situation seem to have risen, as a group, above the status of their darker kin, while the individuals of talent who have appeared—the individuals who have made some conspicuous success in life—are, with rare exception, men of mixed blood." See Reuter, *The Mulatto in the United States, Including a Study of the Rôle of Mixed-Blood Races Throughout the World* (Boston: Richard G. Badger, 1918), 187–88.

129 **Marcus Garvey and his fast-growing Universal Negro Improvement Association** For a definitive history on the Garvey movement, see Tony Martin, *Race First: The Ideological and Organizational Struggles of Marcus Garvey and the Universal Negro Improvement Association* (Westport, CT: Greenwood Press, 1976).

129 **"American Negroes recognize no color line in or out of the race"** W.E.B. Du Bois, "Marcus Garvey," *The Crisis* 21, no. 3 (January 1921), 114.

129 **"If you're white, you're right"** Daryl Cumber Dance, ed., *From My People: 400 Years of African American Folklore* (New York: W. W. Norton, 2003), 484.

129 **his own "Talented Tenth" essay in 1903** See W.E.B. Du Bois, "The Talented Tenth," in *The Negro Problem: A Series of Articles by Representative American Negroes of Today* (New York: James Pott & Company, 1903), 31–75.

129 **the Dark masses needed "proper grooming"** See Charlotte Hawkins Brown, "Clipping," Charlotte Hawkins Brown Papers, Reel 2, Schlesinger

Library, Radcliffe College, Cambridge, MA; and Constance Hill Mareena, *Lengthening Shadow of a Woman: A Biography of Charlotte Hawkins Brown* (Hicksville, NY: Exposition Press, 1977).

129 **John McWhorter's avowal of a post-racial America** John McWhorter, "Racism in American Is Over," *Forbes,* December 30, 2008, www .forbes.com/2008/12/30/end-of-racism-oped-cx_jm_1230mcwhorter .html#50939eb949f8.

129 **White people are wealthier, healthier, and more powerful** Black families claim just 12 cents per dollar of White wealth, and Black people are more than one-and-a-half times as likely as White people to report fair or poor health (13.8 percent compared to 8.3 percent). White people also hold the reins of power; in 2020, *The New York Times* studied the backgrounds of "922 of the most powerful people in America," including lawmakers, officials, and executives and reported that 80 percent are White. On the wealth gap, see Ana Hernández Kent and Lowell Ricketts, "Wealth Gaps between White, Black and Hispanic Families in 2019," Federal Reserve Bank of St. Louis, January 5, 2021, www.stlouisfed.org/on-the-economy /2021/january/wealth-gaps-white-black-hispanic-families-2019; on health disparities, see Sofia Carratala and Connor Maxwell, "Health Disparities by Race and Ethnicity," Center for American Progress, May 7, 2020, www .americanprogress.org/article/health-disparities-race-ethnicity/; on White consolidation of power, see Denise Lu, Jon Huang, Ashwin Seshagiri, Haeyoun Park, and Troy Griggs, "Faces of Power: 80% Are White, Even as U.S. Becomes More Diverse," *The New York Times,* September 9, 2020, www .nytimes.com/interactive/2020/09/09/us/powerful-people-race-us.html.

130 **"absolutely repudiated by every thinking Negro"** Du Bois, "Marcus Garvey," 114.

130 **shied away from defending the Dark and impoverished Scottsboro Boys** The NAACP at this time avoided cases in which Black men were accused of raping White women. See Erin Blakemore, "Why the Communist Party Defended the Scottsboro Boys," *History Stories,* May 1, 2018, www .history.com/news/scottsboro-boys-naacp-communist-party.

130 **reportedly believed that "unmixed" Negroes were "inferior"** Walter White quoted in David Levering Lewis, *W.E.B. Du Bois: The Fight for Equality and the American Century, 1919–1963* (New York: Macmillan, 2000), 341.

130 **"Walter White is white"** W.E.B. Du Bois, "Postscript: Segregation in the North," *The Crisis* 41, no. 4 (April 1934), 115.

130 **as Walter White had** See Walter White, "I Investigate Lynchings," *American Mercury,* January 1929, nationalhumanitiescenter.org/pds/maai3 /segregation/text2/investigatelynchings.pdf.

130 **The post–World War I craze of the conk** Ayana D. Byrd and Lori L.

Tharps, *Hair Story: Untangling the Roots of Black Hair in America* (New York: St. Martin's Press, 2002), 43–47.

130 **"I had joined that multitude of Negro men and women in America"** Malcolm X recalled in Malcolm X and Alex Haley, *The Autobiography of Malcolm X* (New York: Grove Press, 1965), 53–55.

130 **Skin-lightening products received a boost** Russell, Wilson, and Hall, *The Color Complex*, 51–52.

130 **Some Dark people took too much pride** For example, see George Napper, *Blacker Than Thou: The Struggle for Campus Unity* (Grand Rapids, MI: Eerdmans, 1973).

131 **Light children were adopted first . . . public housing and prisons** Russell, Wilson, and Hall, *The Color Complex*, 99–100, 37, 38.

131 **"The lighter the skin, the lighter the sentence"** Ibid., 38.

131 **Imus compared Rutgers's Dark basketball players** Ryan Chiachiere, "Imus Called Women's Basketball Team 'Nappy-Headed Hos,'" Media Matters for America, April 4, 2007, www.mediamatters.org/msnbc/imus-called -womens-basketball-team-nappy-headed-hos.

131 **casting call for the movie *Straight Outta Compton*** Danielle Cadet, "The 'Straight Outta Compton' Casting Call Is So Offensive It Will Make Your Jaw Drop," *Huffington Post,* July 17, 2014, www.huffingtonpost.com/2014 /07/17/straight-out-of-compton-casting-call_n_5597010.html.

131 **Skin-bleaching products were raking in millions** "Lighter Shades of Skin," *The Economist,* September 28, 2012, www.economist.com/baobab /2012/09/28/lighter-shades-of-skin.

131 **In India, the manufacturer of the bestselling "fairness" cream** Geeta Pandey, "Fair and Lovely: Can Renaming a Fairness Cream Stop Colourism?" BBC, June 26, 2020, www.bbc.com/news/world-asia-india-53182169.

131 **70 percent of women in Nigeria . . . 40 percent in China, Malaysia, the Philippines, and South Korea** See "Mercury in Skin Lightening Products," News Ghana, June 13, 2012, newsghana.com.gh/mercury-in-skin-lightening -products/. In 2019, the World Health Organization reported "Mercury is a common but dangerous ingredient found in skin lightening creams and soaps" and called for increased governmental regulation on such products. See World Health Organization, *Mercury in Skin Lightening Products,* November 3, 2019, www.who.int/publications/i/item/WHO-CED-PHE-EPE-19.13.

131 **Some White people have their own skin-care "addiction"** In 2010, nearly 32 percent of White women aged eighteen to twenty-one, and about 8 percent of all White adults, used indoor tanning beds. Numbers have declined in recent years due to greater awareness of the deleterious effects of tanning, but recent "research indicates that more than one-fifth of white women age 18–30 years old who tan indoors exhibit indoor tanning dependence." See Centers for Disease Control and Prevention (CDC), "Use of Indoor Tanning

Devices by Adults—United States, 2010," *Morbidity and Mortality Weekly Report,* May 11, 2012, www.cdc.gov/mmwr/preview/mmwrhtml/mm6118a2 .htm; and American Academy of Dermatology, "Indoor Tanning," June 21, 2022, www.aad.org/media/stats-indoor-tanning.

131 **the United States elected the "orange man"** See Jennifer Brett, "NeNe Leakes Once Liked Donald Trump but Not 'This Orange Man Talking on TV,'" *Atlanta Journal-Constitution,* September 7, 2016, www.ajc.com /entertainment/celebrity-news/nene-leakes-once-liked-donald-trump-but -not-this-orange-man-talking/ZHtnTxZcN5anIJdcqr9maO/.

131 **tanning bed every morning** Emily Zauzmer, "Omarosa Manigault New-man Says Trump Uses a Tanning Bed in the White House Every Morning," *Yahoo! Life,* August 14, 2018, www.yahoo.com/lifestyle/omarosa-manigault -newman-says-trump-154402249.html.

132 **Research shows that people consider tanned skin . . . more attractive** Cynthia M. Frisby, "'Shades of Beauty': Examining the Relationship of Skin Color to Perceptions of Physical Attractiveness," *Facial Plastic Surgery* 22, no. 3 (August 2006), 175–79.

Chapter 10: White

134 **ANTI-WHITE RACIST IDEA** The definition in the hardcover edition was for ANTI-WHITE RACIST, which I now define as: One who is clas-sifying White people as inferior or hating everyday White people, which distracts from and reinforces the power of racist White elites and their poli-cies that harm people of color and everyday White people.

135 **Jeb Bush's termination of affirmative-action programs** Peter T. Kilborn, "Jeb Bush Roils Florida on Affirmative Action," *The New York Times,* February 4, 2000, www.nytimes.com/2000/02/04/us/jeb-bush-roils-flor ida-on-affirmative-action.html.

135 **Al Gore's winning face flash on the screen** Peter Marks, "The 2000 Elections: The Media; A Flawed Call Adds to High Drama," *The New York Times,* November 8, 2000, www.nytimes.com/2000/11/08/us/the-2000 -elections-the-media-a-flawed-call-adds-to-high-drama.html.

135 **a narrow lead in Florida of 1,784 votes** David Barstow and Don van Natta Jr., "Examining the Vote; How Bush Took Florida: Mining the Over-seas Absentee Vote," *The New York Times,* July 15, 2001, www.nytimes.com /2001/07/15/us/examining-the-vote-how-bush-took-florida-mining-the -overseas-absentee-vote.html.

135 **Jeb Bush's appointees were overseeing the recount** Lisa Getter, "Jeb Bush's Recount Role Examined," *Los Angeles Times,* July 14, 2001, www .latimes.com/archives/la-xpm-2001-jul-14-mn-22362-story.html.

136 **stories of FAMU students and their families back home not being able to vote** For example, see Linda Meggett Brown, "FAMU Students

Protest Election Day Mishaps in Florida," *Diverse: Issues in Higher Education,* December 6, 2000, www.diverseeducation.com/home/article/15077340 /famu-students-protest-election-day-mishaps-in-florida; and Jerry White, "Florida A&M Students Describe Republican Attack on Voting Rights," *World Socialist Web Site,* December 6, 2000, www.wsws.org/en/articles /2000/12/flor-d06.html.

136 **11 percent of registered voters but comprised 44 percent of the purge list** Ari Berman, "How the 2000 Election in Florida Led to a New Wave of Voter Disenfranchisement," *The Nation,* July 28, 2015, www.thenation .com/article/archive/how-the-2000-election-in-florida-led-to-a-new -wave-of-voter-disenfranchisement/. For a fuller account of disfranchise- ment schemes in Florida and beyond, see Ari Berman, *Give Us the Ballot: The Modern Struggle for Voting Rights in America* (New York: Farrar, Straus & Giroux, 2015).

136 **Palm Beach County** Henry E. Brady, Michael C. Herron, Walter R. Me- bane Jr., Jasjeet Singh Sekhon, Kenneth W. Shotts, and Jonathan Wand, "Law and Data: The Butterfly Ballot Episode," in *The Longest Night: Polemics and Perspectives on Election 2000,* eds. Arthur J. Jacobson and Michel Rosen- feld (Berkeley: University of California Press, 2002), 51.

136 **Florida's highest percentage of Black voters and the highest spoil- age rate** Greg Palast, "1 Million Black Votes Didn't Count in the 2000 Presidential Election," *San Francisco Chronicle,* June 20, 2004, www.sfgate .com/opinion/article/1-million-black-votes-didn-t-count-in-the-2000 -2747895.php.

136 **ten times more likely than their White peers** Ibid.

136 **a *New York Times* statistical analysis** Ford Fessenden, "Examining the Vote: The Patterns; Ballots Cast by Blacks and Older Voters Were Tossed in Far Greater Numbers," *The New York Times,* November 12, 2001, www .nytimes.com/2001/11/12/us/examining-vote-patterns-ballots-cast-blacks -older-voters-were-tossed-far-greater.html.

136 **179,855 ballots were invalidated by Florida election officials** Palast, "1 Million Black Votes Didn't Count in the 2000 Presidential Election."

136 **a race ultimately won by 537 votes** Doyle McManus, Bob Drogin, and Richard O'Reilly, "Bush Wins, Gore Wins—Depending on How Ballots Are Added Up," *Chicago Tribune,* November 13, 2001, www.chicagotribune .com/news/sns-ballots-story.html.

136 **Ted Cruz served on Bush's legal team** Berman, *Give Us the Ballot: The Modern Struggle for Voting Rights in America,* 210.

137 **a silent march of two thousand FAMU and Florida State University students** See Brown, "FAMU Students Protest Election Day Mishaps in Florida"; and White, "Florida A&M Students Describe Republican Attack on Voting Rights."

137 **those thousands of FAMU students who did not vote** It is estimated that 10,000 out of 12,000 students at FAMU were not voters. Brown, "FAMU Students Protest Election Day Mishaps in Florida."

137 **the U.S. Supreme Court stopped Florida's recount** "Gore Concedes in Speech Before the Nation," *The New York Times,* December 13, 2000, www.nytimes.com/2000/12/13/politics/gore-concedes-in-speech-before-nation.html.

137 *Message to the Blackman in America* Elijah Muhammad, *Message to the Blackman in America* (Chicago: Muhammad Temple No. 2, 1965), 103–22.

137 **led the unorthodox Nation of Islam** Nafeesa Muhammad, "The Nation of Islam's Economic Program, 1934–1975," *BlackPast,* April 1, 2020, www.blackpast.org/african-american-history/the-nation-of-islams-economic-program-1934-1975/.

137 **According to the theology he espoused** For this story, I used the even clearer theology that Malcolm X espoused in his autobiography, as taught to him by Elijah Muhammad. Malcolm X and Alex Haley, *The Autobiography of Malcolm X* (New York: Grove Press, 1965), 165–69.

138 **despite all sorts of "aid" from the former mother countries** British writer Kenan Malik explains that foreign aid from the UK and United States does not correlate to the poverty rates of the top recipient countries, but rather is motivated by "reasons of geopolitics and trade." See Malik, "As a System, Foreign Aid Is a Fraud and Does Nothing for Inequality," *The Guardian,* September 2, 2018, www.theguardian.com/commentisfree/2018/sep/02/as-a-system-foreign-aid-is-a-fraud-and-does-nothing-for-inequality.

139 **"our unity as a people and the strength of our democracy"** "Gore: 'It Is Time for Me to Go,'" *The Guardian,* December 14, 2000, www.theguardian.com/world/2000/dec/14/uselections2000.usa14.

139 **"The white man is the devil"** Malcolm X and Haley, *The Autobiography of Malcolm X,* 159.

139 **He saw White people** Ibid., 159–60.

139 **"no realistic goal"** Ibid., 37.

139 **left prison in 1952 and quickly began to grow Elijah Muhammad's Nation of Islam** "The Life of Malcolm X: The Prison Years and Early Ministry," The Malcolm X Project at Columbia University, www.columbia.edu/cu/ccbh/mxp/prison.html.

140 *The Hate That Hate Produced* See "The Hate That Hate Produced (1959): Malcolm X First TV Appearance," www.youtube.com/watch?v=BsYWD2EqavQ. On Malcolm X's assessment of and reaction to public reception, see Malcolm X and Haley, *The Autobiography of Malcolm X,* 240–41.

140 **Malcolm X made the hajj to Mecca** "The Life of Malcolm X: The Silencing, Muhammad Ali, and Out: December 1963–April 1964," The Malcolm X Project at Columbia University, www.columbia.edu/cu/ccbh/mxp

/ali.html; and "The Life of Malcolm X: A New Vision? The Epiphany of Mecca," The Malcolm X Project at Columbia University, www.columbia .edu/cu/ccbh/mxp/mecca.html.

140 **"Never have I witnessed such"** Malcolm X, "Mecca," in *The Columbia Documentary History of Religion in America Since 1945,* eds. Paul Harvey and Philip Goff (New York: Columbia University Press, 2005), 167.

140 **"I totally reject Elijah Muhammad's racist philosophy"** M. S. Handler, "Malcolm Rejects Racist Doctrine," *The New York Times,* October 4, 1964, timesmachine.nytimes.com/timesmachine/1964/10/04/97278378.html ?pageNumber=59.

141 **"racial prejudice, not racism"** One source that provides this definition is Alberta Civil Liberties Research Centre, Calgary Anti-Racism Education, "The Myth of Reverse Racism," www.aclrc.com/myth-of-reverse-racism.

142 **Note on "prejudice plus power"** Patricia A. Bidol, then the superintendent of Michigan schools, introduced the definition of racism as "prejudice plus institutional power" in 1970. Patricia A. Bidol, *Developing New Perspectives on Race: An Innovative Multi-media Social Studies Curriculum in Race Relations for the Secondary Level* (Detroit: New Detroit, 1970); and A. Sivanandan, *Communities of Resistance: Writings on Black Struggles for Socialism* (London: Verso, 1990), 99.

142 **massacred and enslaved millions of Indigenous and African peoples** Historian Linford D. Fisher estimates that between 2 million and 5.5 million Indigenous people, in addition to 12.5 million African people, were enslaved in the Americas between 1492 and 1880. Gillian Kiley, "Colonial Enslavement of Native Americans Included Those Who Surrendered, Too," *News from Brown,* February 15, 2017, www.brown.edu/news/2017-02-15 /enslavement.

142 **colonized and impoverished millions of people of color** For a visual representation of the scope of European colonization between the 1500s and the 1960s, see Max Fisher, "Map: European Colonialism Conquered Every Country in the World but These Five," *Vox,* February 24, 2015, www .vox.com/2014/6/24/5835320/map-in-the-whole-world-only-these-five -countries-escaped-european.

143 **as the resistance within White nations shows** See, for example, Sarah Jaffee, *Necessary Trouble: Americans in Revolt* (New York: Nation Books, 2016).

143 **Note on antiracist work and CRT: approximately three in four White Americans** 71 percent of White respondents ranked "racial and ethnic discrimination" as a "big problem." Monmouth University Poll, "National: Protestors' Anger Justified Even if Actions May Not Be," www.monmouth .edu/polling-institute/documents/monmouthpoll_us_060220.pdf/, 4.

143 **Note on antiracist work and CRT: even though CRT was born in 1981** See Ibram X. Kendi, "There Is No Debate Over Critical Race Theory,"

The Atlantic, July 9, 2021, www.theatlantic.com/ideas/archive/2021/07/opponents-critical-race-theory-are-arguing-themselves/619391/.

143 **Note on antiracist work and CRT: Senator Ted Cruz said** Ted Cruz quoted in Alexandra Hutzler, "Ted Cruz Says Critical Race Theory Is 'Every Bit as Racist as Klansmen in White Sheets,'" *Newsweek,* June 18, 2021, www.newsweek.com/ted-cruz-says-critical-race-theory-every-bit-racist-klansmen-white-sheets-1602105.

143 **Note on antiracist work and CRT: Alabama state legislator Chris Pringle misleadingly said** Chris Pringle quoted in Philip Bump, "The Scholar Strategy: How 'Critical Race Theory' Alarms Could Convert Racial Anxiety into Political Energy," *The Washington Post,* June 15, 2021, www.washingtonpost.com/politics/2021/06/15/scholar-strategy-how-critical-race-theory-alarms-could-convert-racial-anxiety-into-political-energy/.

144 **racist power contributed to stagnating wages.** For a definitive overview of racist policies and their negative impacts on Americans of all races, see Heather McGhee, *The Sum of Us: What Racism Costs Everyone and How We Can Prosper Together* (New York: One World, 2021).

144 **a popular presidential campaign against the "billionaire class" in 2016** Paul Kane and Philip Rucker, "An Unlikely Contender, Sanders Takes on 'Billionaire Class' in 2016 Bid," *The Washington Post,* April 30, 2015, www.washingtonpost.com/politics/sanders-takes-on-billionaire-class-in-launching-2016-bid-against-clinton/2015/04/30/4849fe32-ef3a-11e4-a55f-38924fca94f9_story.html.

144 **not nearly as much as they could from a just society** See McGhee, *The Sum of Us.*

144 **convincing everyday White people that injustice and inequity are rooted in "personal failure"** Even people most harmed by these narratives and correlated policies perpetuate these ideas. Researchers have found that people living in poverty often try to distinguish themselves from people in similar situations by attributing their own struggles to structural causes and the struggles of others to personal failure. See Wendy Bottero, *A Sense of Inequality* (London: Rowman & Littlefield, 2020), 75–76.

145 **identified anti-White discrimination as a serious problem** Don Gonyea, "Majority of White Americans Say They Believe Whites Face Discrimination," NPR, October 24, 2017, www.npr.org/2017/10/24/559604836/majority-of-white-americans-think-theyre-discriminated-against.

145 **"they seem to give the Blacks the first crack at it"** Tim Hershman quoted in Ibid.

145 **it was actually another White person** Ibid.

145 **"by reason of [their] color or race"** Civil Rights Act of 1866, 14 Stat. 27 (1866), memory.loc.gov/cgi-bin/ampage?collId=llsl&fileName=014/llsl014.db&recNum=058.

145 **President Andrew Johnson reframed this Civil Rights Act** Andrew

Johnson, "Veto of the Civil Rights Bill," March 27, 1866, in Teaching American History, teachingamericanhistory.org/library/document/veto-of -the-civil-rights-bill/.

145 **"hard-core racists of reverse discrimination"** Robert Bork, "The Unpersuasive Bakke Decision," *The Wall Street Journal,* July 21, 1978.

145 **Alicia Garza typed "Black Lives Matter" on Facebook** Jessica Guynn, "Meet the Woman Who Coined #BlackLivesMatter," *USA Today,* March 4, 2015, www.usatoday.com/story/tech/2015/03/04/alicia-garza-black-lives-matter /24341593/.

145 **Giuliani called the movement "inherently racist"** Naomi Lim, "Rudy Giuliani: Black Lives Matter 'Inherently Racist,'" CNN, July 11, 2016, www.cnn.com/2016/07/11/politics/rudy-giuliani-black-lives-matter -inherently-racist/index.html.

145 **soldiers of racist power** See, for example, a list of ridiculous reasons why White people called police on Black people in 2018 alone. Brandon Griggs, "Living While Black," CNN, December 28, 2018, www.cnn.com/2018/12 /20/us/living-while-black-police-calls-trnd/index.html.

146 **bold black letters against a yellow background** Madison Underwood, "Where Does That Billboard Phrase, 'Anti-Racist Is a Code Word for Anti-White,' Come From? It's Not New," *AL.com,* June 30, 2014, www.al.com /news/birmingham/2014/06/where_does_that_billboard_phra.html; and Rhonesha Byng, "Arkansas Town Responds to Controversial 'Anti-Racist Is a Code Word for Anti-White' Sign," *Huffington Post,* November 7, 2013, www.huffpost.com/entry/harrison-arkansas-antiracist-code-word-anti white_n_4227769.

146 **Robert Whitaker, who ran for vice president** Keegan Hankes, "Robert Whitaker of 'Mantra' Fame Announced as AFP Vice Presidential Candidate," Southern Poverty Law Center, March 12, 2015, www.splcenter.org /hatewatch/2015/03/12/robert-whitaker-mantra-fame-announced-afp -vice-presidential-candidate-%C2%A0.

146 **"ongoing program of genocide against my race, the white race"** Ryan Lenz, "Following the White Rabbit: Tim Murdock Sits Atop an Online Cult, Spreading Fears of 'White Genocide' That Have Fueled Violence and Terrorism," Southern Poverty Law Center, August 21, 2013, www.splcenter .org/fighting-hate/intelligence-report/2013/following-white-rabbit.

146 **White supremacists claim to be pro-White but** For the white supremacist positions (and conflicting evidence) cited in this paragraph, see Janice Gassam Asare, "4 Ways That White Supremacy Harms White People," *Forbes,* September 18, 2020, www.forbes.com/sites/janicegassam/2020/09/18/4 -ways-that-white-supremacy-harms-white-people/?sh=2af2b772199e.

146 **refuse to acknowledge that climate change** While many white supremacists refuse to acknowledge climate change, some of them cite global warming and other environmental concerns to support racist policies targeting

immigrants of color. This association is not entirely new: Many of the founders of the conservation movement prior to the 1970s were white supremacists. See Beth Gardiner, "White Supremacy Goes Green," *The New York Times,* February 28, 2020, www.nytimes.com/2020/02/28/opinion /sunday/far-right-climate-change.html; and Ari Shapiro, Matt Ozug, and Casey Morell, "The Far-Right and Environmentalism Overlap Is Bigger Than You Think—and Growing," NPR, *All Things Considered,* April 1, 2022, www.npr.org/2022/04/01/1089990539/climate-change-politics.

147 **despite White women** Asare, "4 Ways That White Supremacy Harms White People."

147 **43 percent of the people who gained lifesaving health insurance** Asare, "4 Ways That White Supremacy Harms White People"; and Bowen Garrett and Anuj Gangopadhyaya, *Who Gained Health Insurance Coverage Under the ACA, and Where Do They Live,* Urban Institute, December 2016, www .urban.org/sites/default/files/publication/86761/2001041-who-gained -health-insurance-coverage-under-the-aca-and-where-do-they-live.pdf.

147 **destroyed the lives of more than forty million White people** "Research Starters: Worldwide Deaths in World War II," The National WWII Museum, www.nationalww2museum.org/students-teachers/student-resources /research-starters/research-starters-worldwide-deaths-world-war.

147 **more than five hundred thousand White American lives lost** "The Cost of War: Killed, Wounded, Captured, and Missing," American Battlefield Trust, www.battlefields.org/learn/articles/civil-war-casualties.

147 **"welcomed" the spread of COVID-19** White supremacists intensified online recruitment efforts as people spent more time at home and on the web during the COVID-19 pandemic. See Billy Perrigo, "White Supremacist Groups Are Recruiting with Help from Coronavirus—and a Popular Messaging App," *Time,* April 8, 2020, time.com/5817665/coronavirus -conspiracy-theories-white-supremacist-groups/.

147 **killed approximately half a million White Americans to date** These figures reflect only deaths reported to the CDC (as of May 11, 2022) and are therefore likely an undercount. CDC, "Demographic Trends of COVID-19 Cases and Deaths in the US Reported to the CDC," covid.cdc.gov/covid -data-tracker/#demographics.

147 **teeming with 15.9 million White people** "Basic Statistics," Talk Poverty, talkpoverty.org/basics/.

147 **a nuclear ideology that poses an existential threat to human existence** Ibram X. Kendi, "A House Still Divided," *The Atlantic,* October 2018, www .theatlantic.com/magazine/archive/2018/10/a-house-still-divided/568348/.

147 **Diop's two-cradle theory** Cheikh Anta Diop, *The Cultural Unity of Negro Africa: The Domains of Patriarchy and of Matriarchy in Classical Antiquity* (Paris: Présence Africaine, 1962).

148 **Bradley's version of the same** Michael Bradley, *The Iceman Inheritance:*

Prehistoric Sources of Western Man's Racism, Sexism and Aggression (Toronto: Dorset Publishing, 1978).

148   *The Isis Papers* Frances Cress Welsing, *The Isis Papers: The Keys to the Colors* (Chicago: Third World Press, 1991).

148   the "great replacement" conspiracy theory See Jason Wilson and Aaron Flanagan, "The Racist 'Great Replacement' Conspiracy Theory Explained," Southern Poverty Law Center, May 17, 2022, www.splcenter.org/hatewatch /2022/05/17/racist-great-replacement-conspiracy-theory-explained.

148   *The Rising Tide of Color Against White World-Supremacy* Lothrop Stoddard, *The Rising Tide of Color Against White World-Supremacy* (New York: Charles Scribner's Sons, 1920).

Chapter 11: Black

152   Chris Rock in his 1996 HBO special See "Chris Rock—Bring the Pain," HBO, June 1, 1996, www.youtube.com/watch?v=coC4t7nCGPs.

153   "the great truth that the negro is not equal to the white man" Alexander H. Stephens, "Cornerstone Address, March 21, 1861," in *The Rebellion Record: A Diary of American Events with Documents, Narratives, Illustrative Incidents, Poetry, etc.,* ed. Frank Moore (New York: G. P. Putnam, 1861), 1:45.

153   Chris Rock stopped performing this routine During an interview in 2005, Chris Rock said, "I've never done that joke again, ever, and I probably never will. 'Cause some people that were racist thought they had license to say n——'. So, I'm done with that routine." See Rebecca Leung, "Rock: Bring On Oscar 'Safety Net,'" CBS News, February 17, 2005, www.cbsnews.com/news/rock-bring-on-oscar-safety-net/.

154   53 percent of Black people were surveyed Frank Newport, "Fewer Blacks in U.S. See Bias in Jobs, Income, and Housing," Gallup, July 19, 2013, news .gallup.com/poll/163580/fewer-blacks-bias-jobs-income-housing.aspx.

154   59 percent of Black people expressed "The Partisan Divide on Political Values Grows Even Wider: 4. Race, Immigration and Discrimination," Pew Research Center, October 5, 2017, www.people-press.org/2017/10/05/4 -race-immigration-and-discrimination/.

154   95 percent of Black Americans This section provides necessary updates on data following the uprising of 2020. Andrew Daniller, "Majorities of Americans See at Least Some Discrimination Against Black, Hispanic, and Asian People in the U.S.," Pew Research Center, March 18, 2021, www .pewresearch.org/fact-tank/2021/03/18/majorities-of-americans-see-at -least-some-discrimination-against-black-hispanic-and-asian-people-in-the -u-s/.

156   recent works on Asian Americans, Native Americans, and Latinx Americans See Cathy Park Hong, *Minor Feelings: An Asian American Reckoning* (New York: One World, 2020); Kyle T. Mays, *An Afro-Indigenous History of the United States* (Boston: Beacon Press, 2021); and Laura E. Gómez,

Inventing Latinos: A New Story of American Racism (New York: New Press, 2020).

156 **racist power dismissing antiracist policies and ideas as racist** It is most obvious through the attack on Black power activists. See M. S. Handler, "Humphrey Backs N.A.A.C.P. in Fight on Black Racism," *The New York Times,* July 7, 1966, timesmachine.nytimes.com/timesmachine/1966/07/07/82473204.html?pageNumber=1.

156 **"Black people can't be racist"** Here is a typical argument: "Black People Cannot Be Racist, and Here's Why," *The University Star,* February 15, 2016.

157 **175 Black Americans who have served in Congress** At the time of first publication, about 154 Black Americans had served in Congress. As of May 11, 2022, the number is 175; 62 of the 175 Black Americans who have served in Congress are current members as of this writing. See U.S. House of Representatives, Office of the House Historian, "Black Americans in Congress: Historical Data," history.house.gov/Exhibitions-and-Publications/BAIC/Historical-Data/Historical-Data---Nav/.

157 **the thousands of state and local Black politicians** Jabari Simama, "Black Elected Officials and the Nuanced Issue of Expectations," *Governing,* March 29, 2022, www.governing.com/now/black-elected-officials-and-the-nuanced-issue-of-expectations.

158 **more than two hundred Black judges on federal courts** "African American Judges on the Federal Courts," Federal Judicial Center, www.fjc.gov/history/judges/search/african-american.

158 **more than fifty thousand Black police officers** Shelley S. Hyland and Elizabeth Davis, "Local Police Departments, 2016: Personnel," Bureau of Justice Statistics, U.S. Department of Justice, October 2019, 6, bjs.ojp.gov/content/pub/pdf/lpd16p.pdf.

158 **hundreds of Black police chiefs, assistant chiefs, and commanders** See Ibid., 8; and Lauren Leatherby and Richard A. Oppel Jr., "Which Police Departments Are as Diverse as Their Communities?" *The New York Times,* September 23, 2020, www.nytimes.com/interactive/2020/09/23/us/bureau-justice-statistics-race.html?searchResultPosition=1.

158 **more than forty-five thousand full-time Black faculty** "Table 315.20. Full-time Faculty in Degree-Granting Postsecondary Institutions, by Race/Ethnicity, Sex, and Academic Rank: Fall 2015, Fall 2017, and Fall 2018," Digest of Education Statistics, National Center for Education Statistics, nces.ed.gov/programs/digest/d19/tables/dt19_315.20.asp.

158 **fifteen Black billionaires and the 340,000 Black millionaire families** Avery Newmark, "Forbes: These Are the World's 15 Black Billionaires," *The Atlanta Journal-Constitution,* February 4, 2022, www.ajc.com/life/celebrities/forbes-these-are-the-worlds-15-black-billionaires/PRWODTCBXNHZLLSQTZOHU5Y3B4/; and Shelley Stewart III, Michael Chui, James Manyika, et al., *The Economic State of Black America: What It*

Is and What It Could Be, McKinsey Global Institute, June 17, 2021, www
.mckinsey.com/featured-insights/diversity-and-inclusion/the-economic
-state-of-black-america-what-is-and-what-could-be.

158 **eighteen Black CEOs** John Csiszar, "There Are Only 4 Black Fortune 500
CEOs," Yahoo!, February 2, 2022, www.yahoo.com/video/only-4-black
-fortune-500-233221901.html.

158 **said he didn't have executive power** For analyses of Obama's use of ex-
ecutive power, see Binyamin Appelbaum and Michael D. Shear, "Once
Skeptical of Executive Power, Obama Has Come to Embrace It," *The New
York Times,* August 13, 2016, www.nytimes.com/2016/08/14/us/politics
/obama-era-legacy-regulation.html; and Kristen Bialik, "Obama Issued
Fewer Executive Orders on Average Than Any President Since Cleveland,"
Pew Research Center, January 23, 2017, www.pewresearch.org/fact-tank
/2017/01/23/obama-executive-orders/.

158 **"When you control a man's thinking"** Carter G. Woodson, *The Mis-
education of the Negro* (1933; Trenton, NJ: Africa World Press, 1990), xiii.

159 **Justice Clarence Thomas's murderous gang of anti-Black judgments** For
a recent recap of Clarence Thomas's opposition to affirmative action, voting
rights, and abortion, see Danny Hakim and Jo Becker, "The Long Crusade
of Clarence and Ginni Thomas," *The New York Times,* February 22, 2022,
www.nytimes.com/2022/02/22/magazine/clarence-thomas-ginni-thomas
.html.

159 **Blackwell directed county boards** See Andy Kroll, "GOPer Behind Ohio's
Botched 2004 Election Eyes Senate Run," *Mother Jones,* April 21, 2011, www
.motherjones.com/politics/2011/04/ken-blackwell-ohio-brown-senate/.

159 **to limit voters' access to the provisional ballots** "Playing with the Election Rules," *The New York Times,* September 30, 2004, www.nytimes.com
/2004/09/30/opinion/playing-with-the-election-rules.html?_r=0.

159 **newly registered voters . . . more likely to be Black** Erik David Heide-
mann, "New Voters in American Elections: Participation, Partisan Mobili-
zation, and the Future of Representative Democracy," Ph.D. diss. (The Ohio
State University, 2011), 130.

159 **falsely telling formerly incarcerated people they could not vote** "Holmes
County Named in PRAC Lawsuit," *The Daily Record,* August 28, 2004,
www.the-daily-record.com/story/news/2004/08/28/holmes-county
-named-in-prac/19571543007/.

159 **according to one post-election study** Democratic National Committee, Voting Rights Institute, *Democracy at Risk: The 2004 Election in Ohio,*
2005, Section I, 2, www-personal.umich.edu/~wmebane/Ohio2004/Ohio
ReportCover2Cover.pdf.

159 **Long lines caused about 3 percent of Ohio voters to leave** Ibid., Section II, 5.

159 **approximately 129,000 potential votes walked away** Ibid., Section III, 2.

159 **"Blackwell made Katherine Harris look like a cupcake"** Rep. John Conyers (D-MI) quoted in Robert F. Kennedy Jr., "Was the 2004 Election Stolen?" *Common Dreams,* June 1, 2006, www.commondreams.org/views /2006/06/01/was-2004-election-stolen.

159 **certified Bush as winner of the election in 2000** Michael S. Rosenwald, "How Katherine Harris Became a Celebrity during the 2000 Recount in Florida," *The Washington Post,* November 6, 2020, www.washingtonpost .com/history/2020/11/06/katherine-harris-florida-recount-bush-trump/.

160 **joined Trump's Presidential Advisory Commission on Election Integrity** "President Announces Formation of Bipartisan Presidential Commission on Election Integrity," White House, May 11, 2017, trumpwhitehouse.archives .gov/briefings-statements/president-announces-formation-bipartisan -presidential-commission-election-integrity/.

160 **to find new ways to suppress the voting power** At the time, the Brennan Center for Justice reported, "There is strong reason to suspect this Commission is not a legitimate attempt to study elections, but is rather a tool for justifying discredited claims of widespread voter fraud and promoting vote suppression legislation." See "Background on Trump's 'Voter Fraud' Commission," Brennan Center for Justice, July 18, 2017, www.brennancenter.org /our-work/analysis-opinion/background-trumps-voter-fraud-commission.

160 **Trump officials had not forgotten Blackwell's state-of-the-art racist work** Ken Blackwell, "Time to Clean Up Our Elections," CNS News, July 17, 2017, www.cnsnews.com/commentary/ken-blackwell/time-clean -our-elections.

161 **kidnapped after he visited sub-Saharan Africa** Elizabeth Heath, "Leo Africanus," in *Africana: The Encyclopedia of the African and African American Experience,* eds. Kwame Anthony Appiah and Henry Louis Gates Jr. (New York: Basic Books, 1999), 1146-47.

161 **when the British, French, and Dutch were diving into human trading** The British, French, and Dutch began participating in the African human trade around the mid-sixteenth century and were "a major presence with forts and permanent trading links" by the seventeenth century. Herbert S. Klein, *The Atlantic Slave Trade* (New York: Cambridge University Press, 1999), 76.

161 **"Negroes . . . leade a beastly kind of life"** Leo Africanus, *The History and Description of Africa,* trans. John Pory and ed. Robert Brown (London: Hakluyt Society, 1896), 1: 187.

161 **to secure favor from the pope** Leo Africanus's arrival in Rome coincided with Pope Leo X's planning of a crusade in northern Africa. Africanus completed his *Description of Africa* upon returning to Rome during the papacy of Clement VII. Pekka Masonen, "Africanus, Leo," in *Encyclopedia of African History,* ed. Kevin Shillington (New York: Fitzroy Dearborn, 2005), 1:29–32.

161 "but an act of Justice," replied Sambo Richard Ligon, *A True and Exact History of the Island of Barbadoes* (London: Prince's Armes, 1657), 53-54.

161 authored the first known slave narrative *A Narrative of the Most Remarkable Particulars in the Life of James Albert Ukawsaw Gronniosaw, an African Prince* was "the first text ever published in Britain by a black author." See Ryan Hanley, *Beyond Slavery and Abolition: Black British Writing, c. 1770–1830* (Cambridge, UK: Cambridge University Press, 2019), 99.

161 Born to Nigerian royalty James Albert, *A Narrative of the Most Remarkable Particulars in the Life of James Albert Ukawsaw Gronniosaw, an African Prince* (1772; Dublin: B. Dugdale, 1790), iv, 11–13.

161 "My master grew very fond of me" Ibid., 14.

162 "a black man called the Devil that lives in hell" Ibid., 15–16.

162 "a poor heathen" Ibid., 16–21.

162 A fifty-one-year-old free Black carpenter For details on this uprising, see David M. Robertson, *Denmark Vesey: The Buried Story of America's Largest Slave Rebellion and the Man Who Led It* (New York: Vintage Books, 2000).

162 "to those waiting men who receive presents of old coats" Quoted in Ibid., 70.

162 bestowed on him a lifetime annual pension Ibid., 123.

162 By 1840, he'd acquired seven enslaved people of his own Ibid.

163 "next to Mr. Booker T. Washington, the best American authority" "The Negro Arraigned," *The New York Times,* February 23, 1901, timesmachine.nytimes.com/timesmachine/1901/02/23/117955436.html ?pageNumber=17. For an excellent analysis of how William Hannibal Thomas fits into discussions of Blackness at this time, see Khalil Gibran Muhammad, *The Condemnation of Blackness: Race, Crime, and the Making of Modern Urban America* (Cambridge, MA: Harvard University Press, 2010).

163 "intrinsically inferior type of humanity" William Hannibal Thomas, *The American Negro: What He Was, What He Is, and What He May Become* (New York: Macmillan Company, 1901), 139.

163 "record of lawless existence" Ibid., 129.

163 "unable practically to discern between right and wrong" Ibid., 134.

163 "in bondage to physical pleasure" Ibid., 195.

163 Thomas's "list of negative qualities of Negroes seemed limitless" John David Smith, *Black Judas: William Hannibal Thomas and The American Negro* (Athens: University of Georgia Press, 2000), 181.

163 But this "saving remnant" was set "apart" Thomas, *The American Negro,* xxiii, 68–69.

163 "the redemption of the negro is" Ibid., 410.

163 "national assimilation" Ibid., 397–432, 386.

163 stamped William Hannibal Thomas as the "Black Judas" See Smith, *Black Judas.*

163 **the diversifying of Amerca's police forces** The Kerner Commission, assembled by President Lyndon B. Johnson to investigate the causes of urban uprisings, recommended that "police departments should intensify their efforts to recruit more Negroes." National Advisory Commission on Civil Disorders, *Report of the National Advisory Commission on Civil Disorders* (Washington, DC: Government Printing Office, 1968), 166.

164 **Black officers were as abusive** James Forman Jr., *Locking Up Our Own: Crime and Punishment in Black America* (New York: Farrar, Straus & Giroux, 2017), 107–8. The subsequent quotes in this paragraph are also pulled from these pages.

164 **killer in 2012 of Brooklyn's Shantel Davis** Matt Flegenheimer, "Record of Detective in Fatal Shooting Is Defended," *The New York Times,* June 15, 2012, www.nytimes.com/2012/06/16/nyregion/woman-killed-by-detective -had-lengthy-arrest-record.html.

164 **the 2015 death of Freddie Gray** Rebecca R. Ruiz, "Baltimore Officers Will Face No Federal Charges in Death of Freddie Gray," *The New York Times,* September 12, 2017, www.nytimes.com/2017/09/12/us/freddie-gray -baltimore-police-federal-charges.html.

164 **in 2016 of Charlotte's Keith Lamont Scott** Holly Yan, Rolando Zenteno, and Brian Todd, "Keith Scott Killing: No Charges against Officer," CNN, November 30, 2016, www.cnn.com/2016/11/30/us/keith-lamont-scott -case-brentley-vinson/index.html.

164 **in 2018 of Sacramento's Stephon Clark** Chris Hagan, Nick Miller, Sammy Caiola, et al., "No Criminal Charges for Sacramento Police Officers Who Fatally Shot Stephon Clark," NPR, March 2, 2019, www.npr .org/2019/03/02/699719214/officers-in-stephon-clark-shooting-wont-be -charged-says-sacramento-d-a.

164 **one of the two police officers who assisted George Floyd's murderer** Kim Barker, "The Black Police Officer Who Detained George Floyd Had Pledged to Fix the Police," *The New York Times,* June 27, 2020, www .nytimes.com/2020/06/27/us/minneapolis-police-officer-kueng.html.

164 **survey of nearly eight thousand sworn officers** White officers (92 percent) and Black officers (29 percent) are far more likely than White (57 percent) and Black (12 percent) members of the general public to conclude "our country has made the changes needed to give blacks equal rights with whites." See John Gramlich, "Black and White Officers See Many Key Aspects of Policing Differently," Pew Research Center, January 12, 2017, www.pewresearch.org/fact-tank/2017/01/12/black-and-white-officers -see-many-key-aspects-of-policing-differently/.

165 **The new crop of Black politicians, judges, police chiefs, and officers** Forman Jr., *Locking Up Our Own,* 147.

165 **Note on "criminal": people who occasionally do bad things** I adopted this framing from prison abolitionist Mariame Kaba. See Mariame Kaba,

We Do This 'Til We Free Us: Abolitionist Organizing and Transforming Justice (Chicago: Haymarket Books, 2021), 160.

165 **cancers, heart diseases, and respiratory diseases killing them** 163,265 Black people in the United States died from cancer, heart disease, and chronic lower respiratory diseases in 2019 alone. For most cancers, Black Americans have the highest death rate and shortest survival of any racial or ethnic group. Black Americans are also 30 percent more likely than White Americans to die from heart disease. See Melonie Heron, *Deaths: Leading Causes for 2019,* National Vital Statistics Reports 70, no. 9 (Hyattsville, MD: National Center for Health Statistics, 2021) 13, www .cdc.gov/nchs/data/nvsr/nvsr70/nvsr70-09-508.pdf; American Cancer Society, "Cancer Facts & Figures for African American/Black People, 2022–2024," www.cancer.org/research/cancer-facts-statistics/cancer-facts -figures-for-african-americans.html; and U.S. Department of Health and Human Services, Office of Minority Health, "Heart Disease and African Americans," January 31, 2022, minorityhealth.hhs.gov/omh/browse .aspx?lvl=4&lvlid=19.

165 **"Black on Black crime has reached a critical level"** John H. Johnson, "Publisher's Statement," *Ebony,* August 1979.

166 **doubled the number of racist discrimination cases it dismissed** See Manning Marable, *Race, Reform, and Rebellion: The Second Reconstruction and Black America, 1945–2006,* 3rd ed. (Jackson: University Press of Mississippi, 2007), 196.

166 **redirected billions of dollars in federal funds** Ibid., 198, 206–7.

Chapter 12: Class

168 **CLASS RACIST IDEA** The definition in the hardcover edition was for CLASS RACIST, which I now define as: One who suggests a race-class is superior or inferior to another race-class in any way, and justifies the relative disparities in poverty and wealth between the race-classes brought on by racial capitalism.

168 **two of the most dangerous neighborhoods in Philadelphia** And they are still being told this. See Nick Johnson, "These Are the 10 Worst Philadelphia Neighborhoods for 2022," *Road Snacks,* April 6, 2022, www.roadsnacks .net/worst-philadelphia-neighborhoods/.

169 **millions of Black people migrating from the South** For more on the migration and what happened to them when they arrived, see Isabel Wilkerson, *The Warmth of Other Suns: The Epic Story of America's Great Migration* (New York: Vintage Books, 2010); and Thomas J. Sugrue, *The Origins of the Urban Crisis: Race and Inequality in Postwar Detroit* (Princeton, NJ: Princeton University Press, 1996).

169 **The combination of government welfare . . . along with often racist developers** See Richard Rothstein, *The Color of Law: A Forgotten History*

of How Our Government Segregated America (New York: Liveright Publishing Corporation, 2017).

169 **"The dark ghetto is institutionalized pathology"** Kenneth B. Clark, *Dark Ghetto: Dilemmas of Social Power* (New York: Harper & Row, 1965), 81.

169 **"the behavior of the African American underclass"** Dinesh D'Souza, *The End of Racism: Principles for a Multicultural Society* (New York: Free Press, 1995), 527.

170 **impoverished White people as "White trash"** See Nancy Isenberg, *White Trash: The 400-Year Untold History of Class in America* (New York: Viking, 2016).

171 **a 1959 ethnography of Mexican families** Oscar Lewis, *Five Families: Mexican Case Studies in the Culture of Poverty* (New York: Basic Books, 1959).

171 **explored the role of policy in the "cycle of poverty"** President Lyndon B. Johnson, informed by his Council of Economic Advisers, used the language of a "cycle of poverty." Johnson's economic report in 1964 lamented "the cycle of poverty" perpetuated by "inadequate schools, drop-outs, poor health, [and] unemployment," and recommended community action backed by federal assistance. In 1968, Johnson called for policies and programs (including income support) to help "break the cycle of deprivation and dependency." See Lyndon B. Johnson and U.S. Council of Economic Advisers, *Economic Report of the President Transmitted to the Congress* (Washington, D.C.: U.S. Government Printing Office, 1964), 16; and *Economic Report of the President Transmitted to the Congress* (Washington, D.C.: U.S. Government Printing Office, 1968), 16–17.

171 **"People with a culture of poverty"** Oscar Lewis, "The Culture of Poverty," *Trans-action* 1 (1963), 17–19.

171 **"We have got this tailspin of culture"** Paul Ryan quoted in Zak Cheney-Rice, "Paul Ryan's Racist Comments Are a Slap in the Face to 10.5 Million Americans," *Mic,* March 13, 2014, mic.com/articles/85223/paul-ryan -s-racist-comments-are-a-slap-in-the-face-to-10-5-million-americans.

171 **In Clark's work** Clark, *Dark Ghetto.*

171 **"transforms the individual"** Barry Goldwater, *The Conscience of a Conservative* (New York: Macfadden Books, 1960), 75.

171 **rich White people who depended on the welfare** For examples of government handouts to the wealthy, see Emily Badger and Christopher Ingraham, "The Rich Get Government Handouts Just Like the Poor. Here Are 10 of Them," *The Washington Post,* April 9, 2015, www.washingtonpost .com/news/wonk/wp/2015/04/09/the-rich-get-government-handouts -just-like-the-poor-here-are-10-of-them/.

171 **White middle class depending on the welfare** See Ira Katznelson, *When Affirmative Action Was White: An Untold History of Racial Inequality in Twentieth-Century America* (New York: W. W. Norton & Company, 2005).

172 **"The evidence of this failure is all around us"** Kay Coles James, "Why

We Must Be Bold on Welfare Reform," The Heritage Foundation, March 12, 2018, www.heritage.org/welfare/commentary/why-we-must-be-bold-welfare-reform.

172 **"within the walls of the ghetto"** Clark, *Dark Ghetto,* xv.

172 **"The white poor and slum dweller"** Ibid., xxii.

172 **Obama made a similar case** "Barack Obama's Speech on Race," *The New York Times,* March 18, 2008, www.nytimes.com/2008/03/18/us/politics/18text-obama.html.

172 **impoverished Black people are more optimistic** See Carol Graham, *Happiness for All? Unequal Hopes and Lives in Pursuit of the American Dream* (Princeton, NJ: Princeton University Press, 2017).

172 **"wage" of Whiteness** W.E.B. Du Bois, *Black Reconstruction in America, 1860–1880* (New York: Harcourt, Brace and Company, 1935), 700. See also David R. Roediger, *The Wages of Whiteness: Race and the Making of the American Working Class* (New York: Verso, 1991).

173 **as the "Talented Tenth"** See W.E.B. Du Bois, "The Talented Tenth," in *The Negro Problem: A Series of Articles by Representative American Negroes of Today* (New York: James Pott & Company, 1903), 33-75.

173 **As Martin Luther King said in his critique of capitalism in 1967** Martin Luther King Jr., "Where Do We Go from Here?" August 16, 1967, The Martin Luther King, Jr. Research and Education Institute, Stanford University, kinginstitute.stanford.edu/where-do-we-go-here.

173 **what world-systems theorists term the "long sixteenth century"** Immanuel Wallerstein, *The Modern World-System: Capitalist Agriculture and the Origins of the European World-Economy in the Sixteenth Century* (New York: Academic Press, 1974), 63.

173 **Prince Henry's Portugal birthed conjoined twins** For histories of the conjoined origins of racism and capitalism, see Ibram X. Kendi, *Stamped from the Beginning: The Definitive History of Racist Ideas in America* (New York: Nation Books, 2016); Eric Williams, *Capitalism & Slavery* (1944; Chapel Hill: University of North Carolina Press, 1994); and Edward E. Baptist, *The Half Has Never Been Told: Slavery and the Making of American Capitalism* (New York: Basic Books, 2014).

174 **England, France, and the Netherlands competed for dominance** Portugal transported the most enslaved captives until the period spanning 1726 to 1750, when Great Britain surpassed Portugal as the leading slave-trading country. By the end of the eighteenth century, the numbers of enslaved people carried away by Portugal, Great Britain, France, and the Netherlands were as follows: 3,224,196 by Portugal; 2,973,560 by Great Britain; 1,177,449 by France; and 549,945 by the Netherlands. For corresponding data tables, see "Trans-Atlantic Slave Trade—Estimates," Slave Voyages: The Trans-Atlantic Slave Trade Database, www.slavevoyages.org/assessment/estimates.

174 **The Black poverty rate in 2020 stood at 19.8 percent** The White poverty rate was 8.3 percent. "Poverty Rate by Race/Ethnicity," Kaiser Family Foundation Database, www.kff.org/75afb53/.

174 **The Black unemployment rate has consistently been about twice as high** See U.S. Bureau of Labor Statistics, "Labor Force Statistics by Race and Ethnicity, 2020," Report 1095, November 2021, 61–63, www.bls.gov/opub/reports/race-and-ethnicity/2020/pdf/home.pdf.

174 **about as large as it was in 1950** David Leonhardt, "The Black-White Wage Gap Is as Big as It Was in 1950," *The New York Times,* June 25, 2020, www.nytimes.com/2020/06/25/opinion/sunday/race-wage-gap.html.

174 **median net worth of White families is about eight times that of Black families** Emily Moss, Kriston McIntosh, Wendy Edelberg, and Kristen Broady, "The Black-White Wealth Gap Left Black Households More Vulnerable," Brookings, December 8, 2020, www.brookings.edu/blog/up-front/2020/12/08/the-black-white-wealth-gap-left-black-households-more-vulnerable/.

175 **By 2053, the median wealth** Dedrick Asante-Muhammad, Chuck Collins, Josh Hoxie, and Emanuel Nieves, "The Road to Zero Wealth: How the Racial Wealth Divide Is Hollowing Out America's Middle Class," Institute for Policy Studies and Prosperity Now, September 2017, 5, ips-dc.org/wp-content/uploads/2017/09/The-Road-to-Zero-Wealth_FINAL.pdf.

175 **Africa's unprecedented capitalist growth over the last two decades** "Africa's unprecedented growth in the 2000s has not translated into significantly improved livelihoods for most Africans, as the income gap between rich and poor has widened. . . . About 34 per cent of African households live below the $1.90 per day international poverty line, and around 40 per cent of the total wealth is owned by approximately one ten-thousandth per cent of the continent's population." See United Nations, "Africa Free Trade Area, Likely Spur for Growth and Development," *UN News,* December 8, 2021, news.un.org/en/story/2021/12/1107482.

175 **nearly nine in ten extremely impoverished people will live in Sub-Saharan Africa by 2030** Divyanshi Wadhwa, "The Number of Extremely Poor People Continues to Rise in Sub-Saharan Africa," The World Bank, September 19, 2018, blogs.worldbank.org/opendata/number-extremely-poor-people-continues-rise-sub-saharan-africa.

175 **In Latin America, people of African descent** People of African descent "account for about one-quarter of Latin America's population, and are overrepresented among the poor in every country." To learn more about the racial inequities in wealth and other sectors, see Germán Freire, Ede Ijjasz-Vasquez, and Carolina Diaz-Bonilla, *Afro-Descendants in Latin America: Toward a Framework of Inclusion* (Washington, D.C.: World Bank, 2018), openknowledge.worldbank.org/handle/10986/30201.

175 **The global gap** Jason Hickel, "Global Inequality May Be Much Worse Than We Think," *The Guardian,* April 8, 2016, www.theguardian.com/global -development-professionals-network/2016/apr/08/global-inequality-may -be-much-worse-than-we-think.

175 **the global non-White middle class has grown** See Homi Kharas, *The Un- precedented Expansion of the Global Middle Class: An Update,* Global Economy and Development Working Paper 100, Brookings, February 2017, www .brookings.edu/wp-content/uploads/2017/02/global_20170228_global -middle-class.pdf.

175 **upward mobility is a struggle for all racial groups** Marcus Lu, "Is the American Dream Over? Here's What the Data Says," World Economic Forum, September 2, 2020, www.weforum.org/agenda/2020/09/social -mobility-upwards-decline-usa-us-america-economics/.

175 **Upward mobility is still greater for White people** Raj Chetty, Nathaniel Hendren, Maggie R. Jones, and Sonya R. Porter, "Race and Economic Opportunity in the United States: An Intergenerational Perspective," *The Quarterly Journal of Economics* 135, no. 2 (May 2020), 711–83.

175 **the highest-income quintile** Dedrick Asante-Muhammad, "The Racial Wealth Divide Holds Back Black Earners at All Levels," *AlterNet,* April 3, 2018, www.alternet.org/2018/04/racial-wealth-divide-holds-back-black-ear ners/.

175 **Black middle-income households have less wealth** See Christopher Pul- liam, Richard V. Reeves, and Ariel Gelrud Shiro, "The Middle Class Is Al- ready Racially Diverse," October 30, 2020, Brookings, www.brookings.edu /blog/up-front/2020/10/30/the-middle-class-is-already-racially-diverse/.

175 **whose homes are valued higher** A recent study by Freddie Mac shows that home appraisal values decrease as the concentration of Black or Latinx people increases. For census tracts that are more than 50 percent Black, the appraisal value for a single-family home is 5.2 percent lower than for a comparable home in a White tract (a disparity called "the appraisal gap"). For census tracts that are more than 50 percent Latinx, the appraisal gap is 8 percent. See "Ra- cial and Ethnic Valuation Gaps in Home Purchase Appraisals," Freddie Mac, September 20, 2021, www.freddiemac.com/research/insight/20210920 -home-appraisals. For one Black family's recent experience with a racist undervaluation of their home, see Debra Kamin, "Home Appraised With a Black Owner: $472,000. With a White Owner: $750,000," *The New York Times,* August 18, 2022, www.nytimes.com/2022/08/18/realestate/hous ing-discrimination-maryland.html.

175 **the wealth distribution of White low-income families** See William Dar- ity Jr., Fenaba R. Addo, and Imari Z. Smith, "A Subaltern Middle Class: The Case of the Missing 'Black Bourgeoisie' in America," *Contemporary Eco- nomic Policy* 39, no. 3 (July 2021), 494–502.

175 **White poverty is not as distressing as Black poverty** For this claim and the following claims in this paragraph, see Emily Badger, "Black Poverty Differs from White Poverty," *The Washington Post,* August 12, 2015, www.washingtonpost.com/news/wonk/wp/2015/08/12/black-poverty-differs-from-white-poverty/.

176 **Antiracist policies in the 1960s and 1970s narrowed these inequities** Richard Wolf, "Equality Still Elusive 50 Years After Civil Rights Act," *USA Today,* January 19, 2014, www.usatoday.com/story/news/nation/2014/01/19/civil-rights-act-progress/4641967/.

176 **economic inequities within the races have broadened** Rakesh Kochhar and Anthony Cilluffo, "Income Inequality in the U.S. Is Rising Most Rapidly Among Asians," Pew Research Center, July 12, 2018, www.pewresearch.org/social-trends/2018/07/12/income-inequality-in-the-u-s-is-rising-most-rapidly-among-asians/#fn-24708-2.

176 **as chronicled by historian Devyn Spence Benson** Devyn Spence Benson, *Antiracism in Cuba: The Unfinished Revolution* (Chapel Hill: University of North Carolina Press, 2016), 30–71.

176 **Socialist Party of America (SPA) in 1901 refused to adopt an anti-lynching petition** Paul D'Amato, "Race and the U.S. Socialist Tradition," *Socialist Worker,* November 18, 2010, socialistworker.org/2010/11/18/race-and-us-socialist-tradition.

176 **decrying "identity politics"** See Helen Gilbert, "Opinion—The Meltdown of International Socialist Organization: How Anti-Feminism, Racism, and Bureaucracy Led to Its Demise," *South Seattle Emerald,* June 4, 2019, southseattleemerald.com/2019/06/04/opinion-the-meltdown-of-international-socialist-organization-how-anti-feminism-racism-and-bureaucracy-led-to-its-demise/.

176 **"The discovery of gold and silver in America"** Karl Marx, *Capital: A Critique of Political Economy* (1867; New York: Modern Library, 1906), 1:823.

177 **depressed the Black poor worse than the White poor** See Katznelson, *When Affirmative Action Was White.*

177 **pleaded with Du Bois to reconsider** David Levering Lewis, *W.E.B. Du Bois, 1919–1963: The Fight for Equality and the American Century* (New York: Macmillan, 2000), 309–10.

177 **what scholars now call racial capitalism** See Robin D. G. Kelley, "What Did Cedric Robinson Mean by Racial Capitalism," *Boston Review,* January 12, 2017, bostonreview.net/articles/robin-d-g-kelley-introduction-race-capitalism-justice/.

177 **"The lowest and most fatal degree"** W. E. B. Du Bois, "Marxism and the Negro Problem," *The Crisis,* May 1933, 103–104.

177 **the development of a "petty bourgeoisie"** Ibid.

177 **started to think beyond Marx and Russian communists** See Cedric J.

NOTES • 325

Robinson, *Black Marxism: The Making of the Black Radical Tradition* (Chapel Hill: University of North Carolina Press, 2000).

177 **"Instead of a horizontal division of classes"** W.E.B. Du Bois, *Dusk of Dawn: An Essay Toward an Autobiography of a Race Concept* (New York: Harcourt, Brace and Company, 1940), 205.

178 **called for a "Guiding One Hundredth"** See W.E.B. Du Bois, "The Talented Tenth: Memorial Address," in *W.E.B. Du Bois: A Reader*, ed. David Levering Lewis (New York: Henry Holt, 1995), 347–53.

178 **the red scares of the 1950s** To understand how policymakers exploited American fears of communism to suppress the civil rights movement, see Jeff R. Woods, *Black Struggle, Red Scare: Segregation and Anti-Communism in the South, 1948–1968* (Baton Rouge: Louisiana State University Press, 2003).

178 **"inextricable link between racism and capitalism"** Keeanga-Yamahtta Taylor, "Race, Class and Marxism," *Socialist Worker,* January 4, 2011, social istworker.org/2011/01/04/race-class-and-marxism.

178 **Note on Marxism: segregationists called Martin Luther King Jr. a "communist"** See "Communism," *Martin Luther King, Jr. Encyclopedia,* The Martin Luther King, Jr. Research and Education Institute, Stanford University, king institute.stanford.edu/encyclopedia/communism.

178 **regularly say their opponents fighting for economic justice for all people** For a recent summary of conservative accusations of anti-capitalism, see Max Boot, "There They Go Again. For 90 Years, Republicans Have Been Crying Wolf about Democratic 'Socialism,'" *The Washington Post,* November 2, 2021, www.washingtonpost.com/opinions/2021/11/02/here-we-go-again-90-years-republicans-have-been-crying-wolf-about-democratic-socialism/.

179 **The history of capitalism** For honest histories of capitalism and the United States, see Howard Zinn, *A People's History of the United States, 1492–Present*, rev. ed. (New York: Harper Perennial, 1995); and Sven Beckert and Seth Rockman, eds., *Slavery's Capitalism: A New History of American Economic Development* (Philadelphia: University of Pennsylvania Press, 2016).

179 **"capitalist to the bone"** Franklin Foer, "Elizabeth Warren's Theory of Capitalism," *The Atlantic,* August 28, 2018, www.theatlantic.com/politics/archive/2018/08/elizabeth-warrens-theory-of-capitalism/568573/.

179 **a series of regulations and rules** One such proposal was Warren's Ultra-Millionaire Tax Act, which she introduced in March 2021. See Naomi Jagoda, "Warren Bill Would Impose Wealth Tax on $50M Households," *The Hill,* March 1, 2021, thehill.com/policy/finance/540968-warren-offers-bill-to-create-wealth-tax-on-net-worth-above-50-million/.

180 **The top 1 percent now own around half** The top 1 percent owns 46 percent of the world's wealth. See Anthony Shorrocks, James Davies, and Rodridgo Lluberas, *Global Wealth Report* 2021 (Credit Suisse Research

Institute, June 2021), 18, www.credit-suisse.com/about-us/en/reports-research/global-wealth-report.html.

180 **42.5 percent at the height of the Great Recession in 2008** Rupert Neate, "Richest 1% Own Half the World's Wealth, Study Finds," *The Guardian,* November 14, 2017, www.theguardian.com/inequality/2017/nov/14/worlds-richest-wealth-credit-suisse.

180 **The world's 2.9 billion poorest adults** This is the most recent data. The world's poorest working-age adults now own significantly less (1.3 percent vs. 2.7 percent) of global wealth. Experts cite the COVID-19 pandemic for this growing gap. See Shorrocks, Davies, and Lluberas, *Global Wealth Report* 2021, 17.

181 **taken through force with the threat of "economic sanctions"** See Stuart Davis and Immanuel Ness, eds., *Sanctions as War: Anti-Imperialist Perspectives on American Geo-Economic Strategy* (Leiden, Netherlands: Brill, 2021).

181 **one of the richest countries in the world belowground** The Democratic Republic of the Congo has valuable minerals like cobalt and copper but also "the third largest population of poor people globally." See World Bank, "The World Bank in DRC: Overview," May 9, 2022, www.worldbank.org/en/country/drc/overview#1.

182 **the Blaxploitation films of the late 1960s and early 1970s** On Blaxploitation films, see Ed Guerrero, *Framing Blackness: The African American Image in Film* (Philadelphia: Temple University Press, 1993), 69–111.

182 **"I made this film for the black aesthetic"** Van Peebles quoted in Lerone Bennett Jr., "The Emancipation Orgasm: Sweetback in Wonderland," *Ebony,* September 1971, 112.

182 **Bennett blasted Van Peebles** Ibid., 106–18.

183 **E. Franklin Frazier's *Black Bourgeoisie*** E. Franklin Frazier, *Black Bourgeoisie: The Rise of a New Middle Class* (Glencoe, IL: Free Press, 1957).

183 **"the Negro middle class contributes very little"** Nathan Glazer, "The Negroes," in Nathan Glazer and Daniel Patrick Moynihan, *Beyond the Melting Pot: The Negroes, Puerto Ricans, Jews, Italians, and Irish of New York City* (Cambridge, MA: MIT Press, 1963), 53.

184 **Martin Luther King Jr. and a generation of elite Black youngsters** Lewis, *W.E.B. Du Bois, 1919–1963,* 557–58.

Chapter 13: Space

185 **SPACE RACIST IDEA** The definition in the hardcover edition was for SPACE RACISM, which I now define as: A powerful collection of inequitable and unjust policies that lead to injustice and resource inequity between racialized spaces or the elimination of certain racialized spaces, which are substantiated by ideas of racial hierarchy about racialized spaces.

185 **SPACE ANTIRACIST IDEA** The definition in the hardcover edition was for SPACE ANTIRACISM, which I now define as: A powerful collection

of equitable and just policies that lead to justice and equity between integrated and protected racialized spaces, which are substantiated by ideas of racial equality about racialized spaces.

185 first printed the *Journal of Black Studies* SAGE, "50 Years of the Journal of Black Studies," September 29, 2021, group.sagepub.com/blog/50-years-of -the-journal-of-black-studies.

185 "looking out" at the world from a European "center" Molefi Kete Asante, *Afrocentricity,* rev. ed. (Trenton, NJ: Africa World Press, 1988), 1.

186 "The rejection of European particularism" Ibid., 104.

186 the nation's first African American studies doctoral program Ronald Roach, "Despite Struggles, Pioneering Black Studies Department Presses Forward," *Diverse: Issues in Higher Education,* December 9, 2009, www .diverseeducation.com/students/article/15089161/despite-struggles -pioneering-black-studies-department-presses-forward.

186 to speak on her research Ama Mazama and Garvey Musumunu, *African Americans and Homeschooling: Motivations, Opportunities, and Challenges* (New York: Routledge, 2015); Molefi Kete Asante and Ama Mazama, eds., *Encyclopedia of African Religion,* 2 vols. (Thousand Oaks, CA: SAGE, 2009); and Ama Mazama, ed., *The Afrocentric Paradigm* (Trenton, NJ: Africa World Press, 2003).

186 "collective subjectivity" Molefi Kete Asante, *The Afrocentric Idea* (Philadelphia: Temple University Press, 1987), 3.

187 "creeping blight" Kenneth B. Clark, *Dark Ghetto: Dilemmas of Social Power* (New York: Harper & Row, 1965), 25.

187 "juvenile delinquency" Ibid., 87.

187 "widespread violence" Ibid., 109.

188 "banksters," as radio personality Thom Hartmann calls them Thom Hartmann, "How to Take on the Banksters," *The Hartmann Report,* September 21, 2016, www.thomhartmann.com/blog/2016/09/how-take-banksters.

188 Americans lost trillions during the Great Recession John Carney, "America Lost $10.2 Trillion in 2008," *Business Insider,* February 3, 2009, businessinsider.com/2009/2/america-lost-102-trillion-of-wealth-in-2008.

188 largely triggered by financial harms See Charles Ferguson, "Heist of the Century: Wall Street's Role in the Financial Crisis," *The Guardian,* May 20, 2012, www.theguardian.com/business/2012/may/20/wall -street-role-financial-crisis; and Erin Coghlan, Lisa McCorkell, and Sara Hinkley, "What Really Caused the Great Recession?" Institute for Research on Labor and Employment, University of California, Berkeley, September 19, 2018, irle.berkeley.edu/what-really-caused-the-great-recession/.

188 White-collar harms increased "White-Collar Crime in the Post-COVID-19 Landscape," *Financier Worldwide Magazine,* February 2022, www.financierworldwide.com/white-collar-crime-in-the-post-covid-19 -landscape#.YoughvPMLPY.

188 **"roughly double" the wealth** Martha C. White, "Wall Street Minted 56 New Billionaires Since the Pandemic Began—But Many Families Are Left Behind," NBC News, December 30, 2020, www.nbcnews.com/business /business-news/wall-street-s-best-year-ever-why-pandemic-has-been -n1252512.

188 **Estimated losses from white-collar harms** To better understand the scope of white-collar harms, consider that the estimated annual losses from street-level harms (e.g., burglary, theft, and larceny) add up to $16 billion. Robin Kaiser-Schatzlein, "How White-Collar Criminals Get Away With It," *The New Republic,* September 15, 2020, newrepublic.com/article/159361/white -collar-criminals-get-away.

188 **the combined costs of burglary and robbery** Patrick Colm Hogan, *The Culture of Conformism: Understanding Social Consent* (Durham, NC: Duke University Press, 2001), 15.

188 **the disproportionate number of White males who engage in mass shootings** The Violence Project, "Why Are Almost All Mass Shooters Men?" The Violence Project, March 29, 2021, www.theviolenceproject.org/media/why -are-almost-all-mass-shooters-men/.

188 **deliver mostly White suburbanites to their homes** See Deborah N. Archer, "'White Men's Roads Through Black Men's Homes': Advancing Racial Equity Through Highway Reconstruction," *Vanderbilt Law Review* 73, no. 5 (October 2020), 1259–1330, cdn.vanderbilt.edu/vu-wp0/wp-content /uploads/sites/278/2020/10/19130728/White-Mens-Roads-Through -Black-Mens-Homes-Advancing-Racial-Equity-Through-Highway -Reconstruction.pdf.

188 **3,380 more Americans died from alcohol-related traffic deaths** Ibram X. Kendi, *Stamped from the Beginning: The Definitive History of Racist Ideas in America* (New York: Nation Books, 2016), 437.

189 **"are living in hell"** Matthew Nussbaum, "Trump at Debate: Minorities in Cities 'Are Living in Hell,'" *POLITICO,* September 26, 2016, www .politico.com/story/2016/09/trump-minorities-living-in-hell-228726.

189 **"from shithole countries"** Josh Dawsey, "Trump Derides Protections for Immigrants from 'Shithole' Countries," *The Washington Post,* January 12, 2018, www.washingtonpost.com/politics/trump-attacks-protections-for-im migrants-from-shithole-countries-in-oval-office-meeting/2018/01/11 /bfc0725c-f711-11e7-91af-31ac729add94_story.html.

190 **HBCUs do not represent "the real world"** Evelyn Diaz, "Hold Up: Aisha Tyler Thinks HBCUs Are Bad for Black Students?" BET, April 28, 2016, www.bet.com/article/4pyiku/aisha-tyler-thinks-hbcus-are-bad-for-black -students.

190 **Black Americans live in majority-Black neighborhoods** "Just as white neighborhoods continue to remain 'whiter' than their surrounding met-

ropolitan areas, it's also the case that neighborhoods where average Black and Latino or Hispanic populations reside continue to include overrepresentations of those groups." William H. Frey, "Even as Metropolitan Areas Diversify, White Americans Still Live in Mostly White Neighborhoods," Brookings, March 23, 2020, www.brookings.edu/research/even-as-metropolitan-areas-diversify-white-americans-still-live-in-mostly-white-neighborhoods/.

190 **work in majority-Black sites of employment** "Blacks made up 12 percent of all employed workers, but were substantially overrepresented in several detailed occupational categories, including home health aides (37 percent), transit and intercity bus drivers (37 percent), nursing assistants (35 percent), correctional officers and jailers (33 percent), and security guards and gaming surveillance officers (31 percent)." U.S. Bureau of Labor Statistics, "Labor Force Characteristics by Race and Ethnicity, 2020," BLS Reports, Report 1095, November 2021, www.bls.gov/opub/reports/race-and-ethnicity/2020/home.htm.

190 **socialize in majority-Black spaces** A study found that the average Black person has eighty-three Black friends for every one hundred friends. See Christopher Ingraham, "Three Quarters of Whites Don't Have Any Non-White Friends," *The Washington Post,* August 25, 2014, www.washingtonpost.com/news/wonk/wp/2014/08/25/three-quarters-of-whites-dont-have-any-non-white-friends/.

190 **attend majority-Black churches** Sixty percent of Black Americans who attend religious services are members of Black congregations. Besheer Mohamed, Kiana Cox, Jeff Diamant, and Claire Gecewicz, "Faith Among Black Americans," Pew Research Center, February 16, 2021, www.pewresearch.org/religion/2021/02/16/faith-among-black-americans/.

190 **send their children to majority-Black schools** 42 percent of Black students attend schools where more than half of the student population is Black. Katherine Schaeffer, "U.S. Public School Students Often Go to Schools Where at Least Half of Their Peers Are the Same Race or Ethnicity," Pew Research Center, December 15, 2021, pewrsr.ch/3dSCmlx.

190 **"Even the best black colleges and universities do not approach"** Thomas Sowell, "The Plight of Black Students in America," *Daedalus* 103 (Spring 1974), 189.

190 **Sowell's "description remains accurate"** Jason L. Riley, "Black Colleges Need a New Mission," *The Wall Street Journal,* September 28, 2010, www.wsj.com/articles/SB10001424052748704654004575517822124077834.

191 **The endowment of the richest HBCU, Howard** Howard's endowment was $712,500,000, compared to $31,958,313,000 for the University of Texas System, $28,948,000,000 for Stanford University, and $31,201,700,000 for Yale. See Mirtha Donastorg, "Database: All 2020 HBCU Endowments Combined

Just a Fraction of One Ivy League," *The Plug,* January 5, 2022, www.tpinsights
.com/free-articles/database-all-2020-hbcu-endowments-combined-just
-a-fraction-of-one-ivy-league; and Emma Whitford, "College Endowments Boomed in Fiscal 2021," *Inside Higher Ed,* February 18, 2022, www
.insidehighered.com/news/2022/02/18/college-endowments-boomed-fiscal
-year-2021-study-shows.

191 **produces a giving gap** Kristen Broady, Andre M. Perry, and Carl Romer,
"Underfunding HBCUs Leads to an Underrepresentation of Black Faculty,"
Brookings, August 4, 2021, www.brookings.edu/blog/the-avenue/2021/08
/04/underfunding-hbcus-leads-to-an-underrepresentation-of-black-faculty/.

191 **racist policies steer more funds to HWCUs** See Andre M. Perry, "HBCUs
Are Leading Centers of Education—Why Are They Treated as Second-
Class Institutions?" Brookings, November 22, 2019, www.brookings.edu
/blog/brown-center-chalkboard/2019/11/22/hbcus-are-leading-centers
-of-education-why-are-they-treated-as-second-class-institutions/.

191 **like the current "performance based" state models** Education policy
experts recently observed that "high-dosage [performance-based funding]
(PBF) policies had a negative impact on state funding for four-year HBCUs
and four-year institutions serving an above-average share of racially minoritized students. . . . Specifically, the adoption of a high-dosage PBF system decreased state appropriations per [full-time] student for HBCUs ($1,288.04),
[minority-serving institutions] (MSIs) ($486.57), and institutions serving an
above-average share of racially minoritized students ($568.48)." See Justin C.
Ortagus, Kelly Ochs Rosinger, Robert Kelchen, Garam Chu, and Mitchell
Lingo, "The Unequal Impacts of Performance-Based Funding on Institutional Resources in Higher Education," InformEd States Working Paper,
January 2022, static1.squarespace.com/static/5d9f9fae6a122515ee074363
/t/61f42ff33d2a6053c9889514/1643393013933/InformedStates_Paper
_UnequalImpactsofPBFinResources.pdf.

191 **HBCUs have equal rates of Black graduation** Bryan J. Cook, "Black Students Find Greater Satisfaction Attending Historically Black Colleges and
Universities," Urban Institute, February 18, 2022, www.urban.org/urban
-wire/black-students-find-greater-satisfaction-attending-historically-black
-colleges-and-universities.

191 **HBCU graduates are, on average, more likely** Sean Seymour and Julie
Ray, "Grades of Historically Black Colleges Have Well-Being Edge," Gallup,
October 27, 2015, news.gallup.com/poll/186362/grads-historically-black
-colleges-edge.aspx.

192 **Banks remain twice as likely to offer loans to White entrepreneurs**
Furthermore, approval rates for Black-owned low-credit risk businesses are
nearly the same as the approval rates for White-owned high- and medium-
credit risk businesses. See Federal Reserve Banks, *Small Business Credit*

Survey: 2021 Report on Firms Owned by People of Color, 2021, 28, www.new yorkfed.org/medialibrary/FedSmallBusiness/files/2021/sbcs-report-on -firms-owned-by-people-of-color.

192 **Customers avoid businesses in Black neighborhoods** Andre M. Perry, Jonathan Rothwell, and David Harshbarger, "Five-Star Reviews, One-Star Profits: The Devaluation of Businesses in Black Communities," Brookings, February 18, 2020, www.brookings.edu/research/five-star-reviews-one-star -profits-the-devaluation-of-businesses-in-black-communities/.

192 **"does that inequitable treatment excuse bad service?"** "Should Black Owned Businesses Get a Hall Pass for Bad Service?," *Blavity,* May 14, 2017, blavity.com/black-owned-businesses-get-pass-for-bad-service.

192 **"carry back to the country of their origin, the seeds of civilization"** Thomas Jefferson, "Letter to John Lynch, January 21, 1811, Monticello," in *The Writings of Thomas Jefferson,* ed. H. A. Washington (New York: Riker, Thorne & Co., 1854), 5:564.

192 **redeeming Africa "from ignorance and barbarism"** Henry Clay quoted in Isaac V. Brown, *Biography of the Rev. Robert Finley, D.D., of Basking Ridge, N.J., with an Account of His Agency as the Author of the American Colonization Society,* 2nd ed. (Philadelphia: John W. Moore, 1857), 105.

192 **"savage wilds of Africa"** Quoted in Claude A. Clegg III, *The Price of Liberty: African Americans and the Making of Liberia* (Chapel Hill: University of North Carolina Press, 2004), 35.

192 **A writer for the South's *De Bow's Review* searched** "Free Negro Rule," *DeBow's Review* 3, no. 4 (April 1860), 440.

193 **Sherman and U.S. secretary of war Edwin M. Stanton met** For an account of this meeting, see *The War of the Rebellion: A Compilation of the Official Records of the Union and Confederate Armies* (Washington, D.C.: U.S. Government Printing Office, 1895), 37–41.

193 **"will be left to the freed people themselves"** "Sherman's Special Field Orders, No. 15," in *The Empire State of the South: Georgia History in Documents and Essays,* ed. Christopher C. Meyers (Macon, GA: Mercer University Press, 2008), 174.

193 **the most eminent newspaper editor of the day** James M. Lundberg, "How Horace Greeley Turned Newspapers Legitimate and Saved the Media from Itself," *Smithsonian Magazine,* March 6, 2020, www.smithsonianmag.com /history/how-horace-greeley-invented-persona-crusading-journalist-180 974348/.

193 **Sherman's order deprived the Negroes** Horace Greeley, "Gen. Sherman and the Negroes," *New York Daily Tribune,* January 30, 1865.

194 **roughly forty thousand Black people had settled** William A. Byrne, "'Uncle Billy' Sherman Comes to Town: The Free Winter of Black Savannah," *Georgia Historical Quarterly* 79, no. 1 (Spring 1995), 112–14.

195 "on the platform of equal accommodations" Henry W. Grady, "In Plain Black and White: A Reply to Mr. Cable," *Century Magazine* 29 (April 1885), 911.

195 in the 1896 *Plessy v. Ferguson* decision See *Plessy v. Ferguson*, 163 U.S. 537 (1896), available courtesy of Cornell Law School's Legal Information Institute, www.law.cornell.edu/supremecourt/text/163/537.

195 diverted resources toward exclusively White spaces Education is a prime example. For the school funding disparities mentioned in this paragraph, see Peter Irons, "Jim Crow's Schools," *American Educator*, Summer 2004, www .aft.org/periodical/american-educator/summer-2004/jim-crows-schools, reprinted from Irons, *Jim Crow's Children* (New York: Viking, 2002).

195 switched tactics to taking down "separate" Robert J. Cottrol, Raymond T. Diamond, and Leland B. Ware, "NAACP v. Jim Crow: The Legal Strategy That Brought Down 'Separate but Equal' by Toppling School Segregation," *American Educator*, Summer 2004, www.aft.org/periodical/american -educator/summer-2004/naacp-v-jim-crow.

195 "the enforced separation of the two races stamps the colored race" *Plessy v. Ferguson*, 163 U.S. 537 (1896).

195 Marshall asked psychologists Kenneth and Mamie Clark Ernie Suggs, "How Mamie and Kenneth Clark Used Dolls to Overturn School Segregation Law," *Atlanta Journal-Constitution*, February 8, 2022, www.ajc.com /news/martin-luther-king-jr/black-doll-white-doll-and-racial-shame-thats -nothing-to-play-with/KPFSRBF5PZHKPLDNMKXMYZXZIA/.

195 the majority of Black children preferred White dolls For essays on their doll experiments, see Kenneth B. Clark and Mamie P. Clark, "Racial Identification and Preference in Negro Children," in *Readings in Social Psychology*, ed. E. L. Hartley (New York: Holt, Rinehart & Winston, 1947); Clark and Clark, "Emotional Factors in Racial Identification and Preference in Negro Children," *Journal of Negro Education* 19, no. 3 (Summer 1950), 341–50; Kenneth B. Clark, *Prejudice and Your Child* (Boston: Beacon Press, 1955).

195 argued the harm could be permanent See John P. Jackson, Jr., *Social Scientists for Social Justice: Making the Case Against Segregation* (New York: New York University Press, 2001).

195 "To separate [colored children] from others" *Brown v. Board of Education of Topeka*, 347 U.S. 483 (1954), available courtesy of Cornell Law School's Legal Information Institute at www.law.cornell.edu/supremecourt/text /347/483%26gt#writing-ZS.

196 *San Antonio Independent School District v. Rodriguez* See Paul A. Sracic, *San Antonio v. Rodriguez and the Pursuit of Equal Education: The Debate Over Discrimination and School Funding* (Lawrence: University Press of Kansas, 2006); and *San Antonio Independent School District v. Rodriguez*, 411 U.S. 1 (1973), available courtesy of Cornell Law School's Legal Information Institute at www.law.cornell.edu/supremecourt/text/411/1.

196 **"there are adequate Negro schools and prepared instructors"** Zora Neale Hurston, "Court Order Can't Make Races Mix," *Orlando Sentinel,* August 11, 1955.

196 **"I think integration in our public schools is different"** "Deacon John Feagin Sr." in *Reflections on Our Pastor: Dr. Martin Luther King, Jr. at Dexter Avenue Baptist Church, 1954–1960,* eds. Wally G. Vaughn and Richard W. Wills (Dover, MA: The Majority Press, 1999), 129.

197 **a 79 percent-White teaching force** For reference, 47 percent of public elementary and secondary school students are White; 27 percent are Latinx; 15 percent are Black; 5 percent are Asian; 4 percent are mixed race; and about 1 percent are Native. Katherine Schaeffer, "America's Public School Teachers Are Far Less Racially and Ethnically Diverse Than Their Students," Pew Research Center, December 10, 2021, www.pewresearch.org/fact-tank /2021/12/10/americas-public-school-teachers-are-far-less-racially-and -ethnically-diverse-than-their-students/.

197 **40 percent less likely to believe the student will finish high school** Seth Gershenson, Stephen B. Holt, and Nicholas W. Papageorge, "Who Believes in Me? The Effect of Student-Teacher Demographic Match on Teacher Expectations," *Economics of Education Review* 52 (June 2016), 209–24.

197 **Low-income Black students who have at least one Black teacher** Seth Gershenson, Cassandra M. D. Hart, Constance A. Lindsay, and Nicholas W. Papageorge, "IZA DP No. 10630: The Long-Run Impacts of Same-Race Teachers," IZA—Institute of Labor Economics, March 2017, www.iza.org /publications/dp/10630.

197 **Integration had turned into "a one-way street"** Barack Obama, *Dreams from My Father: A Story of Race and Inheritance* (1995; New York: Crown, 2007), 99–100.

198 **one Pew Research Center study found that** Schaeffer, "U.S. Public School Students Often Go to Schools Where at Least Half of Their Peers Are the Same Race or Ethnicity."

198 **"The experience of an integrated education"** David L. Kirp, "Making Schools Work," *The New York Times,* May 19, 2012, www.nytimes.com/2012 /05/20/opinion/sunday/integration-worked-why-have-we-rejected-it.html.

198 **"I had always thought the ultimate goal of better race relations was integration"** Tamar Jacoby, "What Became of Integration," *The Washington Post,* June 28, 1998.

198 **erases the actual King** See Ibram X. Kendi, "The Second Assassination of Martin Luther King Jr.," *The Atlantic,* October 14, 2021, www.theatlan tic.com/ideas/archive/2021/10/martin-luther-king-critical-race-theory /620367/.

198 **"using Negro workmen, Negro architects, Negro attorneys, and Negro financial institutions"** Martin Luther King Jr., "Where Do We Go from Here?" August 16, 1967, The Martin Luther King, Jr. Research and Educa-

tion Institute, Stanford University, kinginstitute.stanford.edu/where-do-we -go-here.

199 **A Black (13.4 percent) person would not see another** Black (13.4 percent vs. 12.7 percent), Latinx (18.5 percent vs. 17.8 percent), Asian (5.9 percent vs. 4.8 percent), and Native (1.3 percent vs. 0.9 percent) populations have increased since first publication, while the White population (60.1 percent vs. 61.3 percent) has decreased. However, White people remain the racial majority in the United States. Population estimates and corresponding calculations are based on U.S. Census Bureau, "Quick Facts: Population Estimates, July 1, 2021," www.census.gov/quickfacts/fact/table/US /PST045221.

199 **"only white men" with different "skins"** Kenneth M. Stampp, *The Peculiar Institution: Slavery in the Ante-Bellum South* (New York: Vintage Books, 1956), vii.

Chapter 14: Gender

201 **GENDER RACIST IDEA** The definition in the hardcover edition was for GENDER RACISM, which I now define as: A powerful collection of inequitable and unjust policies that lead to injustice and inequity between race-genders and are substantiated by ideas of racial hierarchy about race-genders.

201 **GENDER ANTIRACIST IDEA** The definition in the hardcover edition was for GENDER ANTIRACISM, which I now define as: A powerful collection of equitable and just policies that lead to justice and equity between race-genders and are substantiated by ideas of racial equality about race-genders.

202 **just as many parents rarely talk explicitly about people of color** For research on the dangers of color-blind caregiving, and the demonstrated benefits of antiracist alternatives, see Ibram X. Kendi, *How to Raise an Antiracist* (New York: One World, 2022).

203 **Alice Walker's** *The Color Purple* Alice Walker, *The Color Purple* (New York: Harcourt Brace Jovanovich, 1982).

203 **saw as a hit job on Black masculinity** For a synopsis of what some Black male critics said about *The Color Purple,* see Jacqueline Bobo, "Sifting Through the Controversy: Reading *The Color Purple*," *Callaloo* 39 (Spring 1989), 332–42.

203 *The Negro Family: The Case for National Action* U.S. Department of Labor, Office of Policy Planning and Research, *The Negro Family: The Case for National Action* (Washington, D.C.: U.S. Government Printing Office, 1965).

203 **Nearly one-fourth of Black families** Ibid., 9.

204 **"forced into a matriarchal structure"** Ibid., 29.

204 **"Keeping the Negro 'in his place'"** Ibid., 16.

204 **"The reverberations" from the Moynihan report "were disastrous"** Deborah Gray White, *Too Heavy a Load: Black Women in Defense of Themselves, 1894–1994* (New York: W. W. Norton, 1999), 200.

204 **"immediate goal of the Negro woman today"** "For a Better Future," *Ebony,* August 1966, 150.

204 **Racism had "clearly" and "largely focused" on the Black male** Charles Herbert Stember, *Sexual Racism: The Emotional Barrier to an Integrated Society* (New York: Elsevier, 1976), 66.

204 **"sexual rejection of the racial minority"** Ibid., ix.

204 **For too many Black men, the Black Power movement** See Eldridge Cleaver, *Soul on Ice* (New York: Dell, 1968).

205 **growing percentage of Black children being born into single-parent households** For relevant data see Spencer Rich, "Single-Parent Families Rise Dramatically," *The Washington Post,* May 3, 1982, www.washingtonpost.com/archive/politics/1982/05/03/single-parent-families-rise-dramatically/cc4afac4-2764-419e-8bda-66f14bad3dd0/; and George A. Akerlof and Janet L. Yellen, "An Analysis of Out-of-Wedlock Births in the United States," Brookings, August 1, 1996, www.brookings.edu/research/an-analysis-of-out-of-wedlock-births-in-the-united-states/.

205 **"has now reached 68 percent"** Charles Murray, "The Coming White Underclass," *The Wall Street Journal,* October 29, 1993.

205 **married Black women having fewer children** Angela Y. Davis, *Women, Culture & Politics* (New York: Random House, 1989), 75–85; and Ta-Nehisi Coates, "The Math on Black Out of Wedlock Births," *The Atlantic,* February 17, 2009, www.theatlantic.com/entertainment/archive/2009/02/the-math-on-black-out-of-wedlock-births/6738/.

206 **Only Black feminists like Dorothy Roberts** See Dorothy Roberts, *Killing the Black Body: Race, Reproduction, and the Meaning of Liberty* (New York: Pantheon, 1997).

206 **Kimberly Springer calls the "Black feminist movement"** See Kimberly Springer, *Living for the Revolution: Black Feminist Organizations, 1968–1980* (Durham, NC: Duke University Press, 2005).

207 **more Black babies for the "Black nation"** Patricia Hill Collins, *From Black Power to Hip Hop: Racism, Nationalism, and Feminism* (Philadelphia: Temple University Press, 2006), 107–11.

207 **fought sexism in Black spaces and racism in women's spaces** See Springer, *Living for the Revolution.*

207 **launched the gay-liberation movement** Of course, the freedom struggles of lesbian, gay, bisexual, transgender, and gender nonconforming people predated 1969. See Thomas A. Foster, ed., *Long Before Stonewall: Histories of Same-Sex Sexuality in Early America* (New York: New York University Press, 2007); Susan Stryker, *Transgender History* (Berkeley, CA: Seal Press, 2008); Jim Downs, *Stand by Me: The Forgotten History of Gay Liberation* (New York:

Basic Books, 2016); and Marc Stein, ed., *The Stonewall Riots: A Documentary History* (New York: New York University Press, 2019).

207 **the Combahee River Collective** See Keeanga-Yamahtta Taylor, ed., *How We Get Free: Black Feminism and the Combahee River Collective* (Chicago: Haymarket, 2017).

207 **named for the Combahee River slave raid of 1863 led by Harriet Tubman** Combahee River Collective, *Combahee River Collective Statement: Black Feminist Organizing in the Seventies and Eighties* (Albany, NY: Kitchen Table: Women of Color Press, 1986), 9.

207 **"To be recognized as human, levelly human, is enough"** Combahee River Collective Statement, April 1977, in Taylor, *How We Get Free,* 19.

207 **"the shared belief that Black women are inherently valuable"** Ibid., 18.

207 **America's first feminist known to give a public address to a coed audience** See Marilyn Richardson, ed., *Maria W. Stewart: American's First Black Woman Political Writer: Essays and Speeches* (Bloomington: Indiana University Press, 1987).

208 **So did Frances Beal** See Beverly Guy-Sheftall, ed., *Words of Fire: An Anthology of African-American Feminist Thought* (New York: The New Press, 1995).

208 **"double jeopardy" of racism and sexism** Frances M. Beal, "Double Jeopardy: To Be Black and Female," in *Sisterhood Is Powerful: An Anthology of Writings from the Women's Liberation Movement*, ed. Robin Morgan, (New York: Vintage Books, 1970), 340–53.

208 **"preoccupations of the contemporary Black woman in this country"** . . . **"evil Black bitch"** Toni Cade Bambara, "Preface," in *The Black Woman: An Anthology*, ed. Toni Cade Bambara (New York: New American Library, 1970), 11.

208 **"high-tech lynching"** Clarence Thomas quoted in Victoria M. Massie, "How Racism and Sexism Shaped the Clarence Thomas/Anita Hill Hearing," *Vox,* April 16, 2016, www.vox.com/2016/4/16/11408576/anita-hill -clarence-thomas-confirmation.

208 **"In discussing the experiences of Black women"** Philomena Essed, *Understanding Everyday Racism: An Interdisciplinary Theory* (Newbury Park, CA: SAGE, 1991), 31.

209 **"racism and sexism readily intersect in the lives of real people"** Kimberlé Crenshaw, "Mapping the Margins: Intersectionality, Identity Politics, and Violence Against Women of Color," *Stanford Law Review* 43, no. 6 (July 1991), 1242.

209 **Note on misogynoir: coined in 2008 by queer Black feminist Moya Bailey** See Moya Bailey, "More on the Origin of Misogynoir," *Moyazb* (blog), April 27, 2014, moyazb.tumblr.com/post/84048113369/more-on-the-origin -of-misogynoir.

209 **involuntary sterilizations of Black women** See Dorothy Roberts, *Killing the Black Body*, 90–98.

209 **Black women with some collegiate education making just $29 more per week** Black women with some college education or associate degrees have median weekly earnings of $714, compared to $797 for White women with some college education and $685 for White women with high school diplomas. U.S. Department of Labor, Women's Bureau, "Women's Median Weekly Earnings by Educational Attainment, Race, and Hispanic Ethnicity (Annual)," 2020, www.dol.gov/agencies/wb/data/earnings/Women-median-weekly-earnings-educational-attainment-race-Hispanic-ethnicity.

209 **Black women having to earn advanced degrees before they earn more** Ibid. Black women with advanced degrees have median weekly earnings of $1,323, compared to $1,406 for White women with advanced degrees and $1,142 for White women with bachelor's degrees.

209 **median wealth of single White women being $81,200** Single White men's median wealth is $78,200, and single Black men's median wealth is $10,100. Dedrick Asante-Muhammad, Esha Kamra, and Connor Sanchez, "Racial Wealth Snapshot: Women, Men, and Racial Wealth Divide," National Community Reinvestment Coalition, March 3, 2022, ncrc.org/racial-wealth-snapshot-women-men-and-racial-wealth-divide/.

210 **Native women and Black women experience poverty at higher rates** 24.6 percent of Native women live in poverty, followed by 22.5 percent of Black women, 19.4 percent of Latinx women, 15.4 percent of mixed-race women, 10.0 percent of Asian or Pacific Islander women, and 9.0 percent of White women. Robin Bleiweis, Diana Boesch, and Alexandra Cawthorne Gaines, "The Basic Facts about Women in Poverty," Center for American Progress, August 3, 2020, www.americanprogress.org/article/basic-facts-women-poverty/.

210 **Black and Latinx women still earn the least** During the first quarter of 2022, Latinx women had median weekly earnings of $732 and Black women had median weekly earnings of $811. Asian men and White men took home $1,452 and $1,148 per week, respectively. U.S. Bureau of Labor Statistics, "Usual Weekly Earnings of Wage and Salary Workers, First Quarter 2022," news release, April 15, 2022, www.bls.gov/news.release/archives/wkyeng_04152022.pdf. See page 6, Table 2 for median weekly income data by sex, age, and race.

210 **Black women are three times more likely to die** Centers for Disease Control and Prevention, "Working Together to Reduce Black Maternal Mortality," April 6, 2022, www.cdc.gov/healthequity/features/maternal-mortality/index.html.

210 **A college-educated Black woman is three times more likely to lose her baby** Samuel H. Fishman, Robert A. Hummer, Gracia Sierra, Taylor

Hargrove, Daniel A. Powers, and Richard G. Rogers, "Race/Ethnicity, Maternal Educational Attainment, and Infant Mortality in the United States," *Biodemography and Social Biology* 66, no. 1 (March 2021), doi.org/10.1080/19485565.2020.1793659.

210 **Black women remain nearly twice as likely to be incarcerated** Black women are 1.7 times more likely than White women to be incarcerated in prison or jail. The Sentencing Project, "Incarcerated Women and Girls," May 12, 2022, 2, www.sentencingproject.org/publications/incarcerated-women-and-girls/.

210 **as much about controlling the sexuality of White women** For a full study on the politics of women during the lynching era, see Crystal N. Feimster, *Southern Horrors: Women and the Politics of Rape and Lynching* (Cambridge, MA: Harvard University Press, 2009).

210 **were re-creating the enslavement era all over again** Rachel A. Feinstein, *When Rape Was Legal: The Untold History of Sexual Violence During Slavery* (New York: Routledge, 2018); and Daina Ramey Berry and Leslie M. Harris, eds., *Sexuality and Slavery: Reclaiming Intimate Histories in the Americas* (Athens: University of Georgia Press, 2018).

211 **Male resistance to Black feminism and intersectional theory** Patricia Hill Collins, *Black Feminist Thought: Knowledge, Consciousness, and the Politics of Empowerment,* rev. ed. (New York: Routledge, 2000), 158.

211 **Casey Anthony, the White woman a Florida jury exonerated** Breeanna Hare, " 'What Really Happened?': The Casey Anthony Case 10 Years Later," CNN, June 30, 2018, www.cnn.com/2018/06/29/us/casey-anthony-10-years-later/index.html.

211 **Black men spend years in prisons for wrongful convictions** For example, innocent Black people are seven times more likely than innocent White people to be convicted of murder. Innocent Black people on death row spend, on average, 13.8 years wrongfully imprisoned before their exoneration, 45 percent longer than their White counterparts. Daniele Selby, "8 Facts You Should Know About Racial Injustice in the Criminal Legal System," The Innocence Project, February 6, 2022, innocenceproject.org/facts-racial-discrimination-justice-system-wrongful-conviction-black-history-month/#:~:text=On%20average%2C%20they%20spend%204.5,they%20are%20on%20death%20row.

211 **the imprisonment rate of Black men dropped 45 percent** The Black male incarceration rate per 100,000 is 1,890, the White male rate is 332, the Black female rate is 65, and the White female rate is 38, according to the Bureau of Justice Statistics. See Allen J. Beck and Paige M. Harrison, "Prisoners in 2000," Bureau of Justice Statistics Bulletin, U.S. Department of Justice, August 2001, 11, bjs.ojp.gov/content/pub/pdf/p00.pdf; and E. Ann Carson, "Prisoners in 2020—Statistical Tables," Bureau of Justice Statistics,

U.S. Department of Justice, December 2021, 24, bjs.ojp.gov/content/pub /pdf/p20st.pdf. Change in imprisonment rate between 2000 and 2020 has been calculated using the same method as deployed to show fluctuations between 2000 and 2015 in Eli Hager, "A Mass Incarceration Mystery," The Marshall Project, December 15, 2017, www.themarshallproject.org/2017 /12/15/a-mass-incarceration-mystery.

211 **Black men raised in the top 1 percent by millionaires** Emily Badger, Claire Cain Miller, Adam Pearce, and Kevin Quealy, "Extensive Data Shows Punishing Reach of Racism for Black Boys," *The New York Times,* March 19, 2018, www.nytimes.com/interactive/2018/03/19/upshot/race-class-white -and-black-men.html.

212 **"Contemporary feminist and antiracist discourses have failed to consider intersectional identities"** Crenshaw, "Mapping the Margins," 1242–43.

Chapter 15: Sexuality

213 **QUEER RACIST IDEA** The definition in the hardcover edition was for QUEER RACISM, which I now define as: A powerful collection of inequitable and unjust policies that lead to injustice inequity between race-sexualities and are substantiated by ideas of racial hierarchy about race-sexualities.

213 **QUEER ANTIRACIST IDEA** The definition in the hardcover edition was for QUEER ANTIRACISM, which I now define as: A powerful collection of equitable and just policies that lead to justice and equity between race-sexualities and are substantiated by ideas of racial equality about race-sexualities.

213 **32 percent of children being raised by Black male same-sex couples live in poverty** Movement Advancement Project, Family Equality Council, and Center for American Progress, *LGBT Families of Color: Facts at a Glance,* January 2012, 3, www.lgbtmap.org/file/lgbt-families-of-color-facts-at-a-glance .pdf.

213 **four times as likely as White children to be in foster care** For this statistic and the statistic about Black mothers who identify as lesbian or bisexual, see Kathi L. H. Harp and Carrie B. Oser, "Factors Associated with Two Types of Child Custody Loss Among a Sample of African American Mothers: A Novel Approach," *Social Science Research* 60 (November 2016), 283–96, doi.org/10.1016/j.ssresearch.2016.06.007.

214 **their parents are more likely than Black heterosexual and White queer couples to be impoverished** 30.8 percent of Black LGBT people live in poverty, compared to 25.3 percent of Black cisgender and straight people, 15.4 percent of White LGBT people, and 9.1 percent of White cisgender and straight people. M. V. Lee Badgett, Soon Kyu Choi, and Bianca D. M. Wilson, *LGBT Poverty in the United States: A Study of Differences Between*

Sexual Orientation and Gender Identity Groups, Williams Institute at UCLA Law, October 2019, 13, williamsinstitute.law.ucla.edu/wp-content/uploads/National-LGBT-Poverty-Oct-2019.pdf.

214 **known for popularizing the term "homosexual"** Ellis co-wrote *Sexual Inversion* (London: Wilson and Macmillan, 1897), the first English book on homosexuality. However, Ellis and John Addington Symonds, his co-author, derided the term as "a barbarously hybrid word," and insisted that they claimed "no responsibility for it." See Ellis and Symonds, *Sexual Inversion,* 1.

214 **"the question of sex"** Havelock Ellis, "Preface," in *Sexual Inversion,* x.

214 **regarded homosexuality as a congenital physiological abnormality** Ellis and Symonds wrote, "Sexual inversion [homosexuality], therefore, remains a congenital abnormality to be classed with the other congenital abnormalities which have psychic concomitants." Ellis and Symonds, *Sexual Inversion,* 137.

214 **a popular summary of Lombroso's writings** Havelock Ellis, *The Criminal* (New York: Scribner & Welford, 1890).

214 **"As regards the sexual organs it seems possible"** Havelock Ellis, *Studies in the Psychology of Sex,* 3rd ed. (Philadelphia: F. A. Davis, 1933), 2:256.

214 **racist physicians were contrasting** Robert T. Morris, "Is Evolution Trying to Do Away with the Clitoris?" Paper presented at the meeting of the American Association of Obstetricians and Gynecologists, St. Louis, September 21, 1892, archive.org/stream/39002086458651.med.yale.edu/39002086458651_djvu.txt.

214 **"will in practically every instance disclose"** Perry M. Lichtenstein, "The 'Fairy' and the Lady Lover," *Medical Review of Reviews* 27 (August 1921), 372.

214 **which "is particularly so in colored women"** Ibid.

216 **Black gay men are less likely to have condomless sex** Jacob Anderson-Minshall, "What's at the Root of the Disproportionate HIV Rates for Black Men?" *Plus,* March 6, 2017, www.hivplusmag.com/stigma/2017/3/06/whats-root-disproportionate-hiv-rates-their-queer-brothers.

216 **Note on "gaydar": a homophobic term that emerged in the 1980s** William Cox, "The Truth about 'Gaydar,'" CNN, March 24, 2017, www.cnn.com/2017/03/24/health/gaydar-stereotypes-partner/index.html.

216 **perform masculinity and actually prefer** Researchers have found that some gay men "defeminize" certain childhood behaviors when they reach their teenage years, likely to shield themselves from homophobic violence and discrimination sustained by our heteronormative and patriarchal society. To better understand this masculinization and its sometimes damaging effects, see Kittiwut Jod Taywaditep, "Marginalization Among the Marginalized: Gay Men's Anti-Effeminacy Attitudes," *Journal of Homosexuality* 42, no. 1 (2002), 1–28, doi.org/10.1300/J082v42n01_01; Francisco J. Sánchez, Stefanie T. Greenberg, William Ming Liu, and Eric Vilain, "Reported Effects of Masculine Ideals on Gay Men," *Psychology of Men & Masculinities* 10, no. 1 (Janu-

ary 2009), www.ncbi.nlm.nih.gov/pmc/articles/PMC2902177/; and Adam Davies and Rhea Ashley Hoskin, "10-Year Challenge Reveals Femmephobia in Gay Communities," *The Conversation,* December 9, 2019, theconversation .com/10-year-challenge-reveals-femmephobia-in-gay-communities-127783. However, it is wrong to limit our understandings of gender-based expressions to a binary, and would be equally problematic to dismiss all gay men's traits and behaviors as inauthentic.

216 **gender being an authentic performance** See Judith Butler, *Gender Trouble: Feminism and the Subversion of Identity* (New York: Routledge, 1990); Judith Butler, *Bodies That Matter: On the Discursive Limits of Sex* (New York: Routledge, 1993).

217 **"affirm that all Black lives matter"** Opal Tometi quoted in Foluké Tuakli and Chandelis R. Duster, "Black Lives Matter Movement Awarded Sydney Peace Prize for Activism," NBC News, November 2, 2017, www.nbcnews .com/news/nbcblk/black-lives-matter-movement-awarded-sydney-peace -prize-activism-n816846.

217 **average life expectancy of a transgender woman of color in the Americas** Inter-American Commission on Human Rights, *An Overview of Violence Against LGBTI Persons: A Registry Documenting Acts of Violence between January 1, 2013 and March 31, 2014,* 2014, 3, www.oas.org/en/iachr/lgtbi/docs /Annex-Registry-Violence-LGBTI.pdf.

217 **from the personal stories of transgender activist Janet Mock** See Janet Mock, *Redefining Realness: My Path to Womanhood, Identity, Love & So Much More* (New York: Simon & Schuster, 2014); Janet Mock, *Surpassing Certainty: What My Twenties Taught Me* (New York: Atria, 2017).

218 **voter-ID laws** Experts estimated that "260,000 transgender people who live in the 35 states with voter ID laws did not have a form of ID that accurately reflected their name and/or gender identity to use in the 2020 general election. This number represents more than one quarter of the transgender adult population eligible to vote in the 2020 general election." See Stuart Baum, Izabela Tringali, and Mikael Morelión, "How Voter ID Laws Threaten Transgender Voters," Brennan Center for Justice, November 20, 2020, www .brennancenter.org/our-work/analysis-opinion/how-voter-id-laws-threaten -transgender-voters.

218 **book bans** I've added more recent examples to this paperback edition to illustrate the ongoing battles of all antiracists. Sadly, there has been no shortage of anti-LGBTQ attacks in Republican-led legislatures. On anti-LGBTQ book bans, see Matt Lavietes, "From Book Bans to 'Don't Say Gay' Bill, LGBTQ Kids Feel 'Erased' in the Classroom," NBC News, February 20, 2022, www.nbcnews.com/nbc-out/out-news/book-bans-dontsay-gay-bill -lgbtq-kids-feel-erased-classroom-rcna15819.

218 **"Don't Say Gay" bills** Dustin Jones and Jonathan Franklin, "Not Just Florida: More Than a Dozen States Propose So-Called 'Don't Say Gay' Bills," NPR,

April 10, 2022, www.npr.org/2022/04/10/1091543359/15-states-dont-say
-gay-anti-transgender-bills.

218 **legislation criminalizing trans children and their supportive parents**
See "Legislative Tracker: Anti-Transgender Legislation," Freedom for All
Americans, freedomforallamericans.org/legislative-tracker/anti-transgender
-legislation/; and Arthur Jones II and Aaron Navarro, "This Year on Pace
to See Record Anti-Transgender Bills Passed by States, Says Human Rights
Campaign," CBS News, April 22, 2022, www.cbsnews.com/news/2022
-anti-transgender-legislation-record-human-rights-campaign/.

219 **I gobbled up** See Audre Lorde, *Sister Outsider: Essays and Speeches* (Berkeley,
CA: Crossing Press, 1984); E. Patrick Johnson, *Sweet Tea: Black Gay Men
of the South* (Chapel Hill: University of North Carolina Press, 2008); bell
hooks, *Ain't I a Woman: Black Women and Feminism* (Boston: South End
Press, 1981); Joan Morgan, *When Chickenheads Come Home to Roost: A Hip-
Hop Feminist Breaks It Down* (New York: Simon & Schuster, 1999); Dwight
A. McBride, *Why I Hate Abercrombie & Fitch: Essays on Race and Sexuality*
(New York: New York University Press, 2005); Patricia Hill Collins, *Black
Sexual Politics: African Americans, Gender, and the New Racism* (New York:
Routledge, 2004); and Kimberlé Crenshaw, "Mapping the Margins: Inter-
sectionality, Identity Politics, and Violence Against Women of Color," *Stan-
ford Law Review* 43, no. 6 (July 1991), 1241–99.

220 **Amy Coney Barrett vote to overturn** *Roe v. Wade* Nina Totenberg
and Sarah McCammon, "Supreme Court Overturns Roe v. Wade, Ending Right to Abortion Upheld for Decades," NPR, June 24, 2022, www
.npr.org/2022/06/24/1102305878/supreme-court-abortion-roe-v-wade
-decision-overturn.

220 **the majority of White women voters persistently support Donald
Trump** In 2016, one exit poll found that 52 percent of White women supported Trump. In 2020, that same exit poll reported that 55 percent voted
for Trump. See Amanda Becker, "White Women Had Doubts. They Voted
for Trump Anyway." *The 19th,* November 7, 2020, 19thnews.org/2020/11
/white-women-had-doubts-they-voted-for-trump-anyway/.

220 **accused of sexual harassment or assault by at least eighteen women**
Meghan Keneally, "List of Trump's Accusers and Their Allegations of Sexual
Misconduct," ABC News, September 18, 2020, abcnews.go.com/Politics
/list-trumps-accusers-allegations-sexual-misconduct/story?id=51956410.

220 **watching Kayla Moore defend her husband** Jenna Johnson, Ellie Silverman, and Lindsey Bever, "Kayla Moore Emerges as Her Husband's Fierc-
est and Most Vocal Defender," *The Washington Post,* November 15, 2017,
www.washingtonpost.com/politics/kayla-moore-emerges-as-her-husbands
-fiercest-and-most-vocal-defender/2017/11/15/5c8b7d82-ca19-11e7-8321
-481fd63f174d_story.html.

220 **"even though we had slavery"** Roy Moore quoted in Lisa Mascaro, "In

Alabama, the Heart of Trump Country, Many Think He's Backing the Wrong Candidate in Senate Race," *Los Angeles Times,* September 21, 2017, www.latimes.com/politics/la-na-pol-alabama-senate-runoff-20170921 -story.html.

220 **publicly attacking the women saying #MeToo** See Martha Gill, "#MeToo Is Over If We Don't Listen to 'Imperfect Victims' Like Amber Heard," *The Guardian,* May 22, 2022, www.theguardian.com/commentisfree/2022/may /22/metoo-is-over-if-we-dont-listen-to-imperfect-victims-like-amber -heard.

Chapter 16: Failure

223 **"our parental care"** Minutes of Proceedings of Tenth American Convention for the Abolition of Slavery, 1805, in David Scholfield and Edmund Haviland, "The Appeal of the American Convention of Abolition Societies to Anti-Slavery Groups," *The Journal of Negro History* 6, no. 2 (April 1921), 225.

223 **Black "conduct must, in some measure"** Minutes of the Proceedings of a Convention of Delegates from the Abolition Societies, 1804, in Scholfield and Haviland, "The Appeal of the American Convention of Abolition Societies to Anti-Slavery Groups," 221.

223 **"The further decrease of prejudice"** "Raising Us in the Scale of Being," *Freedom's Journal,* March 16, 1827.

224 **the first African American newspaper** Malea Walker, "Honoring African American Contributions: The Newspapers," *Headlines & Heroes: Newspapers, Comics & More Fine Print,* Library of Congress, July 30, 2020, blogs.loc.gov /headlinesandheroes/2020/07/honoring-african-american-contributions -the-newspapers/.

224 **the judges of "uplift suasion"** See Ibram X. Kendi, *Stamped from the Beginning: The Definitive History of Racist Ideas in America* (New York: Nation Books, 2016), 124–25.

226 **"Have you not acquired the esteem"** William Lloyd Garrison, *An Address, Delivered before the Free People of Color, in Philadelphia, New-York, and Other Cities, During the Month of June, 1831,* 3rd ed. (Boston: S. Foster, 1831), 5.

226 **"accomplish the great work of national redemption"** "What we have long predicted . . . has commenced its fulfillment," *The Liberator,* September 3, 1831, in David Brion Davis and Steven Mintz, eds. *The Boisterous Sea of Liberty: A Documentary History of America from Discovery through the Civil War* (New York: Oxford University Press, 1998), 390.

226 **fit his personal upbringing** For a good biography of Garrison, see Henry Mayer, *All on Fire: William Lloyd Garrison and the Abolition of Slavery* (New York: W. W. Norton, 2008).

226 **astounding growth of slavery** As cotton lured enslavers south and west, the enslaved population in the South grew from 1.6 million to 2.2 million

people between 1850 and 1860. Edward E. Baptist, *The Half Has Never Been Told: Slavery and the Making of American Capitalism* (New York: Basic Books, 2016), 361.

227 **to paraphrase Malcolm X** Malcolm X instructed Black nationalists, "Don't change the white man's mind—you can't change his mind, and that whole thing about appealing to the moral conscience of America—America's conscience is bankrupt. She lost all conscience a long time ago. Uncle Sam has no conscience. They don't know what morals are." Malcolm X, "The Ballot or the Bullet," April 3, 1964, in *Malcolm X Speaks: Selected Speeches and Statements,* ed. George Breitman (1965; New York: Grove Weidenfeld, 1990), 40.

227 **to paraphrase Assata Shakur** Assata Shakur said, "Nobody in the world, nobody in history, has ever gotten their freedom by appealing to the moral sense of the people who were oppressing them." Assata Shakur, *Assata: An Autobiography* (Westport, CT: Lawrence Hill Books, 1987), 139.

227 **"If I could save the Union without freeing any slave"** Abraham Lincoln, "To Horace Greeley," in *The Collected Works of Abraham Lincoln,* ed. Roy P. Basler (New Brunswick, NJ: Rutgers University Press, 1953), 5:388.

227 **"necessary war measure"** Abraham Lincoln, Emancipation Proclamation, January 1, 1863, National Archives, www.archives.gov/milestone-documents /emancipation-proclamation#.YpD7uYFuWuw.

227 **After winning the Civil War** See Eric Foner, *Reconstruction: America's Unfinished Revolution, 1863–1877* (New York: Harper & Row, 1988); and Eric Foner, *The Second Founding: How the Civil War and Reconstruction Remade the Constitution* (New York: W. W. Norton, 2019).

227 **"want nothing to do with the negroes"** Lyman Trumbull quoted in Adam I. P. Smith, *No Party Now: Politics in the Civil War North* (New York: Oxford University Press, 2006), 55.

227 **one of the laws' main sponsors** Trumbull was far from a fierce advocate for Black voting rights. Defending his proposal for what became the Civil Rights Act of 1866, Trumbull insisted he did not intend to confer political power or voting rights to any Black people. See Horace White, *The Life of Lyman Trumbull* (Boston: Houghton Mifflin, 1913), 257–68.

227 **The "White man's party"** Lyman Trumbull speech, August 7, 1858, quoted in Francis P. Blair Jr., "Appendix," in *The Destiny of the Races of this Continent: An Address Delivered before the Mercantile Library Association of Boston, Massachusetts, on the 26th of January, 1859* (Washington, D.C.: Buell & Blanchard, 1859), 30.

227 **militarily defending the Negro from the racist terrorists** See Foner, *Reconstruction.*

227 **"Expediency on selfish grounds"** William Lloyd Garrison quoted in Mayer, *All on Fire,* 617.

228 **"For many years it was the theory of most Negro leaders"** W.E.B.

Du Bois, "A Negro Nation Within a Nation," in *Ripples of Hope: Great American Civil Rights Speeches*, ed. Josh Gottheimer (New York: Basic Civitas Books, 2003), 176.

228 **"the ultimate evil was stupidity"** W.E.B. Du Bois, *Dusk of Dawn: An Essay Toward an Autobiography of a Race Concept* (1940; New York: Schocken Books, 1970), 58.

228 **"we have striven by book and periodical"** Du Bois, "A Negro Nation Within a Nation," in *Ripples of Hope*, 176.

228 **"astonishing ignorance"** Gunnar Myrdal, *An American Dilemma: The Negro Problem and Modern Democracy* (New York: Harper & Brothers, 1944), 1:48.

228 **"Gunnar Myrdal had been astonishingly prophetic"** Gene Roberts and Hank Klibanoff, *The Race Beat: The Press, the Civil Rights Struggle, and the Awakening of the Nation* (New York: Vintage Books, 2006), 406. Aside from this assessment, this is a stunning work of journalism history.

228 **"discrimination against minority groups in this country has an adverse effect"** Brief for the United States as Amicus Curiae, p. 7, *Brown*, 347 U.S. 483, quoted in Mary L. Dudziak, *Cold War Civil Rights: Race and the Image of American Democracy* (Princeton, NJ: Princeton University Press, 2000), 100.

228 **as historian Mary L. Dudziak documents** See Dudziak, *Cold War Civil Rights*, 90–107.

228 **the racist abuse and segregated businesses African diplomats faced** For example, on several occasions, White restaurant owners refused to serve African diplomats who stopped for food on their drive from the United Nations in New York to Washington, D.C. Ibid., 152–53, 167.

228 **"in waging this world struggle"** U.S. Senate Committee on Commerce, Hearings on S. 1732, quoted in Dudziak, *Cold War Civil Rights*, 185.

229 **Seventy-eight percent of White Americans agreed** Dudziak, *Cold War Civil Rights*, 187.

229 **stopped out of self-interest** Ibid., 202–48.

229 **In 1967, Martin Luther King Jr. admitted** Martin Luther King Jr., "Where Do We Go from Here?" August 16, 1967, The Martin Luther King, Jr. Research and Education Institute, Stanford University, kinginstitute.stanford.edu/where-do-we-go-here.

229 **Look at the soaring White support** Lawrence D. Bobo, Camille Z. Charles, Maria Krysan, and Alice D. Simmons, "The *Real* Record on Racial Attitudes," in *Social Trends in American Life: Findings from the General Social Survey Since 1972*, ed. Peter V. Marsden (Princeton, NJ: Princeton University Press, 2012), 47.

229 **Look at the soaring support for Obamacare** Hannah Fingerhut, "Support for 2010 Health Care Law Reaches New High," Pew Research Center, February 23, 2017, www.pewresearch.org/fact-tank/2017/02/23/support-for-2010-health-care-law-reaches-new-high/.

230 **the Jena 6** For an interview that details the case, see "The Case of the Jena Six:

Black High School Students Charged with Attempted Murder for Schoolyard Fight After Nooses Are Hung from Tree," *Democracy Now*, July 10, 2007, www .democracynow.org/2007/7/10/the_case_of_the_jena_six.

230 **under the "White tree"** American Civil Liberties Union (ACLU), "Background: Jena 6," www.aclu.org/other/background-jena-6.

230 **charged with attempted murder and conspiracy to commit murder** "Judge Removed From 'Jena Six' Case," NPR, August 1, 2008, www.npr .org/2008/08/01/93196840/judge-removed-from-jena-six-case.

230 **"When you are convicted"** Reed Walters quoted in "The Case of the Jena Six," *Democracy Now*.

230 **An all-White jury had already found him guilty** Ron Claiborne, "Charges Dropped for One of 'Jena Six,'" ABC News, January 8, 2009, abcnews.go .com/GMA/story?id=3607084.

230 **as much as twenty-two years** "The Case of the Jena Six," *Democracy Now*.

232 **used the Malcolm X line out of context** The full quote is, "When I was in prison, I read an article—don't be shocked when I say I was in prison. You're still in prison. That's what America means: prison." See Malcolm X, "Message to the Grassroots," December 10, 1963, in *Malcolm X Speaks*, 8.

233 **"The action of President Roosevelt in entertaining"** Ben Tillman quoted in Stephen Kantrowitz, *Ben Tillman & the Reconstruction of White Supremacy* (Chapel Hill: University of North Carolina Press, 2000), 259.

234 **his involvement in the Hamburg Massacre** Kantrowitz, *Ben Tillman & the Reconstruction of White Supremacy*, 64–71.

234 **trooped on lynched heads** Ibid., 112–13, 166–70, 161–62.

234 **"The purpose of our visit to Hamburg was to strike terror"** Benjamin R. Tillman, Address Delivered at the Red Shirt Reunion, Anderson, SC, August 25, 1909, in *The Struggles of 1876: How South Carolina Was Delivered from Carpet-Bag and Negro Rule* (Anderson, SC: s.n., 1909), 24.

236 **loudly marched down North Broad Street and rallied on campus** See Vernon Clark, Larry King, and Andrew Maykuth, "Region Adds a Voice to Jena Protests," *The Philadelphia Inquirer*, September 21, 2007, www.inquirer .com/philly/news/breaking/20070920_Rally_in_support_of_Jena_6_draws _hundreds_to_Temple.html.

236 **That day, thousands of us thought we were protesting** See Richard G. Jones, "Thousands Protest Arrests of 6 Blacks in Jena, La.," *The New York Times*, September 21, 2007, www.nytimes.com/2007/09/21/us/21cnd -jena.html.

237 **fundraising behind the scenes** "Plea Agreement Reached in Jena Six Case," Southern Poverty Law Center, June 26, 2009, www.splcenter.org/news/2009 /06/26/plea-agreement-reached-jena-six-case.

237 **quietly got the charges reduced** "Plea Bargain Wraps Up 'Jena 6' Case," CBS News, June 26, 2009, www.cbsnews.com/news/plea-bargain-wraps-up -jena-6-case/.

237 **sustained those courageous Black women** For a fascinating firsthand account of the boycott, see Jo Ann Gibson Robinson, *The Montgomery Bus Boycott and the Women Who Started It: The Memoir of Jo Ann Gibson Robinson* (Knoxville: University of Tennessee Press, 1987).

237 **desegregating businesses because the sit-ins are driving away customers** James Button, "The Outcomes of Contemporary Black Protest and Violence," in *Violence in America,* ed. Ted Robert Gurr (Newbury Park, CA: SAGE, 1989), 2:289.

237 **A judge denied bail** "'Jena 6' Defendant Denied Bail," ABC News, September 21, 2007, abcnews.go.com/TheLaw/story?id=3635867&page=1.

Chapter 17: Success

240 **Joe Biden and other Democratic candidates** Errin Haines and Juana Summers, "Biden: Racism in US Is Institutional, 'White Man's Problem," AP, August 28, 2019, apnews.com/article/election-2020-joe-biden-race-and-ethnicity-donald-trump-ap-top-news-88bd58010e75449eb5748499724df2f2; and Ronald Brownstein, "Why Race Is Moving Center Stage for 2020," CNN, September 17, 2019, www.cnn.com/2019/09/17/politics/2020-candidates-voters-racism-sexism-attitudes/index.html.

240 **activists took to the streets** Dmitry Zaks with AFP Bureaus, "'Burn Down Racism': World Rallies against George Floyd's Death," Yahoo!, June 6, 2020, www.yahoo.com/now/global-race-protests-mark-george-floyds-death-112330622.html.

241 **"Racism is both overt and covert"** Kwame Ture and Charles V. Hamilton, *Black Power: The Politics of Liberation* (New York: Vintage Books, 1967), 4.

241 **Ture and Hamilton distinguished** Ibid.

241 **White impoverished people benefit more than Black impoverished people** Take economic status and income, for example. Poverty persists in Black families longer than in White families, with Black adults most likely to be living in poverty after two generations. White women earn 79 cents for every dollar a White man makes, while Black women earn just 64 cents. Finally, LGBTQ+ people of color earn less than LGBTQ+ White people. See Scott Winship, Christopher Pulliam, Ariel Gelrud Shiro, Richard V. Reeves, and Santiago Deambrosi, "Long Shadows: The Black-White Gap in Multigenerational Poverty," Brookings, June 10, 2021, www.brookings.edu/research/long-shadows-the-black-white-gap-in-multigenerational-poverty/; Robin Bleiweis, Jocelyn Frye, and Rose Khattar, "Women of Color and the Wage Gap," Center for American Progress, November 17, 2021, www.americanprogress.org/article/women-of-color-and-the-wage-gap/; and Aryn Fields, "Human Rights Campaign Foundation Releases New Data on the LGBTQ+ Wage Gap," Human Rights Campaign, January 19, 2022, www.hrc.org/press-releases/human-rights-campaign-foundation-releases-new-data-on-the-lgbtq-wage-gap.

242 **all White people do not benefit equally from racism** See Heather C. McGhee, *The Sum of Us: What Racism Costs Everyone and How We Can Prosper Together* (New York: One World, 2021).

242 **killed four Black girls in a Birmingham church in 1963** Ture and Hamilton, *Black Power*, 4; and "On This Day—September 15, 1963: Four Black Girls Killed in Church Bombing in Birmingham, Alabama," Equal Justice Initiative, calendar.eji.org/racial-injustice/sep/15.

243 **" 'Respectable' individuals can absolve themselves"** Ture and Hamilton, *Black Power*, 5.

244 **The rain fell on his gray hooded sweatshirt** For perhaps the best overview of the Trayvon Martin story, see *Rest in Power: The Trayvon Martin Story*, Paramount Network, www.paramountnetwork.com/shows/rest-in-power -the-trayvon-martin-story.

245 **faced zero tolerance in a policed state** See Nicholas P. Triplett, Ayana Allen, and Chance W. Lewis, "Zero Tolerance, School Shootings, and the Post-Brown Quest for Equity in Discipline Policy: An Examination of How Urban Minorities Are Punished for White Suburban Violence," *The Journal of Negro Education* 83, no. 3 (Summer 2014), 352–70, doi.org/10.7709 /jnegroeducation.83.3.0352; and Charles Bell, "The Hidden Side of Zero Tolerance Policies: The African American Perspective," *Sociology Compass* 9, no. 1 (January 2015), 14–22, doi.org/10.1111/soc4.12230.

245 **buying foreclosed properties and renting them out** Dan Barry, Serge F. Kovaleski, Campbell Robertson, and Lizette Alvarez, "Sanford in the Eye of a Racial Firestorm," NBC News, April 2, 2012, www.nbcnews.com/id /wbna46922042; and Angela Onwuachi-Willig, "Policing the Boundaries of Whiteness: The Tragedy of Being 'Out of Place' from Emmett Till to Trayvon Martin," *Iowa Law Review* 102, no. 3 (March 2017), ilr.law.uiowa .edu/print/volume-102-issue-3/policing-the-boundaries-of-whiteness-the -tragedy-of-being-out-of-place-from-emmett-till-to-trayvon-martin/.

245 **the "rash" of seven burglaries in 2011** Richard Fausset, "In Trayvon Martin Case, a Complex Portrait of Shooter Emerges," *Los Angeles Times,* March 28, 2012, www.latimes.com/nation/la-xpm-2012-mar-28-la-na-zim merman-profile-20120329-story.html.

245 **born a year after me** Ibid.

245 **assault charges and domestic-violence accusations** Barry et al., "Sanford in the Eye of a Racial Firestorm."

245 **"could have been my son"** Mark Memmott, "Obama: 'Trayvon Martin Could Have Been Me 35 Years Ago,'" NPR, July 19, 2013, www.npr.org /sections/thetwo-way/2013/07/19/203660128/obama-trayvon-martin -could-have-been-me-35-years-ago.

245 **on the Black Campus Movement** Ibram X. Kendi, *The Black Campus Movement: Black Studies and the Racial Reconstitution of Higher Education, 1965–1972* (New York: Palgrave, 2012).

246 **Zimmerman told the 911 dispatcher** "Transcript of George Zimmerman's Call to the Police," archive.org/details/326700-full-transcript-zimmerman.

246 **dispatcher told him to stop** Ibid. When Zimmerman confirmed that he was following Trayvon Martin, the dispatcher said, "Ok, we don't need you to do that." Zimmerman replied, "Ok," but pursued Martin anyway.

246 **ended the call and caught up to Martin** Frances Robles, "What Is Known, What Isn't about Trayvon Martin's Death," *Miami Herald,* March 31, 2012, web.archive.org/web/20130718121422/http://www.miamiherald.com /2012/03/31/v-fullstory/2725442/what-is-known-what-isnt-about.html.

246 **A jury agreeing** Lizette Alvarez and Cara Buckley, "Zimmerman Is Acquitted in Trayvon Martin Killing," *The New York Times,* July 13, 2013, www.nytimes.com/2013/07/14/us/george-zimmerman-verdict-trayvon -martin.html.

246 **Garza typed "Black Lives Matter"** Jessica Guynn, "Meet the Woman Who Coined #BlackLivesMatter," *USA Today,* March 4, 2015, www.usatoday.com /story/tech/2015/03/04/alicia-garza-black -lives-matter/24341593/.

Chapter 18: Survival

249 **96 percent of women diagnosed with breast cancer** American Cancer Society, *Breast Cancer Facts & Figures, 2019–2020* (Atlanta, GA: American Cancer Society, 2019), 3, www.cancer.org/content/dam/cancer-org/research /cancer-facts-and-statistics/breast-cancer-facts-and-figures/breast-cancer -facts-and-figures-2019-2020.pdf.

252 **produces public scholarship** For more on this concept of public scholarship, see Keisha N. Blain and Ibram X. Kendi, "How to Avoid a Post-Scholar America," *The Chronicle of Higher Education,* June 18, 2017, www .chronicle.com/article/how-to-avoid-a-post-scholar-america/.

252 **This BU Center for Antiracist Research** To learn more about our work at the BU Center for Antiracist Research, visit www.bu.edu/antiracism-center/.

253 **copies of Confederate flags with cotton balls inside several buildings** Jonah Engel Bromwich, "Confederate Flags with Cotton Found on American University Campus," *The New York Times,* September 27, 2017, www .nytimes.com/2017/09/27/us/american-university-confederate.html.

253 **running and terrorizing the United States** For an overview of white nationalist activity in the United States in 2017, see Heidi Beirich and Susy Buchanan, "2017: The Year in Hate and Extremism," *Southern Poverty Law Center Intelligence Report,* February 11, 2018, www.splcenter.org/fighting -hate/intelligence-report/2018/2017-year-hate-and-extremism.

253 **spreading across the Western world** See Lev Golinkin, "White Supremacy Movement Is More Than Just an American Problem," CNN, November 16, 2017, www.cnn.com/2017/11/16/opinions/global-white-sup remacy-opinion-golinkin/index.html.

254 **the median age for the worst possibility, colon cancer** The median age

at colon cancer diagnosis for men is 67. American Cancer Society, *Colorectal Cancer Facts & Figures, 2020–2022* (Atlanta, GA: American Cancer Society, 2020), 5, www.cancer.org/content/dam/cancer-org/research/cancer-facts -and-statistics/colorectal-cancer-facts-and-figures/colorectal-cancer-facts -and-figures-2020-2022.pdf.

254 **the risk factors for colon cancer** Risk factors for colorectal cancer include "lack of regular physical activity," "a diet low in fruit and vegetables," "a low-fiber and high-fat diet, or a diet high in processed meats," "overweight and obesity," "alcohol consumption," and "tobacco use." See Centers for Disease Control and Prevention, "Colorectal (Colon) Cancer: What Are the Risk Factors for Colorectal Cancer?" February 17, 2022, www.cdc.gov/cancer /colorectal/basic_info/risk_factors.htm.

254 **to help prevent a recurrence of her cancer** The American Cancer Society reports that "dietary patterns rich in plant foods and low in animal products and refined carbohydrates lower risk" of breast cancer. See Cheryl L. Rock, Cynthia Thomson, Ted Gansler, Susan M. Gapstur, et al., "American Cancer Society Guideline for Diet and Physical Activity for Cancer Prevention," *CA: A Cancer Journal for Clinicians* 70, no. 4 (July/August 2020), doi.org/10 .3322/caac.21591.

255 **About 86 percent of people diagnosed with stage-4 colon cancer die within five years** American Cancer Society, "Survival Rates for Colorectal Cancer," March 1, 2022, www.cancer.org/cancer/colon-rectal-cancer /detection-diagnosis-staging/survival-rates.html.

256 **that the heartbeat of racism is denial, the heartbeat of antiracism is confession** Ibram X. Kendi, "The Heartbeat of Racism Is Denial," *The New York Times,* January 13, 2018, www.nytimes.com/2018/01/13/opinion/sunday /heartbeat-of-racism-denial.html. The article also appeared in the Sunday print edition on January 14, 2018.

258 **14 percent of people who survived stage-4 colon cancer** American Cancer Society, "Survival Rates for Colorectal Cancer."

258 **trillions of tax dollars we spend** See David Rogers, "POLITICO Analysis: At $2.3 Trillion Cost, Trump Tax Cuts Leave Big Gap," *POLITICO,* February 28, 2018, www.politico.com/story/2018/02/28/tax-cuts-trump -gop-analysis-430781; Beatrix Lockwood and Nicole Lewis, "The Hidden Cost of Incarceration," The Marshall Project, December 17, 2019, www .themarshallproject.org/2019/12/17/the-hidden-cost-of-incarceration; and Center on Budget and Policy Priorities, "Policy Basics: Where Do Our Federal Tax Dollars Go?" April 9, 2020, www.cbpp.org/research/federal -budget/where-do-our-federal-tax-dollars-go.

INDEX

ableism/ableist, 4n
abolitionist idea/ideas, 85n, 88n, 108, 127, 223–24, 226
Acheson, Dean, 228
activism/activist, 222–37, 314n156
    author and, 230–33, 234
    defined, 222
    demonstration vs. protest, 236
    "failure doctrine" and, 234–35
    goals, 229, 230
    Jena 6 protest, 230–33, 234, 237
    outcome advocacy and, 231
affirmative action, 25, 34, 135, 145, 146–47, 267n25
Affordable Care Act (ACA), 28, 147, 229
Afonso V, King of Portugal, 46, 48
Africa
    capitalist growth in, 175, 322n175
    enslavers, human trade, and, 45–46, 48–49, 67, 142, 161, 174, 175, 177, 275n48, 309n142, 316n161, 321n174

first European book on, 46
genetic diversity in, 61
impoverished people in, 322n175
racial capitalism in, 180
repatriation of enslaved people, 192
undernourished people in, 268n27
Africanus, Leo, 161, 316n161
    Della descrittione dell'Africa, 161
Afrocentric Black people, 185
Afrocentricity (Asante), 185
After Earth (film), 233
Agassiz, Louis, 58, 278n58
ageist discrimination, 22–23, 267n23
Age of Enlightenment, 47, 58, 101–2, 126
Ali, Laila Amaria, 201
Allen, Richard, 43
Allen African Methodist Episcopal Church, Queens, NY, 36
American Dilemma, An (Myrdal), 94, 228, 290–91n94
American Freedom Party, 146
American Negro Academy, 108

White teaching force in public
schools, 197, 333n197
"educational suasion," 226, 228, 234,
251
Ehrlichman, John, 32
Ellis, Havelock
on homosexuality, 214, 340n214
Sexual Inversion, 340n214
Studies in the Psychology of Sex, 214
Emergency Quota Act, 70
End of Racism, The (D'Souza), 56
enslavement
abolitionist ideas and, 116, 223
behavioral racism and, 108–9
Biblical justification, 58, 162,
277n58
biological racist ideas and, 57–58,
276–77n57, 277–78n58
Black slave ownership, 162
capitalism and, 174, 177
colorist ideas and, 46, 126–27
curse theory and, 57–58
Emancipation Proclamation, 227
enslaved population of the South,
226, 343–44n226
ethnic racism and, 66–68, 281n68
Europeans in Africa and, 161,
316n161, 321n174
first enslaved people in America, 67
first known slave narrative, 161
first transatlantic slaver
movement, 58
first White antislavery society, 108,
294n108
freedom revolts, 162
Great Britain and, 174, 321n174
as "human trade," 37, 161, 272n37,
316n161
Islamic human traders, 46
Ligon's Sambo and, 161
Lincoln and, 227
meaning of enslaved/enslaver, vs.
slave/slaveholder, 19n

number of African and Indigenous
people enslaved, 309n142,
321n174
polygenesis vs. monogenesis and,
58, 277–78n58
Portuguese and, 46, 48–49,
275n48, 321n174
profits from, 49
PTSS and, 109
race and, 47
racial capitalism and, 142–43
saving of souls and, 48
segregationist ideas replacing, 109,
127–28
slavery/hypertension thesis, 57,
276–77n57
social Darwinism and, 59,
278–79n59
trauma of, 109
"uplift suasion" ideology and, 226
environmental determinism, 147–48
Equal Justice Initiative, 285n80
Ervin, Sam, 266n21
Essed, Philomena
Understanding Everyday Racism, 208
Essence magazine, 249
ethnic antiracist idea/ideas, 64, 64n,
73, 75, 202
defined, 64, 280n64
perspective on Black
immigrants, 76
ethnic racist idea/ideas, 64, 64n,
65–77
belief in a racial ethnic hierarchy, 71
defined, 64, 280n64
double standard of, 75
enslavers, human traders, and, 67
group behavior stereotyping, 71
history of, 74–75
immigration policy and, 68–70
power relationships and, 71
racializing and, 71
stereotypes and, 72

racist idea/ideas (*cont.*)
  narrative of White colonists and
    language, 58n
  NOI and, 140, 141
  Norton's, 33
  policy and, 75, 105, 140
  power and, 49
  powerless defense, 151, 156–60,
    314n157
  psychological inversion and, 137
  queer racist ideas, 213–21
  racializing behavior as, 103–18
  replacement theory and, 148
  root problem and, 49
  segregationist ideas and, 37–38
  space racist ideas, 185–200
  that White people have all the
    power, 158–59
  "them niggers" and, 151–55
  what it is, 25
  White recognition of, 154
  Zurara as crafter of, 46
racist language, 4n
  anti-Native racist ideas and, 58n
racist policy, 15, 15n, 20, 223
  anti-White racism taking focus off,
    146
  cause of, 49
  climate change and, 26
  colorist ideas and, 122, 129–30
  "cycle of poverty" and, 170–71,
    320n170
  deficiencies of people vs., 34
  defined, 21
  denial of, 10, 142
  dueling White consciousness and,
    38–39
  effect on employment and housing,
    154
  effects of changing, 229
  enslavement and, 48–49
  ethnic racist ideas and, 75, 76
  failed solutions for, 223, 225–27

  fighting for mental and moral
    changes after changing, 229
  focus on changing, 252
  as form of harm and violence, 85n
  how to change, 237, 251
  identifying, 62
  immigration laws and, 68–71
  impoverished people and, 144,
    310n144
  "institutional racism," 240–44
  moral and education suasion and,
    229
  other names for, 21
  power and, 49, 157–60, 314n157
  as producing harm to all, 142
  racial inequities emerging form,
    242–43
  racial inequity as signpost of, 255–56
  racist power as source of, 144
  Reagan and, 31, 33–34, 39
  standardized testing as, 113–14
  steps to change injustice and
    inequity, 252–53
  success of groups and, 105
  "them niggers" and, 153–54
  what it is, 170
  White people benefitting from, 144
racist power, 21, 22, 25, 223
  "by any means necessary" and, 235
  bodily racist idea and, 80
  civil rights legislation and, 228–29
  conflating all White people with,
    134
  ethnic racism and, 76
  fear and, 233–34
  hatred and, 146
  homophobia and, 213
  inequity and, 62
  limited Black power and, 140–41,
    166
  as loser in a just society, 144
  powerless defense and, 151,
    156–60, 314n157

wealth inequality, 39, 144, 174–75,
180–81
  Black women and, 209, 210,
  337n209, 337n210
  giving gap and, 191
  "99 percenters" and, 144
Weaver, Vesla, 122
welfare, 72, 171–72, 205
Wells, Ida B., 43, 208
Welsing, Frances Cress
  "color confrontation theory," 148
  Isis Papers, The, 148, 149, 150
West Indians, 69, 76
Whitaker, Robert, 146
  "The Mantra," 146
White, Deborah Gray, 204
White, Walter, 130
White colonialism/colonists, 58n, 71,
  142, 309n142
White ethnostate, 25
White identity, 44
  post-racial future and, 122
"White judge," 4, 11, 223
White nationalism, 25
White privilege, 27, 44–45

White supremacy, 10, 11, 37, 140,
  146–47, 194, 278n58
  climate change and, 146,
  311–12n146
  COVID-19 and, 147, 312n147
  "great replacement" theory, 148
  Tillman's Red Shirts, 233–34
Wilkins, Roy, 290–91n94
Williams, Robert, 93
Winckelmann, Johann Joachim
  History of the Art of Antiquity, 126
Winfrey, Oprah, 125
Winston, George T., 128
Woodson, Carter G., 158
Words of Revolution (Skinner), 16
Wright, Richard
  Native Son, 17
Wu-Tang Clan, 98

Zimmerman, George, 246–47
Zuazo, Alonso de, 47
Zulu Nation, 81, 285–86n81
Zurara, Gomes de, 46–49, 80
  Chronicle of the Discovery and
    Conquest of Guinea, The, 40, 48

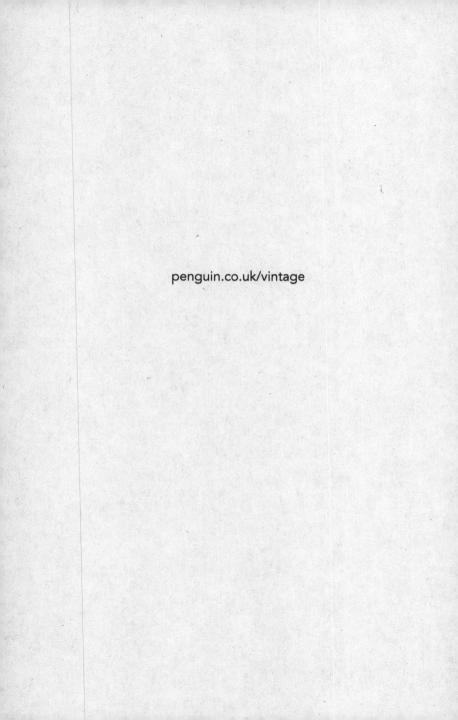

penguin.co.uk/vintage